Karsh

DAVID LOW

AUTOBIOGRAPHY

SIMON AND SCHUSTER · NEW YORK

1957

PUBLISHED BY SIMON AND SCHUSTER, INC.
ROCKEFELLER CENTER, 630 FIFTH AVENUE
NEW YORK 20, N. Y.
FIRST PRINTING

LIBRARY OF CONGRESS CATALOG CARD NUMBER: 57—7304
MANUFACTURED IN THE UNITED STATES OF AMERICA
PRINTED BY THE MURRAY PRINTING COMPANY, WAKEFIELD, MASS.
BOUND BY AMERICAN BOOK-STRATFORD PRESS, INC., NEW YORK

ACKNOWLEDGMENTS

IN writing this book, besides making use of a fifty-year accumulation of personal press cuttings, countless 'I-remember' conversations, a mound of relevant correspondence and a fragmentary diary, I have helped myself freely to my own writings published in a multitude of newspapers and periodicals. Some of the proprietors and editors of these, with their publications, are beyond my felicitations, but to those who survive I make my acknowledgments.

Particularly I should mention that I have borrowed from my book *Ye Madde Designer*, published by The Studio Ltd., some anecdotes, for re-telling here in their appropriate place and sequence as part of Chapters 10 and 17; from the *New Statesman and Nation*, London, and the *New Republic*, New York, part of Chapter 16; from the *New York Times* and *Nash's Magazine* other parts of the same chapter; and from the London *Evening Standard* and *New York Times* passages which appear in Chapters 10, 14 and 18.

I offer my thanks to Lord Beaverbrook, Herbert Morrison, Gilbert Murray and Aldous Huxley; and the executors of the late H. G. Wells, Arnold Bennett, Harold Laski, Chaim Weizmann, Sigmund Freud, Lord Keynes and Lady Oxford and Asquith for their courtesy in permitting me to reprint letters.

To The Sydney Bulletin Co., the Star Newspaper Co. Ltd. and The Evening Standard Co. I am especially indebted for their consent to republication of cartoons which first appeared in their papers. A word of appreciation is due also to the friends and relatives who read the typescript when in progress and encouraged me with constructive suggestions. This I give with grateful thanks.

ILLUSTRATIONS

Photographs

Drawings

AUTOBIOGRAPHY

I

THERE were no artists on my family tree.

Great-grandfather Low was a blacksmith in Fifeshire. Grandfather Low was a marine engineer. After doing a stretch of whaling in the Arctic and ranging the South Seas he found in New Zealand what he thought was a good place to live. So he uprooted his family of five, including my father-to-be, from Carnoustie and sailed the lot of them off to the new settlement at Dunedin in the 1860's. Grandfather Low, according to his daguerreotype, had a sad face and dreamy eyes behind his forest of dark beard. My father had a similar eye. So have I.

Great-grandmother Heenan (on my mother's side) had arrived in Dunedin some years earlier—in 1850—from a village near Dublin, with her husband and the twelve survivors of her seventeen children. Great-grandfather Heenan died a comparatively young man (for the Heenans) at 84, leaving Great-grandmother to grow formidably old, with an endearing peculiarity of interrupting church services by breaking out into loud extempore prayers on her own account. By all reports, in her prime she was an indomitable woman. She had to be. Life was hard in the new settlement. The Heenans had to build their own house, boil salt-water to get salt, make tea from manuka scrub, walk eight miles of track to see the nearest neighbour. The Heenans, judging from their daguerreotypes, were an angry-looking lot of people, with their whiskers and riding-boots and tight little mouths. That is where I get my mouth from.

Grandmother Flanagan (*née* Heenan) who survived them all, was to me as a child the head of the tribe, a matriarch of awe-inspiring dignity gowned in black silk with lace fichu and bonnet. Her husband, Grandfather Flanagan, had vanished into the mist long before I appeared on the scene, leaving a legend of himself as a wild colonial boy who used to ride his horse in to public buildings and in other ways show his contempt for convention. She was a disciplinarian, as hard as nails, who ruled her children—she had had ten by the time she was twenty-eight—with a rod of iron. Like her parents she was fiercely religious in the Presbyterian faith, with a lively abomination of sin. Her method of fighting sin was to place almost everything pleasant or amusing out of bounds for the members of her household—the theatre (a den of iniquity), card-playing (the devil's books), dancing, whistling, smoking, horse-racing, novels, cosmetics, brilliantine, 'loose' music, etc. When Grandmother was asked to contribute an item to a musical evening she invariably obliged with 'The Old Hundredth,' the only tune she could be sure of. She placed great reliance upon cold baths as a reducer of the appetite for sin and insisted upon the daily douche for everyone within reach, even in the dead of winter. Evidently Grandmother's efforts against sin were such as to merit special attention at Headquarters, for according to her own account, sincere and deliberate, Satan in person actually called on her to tempt her and she saw him fair and square standing in the doorway. As evidence in proof of this remarkable occurrence she used to point out two discoloured patches on the verandah, which she maintained (without fear of contradiction) were the burns of his hoof-prints.

Grandmother Flanagan had become Grandmother Dallas before I saw the light. She had got married again to a French university professor with two daughters to add to the copious family. As she grew older, so did the town of Dunedin grow around her. The 'colonial-style' one-storied wooden house in which she lived had been built in the early days on the top of a sandhill, eighty steps and a steep slope up. To accommodate first the street and then the up-to-date brick residences lining it, sections of the sandhill had had to be sheared away. This, combined with subsidences caused by little boys playing mountaineering, gave the old house such a perilous look that fears were expressed lest the occupants one day be precipitated suddenly into the street below. Grandmother relieved the general anxiety by having it propped up with beams and poles, so that it sat out from all the other houses with a stupefying effect suggestive of a nesting yellow hen with a broken leg. But nobody said a word. Grandmother had become an Identity, a Grand Old Lady, respected, feared and loved, a woman of property with responsibilities. She interpreted the latter strictly as involving almost feudal rights over her tenants,

My Mother

particularly over certain Chinese whose occupation of one of her warehouses she could overlook from her lofty verandah. She appeared to have the idea that the saffron complexion of these Chinese was caused by constipation. Accordingly she insisted upon their attendance at her house for a cup of senna tea every Saturday morning—Saturday morning, so that the consequences thereof would not interfere with the conduct of their business. And they came.

The precepts and practice of Grandmother Flanagan had a considerable effect upon the destinies of her posterity, though not in the way she might have anticipated; for her children, as and when they could lead their own lives, proceeded to do so on very different lines from hers. It was of great importance to me that her daughter Caroline, my mother-to-be, who inherited Grandmother Flanagan's resolution but revolted from her everlasting discipline, decided that in all respects save cleanliness and godliness her methods of raising any children she might have would be the opposite of her mother's. She would make a point of giving individual character a chance and not 'bring up' her children too much.

My father's people were cast in very different mould from those of my mother. The Low family were Scottish—very Scottish indeed. Dunedin was a predominantly Scottish settlement and the exiled settlers clung with such sentimental devotion to customs and symbols of their far-off native land that in other parts of New Zealand Dunedin was jokingly spoken of as the capital of Scotland. The Lows played their part in keeping alive the ideas of Hallowe'en, nichts wi' Burrns, and other rites with haggis, the pipes, whisky and mournful folk-songs about the auld hoose, the bonnie glen and Chairlie. Grandmother Low made a gentle kindly widow when Grandfather died at sea, after she had put up so patiently with his marine adventurings after fairy gold.

The expedition to the *General Grant*, for instance. In 1886 the American full-rigged ship *General Grant*, with £50,000 worth of gold and a passenger list of miners bringing home their piles aboard, set sail from Melbourne to London. For some unexplained reason she passed away south of her intended course and found herself before the Auckland Archipelago with a falling wind and a heavy swell on the sea. In the murky night the doomed vessel was caught in the currents near the rocky shores of Adam's Island and sucked into a cave. The rise and fall of the swell within caused her tall masts to punch against the roof of the cave and finally drove the mainmast clean through the keel. The vessel sank in five minutes with great loss of life.

As might be expected, the idea of all that treasure lying on the sea-floor of that cave inflamed the imagination of adventurers everywhere. Expeditions were fitted out, steamers were chartered complete with divers. At this point the story, as handed down by Dad to us children, becomes a little woolly and tinged with fantasy. Grandfather Low, it seems, went into a huddle with a syndicate of kindred spirits to hatch mysterious plans for an attempt of their own. All of the expeditions were said to depend upon the indispensable help of a certain survivor who alone could guide the adventurers to the right spot. Grandfather's syndicate had made special arrangements with this survivor. But just as all was ready and steam was practically up, the survivor was found dead in his hotel bedroom. The question arose : should this stop the intrepid syndicate? Never. Off they go into the blue, Grandfather Low's bushy beard waving in the breeze. . . . After many months, long overdue, the vessel steamed back into Dunedin harbour. But how changed. Except for the shell and essential portions of her deck, practically everything wooden had disappeared, burned up for fuel to enable the company to stay away so long and then get home. The great curiosity aroused by this exploit was not gratified by any sensational revelations from members of the syndicate, who had evidently agreed among themselves to keep their mouths closed. Even Grandfather Low observed the rule of mum's the word to his family. But it was darkly hinted by disappointed neighbours that after a few weeks all those who returned seemed to be leading suspiciously rich lives, wearing new clothes, smoking big cigars, drinking expensive drinks and riding freely in smart carriages. That might have been sheer imagination. On the other hand it was certainly true that Grandfather Low had had a great beano. But poor Grandmother Low . . .

The Lows and the Heenans were antipathetic; and the conflict was amply represented in young David Low and young Caroline Flanagan. In spite of this—or perhaps because of it—they courted, wed and settled down in a house in the shadow of Grandmother's sandy eminence where she could keep an eye on them. In due course, in rapid succession, three sons were born to them, of whom I was the third. If I were asked to stock-take the better qualities of my inheritance and their sources I should say my mother is represented in me by such practicality, resource and

My Father

determination as I possess; my father, by the optimism, romance and curiosity.

Before I was old enough to notice, we had all moved to live farther north at Christchurch, where I was to grow up.

The dawn of consciousness for me synchronized more or less with the South African War and the Relief of Mafeking. Flags, crowds, brass bands, newspapers printed in red, white and blue, the Absent-minded Beggar—hooray! . . . our gallant troops . . . hooray! . . . hooray! . . . lemonade, lollies . . . the Dear Old Queen . . . hooray! the Procession with Our Lads . . . an effigy of silly old Kruger, whiskered, umbrellaed and top-hatted . . . BOO! BOOOOO!! . . . a big stove-pipe marked LONG TOM (an allusion to a field-gun currently famous for its siege-breaking effectiveness) set up at a business-like angle belching forth smoke and loud bangs every few minutes . . . the fairy lamps which Dad hung all over the front of our house at night . . . A kaleidoscopic day of excitement and delight. Dad had said at tea-time that someone called Lloyd George had talked sense about the Boers, but that was above my head. Someone had told us that a cousin had been killed and another had died of enteric fever in camp, but that had no meaning for me.

Dad had an appetite for new experiences and he moved with the times. His business advantages enabled him to enter with enthusiasm into the new developments of photography, wet and dry plate, posed and, later, snapshot, stereoscopic double-view and lantern-slide making. We were among the first in our town to possess one of the new marvellous phonographs. When safety bicycles came in we had five, one for each in different sizes, with a small one for me, aged seven, to fit my small legs. (I can still see the amazed neighbours as we whisked by.) We had one of the new treadle fretsaws and made horrible pipe-racks and book-ends. We collected stamps, with judgment and profit. Dad's only failure as a hobbyist was his attempt to collect half-tone illustrations from the periodicals. He had worked it out that the new form of reproduction had no future and examples must necessarily remain few and would become rare. That was a miscalculation.

Don't imagine we never suffered correction, for we did. Lying, cheating, meanness, gluttony, plain rudeness, sadistic cruelty like chasing the hens with a stick, or breaches of personal hygiene like failing to clean one's teeth, earned shame and tears, even sometimes a clout on the behind. In those far-off days the new methods of child-rearing were yet unknown. My parents had never heard of 'repressions' or 'complexes.' They just used their hearts and heads. I do not say their way of raising children was the best way for others; indeed in the course of my life I have met disgusting brats brought up on similar lines who misbehaved recklessly making life a hell generally for everybody including themselves. But it worked with the Lows—if a natural growth of trust and affection between child and parent is a test.

My father's ideas on equipping us for the battle of life were unconventional. As small boys he took us to the theatre (orchestra stalls, one for each of us at 3s. 6d. apiece) whenever any worthy company of actors visited our town. I was used to the Drama before I could understand what was happening . . . He took us to the races and showed us How to Bet intelligently, with the aid of Turf Register and Handbook of Form. As we passed to early youth he bought us pipes and showed us How to Smoke . . . He showed us How, by a substitution of harmless words, one could Swear without using foul language. 'Crrash the dingled blub!' must have sounded peculiar to the ear of a stranger, but it relieved the feelings wonderfully and usually sublimated anger to laughter. 'Frost!' cursed my father when he dropped the spade on his foot . . . He explained the evils of Irregularity in Alcohol and Sex, and left it at that . . . and he showed us How to Read for pleasure as well as for profit. Our house was full of books and we were encouraged to read in bed, at the dinner-table, in the fields or up a tree . . . He had us always at his table for meals. My father was a disputatious person about political and social subjects (on a theological background) and he was prone to talk at us and to us on the adult level about the State of the Country, the Destiny of Man and the Nature of the Infinite. I groped for opinions and began to develop a precocious interest in the world about me.

Reflections on a tricycle in 1898

14A

2

IF at the beginning of the present century Dunedin were Scottish, Christchurch was definitely English. It was as though the god-fearing settlers, struck on their arrival fifty years before by the charm of the green plains laced with a gently-flowing river and edged with comfortable hills, had said 'Lovely! So different! The very place for an English cathedral town!' The motion was evidently carried unanimously, so they went to work. They built a massive Gothic cathedral, laid down a sensible street system naming all the streets after English cathedrals and, just so that there should not be any mistake, they called it Christchurch.

Fifty years later, in 1900, when I was nine and able to take notice, the succeeding generation had played up to the original conception and had established a clean open pleasant town in which any exile from England could have settled down without feeling too painfully far from home. The climate, except for the inversion of the seasons, was like enough to that which he had left behind. The food was much the same. English flowers, shrubs and trees had been transplanted liberally and flourished everywhere. The river Avon, winding softly around the town, lined with picturesque weeping willows (and full of trout), bore a family likeness to its sister at Stratford. The cathedral now lay to the east of a large open square lined with buildings in the pure English tradition of assorted architecture and containing a central grass plot with statue of The Founder, looking out at his work from a circle of waiting carriers' vans, and London hansom-cabs, a steam-tram terminus, a horse-bus stop and a multitude of cyclists; leaving plenty of room still for the local big-wigs to parade, meet and transact their business in the fresh air.

Doubtless there are, or have been, many such squares in

England. But the number of cyclists was unusual. Christchurch citizens had found this means of travel particularly suitable to their flat terrain and even by 1900 had adopted it so completely that local humorists proudly boasted that all Christchurch babies were born on bicycles. And the houses, of course, were different. Except for main public offices and business premises they were built of wood, not stone, and were single-storied, iron-roofed, with verandahs. No antiquity, no ancient monuments, no manor-house. The people were the familiar sound middle-class stock, healthy and pink-cheeked, though with a new inflection in their speech, slower, harder and with sharper corners than any English accent.

By 1900 New Zealand had got over some of its growing pains and the frozen meat industry had brought prosperity to Christchurch. In a thriving community where there was plenty of work for everybody, tempers were mellow and there were no poor. The social atmosphere was fairly equalitarian and individuals were robustly independent, although there were, of course, snobs to encourage social distinctions on the model of the Old World, as between old families (nobility) and new, land proprietors (landed gentry) and tradesmen, big importing business men (barons of industry) and workmen. At least two silk top-hats were in daily use and on town occasions we could muster about twenty. If our visitor from England happened to have a handle to his name he could reckon on suffering a red carpet reception from our 'best people,' however much he might have thought that the tendency to imitate some manners and customs of the Old World seemed a little incongruous in these surroundings.

But if he wished to sail his model yacht he could do so on the lake in Hagley Park, just as on the Serpentine. He could watch good cricket at Lancaster Park just as at The Oval or Lord's, and good racing at Riccarton in the best Aintree–Epsom tradition. He could have an English day at the seaside, complete with donkeys and Punch and Judy, at New Brighton or Sumner; or an English political argument at the open-air meetings on the Hyde Park model in Cathedral Square. For entertainment, he could go to the Theatre Royal to see stock companies from Australia (and occasionally momentous visiting stars from the Old Country like, say, Mrs. Brown Potter, Mrs. Patrick Campbell, or Wilson Barrett) play London successes; or there was always the local branch of a regular vaudeville circuit, run on lines half Christy-Minstrels, half London music-hall.

There was a roller-skating rink, several well-lit hotels with friendly barmaids and two or three cheerful billiards saloons for young men-about-town. But no cinemas yet. No taxis, no restaurants, no night-clubs, no dance halls, no electric signs, The gay life closed down at about nine o'clock p.m. excepting on Saturday night. That was the big night when the shops kept open until after eleven and the town let itself go. Then one could have a royal time for a couple of shillings: half a dozen oysters at Mr. Fail's the fishmonger, sixpence; or two large beef saveloys piping hot at Mr. Steele's the butcher, twopence; a cup of coffee, a penny; a first-class American cigar, sixpence; a look at the strolling juggler, nothing—or perhaps a penny; and a listen to the political wrangles in the square, nothing; a game of billiards (which one hoped to win), nothing; beer for defeated partner and one's self, sixpence; a copy of the late edition of the *Star*, a sizeable wad of reading, a penny. Then the long walk home, singing. A full life.

Life was not all butter, cheese and Canterbury lamb. Christchurch had a window on the world. We had two morning newspapers, two evenings, all built on the lines of the London *Times*, well served with foreign cables and local reports; two heavyweight weeklies for the farmers, with half-tone picture supplements; and a social-political-gossip weekly that printed cartoons. For a population of one hundred thousand that was not so bad. We had a respectable seat of learning in Canterbury College, an adequate public library and a conservative but well-attended school of art.

New Zealand then had not advanced far enough from pioneering difficulties for people to be as concerned with the encouragement of the graces as with making a living. Still, there were poets, actors, musicians, half a dozen professional painters and two black-and-white artists in Christchurch. But the life artistic offered no glittering prizes, and talent was usually accompanied by ambition to save up and go to seek laurels elsewhere.

It was not until I grew older that I began to see my father in better perspective. As a man of business working at the direction of others he was a square peg in a round hole, a man of ideas chafing at routine, dreaming expansive dreams of bringing off some master-stroke which would put us all on velvet, when he should have been counting pennies. Such men—and their families —are fated to Ups and Downs. His abilities had taken him from junior clerk to a sound and dignified job as Christchurch manager of a big drug importing business, and caught in this trap he

17

should have settled down to respectable frustration like a responsible citizen, and given up trying to spread wings. But he did not—with far-reaching results.

This was the era of patent medicines and my father was in the drug business. The chemists' shops were full of cough cures. My father knew that practically all of these 'cures' were based upon the appropriate standard recipe in the Pharmacopœia, to be found by anybody who liked to look it up, and that they differed only according to a pinch of flavouring, a catchy name and smart advertising. In my father's view, the advertising was the thing. In imagination he conceived of an organization of chemists to produce new and better-flavoured cough cures, with absolutely irresistible names and unprecedentedly stupendous advertising. From imagination to realization proved a short step. Discreetly —obscurely, almost—he became a moving spirit in a small group of retail chemists to make and push a cough cure named 'Benjamin Gum.'

The effect was startling. 'Benjamin Gum' stickers appeared on lamp-posts; householders found visiting-cards with 'Benjamin Gum' beautifully engraved pushed under their doors; cheap little toys imported from Japan by the bale found their way into the hands of little children with the compliments of 'Benjamin Gum'; 'Benjamin Gum' decorated posters and handbills; there were 'Benjamin Gum' competitions, songs, jokes and puzzles. I was deeply impressed. If Mary Tudor had Calais written on her heart, Benjamin Gum was written on mine.

For a time 'Benjamin Gum' did well and no doubt cured many coughs. But its success encouraged expansion, and my father endeavoured to expand. Another patent medicine was born in which he also had a hand. Things became involved and my father found himself caught in a chain of complexities which included, among other surprises, his becoming part-owner of a bioscope, the first to reach New Zealand. I well remember the excitement with which the Low family sat—myself spellbound—in the dress circle of the Christchurch Opera House to see this marvellous new magic lantern which showed pictures that moved; and the privileged visit we made behind the screen to peep, from a fair distance, at Cousin Alick engaged in the dangerous function of guarding the acetylene gas illumination. That was a red letter day. That was one of the Ups.

The end was inevitable. The board of directors of the big drug business of which my father was local manager, learning of his independent activities, took exception and he and they

18

parted. The scene changed. Bioscope, Benjamin Gum and all faded. That was a Down.

The Low fortunes were depressed when suddenly there came a bouncing UP. Among the many and varied sprats tossed by my father to catch Fortune, were his regular 'subscriptions' to the Tattersalls Sweepstakes, the big Australian lottery which was as famous in its day as the Calcutta Sweep or the Irish Sweep in later years. One day the news arrived that he had drawn Maltster, the favourite for the Melbourne Cup. He stood to win £6,750, a fortune in those days. At the time he was in delirium with congestion of the lungs. My mother took charge. Our house was invaded by a procession of sharp-eyed jowled men who came to make offers for either the whole or a piece of the ticket. They did not get far with my mother. With characteristic strength of mind she stood pat on our luck and sent them all packing.

Unfortunately the favourite was pipped on the post. The second prize, however, was £2,250, still a considerable win. How the money was spent is illuminating of the family blend of practicality and romance. Half went to buying Riversleigh, the rambling old house in the country (two miles from the centre of Christchurch was country in those days) which we had been renting; half to going—all six of us, a new sister having arrived—for a glorious spree to Sydney, the fabulous Australian city which stood for pleasure to New Zealanders as Paris does to the English.

But a windfall does not last for ever. With some family financing we began a new chapter. The large hotel bills during our travels had convinced my father that there was a fortune in the hotel business. So naturally we had to go into the hotel business (guest-house division). There *should* have been a fortune in it, especially for people in our position, able to stock, partly, at least, with food grown by ourselves at our country place. Alas! Despite Dad's best efforts in well-printed, attractive publicity, and my mother's newly-discovered talent for the organization of the welfare of from sixty to a hundred and twenty people, there wasn't.

It was during this episode that events happened of the greatest importance in shaping my future. My eldest brother died and in consequence of this I was withdrawn from school. My brother's death was clearly caused by peritonitis, but our parents felt that his vitality had been weakened beforehand by over-study. Desperate with grief, they determined not to make the same mistake with their remaining children. Our formal education at

19

the Boys' High School was suspended indefinitely, while we built up our health running wild in the long grass at Riversleigh.

I was aged eleven. For a space of five years I had a healthy time, partly helping with the horses, cows, pigs and chickens, partly following my own hook. I had time to devote to the occupations I liked most, drawing, reading, or just sitting up a tree or in a dry ditch thinking. I had not much company save for my father, an aunt and our handy-man. My second brother, with most of the neighbouring boys within reach, was in love with engines. He acquired a second-hand steam engine from somewhere and set it up on a concrete bed in one of the out-houses. He and his friends would stoke it up and sit admiring it as the flywheel whizzed around to no purpose whatever. Later he and the others became engrossed with the new motor-cars and motor-cycles that were just coming in. All that had no interest for me.

These were formative years, when the young normally go to school to absorb not merely learning but the postulates of citizen-ship and the canons of behaviour in civilized society. I missed all this, and was left without the modifications of 'team-spirit,' outside the freemasonry of Old Boys. But I had the advantages of my disadvantages. I had no discipline so I had to rule myself; in the absence of companionship I had to be self-contained.

In such circumstances orthodoxy was certainly not to be taken for granted. My natural curiosity, left to itself, led me rather to a questioning approach to accepted standards, and a reluctance to facile conformity which sometimes amounted to mutiny. A brash small boy who, when the band played 'God Save the King,' demanded to know 'Why? What's *he* done?', or who declined to cheer the British Empire without knowing more about it, could be a dreadful pill to worthy citizens who deemed uncatechetical acceptance of the social rules a virtue. Improve-ment in drawing, now my absorbing purpose, depended upon my own self-criticism and private effort, there being nobody about to share my interest, so I naturally valued my own concepts of success and failure above those of outsiders who could not know my aims. And it was but a step from there to being more con-cerned with the satisfaction of my own personal standards than with those of others in matters of honour, self-respect and conduct, too. As the twig bent, so grew the tree.

Life was much changed by my brother's death. Seeking con-solation for the death of his dearly beloved eldest son, my father found it in religion. He was always a disputatious man, and religion mixed with his native radicalism made him considerably vocal. Part of the daily routine was the evening return journey transporting produce between the country and town places which we managed together with the aid of our sleepy white horse Euroclydon—Rocky for short. The circumstances were stimulating to discussion, so he argued with me. I seemed to need little encouragement. By all accounts we could be heard along the road long before we came in sight, in loud dispute usually about matters bearing directly or indirectly on religion. What would Christ do with reference to current private and public problems was a favourite theme capable, I found, of expansion to cover unlimited territories of interest.

Dad held that belief was a matter of the will. It seemed to me dimly that in that contention lay a confusion about words. There was a distinction to be drawn between an idea which one forces upon one's self and an idea which forces itself upon one. I fumbled towards an attitude. It was one thing, I protested (in much less precise terms than I state it here), to act upon principles based upon a set of ideas which one had deliberately chosen without the test of experience, but it was quite another to act upon a set based upon the evidence of one's senses. What is the value of human experience? he would retort. What about the incompleteness and uncertainty of human perception? To which I would reply, well, if our human perception is so frail and hit-or-miss, then it can't matter much what we believe. If all man's judgments are worthless, what is the value of your assertion that there is a God? Ah, Dad would say, you are ignoring the creative and sustaining power of Faith. Determine to act on the assumption that an idea is right and it *will* be right . . . whereupon he would be telling me that if I could convince myself that I was in the desert of Sahara—or in Heaven—for all practical purposes I was there.

We were able to disagree, also, with gusto, about sin and hell fire. In my opinion sin lay in going against the light, and since the light differed with individuals, sin was an individual thing. I could not think that if all were sinful and some were born with the ability to throw off the burden and others not, it was right and proper to punish the latter. This did not convince my father any more than my arguments concerning miracles. I inclined to place clarity of mind as the essential attribute of divinity. I was impressed by wisdom more than by magic, which seemed irrelevant and cheating. Was the teaching sound and true? If so, did walking on the water or turning water into wine make it more so? If not sound and true, did miracles make it sound and true? And why, knowing that knowledge is incomplete and the unexplored territories of the human mind unlimited, should man be so ready to credit strange happenings to supernatural agencies rather than to natural causes as yet unexplained?

Dad stood by the complete acceptance of the Church of England Bible in the most literal sense of its meaning. I emerged from our theological wrestlings calling myself a Protestant, but being in fact an Agnostic, a state which seemed to me then, and does so still, to be the only one for an honest seeker after truth whose knowledge is necessarily limited and who is too stiff-necked to dilute his judgment, so far as it goes, by his wishes.

Bowling along the country road beside the river with voices raised in earnest argument above the clatter of cart-wheels and horse-shoes, my bearded dad and his youngster must have made a queer picture to passers-by. Yet perhaps it was not so queer in the circumstances. Apart from a natural growth of confidence resulting from our family practice of freely admitting my brothers and me to conversation 'beyond our years' with our elders, I had become a voracious and omnivorous reader. It was one of my two principal enjoyments, thanks to Dad's sympathetic understanding in consulting my natural boyish interest at the outset.

That interest had been chained in the first place by 'penny dreadfuls.' Their attractions were obvious. Written in simple words they were easy to read, and you could get on with the exciting story for fun without feeling that you were taking another lesson in grammar or 'doing yourself good.' Although to an adult they would certainly have seemed conventional and repetitious in phrase and idea to the point of absurdity, I was not yet an adult. Once lured so easily and willingly through the back door of the world of imagination, I read and read, graduating painlessly from the first rapture of *Deadwood Dick, Frank Reed's Steam Man, Spring-heeled Jack* and *Claude Duval*, through the sheer delight of *Jack Harkaway, Tom Wildrake, Ned Nimble* and *Pantomime Joe*, and the other priceless schoolday books issued from the thrice-blessed publishing houses of Edwin J. Brett, Aldine House and Hogarth House.

There came a time when over-familiarity with the conventions and *clichés*, both of situation and expression, of these schools of literature urged me towards new and farther fields. Waiting for me there were the pleasures of Jules Verne and R. L. Stevenson. I could never stick Ballantyne, Mayne Reed or Henty, possibly because of the smug sort of people who recommended them to me; I scorned *Eric Or Little by Little* as priggish; *Tom Brown's*

Schooldays was insipid after my *Jack Harkaway* and company; and I was filled with enduring loathing of Kingsley's *Westward Ho!* and Blackmore's *Lorna Doone* because they had had to be read compulsorily at school.

Dad throughout his lifetime could never pass a second-hand bookshop, and consequently he had accumulated a large and varied lot of books. I made the acquaintance of Stanley Weyman, Wilkie Collins, Max Pemberton, Quiller Couch, Rider Haggard and Conan Doyle, and then Dickens and Mark Twain. They all became my meat.

So far, until my brother's death, my reading had been almost entirely of fiction. But a change took place when my father found religion. With that enthusiastic devoutness which usually accompanies conversion, he sought opportunities to divest himself of worldliness, and his eye fell on our library. There took place the burial of the books and the purging of the shelves. He collected all his volumes of Zola, de Maupassant, Daudet, George Sand and others whose works in his opinion could be considered ungodly, and taking them to a quiet part of the vegetable garden, solemnly dug a deep hole and buried them. Then he weeded out from the shelves most of the less dangerous fiction and sent it to the second-hand bookshop. The sad gaps on the shelves were refilled with theology.

Because of this my fare had to become more solid. I tried Paley's *Natural Theology* to help me in argument, but it was heavy going. As I prowled the shelves, I made discoveries. I found history, philosophy and the humane arts could be mighty interesting, too, even entertaining and exciting. I made a useful find in a bundle of fortnightly parts of a popular publication which gave its readers potted versions of 'Great Books of the World.' What a lot of nonsense is talked and written about the harmful effects of 'cheap culture.' A pox on those arrogant snobs who from their positions of vantage deplore the means whereby the thoughts and imaginations of the less fortunate may be kindled and would make the path to understanding more difficult and joyless than need be. The snippets of 'Great Books of the World' led me to Socrates, Jane Austen, Tolstoi, Suetonius, Smollett, Plutarch, Herodotus, Montaigne, Kant, Carlyle and many others whom I subsequently tracked down—many of them in a lucky find of old Bohn's Library editions—and read at greater length for entertainment, not as a duty.

Poets and I did not get on in those days. I had been bored as a small schoolboy at having to learn and parrot off poetry from a volume entitled *Lyra Heroica*, a collection made by W. E. Henley. Many years later in London I came across the same volume in a fourpenny box in Farringdon Street. On the cover was the remembered verse printed in gold, something special:

> Sound, sound the clarion, fill the fife,
> To all the sensual world proclaim,
> One crowded hour of glorious life
> Is worth an age without a name.

A gob of mud in the eye for the humble and the ordinary. I suspected that verse when I first saw it. Now that I have grown old after tasting my crowded hour and learned to appreciate the pleasure of quietness, I know it to be musical bosh. I opened the book and turned the pages . . . I could feel an echo of the impact on the mind of the child of nine that had been me. Poetry was a way of writing about rowdy people who showed off and waved swords about. No poems about calm people who just fixed everything sensibly without violence . . . It was years before I was led back, via Gray's country churchyard Over the Hills and Far Away, to the lands of sweet sadness and lovely joy.

I had to set my teeth and bite my way through Aristotle's *Ethics*, and I could only nibble several corners off Gibbon. By comparison Thucydides' *Peloponnesian War* and Clarendon on the *Rebellion in England* came smoothly. The easiest reading I found was the Bible, which I read from start to finish as a book, side-stepping 'texts' so as to get the whole.

This five years of haphazard grazing in the fields of letters came at an absorptive time in my life. Learning, said a wise man, cannot be transferred, it must be appropriated. I soaked up my reading and it became part of my own thoughts, so much so that to this day I have difficulty in quoting without reference. Just as well, perhaps. The regurgitation of tit-bits is too often evidence of an imperfect digestion.

My chores were easily done and I could organize my spare time as I thought fit. I would do a spell of digging or cutting wood, then climb a tree and do a spell of reading, then climb down and do a spell of drawing. I starved for someone to share my delight in drawing, but although I was sometimes damnably lonely, that was just as well, too, as it turned out. Habits of self-reliance and solitary reflection were useful attributes of character for a youth soon to try asserting himself in the unexplored and somewhat doubtful profession of comic art in New Zealand.

3

I DO not remember when my interest in drawing began; but probably it was given direction by the half-penny comics *Chips, Comic Cuts, Larks, Funny Cuts, The Big Budget.* As I remember at this distance of time the comic and the penny dreadful were distinctly different articles in those days. The comics were not full of detectives, revolvers, sex and trips to Mars. Neither were they tiny tots' animal picture-books of teddy bears and tiger tims. The comics were comic. The comicality was simple, repetitious, farcical and robustly vulgar. The very essence, in fact, of British fun.

I got to know Tom Browne's 'Weary Willie and Tired Tim,' Yorick's 'Airy Alf and Bouncing Billy,' Fred Bennett's burlesqued 'Oliver Twist,' and the 'Josser' of Oliver Veal, that creator of a queer race of people who wore their mouths open under their left ears.

At the age of seven or eight to me these were the British comic artists of the time. Was I wrong? I have an uneasy feeling that if at sixty I had to debate the point with myself at eight, I might have difficulty in proving that the elect of the tasteful few were more fitly representative than these mass entertainers of the unsophisticated millions. It is always difficult to explain artistic values to the uninitiated, even the superiority of quality to quantity; especially so when, as in this case, the achievement of quantity obviously demanded a quality of its own. All very well to scorn, but it is no easier to catch the eye of the primitive mass audience with comic pictures than it is to catch its ear on the modern radio—and that is saying something.

These stars of the comics fascinated me. I squandered my pocket money on them. I was moved to emulation. I got a piano-case and set it on end in a quiet place as a studio, took off the

25

narrow side and put hinges on it for a door, cut a small window and fitted a board for a desk. When I got inside there was no room for anybody else and I was quite private. There I sat and tried hard to be a comic artist without in the least knowing how to start. I could find no books which told me anything useful about the HOW. Books either talked as though Caricature was a 'gift' or gave a history of caricaturists of the past garnished with anecdotes. There were no books such as there are a-plenty in the 1950's to teach How to be a Genius in Six Easy Lessons.

For me it seemed that only by dint of smithing could one become a smith. I filled exercise book after exercise book with copies as meticulous as I was able of the drawings in the comics. I became a very dexterous copyist before it occurred to me that this was but copying and I wanted to make drawings of my own.

I managed with infinite labour to contrive some which seemed suitably comic. Ideas did not bother me because I just dipped into the general stockpot. So far as I could judge, to introduce a new idea to this world of fixed jokes would have been a professional error. London, the source of all the comics, was plainly the place for my drawings. It was a disadvantage that I was 15,000 miles from my potential market, but there was the Post Office. I rolled them up and posted them off, the first of a series of parcels so long and so regularly despatched as almost to deserve classification as an important New Zealand export. Some of these parcels I never heard of again. Some returned with rejection slips, polite and impolite. Otherwise nothing happened.

Drawing my own compositions was a mighty different thing, I found, from copying. My drawings wouldn't flow off the pen. I started to take this art of the comics apart to see what it was made of. I saw it was not really an art at all, but a craft—the piecing together of a lot of established conventions not far from the ideographs of ancient Egyptian writing. Combinations of lines representing a boot, or a hat or an umbrella, for instance, only distantly resembling these objects, but traditionally accepted as shorthand for them.

Not that there was anything wrong in that. For the matter of that, all art is based upon convention. People don't think in words, don't feel in music, don't see in lines or brush-strokes. But the fun of being an artist lies in the creation of one's own conventions, in arrangement of the means to enlarge one's individual field of expression. These were old conventions, obsolete, dull with repetition, so mechanical that they might have been stencilled. They were a bore. I wanted to be an artist.

26

I had made the natural mistake of trying to conjure everything out of my head. It struck me that my trouble was that I was trying to draw a house without knowing what a house looked like and the first thing to do was to look at a house. I took stern measures towards improvement, improvising a system whereby I drew and redrew the same picture over and over, each successive state having to be, by a pact with myself, better than the last. First I would draw a general composition as well as I was able, comprising, say, a figure on a horse in front of a building. The next day I would look for a suitable building, give it a good look over and laboriously make a careful picture of it; find a horse and give that also the same treatment; and persuade our handy man to pose for five minutes on a saddle. Finally, when circumstances allowed, I assembled the components, horse, man and house, and photographed them together so that I could see more clearly where my sketch was weak. The immediate result was a mess more often than not. But after a while the exercise helped me to distinguish good from bad in form and arrangement, not merely in my own drawings but also in those of others. It began to dawn on me that one could draw a thing if one understood it, but usually got lost if one did not.

A pile of old copies of *Punch* I found in the back room of a fatherly second-hand bookseller introduced me to the treasure of Charles Keene. Linley Sambourne, Randolph Caldecott and Dana Gibson came as further revelations. The more I pored over the intricate technical quality of these artists the more difficult did drawing appear. How impossible that one could ever become an artist! But then I came on Phil May, who combined quality with apparent facility. I nearly fell into the pitfall of supposing his facility was real and not studied to accord with the spontaneity of his humour. Fortunately I was reading Ruskin at the time, which balanced my judgment. However, once having discovered Phil May I never let him go.

At this point something happened. One day I opened my *Big Budget* to find one of my own three-picture strips printed—printed in microscopic size, but printed. Victory! I leaped in the air.

Joys, like sorrows, never come singly. Shortly afterwards my entry for a monthly drawing competition run by an Australian magazine won and was printed. And a very little later I ventured my first cartoon on public affairs to the local satirical-political weekly, the *Spectator*, and it went in. This run of triumphs was very encouraging. I repaired and whitewashed a redundant

An early comic strip (1903)

fowl-house and moved from my piano-case to new and larger premises. The net receipts from my three successes were: (*a*) nothing; (*b*) five shillings; and (*c*) two shillings and sixpence; but the important gain was that I now had openings. Alas! a mountain of labour moved the *Big Budget* to only one more small mouse, a tiny illustrated joke (nothing). On the other hand I took such care to hit that Australian magazine competition on the button month by month that I came to regard their five-shilling prize almost as fixed income. Best of all, the proprietor of the *Spectator*, feeling, no doubt, that at the price it would be good business to have at hand a potential reserve cartoonist for his paper, decided to try me at illustrating two jokes per week for two shillings and sixpence each.

With the first ten shillings I had a friendly printer produce for me a box of personal cards, saying:

D. A. C. Low,

Black-and-White Artist.

The sight of my work in print gave me more confidence; and my earnings brought within the range of reasonable expenditure the means of possible improvement which before might have seemed unjustified. I answered an American advertisement and for some time sent a dollar a month to a correspondence school of Caricature in New York. They made it easy—too, too easy. The conventions again, the stale old dodges for evading real drawing. How to become a complete hack. Before long I lost interest and turned to our local school of art. Here was the other end of the stick. How to draw without being able to express any-thing. I was put to drawing and shading up carefully, first, blocks of wood, then a plaster bust of Homer, then a 'life' model whose 'life' was apparent only when she was not posing.

I wanted to be an artist, but not that kind of an artist. I was interested in life, and, when it came to drawing, in the representation of life. Technical instruction in graphic exactitude was good, but I felt I needed even more to study objects on the move, to render impressions and to gain a knowledge of essential characteristics and their relationships that would enable me to draw anything at any angle without hesitation. Knowing the characteristic wrinkles in a coat-sleeve, say, was of more practical use to me than shading ten tons of wood blocks. What I needed was a series of busts of Homer sitting in a row, each wearing a different expression, so that I could study the characteristic disturbance of features in the acts of laughing, crying, sneezing, etc. I needed a *real* life class with a moving model, so that I could closely observe just what happens when one walks, and just what one can and cannot do with arms and legs; a class for drawing from memory at which I could crystallize my impressions; a class for the analysis of character, at which I could discover precisely in line such things as what makes old people look old and young people young; and what it is that makes a given person look different from everybody else, and how that difference—personality—may be most emphatically rendered.

Meanwhile my drawing had become almost a full-time job. Interest was now a passion. I had the fire in my stomach and I worked on my first regular assignment, the two jokes a week for the *Spectator*, with infinite pains and delight.

At first my jokes followed the customary pattern of British humour of that time, with a local twist when necessary. Basically New Zealand humour was much the same as that of the Old Country, since the traditions and conventions that had come with the settlers had been sustained by the regular flow of imported British periodicals, comedians and story-tellers. Copyright was vague and troublesome to enforce in distant lands, so colonial editors supplied themselves by scissors and paste when they wanted generalized jokes.

But even before 1900 much of the illustrated humour 'lifted' from English publications had begun to lose point for second-generation native New Zealanders, who failed to understand its English local allusions or to appreciate its underlying upper-middle-class assumptions.

By the time I came on the scene New Zealanders were discovering their own humour, not differing in pattern from the

English but fitted to their own circumstances—jokes about local characters and prominent citizens, with a strong personal interest; jokes about local conditions, like the difficulty of getting beer in prohibited areas, or the bad state of the roads outback; occupational jokes about shearers, miners, farmers, etc.; and something approaching protective satire in jokes about simple New Zealand farmers outwitting slick confidence-men from Sydney or in plain jibes against remittance-men. In those days New Zealand was one of the dumping-grounds for wasters kicked out to the Colonies with a quarterly allowance by their English families. These remittance-men were popularly supposed by chagrined New Zealanders to be uppish and overlordly, a sore point properly ripe for sublimation in jokes. New Zealand cartoonists in the 1900's used to draw two kinds of Englishman— a swell one with buck teeth, top-hat, spats, monocle, called Featherstonehaugh or Cholmondeley, who was always saying 'Bai Jove!' and a somewhat thicker one with a fat face and cap, the Pommy immigrant, who said 'Ow, I sy!' According to the jokes they tried to milk cows at the wrong end and went out rabbiting in golf suits. If such local material were occasionally to be illustrated the pictures had to be drawn locally too. It was all very good exercise for an aspiring comic artist.

I continued to post drawings to Australia and London on the offchance; and a judicious placing of my professional card had led to occasional jobs such as letterheads, labels, plans, showcards, crayon enlargements of snapshots, and a mural decoration. One of my most curious productions was a series of 'stereoscopic' scenes of the Burns–Johnson world heavyweight championship fight, for a slot machine. It gave satisfaction to the proprietor if not to the patrons. When later a customer was shot dead during a brawl at his Funfair he wanted me to do another series depicting the story of the tragedy. I appreciated the compliment but declined. The other various tasks that came my way I tackled with zest. To me each was an interesting problem to be solved for its own sake. The pay, never more than a few shillings, was useful but the real reward was in the achievement.

Nevertheless, while money was the measure of worth among my customers, I did my best to see that the dignity of my profession was not flouted by cheats. Sometimes my methods were a little high-handed. There was the time, for instance, when I called on the proprietor of a mushroom publication to collect the bill he owed me for one month's hard service as his artist-of-

THE CZAR'S NIGHTMARE

An early political cartoon (1904): Nicholas II of Russia fears revolution at home and defeat in the war against Japan

all-work. He told me the venture had not been a success and he would not pay. The 'agreement' he had given me was a fake, and anyway I was a minor without rights of litigation. 'I'll—I'll—' I stuttered, choking with rage. 'You'll do nothing,' he said. 'Why don't you take the furniture?' he said, sarcastically. I retired fuming, with an idea. Next morning at five o'clock, before the world was awake, I and a carrier friend of mine entered the building and carried off the office desk in his cart, after thoughtfully removing the contents and placing then tidily on the floor. We found the desk a new home in the country at Riversleigh, and I then returned to sniff the wind. I ascended the stairs with beating heart. There was my smart Northcliffe sitting blue in the face, with his papers neatly spread before him on the floor. I had to laugh. 'I could put you in gaol!' he says. And he could have. But after half an hour's mutual threatening, cursing and twitting, the tension slackened. I fitted him up with my old trestle table out of my 'art room' across the hall, and we parted friendly. But I kept his desk.

I did my best to uphold also the honour of my profession when necessary. There is, and I suppose there always will be, a romantic notion among the ignorant that there is something vaguely immoral about art and artists, especially comic artists. The ribald legend of Gillray and Rowlandson dies hard. When I had a telephone call one day from a businessman widely popular and admired I warmed with pleasure and good-will. Would I go to see him, he could put a job in my way. This was success. Appreciation. I called. He wanted me to make an illustration of some obscene joke that had taken his fancy. So that was what the stupid fool thought artists were for. Damn! Damn! Damn! I went white with rage. He was about thirty, I was fifteen. But the occasion had to be marked. His inkpot, conveniently full, stood there and I took it and turned it upside down on his desk, spat 'There! Now you can draw dirty pictures for yourself,' and left.

There were precious few publishing enterprises begun within reach of Christchurch that did not find me waiting on the doorstep. I was connected with a monthly magazine, for which I painted the coloured cover, illustrated the serial and short stories, provided the humorous section and designed advertisements. On publishing day, the proprietor, the editor and I walked up and down Cathedral Square flaunting copies so that the public might think everybody was buying us, but it was no go. The first number was the last. I drew anti-smoking and anti-gambling cartoons for the Salvation Army *War Cry*; and I was appointed occasional police-court sketcher for *New Zealand Truth*, a weekly newspaper specializing in sensational crime and sex news. I had seen that *Truth* printed court drawings but never any from Christchurch, and I decided to try my hand at it. The fact that I was a boy of fifteen still in short pants was a disadvantage. But I had already learned that in journalism one can enter a lot of places if one can avoid being asked who one is. So, giving a masterly impression of being a messenger for somebody or other, I sailed in with ease past the grim doorkeepers of the Police Court and saw what I needed to see. The editor in Wellington who engaged me 'blind' on the drawings I made probably did not know what his new artist—at five bob a nob—was like. He must have been surprised later to hear of my being ignominiously turned out of court because to one eagle eye I had looked too young to remain during the hearing of a divorce case. 'Leave the Coort!' shouted Sergeant Scully.

Throughout my term as a court artist Sergeant Scully was my *bête noire*, with his colleague Sergeant Bird a good second. These two consistently sought to foil my efforts. Whether it was that they considered my youthful presence at the exposure of sordid life at a police court an outrage against public morals, against the dignity of the court, or merely against their own dignity, because I had rubbed them up the wrong way in my caricatures of their persons, I shall never know. Certainly they were both exceptionally good to draw. Scully had sore eyes and an over-hanging paunch; Bird was tall, as thin as a skewer, with a wee wrinkled face.

The law was not always so unsympathetic. It was a kind copper who helped me on one memorable occasion to trick up from an old Rogue's Gallery photograph a plausible drawing of a notorious criminal in time to scoop the press photographers before they could get to him. And I got on better in the Supreme Court, especially after I had put on long trousers. A press photograph of the Court during a famous murder trial of that time shows Mr. Justice Denniston presiding in all his glory while just below him, self-installed with the cheek of the devil, wearing high collar and black tie and carefully looking like somebody's secretary with a perfect right to be there, sit I. In this case, by the way, three toughs were concerned but two turned King's Evidence and were pardoned. Two nights later I had the queer luck to find myself sitting one place away from these two in the gallery of the theatre. They knew me. They had seen their 'pictures in the paper.' And they had a peculiar glint in their eyes as they watched me. Remembering in time the British maxim that the asperities of public life must never be permitted to prejudice social relations, I took the boys out and bought them a soft drink. Never did a lemonade taste so full of lemon. They were not wicked, just ignorant. My contact with them, as with other crooks, was useful, as founding a conviction that there is more stupidity than wickedness in the world.

I kept my police-court sketching going, on and off, for four years. It extended my experience both as an artist and as a human being. In the old days before the law forbade the making of drawings in the British courts during trials, the atmosphere and conditions of a court were almost ideal for the study of character in all its diverse aspects.

Both of my parents had regarded my drawing with sympathetic

33A

THE SUPREME COURT AT CHRISTCHURCH (1907)

'Mr. Justice Denniston presiding in all his glory while just below him, self-installed with the cheek of the devil, wearing high collar and black tie and carefully looking like somebody's secretary with a perfect right to be there, sit I.'

Early caricature (1906)

indulgence, and when I succeeded in having some work published they began to doubt if they knew more than I did about what my life should be. But an artist was something new in our family, and the artistic life was precarious and scandalous, as was clearly to be learned from *Trilby*, *L'Œuvre* and other contemporary novels. They had both cherished a hope that I might one day resume my formal education and become something more recognizably respectable, like a barrister, a doctor or a clergyman. To please them and to see if I could, I had a go. After a couple of years at a business college which accommodated its hours to the peculiar needs of its pupils, and with the aid of an extremely absent minded 'coach,' I set out at sixteen to matriculate. I met complete failure. For several reasons. The examiners didn't ask me the questions I could answer. No questions about the Peloponnesian Wars. An essay on Modern Inventions I turned into a tract against war with some success. I was sunk without a trace in mathematics. My Latin was unorthodox. I failed dismally in drawing.

Something of the fiasco was undoubtedly due not only to lukewarmness in my ambition to follow one of the learned professions, but to the fact that alongside my studies I had continued at full blast as a black-and-white artist. And I had covered the fees of my coach by relaying his instruction to two other fellows at half rates, which provided an uncalculated distraction.

It was painfully clear that I was no good at examinations. I could not have passed an examination in a thousand years. This failure did not shake my confidence in myself, but rather in the educational authorities. In my mortification I came to share the conclusions of Strindberg (which I did not at that time know) about the fraud of examinations. Only an idiot could imagine that a human being could remember the precise answers to all of the questions that could be asked by examiners. What I wanted from education—and quickly—was a lead to comprehension of life in its totality, its far perspectives, its broad horizons, the big

34

sweeps, the universal balances. To what end need I fill my brain with details? It was enough to know where to get those if and when required, from those fitted to provide that service.

My disharmony betokened no silly scorn of scholarship. Far from it. When in later life I sauntered around the cloistered lawns of university colleges I meditated on how happily and gratefully I might have spent some years there acquiring an orderly mind. Learning to think by process of trial and error is the hard way. I was aware that my own efforts had been, to say the worst, catch-as-catch-can, to say the best, unorthodox, in that my search for knowledge had usually begun at the apex and worked back to the base, from effect to cause, from current affairs to historical origins, instead of the other way round. Yet something of my early views persisted; for in my lifetime I had met some men 'ill-educated' in the narrow sense who were most enlightened, and on the other hand some 'well-educated' men who were extraordinarily stupid. Obviously a knowledge of forestry may or may not have much to do with the ability to distinguish the wood from the trees.

My failure to matriculate was the end of my formal education. Thereafter I followed my natural bent in reading and reflection related to my own interests.

It was in 1907 that I had just fluffed my matriculation examination. As consolation I now had a thundering piece of luck. A spurt of local enterprise called forth by the holding of an international exhibition at Christchurch in that year included the publication of a skittish new weekly, the *Sketcher*. Fred Rayner, the proprietor, was a caricaturist himself, the first real caricaturist I had met. In the academic sense he could not draw, but his portraits were penetrating and intimate because he had that rare thing, a sense of individual character and, even rarer, the wit and confidence to represent it freely in line without troubling about technical shortcomings. I was waiting with my brown-paper parcel of drawings of local celebrities when he opened his office. He took me on at two pounds a week. But what I gained watching him taking notes behind a newspaper in the street and working them later into caricature portraits was more precious than rubies.

Cathedral Square was the Piccadilly Circus of Christchurch. If one stood long enough everybody in the local world passed by. It was an excellent observation ground. My maestro, with his red hair, sharp pink nose, twinkling blue eyes bespectacled and shaded by a rakishly-worn straw hat, took full advantage of it, lurking, shadowing and making secret notes. At his elbow I lurked too, fascinated.

'Haven't quite got his mouth, my boy,' he would say, screwing a critical nose at my attempt on the back of an envelope to catch some nob waiting for his tram a couple of yards away. 'That fellow's all in his mouth. Now just watch it. Watch the way it opens and shuts.' So saying he would calmly walk over and politely request the subject to direct him to the next street or to give him a light for his cigarette, while I stood by studying jaw-action.

That kind of direct examination greatly improved my judgment of essentials. So character may reside in a boot, an ear could be the man. The difference between good work and trash in the caricature of personality became clearer. I learned to scorn the so-called 'likenesses' taken from photographs, both the wooden or polite kind and the aimlessly distorted 'funny' kind, and to appreciate the art that lay in the synthesis and emphasis of truth perceived in the living person.

The *Sketcher* ended and Rayner departed, leaving me with enough local reputation to justify, almost immediately, a return to the *Spectator* now to a full-time job as its political cartoonist, no longer a reserve junior. Two full-page cartoons, four small ones, weekly. Two pounds. I was seventeen and growing up. As things were then in New Zealand there was an economic inevitability about my gravitation towards political cartooning. Illustrating jokes would never keep me. Caricaturing personalities offered very limited prospects. But here was a regular job at which, with freelancing additions, I could make a living.

Up till then I had been interested mainly in the drawing, and not in drawing my opinions. Now I had to take a closer interest in public affairs.

4

NEW ZEALAND's world interests at the beginning of the twentieth century, when surveyed from the middle of it, illustrate surprisingly the immutability of change. For example, we were haunted then, as today, by the Yellow Peril, meaning first the Chinese, later including the Japanese. In this we were undoubtedly influenced by Australia, where the emptiness of a continent sitting in close proximity to the dense populations of Asia had inspired an uneasy conscience and an exaggerated feeling of insecurity. There was no colour prejudice about it, for in New Zealand brown Maoris and white pakehas lived together without friction or impolite discrimination. But New Zealanders took their Yellow Peril seriously. And we were a bit disturbed about the Russians. There were too many of them, also. Who knew what the old Dowager Empress of China and the old Czar of Russia would be up to next? We heartily wished them both revolutions as soon as possible.

For protection we depended, of course, upon the ubiquitous British Navy; but we were very glad to see Admiral Sperry's American fleet put in at Auckland.

We left Europe to the British Government, confident that one of Rudyard Kipling's Tommy Atkinses was the equal of ten foreigners. If in practice this didn't always work out, we could be dutifully helpful, and we were rather proud of having sent ten contingents of volunteers to fight for the Old Country in the South African war. While our importers did good business with commercial travellers, we took the patriotic cue that 'Made in Germany' meant poor stuff, and we professed to believe that the Kaiser's armies and navy were made of lead and kept in cardboard boxes.

On the home front there was more originality.

37

It had been my luck to be born into the middle of a twenty-year period of bold radicalism under the successive governments of Ballance, Seddon and Ward. It was a time of ideas, in which an astonishing number and variety of social experiments were carried into law. New Zealand fifty years ago must have seemed dangerously 'advanced' to an English visitor, with its adult suffrage, its free education, its State insurance and State railways, its industrial arbitration, its old age pensions. Nobody had been frightened of a bit of the socialism or State ownership which were such bogies to the British in the Old Country. To me, of course, it all seemed natural.

Finance was sometimes a worry and there was much deploring of the unhappy facility with which our statesmen solved their problems by raising loans from Britain. British capital had been essential to the growth of New Zealand but now its concomitant, the abundant supply of British imports, frustrated the development of local manufacturing industries and threatened to fix New Zealand's destiny as exclusively an agricultural and pastoral appendage to the Old Country. This galled New Zealanders who felt the stirrings of national pride. The crimson bonds of Empire had a way of slipping into a knot under the adam's apple. Protective tariffs were a live issue, hotly discussed.

Long debates were in progress on land tenure, labour laws, Henry George's Single Tax and proportional representation. Liquor control—local option and prohibition—was a lively issue. We had strikes and labour troubles which were duly put down to inflammatory agitators. A fair number of working men were in the House of Representatives voting with the Liberal Government, but a separate Labour Party hardly existed. Outside there was something called the International Workers of the World which was humorously alluded to as the 'Wobblies.' Nobody took it seriously.

The *Spectator*, for which I was to work for the next three years, was ostensibly Liberal in politics and out to advance the policies and ambitions of its proprietor, G. W. Russell, popularly known as 'Rickety' Russell because of his precarious occupation of the parliamentary seat for the constituency of Riccarton. That the *Spectator* did this effectively and that the policies and ambitions were wholesome was shown by the fact that Russell subsequently achieved high office in a New Zealand government. This close proximity to an active politician was a valuable educational experience for me.

Our policy was liberal, but cautious. We were for progress, liberty, land settlement, education, arbitration, cheap money, maternity homes and Home Rule for Ireland; but we were suspicious of State control and we deplored labour agitators. We sat on the fence about Prohibition. Russell provided me with suggestions for the cartoons and week by week I dutifully called Prime Minister Seddon to account, severely denounced the Kaiser for building a navy and chided King Edward VII when he seemed to need it. The *Spectator* stood no nonsense.

Political life was not short of caricaturable personalities. The Premier, Dick Seddon, 'King Dick,' big and bearded, had once been a miner and never allowed anyone to forget it. Always he acted heartily, as though he had just dug up a large nugget. As a contrast, his successor, Sir Joseph Ward, was debonair, waxed-moustached and buttonholed, always dressed as though he had a lunch engagement at Downing Street. On the sidelines were lanky black mop-headed Tommy Taylor, leader of the prohibitionists, beloved voice of the people and incidentally my pet subject; and various men of character, including a popular member from a certain 'dry' constituency, who entered the House one evening during an important pronouncement by the Premier, sat down, took off his boots, placed them on the Treasury table and went to sleep snoring like a foghorn.

I started as the obedient hireling, but after a time, when I got into the swing of it, naturally my own political inclinations began to creep into the cartoons, proving once again that matter and manner of artistic expression are one, and irony and sarcasm are difficult to harness. While the cartoons filled the master's orders as to figures, background and caption, subtle changes in the emphasis and temper during the making sometimes changed the finished picture into something rather different from what might have been expected. On such occasions, when one of Russell's ideas had changed into something 'leftish' without one being able to put a finger on just what had made it so, I could see him beginning to suspect that I had a political axe of my own to grind and to wonder where I had got it.

Reformist politicians, when asked the origins of their opinions, usually talk of some emotional experience in their youth, such as anger at somebody's injustice or pity at somebody's misery. It was not so with me. In the first place I had been born into a 'progressive' society, which I consequently accepted as normal. Further development on equally bold lines seemed only right and proper. Even as a youngster I distrusted the emotional approach to politics. To my mind an ounce of calm deliberation was worth a ton of indignation, righteous or otherwise, when it comes to forming judgments concerning the practical improvement of human conditions. In any case I could never be angry or hate for more than five minutes.

But although it would be tiresome to pursue into pre-natal obscurity the derivations of one's political philosophy, one may recall points of time at which the mixture has jelled into coherence. One day I went to our rich quarter, among the big houses, to draw a retired ironmaster from Canada who had come to live his declining years in Christchurch. He received me kindly and we sat in his beautiful garden while I drew him. This wise, if somewhat forbidding old gentleman, touched off by something I had said, began to talk quietly of the possible beauties of living, the ideal organization of the State and the ultimate triumph of wisdom. He took the world view, moving outside our locality, past New Zealand, beyond the British Empire to the wide horizons of the human race. Secure in his fine house, he rejected the glib assumption of the permanence of social inequality. We sat constructing and reconstructing societies, finding the true balance of order and liberty for the betterment of the lot of mankind. I had read some of this before, but it was new to hear it spoken by a rich and successful business man. The sun was shining, the garden was green, the sky was blue—all that was needed was a fig-tree and we might have been Aristotle and a pupil. When at last I got up to leave, he went to his library and brought to me, as a parting gift to an attentive listener, a copy of Bellamy's *Looking Backward*. I never saw him again, but I still have his book. Peace to the bones of J. T. M'Bride. He little recked of the seed he planted that day. Before that my political ideas had been disconnected. After it, they began to take shape and relationship. *Looking Backward* led me to a course of New Worlds—Plato's *Republic*, Butler's *Erewhon*, Wells's *The Sleeper Awakes*, which I balanced with a good go at Burke, and just to counter-balance Burke, Tom Payne and William Morris.

My new job as regular political cartoonist to the *Spectator* gave me a modest standing in the community. I took a room at five shillings a week in Cathedral Square to work in. I bought myself a good suit. Romance reared its pretty head and I had a few love affairs. I discovered in myself an ability to dance and to sing Scottish songs *à la* Harry Lauder, the latter enabling me to add a few half-guineas to my income by accepting engagements at country concerts. I found at last two or three kindred spirits to talk to. Until then I had had little companionship. The life of an artist on the job demands concentration in solitude, and when I had the time I had not found anyone of about my own age who was at all interested in the things that interested me. The girls I took out certainly didn't want to talk about the nationalization of the land. The two or three local artists who worked for the Press were so much older than I that I could find no ease in their company. My father had been my principal foil for serious talk, but he had found a new interest in writing letters to the newspapers on aspects of religion, such as The Weight of the Soul. Some chap on his deathbed somewhere was reported to have allowed himself to be weighed before and after dying, and in the interim a slight loss of weight was shown. This represented the weight of his soul, claimed my father firmly in what widened into an acrimonious, esoteric and highly satisfying newspaper controversy about the material basis of the spiritual. In between times he felt in duty bound to exasperate orthodox 'Christians' by raising his favourite question: 'What Would Christ Do?' concerning the conduct of public affairs, in particular urging the practical application of Christian principles to Defence and Taxation.

My own political ideas fell together on a lower plane, but I took them seriously, read up the issues, attended meetings, debated, and imperceptibly graduated from bookishness to free-and-easy exchange of ideas with persons—occasionally even with personalities.

Regular attendance at the Saturday night open forum held in a cart with flaring oil torches in Cathedral Square brought me into contact with the speakers and earned me at last the privilege of addressing familiarly as 'Dan,' 'Jack,' and 'Will' local Radicals, some of whom, surprisingly enough, were to become His Majesty's Ministers for this or that twenty or thirty years later. Who could have thought that the frock-coated, top-hatted statesman I ran into in London setting out for Buckingham Palace forty years later was a fire-eater I had heard from the tail of that cart so long ago?

I got a lot of 'isms and 'ologies in and out of my system. The One-Big-Union idea bit me, and I went to great pains to work out a chart of possible industrial organization which would have had me clapped into gaol fifty years later. Finally it horrified even its author and I washed it out as incompatible with my idea of democracy.

With zest I stretched my journalistic privileges to get me around to whatever was going, from opening of Parliament to railway strikes; and to gain me access to notable visitors passing through, like Ernest Shackleton, the explorer, Paderewski, the pianist, and Labour leaders like Will Crooks and Tom Mann (who turned up surprisingly in a frock coat with silk facings). I even had talk with Keir Hardie. ('Good evening, Mr. Hardie.' 'Good-night, my boy.') I hob-nobbed around with some famous American orators on Prohibition whose names I have forgotten.

Prohibition worried me. After a spate of rhetoric on the subject I was left confused. Did the suppression of a pernicious traffic balance the loss of individual liberty? Had a man the right to go to hell in his own way? . . . I inclined to prefer the methods of education and persuasion . . . I was making many cartoons on the subject and it occurred to me that for one who should know his own mind about Prohibition it was a disability that I did not know what it was like to be drunk. So I persuaded a friend to go with me to the park with a half-bottle of whisky, which, sitting on the long grass in the dark, we solemnly tossed off in the interests of enlightenment. In no time at all we were both blind-o. The experiment was no good. When I came round, the issue had not clarified. I could not look a whisky in the face again until I was over forty.

The proprietor of the *Spectator* got back into the House of Representatives and to celebrate his success he took a two months' holiday, leaving a friend of mine, George, to edit the paper. George and I took the opportunity to brighten up the policy a little in his absence. Things were never quite the same after that. George departed suddenly. A firmer hand was felt. I chafed for an outlet for my growing political conscience. Rickety's two pounds had not bought my exclusive services.

Conditions were not softened by the fact that while I was the cartoonist of the *Spectator* I had had myself appointed also as cartoonist to a new Labour weekly, the *Herald*, published in Wellington. On Thursdays I piped in the *Spectator* the circumspect voice of liberalism, on Mondays I was Labour's messenger clad in thunder in the *Herald*. The situation was too piquant to last. Russell and I had a row and parted.

I walked under the weeping willows by the river and made a few plans. First, a long-shot. I tried to persuade the most admirable politician I knew to start a new weekly with me as its cartoonist. Apart from the awkward facts that Tommy Taylor was the leader of the prohibitionists, and that in that capacity he had been a butt for my ridicule in the *Spectator* and other sheets, I had picked him as an honest and, in other respects, enlightened man with whom it would be a pleasure to work. He was surprised and touched. But noble fellows like Tommy Taylor never have any money. 'You cannot start a paper on enthusiasm, my boy,' he said.

Second, the even chance. My two years as a journalist had given me an inside view of the comparative business positions of Christchurch newspapers. Our two bulky weeklies, all solidity and dignity, the Liberal *Canterbury Times* and the Conservative *Weekly Press*, were in cut-throat competition, and I knew the *Canterbury Times* was weakening. The circumstances demanded delicacy and finesse. With Machiavellian craft I 'dummied up' a copy of the *Canterbury Times* with a couple of full pages of lively cartoons, and, choosing a time when I figured the periodical statement of his depressing circulation figures would be lying on his desk, I took it along to the business manager, with a carefully prepared sales-talk explaining how necessary for him it was to engage me. To my delight it came off, hook, line and sinker. I landed a plum job such as I had dreamed of, excellent reproduction at last, large space to spread, sympathetic editor, practically a free hand—all this and the fabulous salary of five pounds a week, too. I was eighteen years old and the world was my oyster. I took my savings, thirty pounds, and gave myself a month off before I started, to go to Australia to see for myself what kind of people ran the Sydney *Bulletin*. They had been accepting a lot of my work latterly, and one never knew where that might lead.

On my return all went very well indeed, artistically. The bigger space gave me a chance to experiment with bolder effects, the excellent reproduction and good printing, a possibility of subtler expression. I worked endlessly and by degrees my touch grew more confident and sensitive. There were signs that my cartoons were being noticed in Australia—not surprising perhaps, since every week I posted twenty copies of the paper marked URGENT PERSONAL to Australian editors, with the general idea that if you shoot enough arrows into the air, you are bound in the end to hit something.

Politically, however, all soon was not so well. General Godley, sent from Britain to advise on New Zealand defence, recommended the Government to initiate a measure of compulsory military training. Immediately the country was filled with argument for and against.

I was against, mainly on political grounds. I was no pacifist, although I believed, of course, that wholesale killing was no way to settle international disputes; but I had to make a distinction between defence and offence. I knew well enough that the rights of individuals rested upon collective responsibility. But to me this Bill was abhorrent because it was obviously the thin end of the wedge of conscription, rightly detested by the free British peoples as a sinister foreign invention for curtailing the liberties of the people and arresting political progress. It was doubly wrong to introduce such a measure in time of peace. Even in time of war, Britain had always done well with voluntary enlistment.

In short, mine was the traditional Liberal attitude. If anyone wants to know what Mr. Gladstone said in 1862, it was probably very like what young Mr. Low said in 1911.

Totalitarian war was not yet thought of.

But the *Canterbury Times* was *for*. Deadlock. The Chairman of the Board, a Very Important Person, had me to his house for private conference. But no conclusion emerged except that everyone was out of step but me. Both sides retreated in good order. For that present I refused to draw cartoons approving the Act, and the paper refused to publish any I drew disapproving it.

But my days were numbered. Governments are not as amenable as individuals. Backed by my father I was preparing to resist medical examination when out of the blue came a telegram from the Sydney *Bulletin*: 'Can you take position as our Melbourne cartoonist for six months?' Could I? Wow! I replied 'Yes' without asking about pay or conditions.

'But has not Australia a similar law?' my Chairman of the Board asked me. 'And is not the *Bulletin* in favour of it?'

'I will attend to that when it arises. Life is full of uncertainties,' replied tight-rope walker Low.

Before I left for Australia something happened which suggested a postscript. Some time before my brother and I had bought for ten pounds a mare allegedly in foal to Ribbonwood, the famous New Zealand champion trotter. Actually the distension of the unfortunate creature's stomach was caused by an equine illness called toot—but we didn't know that. One night a storm came up and blew the poor girl into a ditch. Lying half drowned with all four legs sticking up in the air, there was only one thing to be done. We borrowed a gun and shot her. Then I dug an enormous hole, my high-water mark as a hole-digger, and after persuading an obliging passing teamster to hitch his team to the remains and lug them out into the open to their last rest, I buried her. As I

44

patted the top earth I thought to myself 'This is a cartoon idea.'
The scene could be given an allegorical significance and I could
be burying my policy, my past, my soul, my future or something.
An ambiguous title, say, 'A Fool Fills His Belly with the East
Wind' or 'One Toot and Ye're Oot.' Certainly I felt that in that
hole lay something more than a dead mare. Boyhood, friends,
the local success and recognition I had built up one brick on top
of another.

Two days later I stood in the stern of the ship and shed a tear
of self-pity as I watched New Zealand disappear over the horizon.
It is not easy to uproot yourself for ever from the scenes and
people you love and go and start all over again alone in a
strange land.

5

THERE was a day when New Zealanders, with the good-natured candour of next-door neighbours, used to twit Australians.

'Australia? That penal settlement? No thanks. I'm off to England.'

'England? That place where all the convicts come from?'

Nobody any longer thinks that the early convicts who began the modern New South Wales were everything to be ashamed of. Frequently they were men of spirit and enterprise who refused to stand obediently and rot. There were many whose only fault was the admirable one of resistance to oppression. Occasionally there were martyrs to great causes. The Men of Tolpuddle, forefathers of modern trades unionism, went to Botany Bay.

A century later Sydney had become the fifth biggest port in the Empire, with the third most beautiful harbour in the world and the reputation of being, in contrast to our simple honest New Zealand towns, smart, tough and rather wicked. It was known also as a nursery for poets, writers and caricaturists.

The answer to the question: 'Why did Australia produce so many caricaturists and comic artists?' was the Sydney *Bulletin*, the red-covered weekly known throughout Australia as 'the Bushman's Bible.'

The men behind the *Bulletin*, notably 'Jules François' Archibald, a master journalist, and William Macleod, an artist with solid business ability, had made it a major policy of their paper to encourage native Australian talent. The supply of poets and writers began to flow almost immediately. That of comic artists and caricaturists had to be primed at first by a couple of importations, Livingstone Hopkins ('Hop') from America, and Phil May from Britain. With these first-class masters setting the standard in the eighteen-eighties and nineties, the local talent was not long in appearing, and at the beginning of the century the *Bulletin* had grown a team of social and political artists it would have been hard to beat anywhere in the world. In the matter of style and ability in draughtsmanship, that was good; in the matter of satirical approach and content, it was better.

The *Bulletin* was radical, rampant and free, with an anti-English bias and a preference for a republican form of government. No more imported governors nor doggerel national anthems, no more pompous borrowed generals, foreign titles, foreign capitalists, cheap labour, diseased immigrants, if the *Bulletin* could help it. The Crimson Bonds of Empire be damned. In domestic affairs it had the disrespect for crusted custom proper to the Press of a new country. Its caricaturists found in this spirit the perfect inspiration for caustic satire. The ghost of Gillray, the Scottish eighteenth-century master who in his day had made Britain the home of caricature with his robust gibes at the Georges, came to life again in Australia in Phil May's cartoon of John Bull as the Angel of Deliverance hovering over a possible colony with a Bible in one hand and a bottle of gin in the other; and in Hop's classic THE NATION MOURNS, showing a drunk with his tongue hanging out sitting on the doorstep of a pub closed for the day of Queen Victoria's funeral.

By 1911, the *Bulletin*, like Australia, had had some of its rough edges rubbed off, but there was plenty of life in the old horse still. It was the dearest wish of all black-and-white artists to get into the *Bulletin*. And into it I went for a six months' engagement. What luck!

The *Bulletin* I found was still violently nationalistic, with a free and independent Australia as its aim and White-Australia, Federation, and Protection as its watchwords. That meant rigid immigration laws; a strong defence establishment based upon compulsory military training for home defence; the strengthening of Commonwealth powers at the expense of the States; and a high tariff wall against the world.

All three main ideas were in process of realization. As a side-issue of White Australia, the *Bulletin* still played up the 'Yellow Peril,' and cartoons of Japanese monkeys up to devilish mischief were still a stock dish. Of the latter two, the sort of federation the *Bulletin* wanted had necessitated the scornful rejection of Joseph Chamberlain's imperialism, which had appeared in the light, not of co-operation between partners, but of integration in a plan for exploitation by British capitalists placing other

47

considerations before that of the welfare and progress of Australia. If Australia, said the *Bulletin*, were to become a nation, she must have her own local manufacturing industries. Britain, in the character of a dumper of cheap goods that would hinder the growth of these industries, was as unwelcome as any other foreign dumper. Australia for the Australians! Australia a nation! Advance Australia! Give 'em air, boys!

In pursuit of this theme, the *Bulletin* grew vehement. High protection of local industry became the principle of the Left in politics, and, in contrast, abundant imports became that of the Right, whose adherents were dubbed by the *Bulletin* 'Little Australians.'

The Labour movement and the *Bulletin* had grown up side by side, and the paper, agreeing with and inspiring the party on many issues, especially the tariff issue, became its natural advocate, and the most influential political voice in Australia. Whether the paper supported or supplied the policy of the party or vice versa, might have been a matter of opinion; but certainly, in its palmy days, the *Bulletin* inspired the Labour Party with ideals and ideas to an extent rare in political journalism.

The *Bulletin*'s ideas were not always mine and later I was occasionally to bump up against them. But my subject-matter to start with was to be the small parish-pump stuff of local affairs in the State of Victoria.

I was packed off to live and work in Melbourne, under the care of a fatherly gentleman shining with benevolence who was to see me settled and would advise me on the new environment. I took a liking on the spot to gentle slow-voiced Ed Fisher. No tenderfoot could have had a kinder cicerone. He had begun his literary career writing 'poetry' for In Memoriam notices ('Where Jim has gone we do not know, But how we miss him here below' type of thing), and eventually graduated into management of the sketchy Melbourne office of the *Bulletin*, the tedium of which he relieved by writing light verse and reminiscences. Ed was English to the backbone and showed it by his appearance and deportment, barely concealing a faint contempt for Australians. His connection with the *Bulletin* sometimes gave him inner pain. There had been, for instance, the incident at a restaurant during the celebration of the Relief of Mafeking when he, in reality a devoted patriot, was made the object of public contumely as the only representative present of the *Bulletin* and its pro-Boer policy; the end of the matter being that he was obliged to stand out and sing Rule Britannia solo, as though he had not wished to. This and similar embarrassments had saved him from excessive loyalty to official *Bulletin* policy. This suited me down to the ground, as it promised me elbow-room. Six hundred miles from the head office, we were practically on our own hook. My work was to produce a weekly page of about twelve topical drawings. I was ignorant of the matters from which I was to draw material, but the *Bulletin*, I found, had a practice at that time of 'feeding' its cartoonists with suggestions contributed by journalists and others on a basis of five shillings apiece, if used. Certainly in artistic performance idea and treatment are two sides of the same penny, and a cartoonist that does not supply his own ideas is only half a cartoonist. But at that time the *Bulletin* arrangement was highly convenient to me, arriving green and innocent from afar, especially since I had the selection.

It was summer. I was twenty I was working for the fabulous *Bulletin*. I had real money in my pockets—ten pounds a week. I found new friends with houses by the sea, and I enjoyed for the first time the luxury of sprawling on the grass through the long warm Australian evenings in the congenial company of artists, poets and writers, with the sea pounding the beach a hundred yards away. This was happiness and time passed quickly.

My six months were not marked by historic cartoonable events, except perhaps for the founding of the new capital city of the Commonwealth. A mighty company of notables from the four corners of Australia were assembled on the bare plain of Canberra for the ceremony of laying the foundation-stone. A press photograph of the scene includes me crowding, with prescient tactlessness, William Morris Hughes for a good view, and, a short distance off, a small brown dog, presumably ownerless and uninvited. Of this dog I can now reveal an incident which I prefer to describe not as hushed-up but as merely unrecorded until now. The company had listened to the appropriately lofty discourses, sung the right hymns. The Governor-General's plumes quivered as he tapped the stone with his trowel and solemnly declared it well and truly laid. Whereupon, before anyone could stop it, the small brown dog sociably trotted up and christened it for him.

The work was within my range, but I did not spare myself in trying to set the Yarra river on fire. When at the end of my engagement in Melbourne I found that I had done well enough to merit permanent attachment to the *Bulletin* staff on a modest

49

retainer, I could take stock. I was jaded with overwork. I needed exercise and a quiet think. The annual holiday for everyone, universally accepted later, was not usual then in Australia and although I had travelled about alone and in company, journeys to the country or the seaside with no other purpose than an enjoyable loaf would have seemed absurd. And anyway I had no money to spare. I decided on a cheap idea that met all the points. I would walk the six hundred miles to Sydney. I had to get there anyhow.

It is one thing to sing about 'Waltzing Matilda' and another to do it. Off I went with blanket, tin billy-can and frying-pan. I had heard of the tradition of station hospitality in Australia whereby shearers and seasonal farm workers humping the bluey from station to station could count on handouts of a pinch of tea, a handful of flour and a bunk almost as a right. With my soft hands I was too obviously no shearer, but for all that the tradition often held. A fellow foot-slogger taught me how to cook out of flour and water that Australian standby, a 'damper.' I slept in some queer dumps, when necessary cutting some wood or doing odd jobs for my keep. When I had no luck, I parked under the sky, in Starlight Hotel. I kept off the main roads because in those days the rough macadam was hard on the feet, and in taking short cuts I often blundered far off the mark into little more than tracks. Sometimes it was very lonely and I had the wide open spaces to myself all day. Just me and Nature. What quiet happiness to awaken in the crisp dawn, de-blanket, without having to shave or wash or change shirt, leisurely start a fire, boil up and fry my simple meal, put on a pipe, make a sketch of a tree, and then amble away into the blue with my shadow in front of me . . . What fools we are to forget the delights of simplicity . . .

I made one big mistake. As I had mapped it, I could usually expect to find a pub or some kind of shanty about every fifteen or twenty miles. But I had forgotten the big drought which during the previous summer had baked up the Riverina and driven everybody south. I hadn't bargained for dead pubs.

It was after a long weary day's pull that I arrived in the evening at what should have been, according to my map, a bush pub. I had planned to get a drink, a meal and perhaps a bed here. But things had happened. The place was dried up and deserted, windows out, doors hanging on a screw. Picked clean. The wall off, nary a stray bottle. Not a soul. In the gathering dusk the strange silence brooding over the dead pub began to chill my blood. All the same, I thought, I will doss here for the night.

Clearing a place in the corner, I unhitched my blanket, pulled it around me and was soon dead to the world.

I awoke suddenly. It was black night. Silence hung heavy. I saw with a start two points of light. Eyes. Another pair . . . and another . . . and another. A myriad army was looking at me steadily. I was evidently surrounded. Dread crept over my heart. In the dark I felt for a loose plank nearby and lifting it in both hands I hurled it at the foe. Crash! There was a squeaking scuffle . . . and the eyes resumed their intent gaze as if nothing had happened. More of them than ever. I decided to pack up and get out. If I had to fight for it, I would sell my life dearly. Stealthily gathering together my blanket and roping my bluey over my shoulder, I armed myself with another chunk of wood. Charge! Laying about me right and left with my clumsy club, I took two flying steps through the open wall. There were scurrying shapes and eyes everywhere—millions of them it seemed. I have never seen so many rabbits. Whether emboldened by their numbers or by their needs in this parched habitation, they were certainly not as frightened of me as I was of them, and they hardly bothered to get out of my way as I hurried to put a respectable distance between myself and what felt like an H. G. Wells's nightmare. It has occurred to me since what a newspaper headline it would have made: 'LOW DEVOURED BY RABBITS.'

I was on the road for eight weeks—four hundred and fifty miles walking, the rest lifts. The whole trip cost me four pounds. At the end of it, after a scrub with all the trimmings at the public baths and a day in bed, I felt better than I have ever felt before or since. All ready to tear the town apart in a new assignment.

Hope deferred. There was no regular spot for me in Sydney. Meanwhile the *Bulletin* retained me as a kind of roving contributor to range the length and breadth of Australia, transport charges but not living expenses paid, making caricature portraits of local notables. How I was to do this was to be my own concern. Buzz off.

The distances were enormous and the difficulties such as to strain my ingenuity; but as it worked out, the narrow margin between expenses and earnings left me no time to worry about that. Usually I arrived in a new town not knowing a soul, starting from scratch with perhaps two or three names of leading personalities and the merest smattering of local lie-of-the-land. My method was simple. First I found a good cheap place to live, with a table and a chair and the loan of a long mirror in which

I could pose myself as model for difficult pieces of drawing. The latter was a 'must.' I put up with some dreadful witches of landladies because of my regard for their mirrors. Then I looked around to see what functions were impending and in the photographers' windows to see what local worthies were on show. Then, armed with effrontery and persistence and my beautifully engraved visiting card: 'D. Low, the *Bulletin*, Sydney' (my father's lesson about quality in advertising had left its mark on me), I found the Town Hall and called on the Mayor. Few Australian Mayors were so lacking in vanity as to refuse audience to a representative of the *Bulletin*, however much of a stripling he might turn out to be. Once in, I was usually able to establish pleasant relations by a well-rehearsed routine to the effect that the importance of his town had now become so appreciated in Sydney that it was judged advisable that the leading men of this paragon community should be better known, and for this purpose I was there to draw their portraits, starting with himself as its first citizen. While his Worship posed for me, he would certainly ask: 'Who else are you drawing?' (If he did not, I made it my business to put the question into his mouth.) To which I would reply: 'Whom would you suggest?' After that, usually all that was necessary was to let nature take its course and allow one notable to pass me on to another, sorting out the worthy from the unworthy during the process. It rarely failed. But when it did that made no difference, for I developed a memory technique of drawing with my forefinger on the palm of my hand that so impressed the lines of my Mayor on my mind that I could draw him from memory as soon as I got outside. Whereupon I passed on to my next prospect with a similar routine.

As I moved around and a town opened like a flower to me, my progress was like that of a snowball, beginning with civil importunities and building up cumulatively to favoured-guest invitations. I scooped in an average of eight to ten portraits a week and on the way collected a wide variety of social experiences.

But if I had my share of kindliness and hospitality, I had also some snubs. There was, for instance, the mortifying occasion when I was forcibly ejected after a brawl from an office in Perth, Western Australia. But that was as proxy for the *Bulletin* rather than on my own account, for the man I had come to draw had a grudge against the paper, not particularly against me. Not that that made any difference to my bruises.

An incident in Tasmania was typical of one kind of difficulty. A Hobart city father of very picturesque appearance had agreed to sit for me at his home. After, he asked if he could see my notes. Like a fool I showed him. An expression of horror contorted his face. 'No, No, NO!' he said, tearing the sheets in two and throwing them on the blazing fire. I was speechless with indignation. 'Leave my house!' he said, and I had to, it being his house. It made no real difference anyway, since I remembered the notes. But after that, whenever similar trouble seemed likely to arise, I manufactured two sets of notes—one for use, one for show.

As a contrast, I remember softly an octogenarian philanthropist in Adelaide. I found him sitting at his desk, silk hat on head, with an absent air making piles out of a little heap of golden sovereigns. I was a little embarrassed to find my attempts at polite conversation completely ignored, but I went on making my notes. It was only when I rose to go that my subject opened his mouth. He gave me a foggy look and said: 'Have you any money?' Astounded, I replied: 'Certainly.' 'Here,' he said, carefully removing the topmost sovereign of the heap and handing it to me. I was impelled to rebuff the indignity but I could not frustrate the dear old man's good will.

I see now, through age and experience, that to some my requests for co-operation must have seemed impertinent, and my intent mischievous, if not downright malicious. I was so deeply preoccupied with the business of drawing that I sometimes overlooked the fact that those with only the vulgar conception of caricature as aimless distortion of physical shortcomings could have had no inkling of my own view of it. How could I have explained my eagerness to find its art, my zest to try to capture and reduce to visual terms that most elusive of all qualities, individuality? Whilst so engaged it seemed to me self-evident that to concern myself with the emotional reactions of my subject would be degrading to us both.

Believing this, I bore with private contempt those who childishly assumed that the aim of my caricatures was merely to be 'funny.' Refusal to sit for me I could ascribe only to churlishness or plain damned ignorance. Hindrance was stupidity to be over-ridden or circumvented.

To redress the elusiveness of the 'material' in my New Zealand youth I had discovered that unobtrusiveness in dress and behaviour could get me unnoticed into places and situations where my presence was uninvited, or even prohibited. I became interested in bringing this unobtrusiveness by experiment almost to a science, to be turned on and off like a tap. I dressed deliberately to merge into backgrounds, avoided full stares, noisy coughs, rapid movements, isolated stands, strong lights—anything, in fact, that was in the least likely to attract attention. In addition I made a deliberate attempt to think softly, to contract my personality and subdue my 'rays.' Sometimes, I am sure, I was so unobtrusive you could hardly have told I was present. I got near to invisibility as I sleeked myself into forbidden places.

The technique required minor variations, of course, according to circumstances.

Usually there are enough officials about big public meals or receptions to fall over one another. Any confusion is apt to be put down to the incompetence of other fellows. When I wanted to gate-crash such things I walked into the dining-hall boldly like an official and altered the place-cards so that Mr. Low got a good seat. Sometimes I did it too well. An official luncheon of welcome was given at Adelaide for a number of distinguished people just arrived from England. I had put myself sitting amongst a number of strangers who assumed that I was one of the welcomed. All went well. The principal guest, whose name I forget, was called upon to reply. The Chairman then said: 'It gives me great pleasure to call upon Mr. Henry Stead, the distinguished British journalist, to say a few words.' I suddenly realized that he was looking at me. I was petrified. The most embarrassing moment of my life. Imagine my relief to hear behind me the soothing sound of the words: 'Mr. Chairman and gentlemen . . .' issuing from the real Henry Stead in the corner at which I had placed him when I had taken his seat.

Subsequently Henry Stead became a particular friend of mine; but I never heard him rise to make a speech without a shiver.

When after my travels I looked at my four hundred portrait caricatures collected in a book—my first real book—I saw that, although I had succeeded in avoiding flashy 'lightning-sketch' rubbish, my aim at the psychological essence had achieved, except in a very few cases, only wooden superficiality. The reason was clear. A good piece of caricature represents not only what the artist sees but what he *knows* about what he draws. The nature of the job had not allowed me sufficient time to get to know enough of the people who lived within these visible shells.

Well . . . I had learned that much anyway; and towards the end I was drawing better caricature portraits than at the beginning.

Incidentally, and quite apart from drawing, I had learned also more about myself. The job had demanded a deal of energy and concentration. But I had had some left for other interests. Being

54

for the time a free wanderer, the master of my own time and unhindered by the solicitude of relatives and friends, I took the opportunity to satisfy my curiosity upon some of my own capacities. A period followed which might have been called 'experimental living.' I had wondered what it felt like to starve, and I wanted to know how long I could go without food, so I stopped eating and lived on water. The answer was eight days. On the eighth day I grew alarmingly weak and hysterical. My kind old landlady to whom I babbled an explanation of my condition sent me to bed and broke my fast with a cup of warm diluted milk, followed by a good 'talking-to' as dessert. 'Poor boy! Poor boy!' The dear old soul quite naturally concluded that I had starved myself to pay her the rent. How could I explain to her that I was the result not of destitution but of scientific curiosity?

How cheaply could one live? was another of my personal guinea-pig investigations. It involved my living for a month on 12s. 6d. a week—bed, board, including loan of long mirror and all—while at the same time keeping a respectable front. I was happy enough sleeping in an out-house; but I got very tired of sausages-and-mashed at fourpence a plate, my big meal of the day. Going without alcoholic drinks was no great deprivation for me, since I drank very little; but giving up cigars was misery.

By the time that travelling job was ended for lack of material I had acquired considerable self-confidence and some polish in company. I had viewed the national resources of Australia at first-hand, been personally conducted down gold-mines, through factories, vineyards, orchards, runs and ranges. I had chewed sugar-cane and wheat and prodded cattle and sheep. I had travelled Australia from end to end, visited the Parliaments and institutions of all six States, and made personal contact with practically everyone of importance in the continent from aboriginal King Billy of Budgaree downwards. A useful prelude to a career as a full-blown political cartoonist for the *Bulletin*.

But that had to wait. The *Bulletin's* staff of political cartoonists all seemed aggressively healthy and unlikely to pass away to make a place for me. Rather, I fancied with impatience, the opposite. Meanwhile I moved in as a sort of general utility, having a cut at everything—jokes, portrait caricatures, story illustrations, et cetera.

This was the first—and last—time I ever worked in an editorial office. The experience was of no value to me as a guide to future conduct, because this one in 1913 was like no other office on earth. The *Bulletin* was a magnet to talent in Australia and wisely kept a kind of open house for bush poets, artists and writers, who just naturally came to it as they might come home. The small fry sat on the benches provided in the front office, the big fish, names legendary in Australia, wandered around the building. The place was agog with callers and there was no defensive commissionaire in those days to regulate the traffic up and down the stairs of the editorial department. Heaven knows how the paper ever managed to reach publication. One of the prized decorations in the sub-editor's room was a plaster model of straining figures lugging a demonic shape by the tail out of a pit, with the carved caption: LOOK! WE'VE GOT IT OUT AGAIN!

Camped out in a third-floor room which I appropriated for my workroom, I had the intermittent inspiration of people passing through. Henry Lawson bubbling with secret mirth and making cabalistic signals about his current financial position. (When forty years later I look at a photograph of the Sydney statue of an unfamiliar Henry living up to the character of Australia's most be-loved poet, I wish someone had carved on the plinth his immortal line: 'Beer makes you feel as you ought to feel without beer'); Randolph Bedford, the *Bulletin's* own Pacific traveller, whose adventures would have made Munchausen's hair curl; poets galore, including the gentle Roderick Quin and the uproarious Hugh McCrae; storytellers by the bunch—this chap with some impossible tale of how he seduced a beautiful Spaniard in the stokehold of a sinking ship; that chap airing his theory that Australia was really on top of the world and consequently Britain and Europe were the real Antipodes. Sometimes Norman Lindsay would appear from his Blue Mountains fastness, a birdlike man of rapid speech with sharp intelligent eyes. This was Norman's hey-day when he was busy proving that he was the best penman of his generation, his talent shining so brightly as to dim lesser lights into insignificance. I could hardly speak to him for rever-ence. But his admirers filled the landscape, and, as is usual with admirers, tended to crowd out newcomers anyway. It was queer to find myself plonked down in the midst of these characters, many of whom had been until yesterday remote gods to me.

Sometimes on the doorstep I met Archibald, the genius who had begun it all, who in his latter days had become garrulous and wanted listeners. We would go for a ride. We rode in a buggy through the Sydney Domain eating pickled gherkins from a bottle he found in his pocket, and he told me all about the people he didn't like. We met John Norton, newspaper magnate, the

Day off in Australia (1914)

founder of Norton's *Truth* and himself a most sensational ornament of the 'sensation Press.' He was also the world's prize curser. He decorated his speech quite naturally with the foulest adjectives I have ever heard, and to make matters worse, he seemed to have a fixed idea that everybody was deaf. I was aghast when we pulled up at a tea kiosk and he called at the top of his voice for some '. . . ing tea and sandwiches,' using his favourite adjective. The management, however, evidently accustomed to these invasions, sent a pretty waitress with just their completely sexless tea and sandwiches as usual.

Only one thing was missing from the *Bulletin* office in my day. Music by Offenbach. The atmosphere was saved from outright 'bohemianism' only by the unexpectedly sedate deportment of the managers and editors. 'Hop,' the American father of Australian humour, turned out to be a perfect monument of solemn dignity, whose relaxation was making fiddles and playing bowls. 'Wit,' he said to me, 'is just the sense of proportion. Sensible men (that is to say, witty men) conserve their talents for use in working hours, leaving lesser men to mitigate their disappointments with the cheap consolations of exhibitionism.'

New South Wales State politics were having an unusually violent period. The Government was hanging on to office by one vote, tempers ran high and missiles flew. Sober historians recorded 'a violent and disgraceful exhibition' in the State Assembly, during which 'such unspeakably vile language was used by some Opposition member that the Hansard staff couldn't, or wouldn't, take it down.' There was discord, too, in the Federal arena. The State and Federal Labour leaders were having a family jar and thickening the air with fraternal recriminations.

I found an interest both educational and professional in all this, but 'Hop,' Lindsay and Vincent looked after the big cartoons on national subjects and I got a chance only when someone took a week off. In one way that was just as well. It did not suit me to work in an office drawing ideas to order under the nose of an editor. Within myself I began to fall foul of the paper's policies. To start with, I was sceptical of the White Australia conception, linchpin of *Bulletin* policy, and mistrustful of the ideas that went with it. If it had taken a hundred years to get five million people to Australia, how long was it going to take to fill up the vacant spaces under our policy of severely restricted immigration? It seemed like a fool's paradise notion to me. I was for nationalism as far as was necessary to secure a healthy economic and political balance, but the *Bulletin's* exclusive flag-wagging seemed to me

57

neither good morals nor good politics. How far could Australia get on its own anyway? The root of my heresy lay in that I was in my bones a universalist, inclined to divide people up horizontally, good and bad; rather than vertically, English, French, Germans, Chinese, Russians and so on. My instincts were opposed to the narrow nationalism. The *Bulletin's* provocative gibes at Japan seemed to me boyishly irresponsible. If a European war ever came off, we should be trying to keep Japan sweet on our side instead of spitting in her eye. We should be thinking with our brains, not our blood.

There came a day when in a spasm of integrity I refused to draw one of the editor's Jap monkey ideas, to his great astonishment. James Edmond was a grand editor, one of the best. He looked at me sourly through his thick lens spectacles that magnified his eyes six times larger than life. Now then, this is where you stick, Low, I thought. Man or mouse? 'Sit down,' he said. I did, and explained myself. I got everything off my chest. Militant nationalism, the Imperial Connection and all. I could see him thinking: What the hell's this? Mutiny? Damn and blast, I thought, is my goose cooked? But Jimmy took his gag back. The *Bulletin* was big enough. It was some time, however, before I got another show at a big cartoon.

Of all professions journalism is the most widening to the horizon of the mind, if one has one. The journalist is licensed by custom to find out. To gratify his curiosity becomes a duty. The universal respect for the mysterious powers of publicity and the general yearning for self-revelation ensure him wide co-operation. If the proper study of mankind is man, no other occupation provides such facilities for observation.

I have already described how my association with New Zealand *Truth* gave me a nodding acquaintance with Crime. An assignment to provide boxing cartoons for the *Bulletin* sporting page now began my education in Sport. Those were the big days of boxing in Australia. Champions came from the world over to dispute their titles at the Bushcutters' Bay Stadium at Sydney, built to house the Burns–Johnson world heavyweight championship back in 1908. I had my ringside seat there week by week for two years until I was cooled off because a cartoon I drew of myself with an umbrella up at a particularly bloody encounter aggravated the management, who decided it was bad for business.

I have never had any particular interest in watching sport—other people playing games—but I was mildly curious about boxing, which I sometimes tried myself for fun. Soon I became so bored with my job looking at these professionals that I would not have cared had they been fighting with hatchets. But when individuals in the boxing audience merged into a mass howling excitement at the spectacle of two young men in the pink of health trying to stun one another, the audience interested me more than the performance. The proportion of those taking an interest in self-defence as an 'art' was obviously small. I had no definite ideas about mob psychology, which was a subject not discussed in those days, but I was impressed at the perspiring ferocity of the faces.

'This is uncivilized, Jeff,' I said to a hardened old colleague. 'Is this as far as we've evolved since the Romans tossed the Christians to the lions?'

'Just where you're wrong,' he said. 'Isn't it an evidence of civilization that we can sublimate our natural savage instincts to the point at which five thousand people can come along here and let their passions ride for the evening without a single person being killed?'

'That's right,' I said. But when, on a later occasion, as a protest against an unpopular decision, the audience piled the chairs in a heap and set fire to newspapers beneath them to burn the place down, I had my doubt about the sporting spirit being what it was cracked up to be.

Still, however unedified, one cannot spend two years looking at a game without learning willy-nilly what makes the wheels go round. Visits from ringside to dressing-rooms to see how the boys were getting on, with a few trips to training quarters made me acquainted with the local champs of the time.

I was not surprised to find that behind the scenes the atmosphere was not brutal but merely professional. Our Hughie Mehegan, Herb McCoy and the other gladiators of my day were businessmen engaged in the exploitation of their abilities. Sometimes a loud-mouth arrived on the scene, but he soon learned to shut his big trap while his betters exchanged with almost dispassionate interest new developments in their industry.

'Do those rabbit-killers hurt?' I asked Herb McCoy, conscious again after having been battered insensible by a dreadful tattooed American, Milburn Sayler, with a succession of sledgehammer punches on the nape of his neck, any one of which would have broken my spine.

'Not the first twenty or so. After that, you've got to let your head go with it . . .'

Our Australian boys were good, but not quite good enough. There was a constant flow of American pugs coming over to trim any pretensions they might have to world titles. It had been many a long day since Australia had had a top-class heavyweight. Imagine the joy when one day a boy turned up displaying all the promise of a real champion. Les Darcy was young, only a middle-weight, but he would grow. He looked like IT at last. Intelligent, nimble, unstoppable, with a solid punch in both hands, I found this laughing country youth extraordinarily likeable. The list of his wins grew impressively long, at last all the omens were favourable, and away he sailed to conquer the U.S.A. He landed with toothache, had the molar pulled, developed blood-poisoning and in three days was dead. When I heard it, I wept. There are still Australian boxing fans who talk about how the Americans poisoned Les Darcy to prevent his taking the world heavyweight championship.

Although nobody could say my sporting interlude was particularly fruitful, it was a diversion from politics and I collected some curious moments in famous company. I could just remember how the world had excited itself about the Corbett–Fitzsimmons championship fight in 1898. Now here was old Bob Fitzsimmons himself showing me where my own solar plexus was and, with the hoarse croak he used for a voice since someone delivered a right cross on his adam's apple, telling me what he did to Corbett in that celebrated battle. And then, later, Old Corbett, Gentleman Jim still, turns up in Sydney to give me *his* version of the punch that put him out. . . .

When I shifted for variety from boxing to billiards, I remember George Gray, the wizard of the losing hazard, and Fred Lindrum, the first of the brood of champions of that name, giving me private tips (which utterly failed to improve my game) . . . being invited by old father Lindrum at his billiard saloon to play a hundred up with a lean youngster with a freckled nose—his nephew Horace. 'The kid's pretty good,' says he; 'he'll give you eighty.' I got two shots . . . having a tooth stopped by Ray Noble, the cricketer's idol. . . . It was all experience.

Another refreshing change was the theatre. As a roving journalist properly accredited, I was free of all the shows—no bother about tickets, just drop in—and I got a smattering of the stage and its personalities, which led me in the general good fellowship to have a go myself. I joined a repertory company in Sydney and later another in Melbourne. It was one of the proud moments of my life when I took a curtain amid tumultuous applause for my rendering of Rory O'Moore in Galsworthy's *The Pigeon*. As it was one of the most exciting when Hugh McCrae, my poetic friend, and I acted the two dramatic critics in Arnold Bennett's *What the Public Wants* with such boisterous vim that Hugh broke his straw hat.

6

I WAS settling down to a comfortable round in beautiful Sydney when two things happened to disturb the peace: World War I and an opening at last as the *Bulletin's* resident cartoonist at Melbourne, then the temporary capital and centre of Commonwealth politics.

The first reactions of the Australian public to the fact of war, as I remember, were surprise and complacency. Australia had been minding its own business, which was taken then to include that of Ireland. The large Irish–Australian population was concentrated with expatriate-nationalist fervour on the crisis over the new Home Rule Bill before the British Parliament. It was difficult at first to rearrange one's animosities and decide who was the more important villain—the Kaiser or Carson. Europe had been somebody else's affair. The struttings and ultimatums had made exciting news from far away, but the principal figureheads had remained only half-real. The childish propaganda of belittlement of Germany evolved in late Victorian times to soothe British pride after the Kaiser's insults during the Boer War, the dumping of German goods in British markets, and the building of a German navy, came home to roost. Everyone underestimated the enemy. Berlin-to-Baghdad? What's that? . . . Alsace-Lorraine? Who's he? . . . Belgian Treaty? Where's Belgian Treaty? . . . One Englishman could lick two Germans, and one Australian could lick two Englishmen. All was well.

Faced with dire reality, there were sounds of type-smashing by night as newspapers adjusted their ideas. The *Bulletin* supported the war, reserving the right to criticize any back-sliding from the principle of 'Australia First.' Temporarily it modified slightly its fiscal antagonisms to Britain and France and stopped its monkey cartoons. The British had had more sense than the *Bulletin*, and Japan was now our ally.

The *Bulletin's* attitude suited me well enough, with a few reservations. But no one had pressed me to conform to every comma of its policy anyway. I was by no means convinced of the total wrongness of Germany's claim to a 'place in the sun'; and, influenced by the talk flying around even then of a United Europe, I was sceptical of the divine patronage of Britain's Balance of Power. Yet there was no doubt that Germany had prepared for and deliberately begun the war.

I had taken no part in the *Bulletin's* clamour for military compulsion in peace-time. The word 'conscription' had not yet come up and voluntary enlistment was the national policy for overseas service. I had no reason to doubt my paper's editorial goodwill whatever line I took. But I could not say that the actuality of war made no difference to my peace-time thinking—especially a world war in which defeat would probably mean the utter overthrow of democratic progress by military dictatorship. Suppose the war was of such size and length that the defence resources of voluntaryism became worked out and used up, and still no security in sight? I wore out some boot-leather considering that one.

My boarding-house bedroom in Sydney had expanded into a household with the arrival two years previously of my mother, sister and small brother, which was fortunate for me, because it provided me with a smooth background without domestic distractions other than a growing social life, which I should never have had time to make for myself. And, most important, my mother made excellent soup, my sister had grown creditably pretty and my small brother gave me the excuse to fly kites and let off fireworks. My father, too, had paid us frequent visits from some mysterious new business he had successfully created in New Zealand out of his head.

Winding up our affairs in Sydney, I transported the lot of us to Melbourne. We lived in a flat near the Federal Parliament and friendly Representatives used to drop in to sample my mother's soup and drop political hints, which was very useful. The nearness of the House and my journalist's privilege made it possible for me to get around it to see again many of the politicians I had met during my travels as a peripatetic caricaturist and to make enough 'contacts' to keep abreast, if not a jump ahead, of the times. My old happy relations with Ed Fisher were resumed on firmer ground, and there were always two or three bright *Bulletin* colleagues to supply me with ideas if I needed them. After a few months, however, when I was 'run in,' Ed had the wisdom to leave me alone and I tasted once again the satisfaction of free expression.

In Sydney my eminent senior, Norman Lindsay, was producing dramatic and allegorical war cartoons in the grand manner. From Melbourne I was to present, in humorous contrast, the personalities and the minutiae of the politics involved. Much of my first work was shallow flippancy in the conventional manner of its kind and time, interspersed with some of those *cliché* compositions of the 'blood-and-bones' type, with heavy blacks and massive effects which look 'strong' and 'powerful' but say no more than 'Isn't war terrible?' or 'The enemy is a bad man.' I varied these with a few toots at President Woodrow Wilson for the supposed sycophancy of his diplomatic notes to Germany, and at 'peace societies' for the supposed futility of their appeals to flourishing war-lords. As victory seemed a long, long time in coming, I arrived in due course at more meaningful works on profiteering, recruiting, the salvage of living standards and the immediate need to separate the issues of survival from the growing confusion.

Australia had been on the eve of a Federal general election when the war broke. Party leaders had vied with one another in patriotic declamation, and pledged 'the last man and the last shilling' to the Imperial authorities—a big mouthful for a country where the crops and the livestock had to be grown and where the 'last shilling' was one borrowed from the British moneylender.

Probably anticipating difficulty in reconciling reality with rhetoric, Andrew Fisher, leader of the re-elected Labour Government, went up in a puff of patriotic smoke and disappeared to London as High Commissioner. W. M. Hughes, 'Our Billy,' took office as Prime Minister amid loud cheers.

Roughly speaking, Hughes and I synchronized, and a great part of the remainder of my life in Australia was spent in comment upon his personality and his doings. The time, the place and the man conspired not only to sharpen my abilities but to confirm my future as a political cartoonist.

What is it that makes a man good material for caricature? Billy Hughes had it. Picturesque appearance? That of itself is never enough; but he had plenty of it. Five feet high, thin body with spidery arms, small head, swarthy largish face, mostly nose, slanting glittering eyes, wisp moustache. Ability, energy? There was always something doing when Billy was about. As the dynamic

THE IMPERIAL CONFERENCE (1916)

ASQUITH: 'David, talk to him in Welsh and pacify him!'

policy-maker for Labour the little man with the sharp tongue, waving arms and hearing-aid box that was also an aid to deafness when he didn't want to listen, was always an arresting figure. When World War I provided the big events which enabled his attributes to be deployed on the world stage, he came near to being the stuff of history—not for his compelling width of view, but for the other thing. Billy at the Versailles Peace Conference looking at the future through the wrong end of the telescope was almost a unique personality. Who else could have staggered the assembled world statesmen by insisting that New Guinea was more important than Europe? What other could have told Paderewski, the pianist Prime Minister of Poland, to take his policy home and play it on the piano? Certain weaknesses round the portrait for caricature. Vanity, irascibility, impatience, hysteria— Billy had all these. Like all of those capable of inspiring passionate antagonism, he could also inspire devotion. One could say without detracting from his qualities of greatness that he was never a uniting personality.

After sounding a 'Call to Arms' Hughes left to visit Britain. The spirited oratory of the Welshman from overseas made an immediate impression. The cables hummed with his speeches. It was persistently reported, however, that behind closed doors his habit of talking people down was an embarrassing experience to the Asquith Cabinet.

I recorded the situation in a cartoon showing the Cabinet room at Downing Street with Billy in full cry, thumping one end of the table, blotting pads, books and inkwell in disarray, while Asquith and his Ministers take cover. Asquith implores Lloyd George: 'DAVID, TALK TO HIM IN WELSH AND PACIFY HIM.' I spent three days on this drawing and when I had finished, it looked to me overdrawn. Too full of lines. After all, in good drawing an idea and its treatment are one, and technique of representation should arise from the material. A slight quip should not be represented in laborious technique but with economy of line, or its effect is impaired, the purpose defeated. This little thing was drawn with the authenticity and completeness of detail appropriate to a massive subject. I contemplated tearing it up and starting again, but there was no time, so off it went.

Disconcertingly, that cartoon turned out to be a success. The day after it appeared it rained telegrams and letters of congratulation—even a bunch of flowers. The Governor-General promptly sent an aide in all his military magnificence to my

66

studio to put in a claim for the original drawing. Prints were struck off which I obligingly defaced with my quite superfluous signature, since the drawing was signed already. Billy, the hero of it, was called on to sign twenty copies for members of the British Cabinet, and Lloyd George had to have two. The original now hangs, I am told, in the Federal Parliament Library at Canberra, and some kind critic spoke of it recently as 'the best-known Australian political cartoon.' It has too many lines in it.

Unfortunately as Billy's stock rose in London, it fell in Australia. The fulsome tributes to the new leader from the Antipodes, his gifts and wisdom, his dominating personality, when cabled back to Australia, did not impress Billy's labour supporters favourably. The feeling grew that our Billy was being 'used' by intriguing British politicians, or, worse, that the cunning Imperial authorities were seducing him away from 'Australia First.'

By the time Billy had returned home, so strong were the apprehensions that he found his Labour Party comrades receiving him not with welcome but with dark suspicion. Much water had flowed under bridges in other quarters also. The Easter rising in Dublin and its suppression had greatly upset Irish–Australians, who were deciding with the help of their extremely active nationalists and sectarians that England after all was only 'the land of cant, humbug and hypocrisy' and deserved a hiding anyway. Altogether it was not a propitious moment for Billy to announce his big decision to put the question of conscription to a referendum.

No free people had ever before been invited to vote its men into military service. Voluntary recruiting had done very well. Perhaps Billy had promised too much in London; perhaps to arm, equip, feed, pay and transport 200,000 men per annum would soon strip the country of active man-power and cause an economic breakdown. Decision on the limits of prudence in these respects called for sober detached judgment and balancing of risks; and when made, for implementation with a minimum of social disunity. In short, for statesmanship. Instead, the issue was thrown into the ring and a political dogfight unparalleled for irrelevance and confusion began immediately. The country was torn apart.

There was much that was pertinent for argument. Questions, for instance, as to whether voluntaryism was fairer than conscription, or the other way around; whether it was moral to conscript men before wealth; what was to happen to the troops when the war ended; and how, why and where the troops were needed.

Ireland's grievance against England, on the other hand, had precious little to do with the issue. But this is a contrary world, and so, in the long run, actively fomented by the remarkably able Dr. Mannix, Coadjutor Catholic Archbishop of Melbourne, it proved the decisive element.

The Irish vote in Australia represented nearly twenty-five per cent of the total voting power and was largest by far in New South Wales. Mannix was a striking personality, a spellbinder with a queer combination of dignity and demagogy, direct and provocative, generating heat, excitement and occasionally frenzy. After the Dublin rising, the hostile element in this community, backed up by the entire Roman Catholic Press and hierarchy, with the exception of one protesting Archbishop in Western Australia, dominated the scene and swamped the politicians, experts, economists and worthy citizens who confined themselves merely to relevant debate. Billy made the fatal decision to put this troublesome prelate in his place. That was his mistake, for he was beaten at his own game. A duel began. The Archbishop, settling his biretta firmly on his head, proceeded to switch the issue until it seemed that the Battle of Dublin General Post Office had been moved to that of Sydney Post Office and his audience were about to fire their lethal votes at the oppressor. The blind unreason of expatriate nationalism-cum-sectarianism rose to the surface as the flock consolidated. A few months before these Australians had been eager to deal blows for England. The answer to Billy's referendum was NO.

Through this jungle I ploughed conscientiously, weighing pros and cons. I took my responsibilities as a satirist very seriously and was much concerned that my darts should be at the right targets. In general my cartoons of that time had upheld the war aims in more or less dignified allegory and kept check on passing events. When it came to the point I supported YES, largely because, whatever little confidence I had in the arguments for YES, I had still less in the arguments for NO. I was influenced by reasons as much humane as political and military. I still thought voluntaryism was the only tolerable way of raising fighting forces in a free democracy in time of peace—and in war-time, too, except in conditions of desperate emergency. The war was going badly, and it seemed to me that the point had arrived at which a system of compulsory selection taking account of individual circumstances would be better than the cruel farce 'voluntary' recruiting had become. The means to ensure a continuous stream of recruits had already changed by easy stages from persuasion to pressure, from pressure to persecution. The 'voluntaryism' was becoming merely nominal, the reality a degrading man-hunt. My cartoons recommending YES did not prevent me, however, from an intermittent criticism of the Prime Minister's disastrous mishandling of the whole question in the prevailing conditions.

My cartoons were now being reprinted around and 'quoted' in platform speeches. My mail, both abusive and complimentary kinds, began to increase prodigiously. I was by now made aware, by indications pleasant and unpleasant, that I had attracted notice, and, further, that my 'specialization' in Hughes was considered by some of his supporters to be in fact vilification. When another cartoonist drew *me* in a cartoon about Hughes I had an uneasy feeling that I was on the way to becoming a political symbol myself.

The rebuff to the Prime Minister at the referendum and his expulsion from the Labour Party did not deflate his ego but rather increased it to the point of identifying his own retention of power with the winning of the war. He formed a 'National' Government with the anti-Labour Opposition, and the Press began to wilt under the imposition of a censorship becoming more political than military and seemingly directed rather at preserving Billy's personal prestige than at depriving the enemy of advantage and encouragement.

I had never shared the opinion that Billy Hughes himself and the war aims were inseparable. Rather the opposite. It seemed to me that his dominating personality, from being a national asset, had become a definite liability, if not a positive danger; and that both the country and the war effort would be better off with a less disruptive Prime Minister.

My cartoons reflected this view week by week by featuring Billy carrying a penny balloon inscribed 'D.P.' for Dominating Personality. Since it was easier to censor textual statement than the subtle cumulative implications of caricature, I had a charmed life with the censors until one day Billy's vanity exploded and he took steps to have me suppressed. I quote from the *Bulletin* the following account of one incident:

Low had done a fine war cartoon, which had been duly submitted to the censor and passed. The telephone tinkled.

'Mr. Prior, isn't it? The Editor of the *Bulletin*? About that cartoon you sent along. It must not be published.'

'What's that?'

'It must not be published. Mr. Hughes will not allow it to be published.'

'Mr. Hughes? Who is Mr. Hughes? The censor?'

'No, the Prime Minister.'

'I don't know him in the matter. The cartoon has been passed by the Chief Censor, and you'll see it in the *Bulletin* next week.'

'It mustn't appear, Mr. Hughes says. Don't you understand, the Prime Minister will not allow it to appear.'

'Then the *Bulletin* won't come out next week at all.'

Thank God for an editor who stood by his cartoonist. That was too much for Billy. Upon thought of the uproar that would follow the inevitable explanation of the *Bulletin's* non-appearance, Hughes changed his mind, and the *Bulletin* came out as usual, with the cartoon. But pretty soon life was made more difficult for me. An amendment of the War Precautions Regulations was issued tightening up power to censor cartoons. After that it become a game of hide-and-seek, in which I was not always able to keep my nose above water.

The time was ripe for me to publish *The Billy Book*, a fantastic account in caricature of Hughes's adventures during his travels to and in Britain. One can't be mordantly satirical all the time, so this was an essay in mere humour, 'softening with loving wit the social scene.' It was a publishing success at 2s. and it had sales of about 60,000, bales of it going overseas to the soldiers; but its reception proved to be a good demonstration of the decisive contribution made to the effect of a book of cartoons by the element of time. *The Billy Book* made no particular political point, except that in certain aspects a Prime Minister could be comic. There are always, of course, the dullards who cannot discriminate between farce and satire and incline to think that any liberties taken with the personal dignity of a public man come under the heading of attack not only on his policies but on his very existence. So in the prevailing controversial atmosphere, and in the frame created for me by Billy's admirers, the book took on the semblance of an ambush bristling with malice. Useless for me to say that it was just fun. Since I *was* critical of Hughes in the *Bulletin*, the contention that I was being only jocular in *The Billy Book* seemed obvious nonsense. Hughes himself thought so and when Ted Russell, one of his own Ministers who was also a friend of mine, gave him a copy he ripped it up and threw it in the corner.

The legend of my bitter animosity to Hughes grew and his

admirers began to give me some of my own medicine, his Press representing me as a failure squatting in a corner warped with envious hate at people like Hughes who had got on in the world. Stories were printed that Hughes declined to meet me, that I declined to meet Hughes, that when on a certain occasion I walked into a room, he had walked out, and that he had tried to have me barred from the parliamentary Press gallery.

In fact, however, we met often enough. The first time was in the company of his predecessor as Prime Minister, Andrew Fisher, a very different chap, tough but with gentle black eyes and friendliness towards artists. In Andrew's presence a certain cordiality was constrained all round. Next time, in the lift of Parliament House, was more natural. As we slid downwards— Billy, Hector Lamond, a Labour leader who was the friend of both of us, and I—Hector innocently presented me, whereupon Billy cast doubts on the legitimacy of my birth. I had to reply, of course. The term 'bastard' was a term of endearment, however, in Australia in those days and we preferred to take it as such. There were other occasions, none particularly notable for amiability or courtesy.

Among the roses I received from fans and reviewers arrived a contra supply of raspberries, which grew in number day by day. Among my letters one morning was one in wild calligraphy signed A. J. Whoosh, complimentary and asking for the original of that week's cartoon. 'Another fellow wanting something for nothing,' thought I, poking the letter into my 'File and Forget' pigeon-hole. A week later Hector told me the Prime Minister was wondering why I had not replied to his letter. I looked out Mr. Whoosh's letter and scrutinized it afresh. Good heavens! It was not from Whoosh but Hughes, Mr. Dominating Personality himself. I was surprised. But less so when I turned up the cartoon concerning which he had so kindly expressed his admiration. It represented him as having so completely dominated his Cabinet that his personal characteristics had become superimposed on those of each and every Minister. I had it nicely framed and sent to him. The decencies must be preserved.

If everything were properly stage-managed in this world, I should have hated Billy like poison. I should have been his John Wilkes Booth. But, however disappointing to confess, it was not like that at all. Had I been cast up on a desert island with him (my supreme test of human relations) I have no doubt I would have liked him; though I should certainly have done my damnedest to stop him from making himself king.

After a general election at which the 'National' Government and Billy were victorious, Hughes concluded that the NO vote at the referendum must have been someone else's fault, so he decided he would give history a chance to correct itself by putting the question again at a second referendum. Once more with incredible tactlessness he provided his opponents with all the ammunition they needed to frustrate his purpose. In a final miscalculation of public opinion, as if to make quite sure that Conscription would be defeated, he anticipated a YES victory by calling up potential conscripts in advance.

With my call-up papers as a phantom 'Hughesilier' I attended with the rest, coughed and hopped to the satisfaction of the M.O. and was passed as fit for service, to await call. My conscription attracted some attention and one or two newspapers made no secret of their suspicions that Hughes had deliberately chosen this means of shutting up 'his most pertinacious critic.' My destiny became a matter of concern to the public as well as to myself. The call-up caught me, like many another conscript, at a bad moment in my private affairs; for the paper famine in New Zealand had killed my father's business stone dead, my only adult brother was in camp and I was now the sole earner and support of the whole family. My entering the war might not defeat the enemy but it would certainly defeat the Low family. I could justly have claimed a deferment to put my affairs in workable shape. But in the event my private affairs did not come up, and I could not get a word in edgeways.

The *Bulletin* Company promptly filed a claim for exemption on the grounds of national importance. To add a top note, I caught influenza and I drooped before the court like the last rose of summer as the wrangle went on as to whether I was of more value fighting the Turks at Gallipoli or helping Hughes at home, whether any cartoonist could be of national importance, and what had happened to other cartoonists. Such cartoonists as the court could recollect by name were in khaki as official war artists making drawings of soldiers in the trenches, so by implication I could look forward to a continuation of artistic usefulness, albeit under official instructions; but there would not be, of course, political cartoons about Billy, which would be an offence coming from one wearing the King's uniform. At this point voices began to rise. After an interesting and—to everybody but me—diverting discussion, the court decided to leave things as they were, and I was delivered back sneezing and wheezing to the *Bulletin* unconditionally.

This was front-page stuff. I had a mixed Press—hostility at both political extremes, friendliness in the middle. I judged that many solid citizens found in the basic assumptions of my cartoons a reflection of their own feeling. Among those who had a vested interest in the Prime Minister's political glamour, and in the more rabid quarters where I had become an object of open execration, it had been assumed that I would be finally shut up. It was almost too much to have me back officially stamped IMPORTANT. And there was, of course, the lunatic fringe. One critic argued that for me to draw cartoons about the war when I was not in it was indecent. Another demanded that since my cartoons were now of National Importance, I should turn over a new leaf and in future admire Hughes. All the known puns on my name flew about, and I learned from various sources that I was, according to taste, a sybarite living in immoral ease while others suffered, a hireling, and a clown; or, alternatively, a voice of the people, a defender of the oppressed and a statesman. Probably in connection with an astonishing allegation that I was a war profiteer, I found myself bracketed with W. A. Holman, the Premier of New South Wales, and Willie Watt, the Federal Treasurer, who were both the objects of man-hunt at the time. 'The last man and the last shilling!' said the columnist. 'What a contest it will be between Mr. Watt and Mr. Low—each striving to be last! We guess the honours will be divided. Mr. Watt will be the last man and Mr. Low will have the last shilling.'

The second referendum duly took place. Once more the country was torn apart with a jagged pandemonium in which could be discerned fitfully the shrill howls of the Irish banshee and the angry shouts of Billy. Needless to say, NO was carried again, this time by an overwhelming vote. Voluntary enlistment sagged, its neck broken. A situation of complete frustration was avoided only by the unexpected end of the war.

In that particular chapter of Australian history, I had made some bitter political enemies in both camps. But also some good friends. One was Henry Stead, the same Henry Stead I had dispossessed of his seat at that welcoming luncheon at Adelaide five years or so before. Henry was the son of W. T. Stead, the famous British journalist and social reformer, and he had inherited his father's integrity, besides *Stead's Review*, a property of his family in Australia. Henry was that rare thing, an honest thinker. While all around patriotic citizens were striving to distinguish black from white through a fog of 'loyal' preconceptions, Henry eschewed all loyalties save to the truth as he saw it. Gracious, gentle and eminently sane, he and his *Stead's Review* were a pool of light during some murky periods. We clicked. I admired and liked him, and I profited greatly from his wide European outlook and experience. It was at his house and in his company that I met a new circle.

Like attracts like, and Henry's personality was sufficient to exclude the kind of bone-headed 'realists' who take pride in not looking beyond their noses. His friends, writers, civil servants, politicians and a few Cabinet Ministers, exchanged ideas on the war and the post-war future with eyes on the distant horizons. Most of them were nominally Liberals or Conservatives in politics, I remember. My own intimates had been, with few exceptions, of the political Left, but in this company my belief was confirmed that well-disposed men, whatever their party allegiances, do not differ so much in their essential aims.

7

IN the distortions and suppressions of war I had looked to Henry Stead for an objective view with the undertones and overtones. Now the war was over, the Peace Conference ended, the Versailles Treaty signed, and the League of Nations had taken shape in a fog of scepticism. Among Henry's friends I found something of what I had been looking for—analyses of these events and their significance, a cool estimation of the prospects of the peace, and, in particular, of the League ideas. Only a simpleton could believe that all would be well automatically if representatives of all nations were assembled under one roof; but at least here was something more than rhetorical gas, the practical possibility of a move towards the end of war. I was fired with enthusiasm. Here was a worthy cause. Henry had, I think, a feeling that the Russian revolution would mellow into experimental liberalism. He deplored the Churchill expedition to Archangel in aid of Denikin and Koltchak as wrong-headed as well as immoral. His sympathy in the Polish war was with Brussilov rather than with Pilsudski. . . . Great happenings were afoot. As the world picture widened in the news my interest deepened.

One bright morning, striding down Collins Street to my studio, I ran into Henry. He buttonholed me. 'David, how would you like to go to London?' says he. 'Maybe,' says I. He showed me a cable from the London *Daily News*, asking him to negotiate with me about joining its staff.

Henry evidently expected me to be surprised, so I obligingly was. But for some months I had been studying the British newspapers and shooting arrows into the air in their direction. The *Manchester Guardian* had already reproduced a number of my Hughes cartoons. Following my early practice of making the

75

Post Office work for me, I had posted off about fifty copies of *The Billy Book* to various key people in Britain, writers, publicists and editors. Most of them found their way, I have no doubt, into the waste-paper basket, but one fell into the lap of Arnold Bennett who wrote a useful paragraph about it in the *New Statesman*. I had looked up the files and had read closely and with approval A. G. Gardiner's leaders in the *Daily News* about the Peace terms. I put him and his managing director, Henry Cadbury, without their knowing it, on my posting list for a personal copy of the *Bulletin* every week as a kind of remote hint. I calculated from the look of their paper and the look of their competitors that they could do with a cartoonist. So Henry's cable was not entirely a bolt from the blue.

I agreed. Jubilant, I continued my walk. I met a journalist friend. 'I'm off to London,' I says. 'How much?' he asks. 'Princely, my boy,' I says. The newspapers next day served me right:

PRINCELY SALARY
LOW LEAVES FOR LONDON

I sometimes talk too much. It was £30 a week. Good, in those days when a pound was a pound, but not as good as all that. A minor prince, perhaps. Or a dispossessed prince. It suddenly struck me that in all my eight years in Australia I had been so interested in the drawing and the politics that I had forgotten to ask for a raise. I had had no contract and the piecework terms and rates I ended with were those at my beginning. William Macleod now journeyed from Sydney to offer me a packet of shares in the paper to raise my income to £1,000 a year. But great as was my affection for the old man and the *Bulletin*, I could not have forgone my chance to go a-roving if he had offered me the whole paper. On the other hand, I would have gone to London at half the money.

My 'princely salary' haunted me for quite a while. I found myself clasped and congratulated by all sorts of people, including many I did not know and some whose approval was distinctly unwelcome. Feeling was not, however, unanimous. My hostile critics reawakened to the opportunity with zest. Readers of one vituperative journal opined that the *Daily News* would provide congenial surroundings for me, since 'had it prevailed in wartime, the Britisher would now be humbly walking in the London gutter while the Prussian goose-stepped on the sidewalk.' Readers of another were informed that compliments from Arnold Bennett to me meant nothing, since he was poor stuff himself. I found myself again the subject of unflattering newspaper cartoons by other fellows, showing me being seduced away with heavy bribes from my supposed job of guarding the *Bulletin's* cash-box. *Smith's Weekly* of Sydney, which was no friend of mine, put the case in a nutshell:

> Mr. Low is out of place in White and Anglo-Saxon Australia. He will be thoroughly suited on the Quaker paper to which he is going. It hates Mr. Hughes and loves the coloured races. It stands for pacificism, brotherhood of man, no army, if possible no navy, in fact for defeatism generally. It is welcome to Mr. Low and his works.

Tempers were not improved by 'Billywog.' Among the facetious items I had included in *The Billy Book* was a design for a Hughes toy, 'Billywog,' with instructions for use: 'Blow up with wind until head expands, then release hole in face, whereupon Billy will emit loud noises until he goes flat.'

A Sydney trader was fired with the idea of manufacturing 'Billywog,' so I reduced the idea to tangible form on glove-puppet lines, modelled a head of Hughes in plasticine and sold him the puppet rights outright. In due course puppets of 'Billywog' appeared around and about at Billy's comings and goings, wagging, gesticulating and mocking the indignant original according to the mood of the wearer. My Sydney trader, conducting his business as he thought fit without consulting an outsider like me, had had his toys manufactured in Japan. A Sydney newspaper blew up:

COLLEAGUES
Low and Japgog
Jacob and Esau

sang the headlines. The article went on:

> Mr. W. M. Hughes has two personal enemies—bitter at that. One of them is Mr. David Low, the black-and-white artist. . . . The Prime Minister's other enemy is a nation. . . . These two enemies have co-operated and the result is the production of an article called a 'Billywog,' made by Asiatic labour and purchasable in Australia for eighteenpence. . . . Looked at full-face, it gives a novel Hughes—a purely Japanese one. The Asiatic comrade of Mr. Low has subtly created an

atmosphere odorous of all those things which one can imagine
as being regarded with loathing by those minds, So here unite
the two immemorial factors, the hand of Esau and the voice of
Jacob. . . .

There should have been a million pounds' worth of imaginative
libel in that lot, but I couldn't be bothered.

I did not pack my bags to go without sorrow at leaving many
friends. As a small boy the opinions, too often contemptuous, of
outsiders on my choice of a profession had driven me into a defensive solitariness. As a youth, although I became gregarious
enough to be socially at ease in the world, I had continued to
cultivate a private self-sufficiency and was wary of complicating
loyalties and dependent friendships. In my early twenties, when
not in the window so to speak, I could stand my own company for
long stretches without discontent. But for all that, in those black
depressions which follow over-concentration, when all work
seems fruitless, bad, waste of time, when the mind rattles like a
pea in a hollow drum, and confidence is replaced by despair, I
imagined with longing a second self that could know what one
was at and estimate truly the success or failure of the attempt. At
such times what a priceless boon would be a clear-headed outside
judge, to whom one could toss one's piece with 'Good or bad?'
and accept the verdict with confidence as from one familiar with
the conditions of creation.

In Melbourne I was fortunate enough to count two. I shared a
studio with Hal Gye, caricaturist, and C. J. Dennis, poet, was our
inseparable. Before settling in Melbourne I lived as a fellow-
lodger with Den for a space and finished my cartoons by night on
his wash-stand while he read proofs aloud in bed. After that,
Hal and I took our studio, and Hal arranged to illustrate Den's
book. Thus the association was confirmed.

Hal was a fantastic chap, thin, with long hair parted in the
middle, a way of waving his arms about and an irresistible wit.
When he wasn't drawing theatrical caricatures for the *Bulletin*, or
illustrating Den, he was painting water-colour symphonies with
a dreamy effect which he produced by losing his temper with
them and putting them under the tap. After the second jet of
water the picture almost disappeared leaving plenty to the
imagination, which pleased mightily those who had the imagination. Den's chief claim to fame at first was that he was the author
of the Austrabloodylaise, a vernacular piece known far and wide
in Australia, of which the opening stanza gives the flavour:

> Fellers of Australia, blokes and coves and coots,
> Pull yer bloody pants on, tie yer bloody boots.

But he was then deep in the planning of a volume, *The Sentimental Bloke*, which was to bring him wide fame and an honoured place in Australian poetry. Meanwhile Den filled in as a civil servant complete with two-inch starched collar and vest slip, an effect quite unsuited to his bony-nosed Roman face.

Here were a couple of characters in whose company I found rest and understanding. We could laugh, shout, sing, exult, mourn, curse the wrongdoer in the open, as we wrestled with our work. (I was always one to talk to my work as it came out on my old drawing-board perched on a broken arm-chair.) Our trio expanded into an odd mixture of fellowship. Painters, poets and writers, of course, actors, farmers, civil servants, business men, politicians, an occasional Cabinet Minister, and on one red-letter day even Melba herself, the immortal song-bird. All I remember of her was that she was a bullying woman who ate a good deal and swore a lot. It was all one. Even on the blackest days I found relief in that pool of goodwill. In no other company could I ever have tried the experiment of sharing a studio. I have had many since, but all by comparison have had a touch of loneliness.

Life was not all travail. We had our relaxation; but our studio was for work, not play. I still worked with the laborious and pains-taking method I had improvised for myself as a boy, which was literally the only way I knew how to draw. I could not make easily caricatures of people without watching them move, talk and show what they were made of. If I wanted to draw a horse, I had to go out and find a horse. If a table and chairs were called for in my drawing, to do the job properly I had to set up a table and chairs. I worked an eight-hour—sometimes ten-hour—day and with evenings spent moving around seeing people, it was a busy life. Making a cartoon occupied usually about three full days, two spent in labour and one in removing the appearance of labour.

Sometimes I wondered whether I was not taking too much trouble. But when I learned that the methods of Brueghel, Callot, Daumier, Gillray and the other Old Masters of Caricature had been similarly thorough, that Tenniel took two or three days to make a *Punch* cartoon and that Linley Sambourne kept a huge picture library and rooms full of 'props' and frequently set up models and photographed his compositions in advance . . . I concluded that what had been good enough for them was good enough for me. Old Macleod had a story about a young artist who came to see him looking for encouragement. 'I'm very quick,' said the aspirant; 'I can do a drawing in twenty minutes.' 'We don't want *quick* drawings,' said old Mac. 'We want *good* drawings.'

The passion for authenticity sometimes led to diversions. I remember once having to draw a steam-roller. A steam-roller is hard to 'fake' convincingly, so I telephoned to the Corporation office asking where I could see one at work. The official was most obliging. He enquired where my studio was and sent one along. Soon, sure enough a smoking funnel appeared turning the corner and all I had to do was to lean out of my window and draw it. The driver was proud of being 'took' for the *Bulletin* and drove like a Government House chauffeur. I do not know whether the expense appeared in the rates.

We used a lot of live models, and I bought a lay figure. Besides its usefulness, I had romantic ideas about every studio needing to have a lay figure. Well, a lay figure comes in handy, if you can stand it. The thing is so damnably dead. Personally, when we had ours I kept forgetting it was there and having nervous jumps at finding a foreign and sinister presence in the room. I took a dislike to the fellow and we got rid of him.

We had our 'props' too. I acquired a stuffed British lion, a present from an admirer who thought it might come in handy for war cartoons. It was of heroic size, magnified in the stuffing and posed in the attitude of one about to spring upon the Christian martyrs. The morning after it arrived the unexpected menace nearly killed the charlady with fright. We had to get rid of him, too. Too big, too disturbing.

At odd week-ends when the need for fresh air asserted itself we three would shut up shop, assemble some tins of beans and walk over the hills and far away up to Den's broken-down old house at Toolangi (the same house which was rebuilt magnificently in Den's later affluence to fulfil its destiny as picturesque background when John Masefield visited him about ten years later). In those days we had to light the fire carefully in the old range because a snake lived there, and the only chance of a bath was in an ice-cold water-hole with crayfish on the bottom of it.

Young, romantic, sitting in congenial company on top of the wooded wilderness in the open clear blue Australian night listening to Den's new gramophone, the hills echoing back Lina Cavalieri's honey soprano pouring out *O Sole Mio*. That filled the heart. That was a taste of happiness. Why leave it? Why tear myself up by the roots again to start afresh in the unknown? Money? Only fools think of money as the supreme value. Fame? Fame is an irritating and exasperating thing that never comes for the right reasons. Curiosity? I never could pass the door of Opportunity without trying the handle.

In my four years at Melbourne I had acquired a fairly wide circle. There were places and faces I was going to miss. Tom, old Ed, Bob, Bradish, Ted, Hector, Storky, Frank, Harrison Dan. . . .

Dan was an experience. I had lived long enough to know that politics was not the exclusive province of politicians. I had become aware of mysterious shapes in the sidelines, anonymous outsiders engaged in vague activities concerned with the working of democracy. Dan was one of these. He was never seen in Parliament, but he had the entry to all the political back-rooms and the way to get into touch with a Minister was through Dan. This big, bluff, hard-bitten man exuded a large geniality, I have no doubt with an ulterior motive. Even my little quota of influence was cultivated. I responded, with my own ulterior motive. It was a liberal education to move around in the political jungle with Dan, spreading Corona cigars, calling Ministers by their Christian names, throwing them a word of praise or blame, slapping their backs, and in general behaving as though he had something on each one of them, but would not use it unless he had to. I never knew what Dan's precise function was. When I asked him he always changed the subject. I heard him described as an 'organizer,' but of what there was no clue. I assumed he was a 'fixer.' He was the nearest approach to Personal Power I met in Australia. Such a man should have been sinister, but, surprisingly, he was not. Quite the contrary. Everybody thought him a lovable character.

There were my parliamentary pals. . . . What about Hector Lamond of the A.W.U., the friend of Billy, who was also my friend? Hector, pink of face and wild of eye, was a fanatic with the tenacity of a bulldog with a mouthful of trouser-leg when his passions were aroused. Yet tears would start down his cheek when he sat on our sofa, full of my mother's soup, listening to my sister mournfully singing a saccharine ditty like *Little Grey Home in the West*.

Farewell goes out sighing . . . .

I would miss my own particular familiars of Collins Street. Old Champion, say. Where do wild Social Democrats go in the winter time? Who in 1915 would have identified the mild old gentleman, editor of a tiny literary monthly, walking tremulously with the aid of two sticks in the Melbourne sunshine, with the determined young ex-artillery officer H. H. Champion of the 1880's, who introduced John Burns and Keir Hardie to political life, and who with Burns and Hyndman led a riotous mob of unemployed through London's clubland, leaving a trail of broken windows? No one, I wager. Illness, disappointment and age had long since withdrawn Champion from politics to books. But he retained an interest in justice and right. Whenever I did a cartoon which in content departed from the strictly sane view I was sure next day to run into Champion, advancing slowly down the street like a conscience. He would stop, look me in the eye, smile gently and say, 'Not quite, David, do you think . . .?' Very effective criticism, coming from the old war-horse.

Fare thee well! and if for ever . . .

The politics of peace were reasserting themselves in Australia as I departed. The people were obviously sick of war, Europe and foreigners. The intricacies of world politics were receding again before more evident troubles at home. The chickens were coming home to roost. Bad blood generated in the referenda campaigns simmered ominously and it was plain that there were to be some violent rows about the repatriation of the returned soldiers and the clumsy attempts of the Government to alter the laws concerning trade unionism to the disadvantage of the Left. Go-slow movements and strikes began which threatened to tie the country in a knot.

Labour leadership was weak and negative. People began to ask themselves if Labour as an organized force was proving itself a political and moral failure. Politically it had, for the time being. The assertion of its moral failure was, as usual, loudest from those who held it as a dogma that the responsibility of the worker to society was to work, to dig, shunt, stoke and lump to the glory of God and the happiness of their betters.

Both ends of the social and political scale have their narrow reactionaries, and your stupid Left-winger is only your stupid Right-winger with a different hat on. Mobs, rich or poor, are equally capable of rising or falling to an occasion, according to the active spirits which inspire them at the moment. With weak leadership on the Left, and a determination to stand no nonsense on the Right, when the war-clamps were removed the impelling visions of a better life of love and opportunity all went into cold storage. Faces on the Right grew harder. On the Left the old revolt against the divorce of politics from ethics lost dignity and began to look like a rising of mutinous slaves.

82

The aftermath of war presents great opportunities for new designs for living if architects are available and have the talent. But it is aggravating to have fools about who want to put the roof on before you have the foundations down, and who insist on driving in the nails with a steam-hammer. I was impelled to close my Australian career with the publication of an exasperated Message to Everybody:*

I owe Australia a debt of gratitude which would be ill repaid by flattering praises when the need of home-truths is so evident. Australia is a great country, great in extent and possibilities, but it cannot be sanely maintained that its people have made or are making the best of it. . . . Their capacity for missing opportunities seems to increase as . . . the Australian, his pride in himself fanned by the habitual over-rating of his achievements by the Press and politicians, loses his perspective in admiring the view. . . . Some few Australians have made a sordid progress under a strenuous individualism, but . . . as I interpret it, real progress lies in political and economic altruism . . . and on this kind of progress, in the economic relations between employer and employed the brake has been conspicuously evident, or by this time in Australian history there would have been a co-operation by which the workman might have been elevated to an enlightened self-respect, self-control and independence. The economics of Australia are chaotic to a degree. It cannot be called economy in any sense to suffer valuable assets like men and women to go to waste in dissension and discontent. . . . Nothing is more evident than that the mass of the people regard the present so-called representative institutions with contempt; yet the strikes and agitations disturbing the country are not movements for reconstruction, but (merely) angry and vindictive writhings having behind them the destructive wrath of a cheated crowd. . . . The successive Governments of Australia have arrogated to themselves too much power and have inclined too much to regard the people as if they were herds of unruly cattle . . . etc. etc.

A somewhat naïve and turgid ebullition which might have been expressed better by the old lady who said, 'How much nicer everything would be if only people were nice to one another.' I had the grace to end it with the hope that I should not be regarded as a hostile critic of the land that had been a home to me for eight years. 'Faithful are the wounds of a friend.'

* *The Bulletin* 23/10/1919.

8

Was this London? Bleak, dark and uninviting. Our arrival, at dusk on a November evening in the middle of a big railway strike, was a bad start. In the devil-take-the-hindmost rush to catch a makeshift train from Liverpool, our landing port, I had lost my baggage. I hadn't been able to get to a bank and I was uncomfortably short of ready money. We had to stand all the way packed like cattle without even the solace of a cup of tea. There was no one to meet us, of course, on the ill-lit untidy Euston station with bits of newspaper blowing about in a chill wind. The half-dozen taxis were snapped up, the hansom-cabs likewise. The only vehicle left was an unbelievably ancient growler, looking as though it had been just vacated by Boadicea. As we clattered along the dark back streets, I risked cracking the springs by leaning out of the window. Sadness brooded, gloom lurked, winter was approaching; but romance was everywhere. I could hardly wait.

After dinner, I left my sister unpacking at the hotel and set out for my first London walk. There were few street lights owing to a power shortage, the place was dark, bleak and chill, but with imagination afire I followed my nose along some circuitous route which I have never been able to rediscover, until I found myself at the door of Madame Tussaud's. The door was closed, but what of it? This was palpable confirmation that I was in London at last. What delight! What joyful promise of treading the fabulous streets, entering the enchanted places until then only known at second-hand in books and photographs! I was for evermore a Londoner. But then I had always been a Londoner.

Next evening, after a busy day of discovery and introductions, I took another after-dinner stroll. As I returned through an empty street off Marylebone Road, I came on a deserted newspaper pitch with a string of newsbills, under a dim street-light not yet repaired from the war. One caught my eye.

THE STAR

NEW

CARTOONIST

ARRIVES

That was me. I had arrived.

On succeeding days, until I got my feet, I indulged my zest for rambling the four corners of the Old Town. I discovered the enjoyment of riding on the tops of buses (they were open in those days) through the November fog surrounded by the three-plane effects which gave me the feeling of sailing around inside an etching. I savoured the excitement of travelling to Piccadilly on the Underground. What magic for tuppence! To stand on London Bridge! To walk in the Strand! I found St. James's Street where Gillray had worked. I peeked at Phil May's old house at St. John's Wood. . . . But it was the devil's own job to get the fourteen cups of tea per day my constitution from custom demanded.

The *Daily News* office was very different from the *Bulletin* office I had left in Sydney. All old mahogany and worn stone steps, solemn rooms and dark walls, relieved by engravings of Charles Dickens and old-time cartoons about Chinese slavery by Arthur Moreland. Oh, lor', I thought.

'Charles Dickens was our editor,' said someone.

'Did you say "was" or "is"?' I murmured. Explanations.

'Did you know that Charles Dickens—' started off another chap.

'Charles Dickens? Who's he?' I asked.

The chap gave me a wink. 'Oh, one of our sub-editors. Anyway he only lasted six months around here.' That was Hugh Jones. We became firm friends.

The time came for me to start work. I approached my new job with enthusiasm. Which might have been unfortunate, for it very nearly ended before it had begun. After one cartoon I resigned.

Nothing came out as I had expected. A. G. Gardiner, the editor I had hoped to work with, had left. In any case, I was not to work for the *Daily News*, but for the Company's evening paper, the *Star*. It looked to me a miserable little sheet, badly printed. For the matter of that, ALL the London Evenings—there were about nine of them then—looked miserable little sheets, badly printed, but the *Star* was the littlest and worst printed of the lot.

85

The sort of thing I had been doing in Australia, the stuff that had, in fact, attracted the attention of my new employers, was not the kind of thing they wanted from me at all. They had intended me to be a foil to 'Poy,' the political cartoonist of the *Evening News*, who had been winning circulation away from the other papers with his nightly pleasantries. Rival editors, following their usual bold unoriginality, were staffing up with imitation 'Poys.' The general idea, I gathered with a rising fury, seemed to be that I should be another. The *Star* had even plastered advertising around in the Underground, 'LAUGH WITH LOW' to offset the *Evening News*'s 'SMILE WITH POY.' God!

Now 'Poy,' Percy Fearon, a dear friend of mine in later years, had an outlook and technique as different from mine as chalk from cheese. There could be opposition but no competition. His aim was to amuse. Mine was to ridicule. His line was the creation of impersonal symbols and types, many of which became household words—'Dilly and Dally,' 'Ducks and Drakes,' and especially 'John Citizen.' Mine was the revival of the old Gillray practice of using the persons of the politicians to symbolize their policies. To him the drawing didn't particularly matter, the idea was the thing. He would wait until the last moment for 'hot topicality' and rush his picture out. To me the idea was the excuse to make a drawing. I thought cartoonists should make their own topicality, and I took my time. In short, 'Poy' was a newspaper cartoonist according to prevailing standards, and I was not. Above all, he was not a space-grabber. His cartoon took up only a shallow two-column space in the paper. That's the size, I was told. Maximum for cartoons in London. . . . Could it be that these people knew their jobs? I thought. Could it be that it was I that was the chump? Well, I would try anything once.

My first cartoon in London was such a mess—in two columns— that nobody could have known what it was about. It got a scornful paragraph in a rival paper. With memories of my beautiful well-printed full pages on the Sydney *Bulletin* I was desperate with disappointment and vexation. I was face to face with the realization of fears which up till then I had only vaguely felt, that the newspaper was a good medium for the ideographic illustration of ideas, but not for the art of caricature. A fat chance here of anybody ever becoming a Gillray or a Daumier. Exit art. Enter industry.

Moving on full steam, I sped to the office and caught the Board at the tail-end of a conference. Most of these gentlemen were still at the welcoming stage with me. They had been pleased enough

86

at the cartoon and they were expecting me to come up with some bright quip for tomorrow's paper. I took them by surprise. Slapping half a dozen of my *Bulletin* cartoons on the table and beside them my shameful little first effort for the *Star*, I threw a display of temperament which would have done credit to a prima-donna. The Board was impressed by my passionate harangue. I impressed myself, too. Space was vital. I had to have room to breathe or I would suffocate. 'Gentlemen,' I said, 'there has been a mistake. That' (the *Bulletin* heap) 'is what you engaged me on and that's what I'm anxious to do for you. This' (the *Star* atrocity) 'I am no good at. If you want this you've wasted time and money getting me here. Give me a chance at some half-pages and if at the end of three months I am not justified we will tear up the contract. If not, I'm willing to call the whole thing off right now.'

Consternation. Half-page cartoons! Unprecedented, unheard-of. Worse, other papers had not done it first. Two columns was the size. . . I reached for my hat. Very well. I'm not that kind of a cartoonist. I resign.

What a relief at last to see a twinkle in the eye of old Ernest Parke. That grand old man of Fleet Street gave me a fatherly look. He persuaded the others and I got a half-page to do a bit of drawing in. They would try anything once, too.

Fortunately my half-page next day hit the *Star* public square in the eye (partly because of its large size, no doubt) and drew favourable comment from quarters held in respect by the Board. That made it easier to reach a tolerable compromise on space. (Such battles in a newspaper office, however, are never ended, as I was to find out.) Not only that, but it smoothed the way to the discouragement of interferers who came to tell me how to draw cartoons for a London newspaper. Mr. Low would work at that table in that corner. Mr. Low must not be too political, said the circulation department. Mr. Low must be 'bright.' His cartoons must have a ruled frame and type titles because the features editor thought it neater. Mr. Low would avoid using thick lines and heavy blacks, forsooth, because the printer objected that the ink blotted through . . . I was aghast. I had spent much time working out some technical theories of my own about the best treatment for newspaper cartoons. I must have seemed a prickly quarrelsome fellow about my work during those first weeks at the *Star* office. I stormed and swore. 'Who the hell is the cartoonist round here?' I said, delivering cartoons on subjects anything but 'bright' drawn heavily with plenty of the forbidden solid blacks, with the forbidden freehand frames and titles. 'You do your blasted printing, and I'll do the cartoons.'

After a few more arguments everybody was glad enough to agree that I should do my work at home, or as far from the office as possible; and that I would have the status of a signed contributor responsible for his own opinions. I explained very early that while I would need briefing in local colour and political background, the suggestion of cartoon ideas was a matter for experts, not for amateurs who don't know what is drawable and what isn't, and that probably the fresh approach of a complete stranger to the paper's official policy would be good journalism. The editor, James Douglas, agreed with alacrity. Next day, to my astonishment, I found he himself had resigned in the night and taken a job with Beaverbrook's *Sunday Express*. What sort of a jungle was this Fleet Street? Into his chair came Wilson Pope, a new editor eager for harmony and novelty. All was well. Phew! I had had a busy time getting all that straightened out without making any deadly enemies.

Smooth working conditions were now more or less established. Arrangements for private living were not so simple.

I had been told by Jimmy Edmond in Australia that there were only three things against living in Britain: the place, the climate and the people. With a little adjustment of ideas my sister and I accommodated ourselves to the first and the second. The housing problem was acute. We had fixed ourselves in a fairly ordinary furnished flat off Baker Street at what seemed to me a grotesquely expensive rent of seven guineas per week. It was poorly lit and for six weeks until a heater was installed there was no means of taking a hot bath. Rising in the murk that passed for daylight for a wash in a kettleful of warm water was a depressing beginning to the day. Sugar was scarce, meat rationed, coal difficult. Living was confoundedly dear and it was evident that to live in the comfort to which we had been accustomed in Australia would take all my salary. It was freezing cold to us with our thin Australian blood. I laid out fifteen pounds on the thickest overcoat the tailor could be persuaded to make for me. When I buttoned it up I was practically in bed. Wearing this bed, sitting nearly in the fire and irrigating myself with frequent pots of tea I kept warm enough to draw.

Apart from direct professional contacts, London was uninviting in a social sense. People had got out of the way of 'entertaining' during the war, and I had no particular luck with my letters of introduction. I got the impression that Londoners were still a little shy of people from overseas. They had got themselves a reputation for uninhibited independence and non-conformity.

If I didn't know the people I met, neither did they know me. When I introduced my sister, a pretty goldilocks, to Henry Cadbury, I could see him wondering whether she was really my sister or just an entanglement. Ignorance about the Dominions was astonishing. 'Are these Maoris [he pronounced it May-ories] dangerous?' asked my news-editor, wishing no doubt to open pleasant conversation. 'Only when they are on motor-bicycles,' I replied. Just as well I had grown enough self-sufficiency in my early days to be not discomfited by solitude now. I had just left the warmth of a wide circle of friends in Australia to come to this desert island. The contrast was painful.

'It will take you ten years to learn the English,' said Will Dyson, the Australian cartoonist, whom we found crouching over a sinking fire in a large dark studio, nursing a great grief at the death of his wife. Will, despite his sadness, was a great comfort in that cheerless winter of 1919–20. From his early *Bulletin* days I had been his great admirer as one of the master caricaturist-cartoonists. Partly to celebrate our meeting and partly to cheer ourselves up we organized a Christmas dinner, getting all our Australian connections together for the occasion. I felt my sister and I were already slipping into the error that befalls most over-seas arrivals, of recreating a piece of their own native land to stand on instead of walking confidently into the local way of life. . . . Back to the drawing-board.

Although I had made a great fuss about the working conditions necessary for transferring my Australian forms and styles of drawing cartoons to Britain, I soon saw that my technique would have to become much more elastic if I were to establish contact with London newspaper-readers.

Australian wit and humour, though following English forms, had had, besides its own native tartness, a touch of American smartness. The English, by all the evidence, had much more appreciation of humour than of wit. Wit was rather the diversion of intellectuals, narrowed to more or less obscure or esoteric references and associations. In 1920 there was no radio and Hollywood was young; and the British masses still had not only music, songs, plays, pictures but especially their own local jokes, farce and broad comedy, none of it as yet overlaid by stream-lined American imports. The traditions were plainly discernible in the survival of the popular old robust jokes about drunks, buttocks and mother-in-law, etc., even when their aptness had departed, and in the love of puns and word-play, and endless repetition, and comic 'characters.' It was true that in respect of the art of Caricature there had been much evolution and departure from tradition. By the time the world had arrived at 1920, the original ribald rowdy fun of the old masters in this department, Gillray and Rowlandson, had been considerably watered down. Leech, Doyle, Tenniel, Sambourne and Partridge had rubbed the rough places off the genuine article, and substituted dignity and grace for strength and power in political caricature; so that one no longer laughed—if one laughed—from the stomach, but from the front teeth. The translation of the art of Caricature from the periodical to the daily newspaper had begun in many ways an even more restricting and emasculating change. Satire was shooed up a back street as too vulgar for the vulgus, and its place was filled by facetiousness and whimsy.

Will Dyson had broken up the pattern with his striking Socialist cartoons in the *Herald* from about 1910 onwards, and had led the field during the First World War with his large war cartoons in which the monumental and the satirical had been powerfully blended. But when that phase of his work subsided, the harmony had resumed. In 1920, as Gladstone once said in a similar connection, 'there was a total absence of vulgarity which was very pleasing.' Very pleasing, that was, for those who thought that the aim of satire was merely to be pleasing. In the popular Press the significant features of British graphic political satire (as distinct from purely humorous art) were the classical draughtsmanship of Bernard Partridge; the scrupulous good manners of F. Carruthers Gould ('F. C. G.') rounding off his long career as the doyen of the Tennielesque school; the amiable symbolism of 'Poy'; and the socio-political pleasantries of W. K. Hasleden.

A world war had just passed, taking, by the feel of things, the old social order with it. It did not require a New Zealander standing on London Bridge to see that much of the pre-war inspiration of British graphic wit and humour was outdated, overtaken and run down by events. Gentility seemed anaemic, playfulness misplaced in the tougher and rougher job of building the new world.

During my later years in Melbourne I had gained a working acquaintance with the general lines of British politics and

90

economics. On this background first impressions began to broaden and clarify.

It seemed to me that post-war Britain needed something more than a drastic spring-clean. It needed co-ordination, economic, financial, industrial and commercial. Everything needed money— mines, railways, industries, agriculture. All required reorganization, regrouping, replanning. A vast capital investment was needed to replace its worn-out industrial plant, and at the same time (a matter of delicate balance) a wider distribution of wealth or interest to strengthen its social structure; and, finally, forward-looking politicans to open the way for energetic business men to supply the needs of people devastated or held back in the war. So far as the British domestic scene was concerned it was a case not so much of putting a patch on the past as of building a new future.

The impulse to change and readjustment, I decided, was more likely to come from the Left than the Right, so I inclined left-wards. Temperamentally I was for the quick against the dead. I was not, however, dogma-bound. Neither was I overwhelmed by admiration for the Labour Party as it stood. But its fumblings would be corrected by experience and a Labour–Radical Government, which seemed a likely outcome of the next election, would provide that experience. Most important, a virtue of the Labour Party was that it was not obstructed by its past.

The alternative, the Tory Party, was. In my eyes it had already committed itself to stagnation by yielding to the preponderance within its ranks who, lacking imagination, could have no idea but to return to what had been. The 'realists' were in control. Despite the lip-service to 'Homes for Heroes,' 'A Land Fit For Our Boys to Live In,' and the other promising slogans of the Victory election, the drift was now back to the standards of 1914. No vision of new worlds there. No hope from men who feared the unknown future and had always to cling to the past as the familiar reality. Their party speeches and manifestoes did not put the objection to change quite like that, of course. They conveyed the same meaning, but in the brave words 'tradition' and 'continuity.' It was all too evident that too many interpreted the words in terms of quiescence, not of motion, and that their 'continuity' was to be of power, possessions and privilege rather than of processes of evolution; and their 'tradition' that of the old lady who refused to travel on the new-fangled horseless carriage but was determined to go where she had to go by railway as God intended.

Their practical policy was simplicity (in the dictionary sense of silliness) itself: drastic economy; reduce income tax; cut wages, nominal and actual, to pre-war level; sweep away restrictions, wages-boards and such-like; and let nature take its course. Nature took its course. Profiteers prospered scandalously, houses did not build themselves, the cost of living did not come down, the long dismal road of unemployment stretched forward to the crash of 1931.

Unemployment was one of the two salient features of the early 'twenties. The other was fear. The Russian Bolshevik revolution had scared everybody, just as the French revolution over a century before had scared our great-grandfathers. To the nervous ones any rumble of dissent from the disillusioned populace became 'bolshevism'—something to be nipped in the bud. Whereupon the myopic powers-that-were took the usual 'strong measures,' which as usual went some distance towards creating the reality of their own nightmare. It was just as well that the material was not inflammable. There was some loose talk about Direct Action to threaten the Government, and the three biggest trades unions experimentally allied themselves for the supposed purpose of dictating its policy. But anyone who could have found genuine revolutionary possibilities in the persons of the dull, portly, fumbling trades union leaders of the time and their comparatively mild, patient and respectful followers needed a powerful imagination. No one remotely resembling a Lenin or a Trotsky stood in sight. The opportunity for tidying up Britain into a sane, prosperous community worthy of the British people was there; but the only two master-men who looked like possessing the ability, energy and nerve to do the job along lines of British democracy were the two pre-war Radicals Lloyd George and Winston Churchill—and they were on the other side. The opportunity passed.

Abroad, our foreign policy lay somewhere within the shaky new League of Nations, under a tangled heap of all-in wrestlers called the Supreme Council, arguing interminably about how to Make Germany Pay without ruining themselves. (The problem of how to Hang the Kaiser without setting a precedent had been given up.) The United States, standing aloof, was concerned mainly with getting back the money it had lent its allies during the war. Russia was a pariah seen through a mist of tall tales and unreliable reports. Few Western statesmen appeared to see any likelihood of permanence in the new Bolshevik regime. Egged on by Winston Churchill, the British Government was only checked by the prospect of a general strike from carrying on with France still further attempts to crush it by force.

Within the Empire, India writhed uneasily and the Sinn Fein waged guerrilla war in Ireland. The influence of Carson, Ulster and the Tories moved the British Government to suppression by drastic reprisals in kind. While machine-guns shot bullets, officials squirted milk-and-honey and protested that British rule did not rest on force. 'A very small band of terrorists is imposing its policy on Ireland. We know their names,' said the British Commander-in-Chief, going after a mad bull with a fly-swatter.

There was nothing particularly new to me about the issues raised by most of these questions. I had made plenty of cartoons about them already in Australia. Some things looked different, I found, when viewed from London, and I had to correct some wrong impressions I had brought from overseas. I made a thundering fool of myself once or twice before I learned sense about Kemal's new Turkey and the importance of the Mediterranean. I changed my mind about President Wilson, whom I learned to respect as a stubborn stickler for a democratic peace against a company of 'realists' who were not so particular. At the same time I was not sure about his great dream of self-determination in Middle and Eastern Europe.

With some emphasis I took unpopular lines in my cartoons favouring the bringing of Bolshevik Russia into the 'family of nations' by opening up trade; and advocating conciliation and concession towards Germany. This latter guaranteed me a pretty constant supply of trouble. But after all, I argued, the war was over. The Kaiser and his Prussian junkers were defeated, and representatives of the common people were in power under conditions of political democracy as sound as could be arranged. That was what the Allies had fought for. The plain common sense of it was that we should now buttress this government, strengthen it against more junkers, big industrial bosses and warrior kaisers.

The parliamentary position was like that I had left in Australia on a larger scale, with Lloyd George as a magnified version of Billy Hughes. Left-wing Ll. G., like Left-wing Billy, had risen to be the war-winning Prime Minister with the aid of his former rabid opponents, the Conservatives, shedding the bulk of his Left connections on the way. A snap victory election made him and a handful of his loyal Labour and Liberal friends virtually the prisoners of a vast majority of Conservative 'supporters.' Lloyd George was reluctant to accept that status and was obviously trying to escape. The Tory managers were as obviously determined to capture and finally leg-rope the slippery David. In consequence, the outstanding characteristics of the Lloyd George–Bonar Law Coalition Government in its last phase were indecision, self-contradiction and frustration.

There was no lack of material for cartoons in all that. After a peek at Ll. G. from the Press gallery of the Commons, I saw enough to improvise a recognizable cartoon figure until I could get a good look at him. And, bless the luck, I succeeded in finding a drawable symbol for the Coalition. The thing began with a remark by Lord Birkenhead about 'an invertebrate and undefined body, such as the present Coalition.' Lord B. had sought to give it a reactionary spine, but he had had to desist when he saw he could not do so without killing the patient. James Douglas, just before leaving the *Star*, had written an article for it defining the body more precisely as that of a mule, 'without pride of ancestry or hope of posterity.'

'A present for you, Mr. Low,' said friendly James, passing me the galley-proof.

'A swop for you, Mr. Douglas,' I replied, handing him a word-play—'Wasteminster' for 'Westminster'—for his next article on economy. Thus were born two gags which ran for years. Although the invention of the double-headed Ass saved me a lot of work (until the Government fell off it and had to resign) it was not evolved without a deal of trouble. I tried it first as a mule with two faces, then with two heads at the front end. It looked a rather unpleasant invention that way. After a lot of experiment, during which my table became littered with asses of various kinds, I almost absent-mindedly made what autograph collectors call a 'ghost.' I folded over a piece of paper upon one side of which a portion of drawing was still wet, so that a reproduction in reverse blotted itself upon the blank other side. And there, with a little adjustment of legs, was the Coalition Ass. After that I could have drawn him with my eyes shut.

The Ass 'took on' with *Star* readers. I drew him in all kinds of asinine circumstances suggesting the futility of going both ways at once and getting nowhere. He was Ll. G.'s racehorse, Churchill's charger, Bonar Law's carthorse, Carson's hunter and Austen Chamberlain's four-footed circus marvel, besides doing duty as the Bridge of Asses between Free Trade and Protection, and a

94

Lloyd George
and the double-
headed Ass

foster-mother hatching a large egg representing The Future. The *Daily News* began to reprint him regularly, and he was 'lifted' into provincial Liberal newspapers. Liberal headquarters sent him out in posters and pamphlets to political meetings, and he began to crop up in platform speeches up and down the country. His snowball progress passed him into Parliament when a bundle of thistles was handed to the Prime Minister as a suitable diet for the double-headed Ass during a debate on the Coalition Government's agricultural policy. The P.M. replied irrelevantly, 'Well, anyway, two heads are better than one.' When I went to collect some of my original drawings I found that some of the best Ass pictures were missing. It seemed that the P.M. had sent his private secretary down to the *Star* office and got there first.

It was all very friendly. The Ass being a frankly comic invention, it was difficult to make a row about him without the complainant finishing a bigger fool than when he began. But I soon found plenty of trouble in other connections.

In India, at the country town of Amritsar in the Punjab, a British force had dispersed a nationalist crowd by opening fire causing great loss of life; and the British officer commanding had ordered that all Indians passing through a certain street in which a woman missionary had been attacked should be compelled, as a punitive measure, to crawl instead of walking. At the same time reprisals against the Irish revolutionaries hardened in severity and the notorious Black-and-Tans were being organized. The blood-and-iron school were out to 'stamp out agitators.'

The principles involved in the Coalition Government's handling of India and Ireland had been clear enough from Australia, but I was eager to see how far political considerations on the spot might modify judgment formed at a distance. I had imagined that a closer view of the Irish question would reveal arguments against self-government which were not to be fairly appreciated from the other side of the world. The evidence was quite to the contrary. Indeed, I began to feel that after all, the view from afar of these particular woods was less obstructed by the trees. I certainly did not expect to find such obstinate stupidity on both sides, particularly in some influential British quarters where apparently it had been determined to push conflict to the bitter end rather than concede just terms in time. I became acutely aware that my overseas origin had deprived me of any sympathy with the type of British imperialist who assumed the possession of primitive emotions

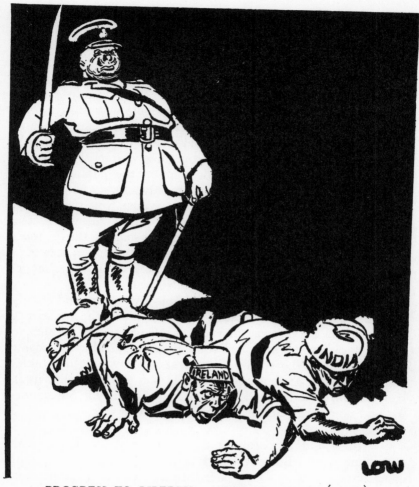

PROGRESS TO LIBERTY—AMRITSAR STYLE (1919)

about one's native land to be patriotism among the British, but treason among the lesser folk. Perhaps if those chaps could be stuck at the receiving end of the imperial connection for a while, I thought, instead of the sending end. . . . On the moral issue, one thing seemed clear about Ireland. The possibility of injustice to the Ulster minority was not to be removed by perpetuating injustice to the Ireland majority. Minority problems were to be justly settled in peace, not in war. All the talk about how the Irish as a people had no talent for government, and how Home Rule would mean Rome Rule left me cold, as subordinate, if not irrelevant, to the main issue. First things first.

97

With these thoughts, I drew a cartoon which pulled no punches. It showed a strutting military popinjay in British uniform, driving India and Ireland wriggling along on their stomachs. The title: PROGRESS TO LIBERTY—AMRITSAR STYLE.

There was a row. This was a cartoon so far removed from the customary pleasantries that it shocked. For some days sizzling letters poured in, the usual spate from people who always complain about a newspaper feature when it means something, and from those who don't like to be told of anything uncomfortable happening in the world; a bagful from those who insist the British can do no wrong, or whose judgment on the public question was smothered by some personal tragedy; some from people agreeing, a few threatening. 'You'll get yours, you swine,' said a postcard, signed, rather surprisingly, 'Yours sincerely.' The cartoon was reprinted in, among other newspapers, the *Freeman's Journal* of Dublin, which was almost immediately suppressed— to achieve partial republication immediately across the Channel within the hospitable pages of the *Daily News*.

The Irish revolt rose to crescendo in bloody murder and ghastly reprisals. The situation became intolerable, and the conscience of the British people was moved. The Government decided to reverse its policy and try conciliation. Everybody suddenly became friendly again. Who should I meet at a party but Sir Hamar Greenwood, the Secretary for Ireland, who was cordiality itself. How British, I thought. All last week I was calling you Sir Shameless and now here I am drinking cocktails with you.

Overtures and preparations for a conference with the Irish took some weeks. But one day I met a fellow *Star*-man on the office stairs. 'Come on,' he said, 'Michael Collins is arriving in half an hour.' A house on the corner of Pont Street and Hans Place in Chelsea was, it appeared, to be his retreat during the negotiations. We arrived barely in time to reach the doorstep and press the bell when a car drove up, the front door opened, the car door opened, several figures leaped out shielding their faces with their hands, sprinted across the footpath carrying us all inside together. The street was empty, but that, I gathered later, was how Irish revolutionary leaders always came and went.

So this was the fabulous Collins—this pink laughing boy. For security reasons he had not allowed himself to be photographed before and no one had known what he looked like. But this was a special occasion. He would certainly pose for me to show him to the world in a drawing. I was surprised to find that he knew of me and my cartoons about Ireland, and that he held me, with warm handshakes, as a friend. Even if the man had not been loaded with charm, that would have been hard to resist. But in fact he was brimming over with life, youth and humour, the sort of personality legends are made of. Admitting that there must be murky passages in the life of every active revolutionary, I prefer them merry. The sour ones with the tight mouths are, I feel, too often impelled by motives quite other than the good of mankind.

Michael Collins

Although Collins was the dominating personality of the delegation, Arthur Griffith was to lead it. He, too, posed for me amiably. To look at he was the very opposite of Collins, the unadventurous suburbanite Ordinary personified, short, plump, a bit behind in the fashions. Was this really the man who created Sinn Fein? His moustache was waxed at the ends in the Victorian style and he wore the wrong collar. It was only under the questioning that he became authoritative and revealed himself as the brains of the party.

The journalists kept arriving and questions were asked. I can remember only two:

'Would Home Rule mean Rome Rule, as your opponents say?'

'The Church has its place in the State, but that place is not in the Government,' replied Griffith. Too careful, I thought.

'Does the delegation look forward to success in the difficult negotiations before it?'

'It's not what we have before us—it's what we have behind us,' replied Collins enigmatically, or, you might say, prophetically.

Had Collins and Griffith survived, no doubt the story of the new Ireland would have been very different. The Irish started their new dispensation with two hungers, one spiritual, one material: the one, to salvage their national pride, by flaunting their own flag, their own language and their Irishness generally, taking the late oppressor Britain down a peg in the process; the other, to create for themselves better and juster standards of life. Unfortunately from the beginning the two hungers occasionally conflicted and they could not have it both ways. Compromising, not uncompromising, statecraft was needed. Collins, I dare swear, would have seen to it that they had less sauce and more pudding.

My portrait of Collins turned out well. After taking such trouble it was a pity I lost it. The damned thing fell out of my pocket in Chancery Lane on my way to Fleet Street. But Collins's lines had impressed themselves so vividly on my mind that I rushed on to the *Star* office and re-drew it from memory in half an hour. To my annoyance it was too late. The original had been picked up and turned in to the office by a *Star* reader ten minutes before I finished the duplicate. It was reprinted all over the world. But Wilson Pope, my editor, was not mollified. He had the *Star* print an announcement that a standing reward would be paid to anyone who found me or my drawings blowing around the streets and returned me or them to the *Star* office.

By contrast the arrival in London of de Valera later was something of an anti-climax. All was scrupulously correct, and consequently less rewarding to journalists. The other delegates grouped punctually at ten o'clock for the photographers, but Dev kept us waiting for an hour. Then Erskine Childers, emaciated and ill-looking, emerged and said: 'Mr. Low, the President will now receive you. You will please address the President as "Mr. President."' 'Blimey!' said somebody.

Soon a by-election at Paisley gave me an opportunity to see something of the British political big guns in action. Liberals, the 'Wee Frees,' decided to get Asquith back into Parliament. With Harry Jones, an admirable character from the *Daily News*, as chaperone, off I went to Paisley, which rapidly became the assembly point for leading figures of the Liberal and Labour Parties—Simon, Runciman, Donald Maclean, Ramsay Mac-Donald and others. Stimulated by the material I worked early and late to cover the opportunity. My *Daily News* connection proved to be the open sesame to Liberal 'Wee Free' meetings, platforms and backroom conferences, giving me a hectic ten days of looking, listening, meeting and drawing. With a few exceptions, my personal contacts were then fleeting as between journalists and public men, and I was too new to do more than put elementary questions while I was drawing, but I came away with a full sketchbook and an extended view on British politics.

The effect of living in an hotel packed with public monuments, who up till then had been for a raw Australian stranger like myself only legendary, was strange. It was a little fluttering, for instance, upon rushing from my bathroom one morning in dressing gown, toothbrush in hand, to find myself bumping almost into the great Asquith himself, sailing along the corridor flanked by Mrs. Asquith and his daughter Violet.

Later, when I talked with Asquith after breakfast as he posed for me in his sitting-room, I found him aloof, old, worn, uncommunicative and more than a little crusty. It was uncomfortable for the old man to have to open his campaign by eating his own words about women's suffrage and to confess that the presence

Marshal Foch

of women in his audience was an act of generosity on their part. Obviously he did not relish the demands being put upon him by his election agent. This I regretted, for the fruitiness of his diction struck my ear, tuned to a comparatively raucous Australian accent, with real pleasure.

His 'line,' about the revolutionary probabilities of a Labour Government, did not impress me, I having experienced eight years of it overseas and survived. But one could forget the matter of his speech in fascination at the voice, suggestive of rich port wine, issuing from the firm lips which he moistened with a nervous recurring flick of the tip of the tongue, like a dignified old lizard. A liberal education in how to speak. I was intensely interested. Here the mechanism of speech was not just operating automatically —thoughts translated into sound and shot from the mouth in one process. This old boy had *control* of it! His mouth said only what he let it. And his released remarks were checked and calculated beforehand. Talk was not aimless but designed. In such company a man who shoots his mouth is as powerless as a baby. After Asquith I looked and listened to other politicians with a sharpened ear to distinguish those who were the masters of their tongues, and those who were not, poor things.

For all that, great old man as he was, I could not see Asquith as the mouthpiece of post-war youth.

The show over the way I found just as interesting, in a different

101A

Asquith poses for me (1919)

way. I was perhaps too greatly impressed by Ramsay MacDonald, who looked to me a real leader. He seemed taller in those days and more craggy, as he stalked up and down. A handsome figure, fine voice, shabby blue serge suit, handlebars moustache solid black against solid white of hair forelock. I enjoyed drawing him. Although I had him all out of proportion, physically and otherwise, I didn't know it. For many years he was to be one of my failures in representation, until I outgrew that windswept-hero first impression.

I had a letter to Ramsay from old Champion in Melbourne. He was courteous and I was soon free of the Labour camp. Of them all I liked best old Bob Smillie, the secretary of the Miners' Federation, who took me aside and said some rash things. More heart than head, I decided.

In between meetings Harry Jones and I ranged the district 'sampling' the voters. Our visits to and with local Labour leaders took us to some stinking dens in Glasgow. This was new to me. There was nothing like this in the Dominions. I had never seen real poverty and degradation before. Eugh, the places crawled. I was filled with rage and disgust, rather than pity, at the blind stupidity that allowed such things to be.

On the whole, if I had had a vote, it would have gone to Labour on the issues. The cartoons I sent down to London reflected my preference, and my editor exercised his contract right to edit two of them out of the paper. I did not complain. The position of the *Star*, like that of the *Daily News*, was ambiguous: Liberal, but friendly to Labour, except that they wished Asquith to win this election. And of course the old man should have been in Parliament.

Asquith won. But I returned to London with the feeling of having come from overseas just in time to catch the twilight of the old pre-war generation. Succeeding weeks intensified this feeling, as a procession of legendary figures passed across my vision. Using all my privileges, and a bit more, I attended all the conferences and meetings within reach—and there were many at that time—rubbing shoulders with Briand and Foch, breathing down the necks of Curzon, Balfour and Robert Cecil, taking a sidelong look at the worn old tiger Clemenceau and a short squint at the first of the post-war Germans, Simons and von Seekt.

A tired-looking lot of old men, all except Lloyd George who was at his top, electric, magnetic. I made a note of him one conference morning arriving across the yard of St. James's Palace. The man radiated vitality. It was probably my best Ll. G.

9

AFTER giving myself about three months to get the wheels running smoothly under my job, I felt it was time to look up H. G. Wells.

I am a Wells man. I came on his books in my early teens and I soon began to think of him as larger than life-size, almost as a god. There was some excuse for this immoderate enthusiasm. In those days, when communications were not as easy as they are today, very few current writers in the Old World could project their personalities with any emphasis across the fifteen thousand miles to New Zealand. To those that did, distance lent enchantment. In that far-off Colony—as it was then—the influence of Wells over the rising generation was in my case surely as great as he could have desired. What a vista of imagination was opened when I lighted on those paper-covered colonial editions of *The Time Machine* and *The Island of Doctor Moreau*; how *Love and Mr. Lewisham* accorded so with my adolescent moods that I walked around dreamily inside the character for weeks looking for my Ethel Henderson; how I waited for the well-thumbed library copy of *Kipps* and became him for a space, too; and when from these I passed fascinated to the procession of socio-political essays and novels, how they stirred me to a livelier interest in the sickness and health of societies, the institution of marriage, the emancipation of women, the bases of good government and the future of mankind.

The worshipper takes a risk in coming to sit at the feet of his oracle. I opened the ball by sending him a note covering a letter of introduction from someone he had probably never heard of. He put me off, saying his bath was out of order. Good-night! I thought. But a month later came a gracious invitation to my sister and myself to week-end at Easton Glebe. Not only was the bath repaired, but Mrs. Wells had now repainted the bathroom with mural designs of fish in submarine effects. Impressed by this apparent obsession with cleanliness, we packed our soap and off we went.

This first visit to see the Wellses was not a howling success. I was tongue-tied with shyness. They lived in one of those roomy country houses with green creeper covering the entire front wall excepting the porticoed door leading into a flagged entrance hall. Before it, against a background of open deer park, lay the lawn on which Mr. Britling played hockey while Seeing It Through; to one side, the sunken garden and the barn in which they played their famous ball game.

Jane was graciously welcoming, H.G. was geniality itself. I felt they had expected us both to be different. After tea, walking across the horizon alongside this plump, high-fluting man with a speech-mannerism of 'dontcher know,' in knickerbockers and yellow moustache, I could not recall the flavour of Hoopdriver, Mr. Lewisham or Kipps, and I got nowhere. It did not seem to me that there could be much between us.

When I found my tongue a little more with Jane, it was only to get off on the wrong foot. When I was asked what struck me so far about the English, I said 'Tips.' Coming from Australia, almost a classless society, I could not understand the greasy ease with which people accepted tips and the humiliating admission of inferior status that came with them. Had these people no pride? Did they not feel as good as the next man? If I had offered a tip to a self-respecting Australian, he would have flipped it back in my face. . . . Jane disagreed.

The other guest was Middleton Murry, already a distinguished critic, who made no concessions. I found myself at odds with him about practically everything, from the derivation of the style of Will Dyson (he thought it was French, whereas I knew it to be German) to the influence of politics on the course of human affairs (he thought it was a minor influence, a view I could not accept for one moment).

Everybody dressed for dinner except the Lows. (How could one guess how Socialists behaved in England?) Table talk about the relative merits of Oxford and Cambridge, about which I knew nothing. I was not familiar with the underlying assumptions and associations of English conversation. My idioms were wrong, my similes were foreign.

'What do they think of Sir Edward Grey in Australia?' asked H.G., Grey being his pet disgust at the time.

'Sir Edward Grey?' I said. 'They don't think about him at all.' Which was true enough. I could see Wells did not think much of Australia.

H.G. and Jane probably felt the party was getting a bit heavy and decided to break it up a bit by organizing some horseplay after dinner. We all put on comic paper hats, one of the boys manned the piano-player, H.G., wearing a tea-cosy and an Oriental dressing-gown and banging a gong, led a capering procession through the house, up and down the stairs, over the chairs, tables and sofas in time to the music. Then we felt better.

Night. Deep silence punctuated by the almighty row made by Lady Warwick's amorous buck deer courting their does in the park without. The sun was up when I fell into a gentle doze . . . s l e e p. . . .

WHAM! I was awakened by Götterdämmerung being played on the piano-player, no holds barred, by a Wells boy. Soothing bath among Mrs. Wells's painted fish. Help-yourself breakfast (bacon and eggs, kipper, toast, jam, coffee), a siesta with the Sunday papers.

'What do you think of Garvin?'

'Oh—ah—I've never been there.'

To the barn for the ball game. A lot of business fossicking out pairs of canvas shoes from an old trunk. Then a large medicine-ball coming at you, it being your business to cannon it off a cross-beam back at a Wells. I am probably wrong but it seemed to me that the Wells family tended to gang up on the visitor, but it wouldn't have mattered if they hadn't because I would never have been any good at it anyway. Properly exhausted, we repaired to lunch, thence to sleep, followed by tea with visitors, whose names escaped me, a long walk, dinner, talk, bed. No unusual routine, but strange to me, accustomed to less deliberately planned relaxation.

Well, well, I thought as I shook hands with H.G. and Jane at parting, I may never see you again. But I did, often, and as time passed and I learned the ways of the English I grew to have a warm affection for them both.

It dawned on me later that if I had not shone as a bright talker at our first meeting, that was all to the good, since H.G., like most men with power of expression and boundless interest in life, had wanted to do all the talking anyway and I had shown myself a good listener.

When I had established myself more soundly in London and

was able to begin returning his hospitality, I bore that in mind. I arranged two or three quiet luncheons at Boulestin's to which I brought select companies of the rising generation of crack commentators on affairs from Fleet Street, and an occasional visiting politician from the Dominions, to whom he could hold forth endlessly without unsympathetic interruption. This pleased him and our friendship improved. In these circumstances my own inhibitions slowly disappeared and there were fewer sterile silences for me. I began to partake of his atmosphere and warm to my own best and liveliest in his company. Now and then stimulated by his evocative talk I forgot my position as acolyte entirely and began to chip in at inordinate length. 'David! David! *I'm* talking!' said H.G., pained.

It could never be said that I talked H.G. out, but once I came near it. It was at Easton Glebe, about the time he was incubating *The Science of Life* and taking a passing interest in psychic phenomena. An outbreak of articles on spiritualism had occurred in the Sunday papers—Vale-Owen in the *Dispatch*, Conan Doyle in the *Express*, and others. H.G. took a poor view of their stuff, and I positively had to open up my own little tale as follows:

When I was twenty-two I discovered that my sister, fifteen, and I had a joint talent at a form of 'spiritualistic phenomena' which some ten years later became widely commercialized as the Oui-ja. Our apparatus was simple: a supple twig, and a sheet of cardboard with the letters of the alphabet and the numerals printed on it in pencil, 'Yes' and 'No' in the top corners to save time. We sat opposite one another, the cardboard alphabet propped up on the table, the twig resting on the tips of our four thumbs and first fingers, not grasped, but barely retained. Soon the twig trembled and a perceptible force seeming to come from without twisted and turned it in mid-air, almost jumping it off our fingers, taking us around the room as we followed its impulses, then leading us back to the alphabet card, where by tapping the letters with its point it proceeded to spell out . . . nonsense. We were both thin, eager, highly-strung youngsters with complete confidence in one another, and there was no possibility of deception. This inexplicable force was disturbing. We decided to go into it further at home in private, and for some weeks the twig had at least one 'seance' daily. The results were alarming—or they would have been had we not agreed to take whatever happened in a friendly spirit. The twig now 'talked' quite freely and sensibly, in several 'personalities,' spelling its words out as quickly as a typist in reply to our spoken conversation. The wisdom and wit of its most constant 'personality,' called Meredith, astonished us. We were no match for its unexpected thrusts in argument. For three engrossing nights we 'listened' to an account of what happened after one died.

This sounds more eerie than it actually was, for the atmosphere of the proceedings was now jovial and light-hearted. With familiarity we advanced to the stage of asking friend Meredith to arrange contacts first with long-dead relatives, then with historical personages. Rather as one pulls a name out of a hat, I asked to talk to Shakespeare.

It took three weeks' hard going to get him, he being much advanced from wherever we were, but at last, one appointed night, Meredith, whose force had waxed to great vitality, handed over. The twig suddenly became weak, almost motionless.

'Hullo! Is that William Shakespeare?' I asked.

The twig had just enough energy to answer: 'Yes.'

'One or two things I want to know, sir,' I said respectfully. 'Were all the plays commonly ascribed to you, written by you or were any, some, or all written by Francis Bacon?'

'All mine.'

'Does a cypher message run through the plays?'

'Yes.'

'What is the message?'

'It reveals ye indiscretions of ye Queene.'

'Oh. What were these indiscretions?'

On this invitation the twig, so to speak, cleared decks for action and spelled out for about five minutes without a break, with great rapidity and energy, a list of names and places.

I realized with surprise that since Shakespeare had arrived the expression and spelling had become Elizabethan with plenty of 'e's' and 'ye's.'

The climax of this story is that I spent the next morning at a public library in Sydney turning up histories of the period. The names and places were authentic, anyway. It was very puzzling.

We resumed with Shakespeare the next evening. With an eye on the main chance, I suggested that he might like to write a new play, and offered myself as the medium and scribe. The proposal was received coldly. He did, however, volunteer a few cartoon ideas. They were no good. We drifted apart and I got into an argument with Voltaire . . . but that is another story.

'What do you make of that, H.G.? Demons? Spirits of the dead? There is no evidence here, except the say-so, of survival after death.

'Released subconscious? Unconscious memory? We felt we were talking to a complete somebody else, coherent, intelligent, eloquent, unpredictable and often quite contrary in view to both of us. The separateness was vivid at times. Neither of us had ever read anything at all detailed about Elizabeth and her Court.

'Thought reception and transmission? To, from or by either of us? Were we open to anybody like a sort of Post Office? Some power as yet unexplained arising from a peculiar juxtaposition of two surrendered wills? Any of these explanations involves a formidable admission of vast uncharted regions of the mind. What do you think, H.G.?'

No reply. He had dozed off.

'Hey! H.G.!' I said, loud enough to wake the sleepy sage. 'What do you think of Oui-ja, automatic writing, messages from the unknown and that kind of thing?'

Wells's explanation was that we human beings were moving about up to our chests perhaps in a kind of sea of thought and ideas. When the emotional weather grew stormy, the waves sometimes swept over our heads. From this sea, one was constantly receiving thoughts and passing them back again. My sister and I, having put ourselves into a state of willing and complete receptivity, would get the maximum intake.

'Good Lord, H.G.!' I said, 'What about the intelligence that selects the ideas for reception and arranges them in relevance and sequence? If you can believe what you have just said, why can't you believe in fairies, Heaven and the resurrection of the dead?'

It was that Wells week-end that started me thinking of religion.

I had heard a lot of talk about God since I arrived in Britain. At Paisley there had been much insistence on Christian principles by all political parties. The *Daily News* and the *Star* were controlled by the old Quaker family of Cadbury, and the reflection of their beliefs was frequently the subject of editorial discussion. Then, my sister had decided to marry a Roman Catholic and preparations were afoot for her entry into his Church. I, as the only member of her family present, found myself unexpectedly involved in responsibilities ranging over a fairly wide area of theological enquiry within the families of both bride and bridegroom. And, finally, I had made the acquaintance of Canon Adderley, 'Father Jim,' the Rector of St. Paul's, Covent Garden, through a publisher who engaged me to illustrate one of his books. He was an admirable character, but our meetings were exasperating. I wanted to talk religion with him, but he seemed to take it for granted that that was the one subject I wouldn't want to talk about. 'You know where you stand, don't you?' he said, puffing his large evil-smelling pipe. 'If not, you'd better find out.'

By Jove, he's right! A man should know himself. He has to be with himself so much.

So far, I had worried out and co-ordinated only some of my ideas about politics and art. For the rest, I was a patchwork of unrelated scraps. It struck me that it was high time, urgent, that I collect myself and try to find out what I believed. When readjustment was the order of the day, one should have something to readjust. If in these strange new surroundings one did not know what one was up to, one might very easily get disconnected from one's sources of strength without knowing it and finish up a mere shell of a man. In the deadly serious moments that come as reaction to the grind of being 'bright,' I began to take stock. During the bitterly cold, rather lonely, hard-working winter of 1919–1920 I went for some long walks and arrived at a row of question marks.

I did not know the secret of life. But neither did anyone else. I heard of infinity, but I was unable to imagine it. I was aware of mysteries but also of unexplored regions of the mind. I could not say whether there was life (in a continuing recognizable individual sense) after death, or even whether there was spiritual life at all, other than that contingent upon physical life. I knew that nobody could know any one thing positively and absolutely unless he knew everything. Yet as I found myself, I could not abdicate my responsibility for using my own powers and perceptions, such as they were, however imperfect they might be, as well as I could. To do otherwise, I felt, would be self-betrayal. 'The real truths are incapable of proof—not to be apprehended by the senses,' I was told. Dangerous words. For I knew that, surrendering reason to emotion I could persuade myself to believe anything, error as easily as truth.

I remained what I had always been—an agnostic, tolerant and enquiring of other views. That is to say, I chose to act upon the assumptions that love ('goodwill' is the better word since 'love' has been monopolized and corrupted by its sex application) and simplicity (meaning not the 'simplicity' of the half-wit, but clarity of understanding and purity of conduct) were the fundamentals of good living.

As for all else, I remained open-minded, ready to be persuaded. But not by threats, promises, organ music, lofty architecture, magic words, intonations, vestments, ritual, massed choirs or the company of vast crowds of people.

My greatest weakness, perhaps, was that I found nothing about that attitude to make me miserable. On the contrary, I was as cheerful as a lark. That's what comes of having a good stomach.

All this spate of ratiocination on Higher Things did not preclude some practical thought on my domestic affairs. When my sister married these appeared to converge to a pointed conclusion. The time had come, I decided, when I must get married, too. An adventurous domestic freedom might frequently be stimulating, especially for artists who need stimulating; but when one had a job to do it was best to adventure freely on a settled domestic background. When I found myself thinking like that, I was certain I was approaching middle age. I was twenty-eight. There have to be two parties to a marriage of course, but so far as I was concerned I was ready.

I was not without experience of the opposite sex. There had been few intervals since I was thirteen when I had not been infatuated with some fair charmer. In the process I had come to dislike fluttering soft women as much as strong hard women; and to detest greedy women, excitable women, envious women, women who played up their sex, women who could not keep their arms and legs still, and women whose mouths opened to emit prattle without their permission. If two qualities more than others attracted me to a woman, they were that she have calm and the excellent thing, a voice low and sweet. I was also as susceptible to beauty and the talents of good housekeeping as most men, but I did not regard these as of paramount importance in marriage, since if one wants a good housekeeper one can hire one, and if all one wants of women is physical attraction, far better not to marry at all but to 'keep' someone. That way one would be doing the Divorce Court a good turn anyway. No, to my mind a wife should be a companion and marriage a partnership.

I sent a cablegram to Madeline Kenning of Auckland, New Zealand, saying: 'Will you marry me?' prepaying address and one word in reply. In due course the answer came: 'Yes,' and in four months she arrived, we were married without fuss in the presence of my sister and her new husband and two friends by Father Adderley in the otherwise starkly empty St. Paul's Church, Covent Garden.

Madeline

Now, I knew this was *not* the way to do it. My wife and I knew very little about one another, the duration of our acquaintance until she stepped off the ship at Southampton having been only three days. We had met during a flying visit I had made to New Zealand from Australia three years before. True, in a New Zealand town in the early days it was difficult for any family to be unknown to all other families, and I had soon become aware of her antecedents, which were very like my own—Scottish–Irish parentage, middle-class, commercial-management division. But what does such data tell?

What is the lure of love? Not beauty alone. The essential physical attractions, certainly, and the indefinable appeal to the imagination which imbues every detail with romantic charm; but more than that, it lies in the flash of recognition, the unspoken understanding, the reassurance, reinforcement. I felt good when she was around. In her big grey eyes lay life. In other words, I loved her.

Instead of revisiting my birthplace, I spent my three days in Auckland where she lived. On the second day we went for a long walk and, sitting on a rock by the sea, we discussed our immediate marriage. Impossible. We both had too many family responsibilities. But this was unfinished business that had one day to be completed. . . .

Her responsibilities had lightened. So had mine. The day had arrived. As I waited on the pier for her to disembark, I thought we might be rushing it a bit. I—she—we—took a frightful risk. Either or both of us might be perverts, drunks or mad, for all the one or the other or both of us might know. By Jove, I thought, if ever we have children, and they are normal (oh, Lord!), I swear I will never allow any of them to do anything like this.

Fortunately our case proved the exception to the rule that calculation is superior to instinct in ordering human affairs, at least so far as the selection of a mate is concerned. It was an ideally happy marriage from the beginning. Mutual attraction had been the one reality of our attachment, all else being vague and of no consequence. There was not only the atmosphere of golden romance but also, as it turned out, a practical advantage in starting from scratch. Where all was uncertain but the central point, it was easier to make mutual compromises in our joint way of life. Once more the Fates had adjusted a pretty balance, for while the Scottish predominated over the Irish in me, the reverse was the case with her. And we were both natural Londoners. A new peace and tranquillity entered my private life.

I thought I loved my wife when I married her, but now I know that I did not fall into adoration until after we had been married about four years and had two bouncing daughters just like her.

A momentary initial misgiving could not have been all on one side. The unknown may be romantic but also extremely disturbing, and I and my world must at first have seemed difficult to measure. My fiancée's arrival in London was marked by an amazing incident which boggled her judgment to start with. We were bowling away in an open car (it was a golden May day) from Victoria Station along Buckingham Palace Road when both of us caught sight of vaguely familiar faces looking over the Palace Garden wall. It was King George the Fifth and Queen Mary with two or three others. Apparently they were sunning themselves on an eminence behind the wall and had leaned over to look at the traffic. 'Oh look!' said Madeline, amazed. 'The King and Queen!' The King's eye fell on my radiant fiancée. He raised his hat solemnly. I raised mine back. The moment passed . . . 'Um, yes,' I said looking at her wrist-watch. 'Punctual . . . I told them 12.30. . . .' A bright spot. It was months before Madeline realized that the stranger she had married was not quite as influential as all that.

It could have been no picnic for her to come alone to a different world full of unheard-of difficulties of living, to make a home for a 'professional' man of uncertain habits and enthusiasms who littered the place with newspapers, talked politics in his bath and made on her the strangest demands. No one was more relieved than my wife when the Irish Peace Treaty was signed, because no longer need she pose for Erin bowed, shackled, and insufficiently clothed against the blasts of Tyranny.

My marriage gave me what I had always needed—a private audience. As soon as we were settled in a small house on the outskirts of London a system organized itself to accord with the needs whereby every morning after breakfast my wife sat offering comments as I thought aloud, and rendered a report on the day's news in my own words; relating it to what had happened yesterday and what was likely to happen tomorrow. This I found was of inestimable benefit to me in getting my views and ideas straight, and it opened the world up to her. Later when the children came we occasionally incorporated them and whoever else happened to be in the house for service in the 'kitchen cabinet,' which as the children grew older became a fixed feature in our way of life. Tedious? Nobody who heard the shouts of laughter, snatches of song and occasional horseplay that punctuated the political conferences of the Low family would have thought so, especially when our dog joined in.

Among the various ideas of the *Star* people for building up their new cartoonist was the publication of a book of my Lloyd George cartoons on the lines of my Australian *Billy Book*. I drew a lively cover for *Lloyd George & Co.*, which pleased everybody, featuring my Ll. G. and the double-headed Coalition Ass. The convention of the time demanded an introduction by a writing man, on the principle that no British public would buy a book of pictures without a wedge of text to read also, for money's-worth of time expended. Who should write my introduction? Who but Arnold Bennett, my 'discoverer'?

Arnold Bennett

The publishers arranged a meeting. I set off to call on Arnold Bennett. Thrill. The door was opened by a neat uniformed maid into a neat dining-sitting room furnished in a conventional style except for two 'modern' water-colour paintings and six Nash woodcuts. Light green centre carpet, polished surround. The Great Man enters, holding writing-block to breast, Mount Sinai fashion. White quiff, pinkish face, heavy supercilious eyes, loose mouth, lumpy receding chin, streaky moustache, chesty carriage, a couple of stone weight more than he should be, neat little hands and feet. Striped suit, the famous fob. Fancy having a watch ticking there, I thought. He didn't look well. Stomach trouble.

'Mr. Low?' he said heavily. There was a touch of condescension in his manner, but how could I resent that from the author of *Clayhanger* and *Hilda Lessways* which had made a mark on my impressionable youth. All the same it was unexpected. I had anticipated someone rushing out with both hands extended saying: 'My dear Low! Welcome!' After all, he had some responsibility for me. I got the idea that he hadn't expected me to be what I was, either. It was, as you might say, two other fellows. I heard later that, as he saw it, I should have found my way into the newspapers of Lord Beaverbrook, with whom he was intimately friendly, and that he was a little annoyed with the *Daily News* and the Cadburys over something. . . . You never know with these English. . . .

113

He took me around the water-colours and woodcuts and appeared slightly pained when I did not enthuse. I explained that my tastes were representational: Velasquez and Rembrandt in paint, Dürer and Daumier in drawing, Rodin and Meunier in sculpture. He thought that was no excuse. Talking to Bennett was easy, although he had the advantage of a slight stammer, which enabled him to keep his thoughts ahead of his utterance. He would start a sentence and hang up in the middle of it, just long enough for one to foretell his meaning, which gave one a pleased feeling at one's own cleverness.

Naturally, since he was to write my preface, and he knew nothing about me except my drawings, what might have been a conversation soon became a cross-examination: full name—birth —nationality and so on. I got tired of the question-and-answer business and twisted an enquiry about my methods into a generalization about the aims and functions of all artists.

'No, Mr. Bennett, I am not an unsuccessful painter drawing cartoons, falling back on journalism to make a living.'

'Well, why do you choose journalism?'

'What do *you* work for, Mr. Bennett?'

'To make a l-living.'

'Oh, that be blowed! You already have a living.'

'Well, what do *you* work for, Mr. Low?'

'Because I like to.'

'You mean that if you hadn't the people who buy the newspapers as your customers, you would go on doing the same sort of stuff for its own sake?'

'Not exactly. In so far as one's stuff is interpretative, one's got to take stock of the receptivity of the customers. What I mean is that an artist has to like and believe in what he's doing. That's the main thing.'

'Don't you want to be famous and make a lot of money?'

'Not that bad.'

Bennett replied: 'Bosh!'

'What about Nash and the other artists who did these pictures on your wall?' I asked.

'They make a sensible compromise.'

He shot at me suddenly: 'D-do you Believe?'

I was taken aback. That opened up too many channels. I felt I had fumbled this meeting and that he had marked me down as a bit above myself. Under these circumstances I had had enough argument for one day. Damn it, how does one handle these English? I could see in his eye that he was not exactly pleased with his *protégé.*

114

I was wrong again. He wrote me a flattering preface for my book—got some of his facts wrong, but all in my favour. I was grateful. But it was years before I was invited to Bennett's house again. By then I had become more established and we had begun to run into one another at other people's parties, and a few words here and a few words there had worn down first impressions and brought an easier association. It was long before I saw what I should have seen in the first place: that the unease of that first meeting was not wholly due to *my* not knowing how to handle *him*, but partly to *his* not knowing how to handle *me*. Behind that façade lay a considerable uncertainty about himself.

But if the personal contact was interrupted, not so the postal. The preparation of the book involved the exchange of a few letters, and after it was done with Bennett continued to write to me from time to time, generally in encouraging terms about this cartoon or that but occasionally admonitory about my efforts to write. For example:

My dear Low,

Your article was good, but something ought to be done about your grammar. You must have been educated at Eton or some such place. Why? Consider the following sentence; and if necessary ask one of your enlightened friends about it. I was shocked.

'He amazed me by recalling out of his marvellous memory cartoons of the past which I am sure everyone but he and I had forgotten.'

Yours ever,
Arnold Bennett.

I was delighted. At last this good man had settled with me a proper relationship of patron and tyro. It was characteristic of the side of Arnold Bennett which wrote books on *Efficiency, How to Live on 24 Hours a Day*, and so on, that he was sensitive about points of punctilious correctitude which to lesser men might have seemed unimportant. When my portrait study of him was published with others in a book for which Rebecca West, under the pseudonym of 'Lynx,' wrote a set of brilliant biographical articles, he had this to say:

75 Cadogan Square,
S.W.1.
9.10.28.

My dear Low,

. . . You ought to have added a note that your caricature of me was done before I had become the sylph I am. There is a grave case of mis-spelling on my first page. And a still graver case of inaccuracy. My shirt-fronts do not give out 'crepitant noises.' Never! For the reason that I never in any circumstances wear a starched shirt-front. (The only other man I know who adheres strictly to this rule is Birkenhead) . . .

Yours ever,
Arnold Bennett.

Lloyd George & Co., my first English book, was not in the same street as *The Billy Book* either in quality or profit, but it went well enough on the bookstalls at half a crown. The reviews were marvellous. With the full weight of the *Daily News* and the *Star* behind it, collecting opinions of all the nobs and using new photographs of Ll. G.'s little daughter Megan handling a copy at Victoria Station, saying 'WHAT A SHAME!', we burst the traditional blindness of Fleet Street newspapers to the performances of journalists outside their own staffs, and got paragraphs from our competitors.

In my temporarily much inflated postbag I was delighted to find one morning a note from Bernard Shaw, the great panjandrum himself:

> Until this man goes back to Australia it will be a case of
> Unhappy Low, lie down
> Uneasy lies the head that wears a crown.

G.B.S. 15/6/1921.

The reception of *Lloyd George & Co.* was a piece of pulse-taking as instructive to me as it was to the *Daily News* Company. It reassured us both and smoothed relations. From then on editorial disputes about the matter of my cartoons became rare and we all got on happily together.

Incidentally the book had given me also a standing of sorts in the Asquithian or 'Wee Free' Liberal Party, based, of course, on the fact of my association with the Radical *Star*, and an easy belief that it's not *what* you are but *where* you are that counts.

I may have been faintly embarrassed at the assumptions. But I was decidedly so when my good friend Hugh Jones brought me an invitation to speak at the National Liberal Club. I accepted, mainly because I wanted to see if I could. 'Speak about what?' 'Anything.' I had made only two speeches in my life—speeches of farewell on leaving Australia. My first was bad. My second was worse. Now we should see.

The speech I made at the National Liberal Club was my third, and probably my worst. The Club was very political then, and the large dining-room was packed to hear me. Everything about me felt wrong. I was acutely conscious of disappointing expectations in my appearance. Despite the impressively solid looks of F. C. Gould, the political cartoonist with most honour among Liberals of the passing generation, there still lingered a general impression that the traditional caricaturist—Gillray to Phil May —should wear loud clothes, drink a lot and exhibit bohemian tastes. I was a thin eager young man with strongly marked eyebrows, weight 9 stone 4, height 5 feet 10, gloomily dressed, preferring tea to strong drink, and argument to funny stories. I was lonely, parked in the middle of a lot of strangers, six of the largest of whom had marched me in to the top table like a military escort. I couldn't see a face I knew—Ah, thank God! . . . Hugh Jones sitting about a quarter of a mile away.

I was vilely nervous; I lost my notes, which were most inappropriate anyway. To say my style was unorthodox was to put it mildly. The marble statue of Gladstone facing me surely turned a shade whiter. It wasn't until I finished and questions came up that I scored a modest little success. Someone asked me how I had invented the double-headed Ass as a symbol of the Coalition. I replied: 'It didn't have to be invented.' Poor stuff, but it brought the house down, probably from relief and partly from loyalty.

I retired as soon as I could, and I was saved from my petty mortification by having a larger private misery. My sister was in hospital dangerously ill and I had to rush to find out whether she would live or die.

Next day when I looked at the Liberal papers, I was genuinely amazed. 'Mr. Low gave a delightful talk full of witticisms' began a half-column notice in the *Westminster Gazette*. 'The large company who listened delightedly to his mordant wit and screaming stories . . .' said another. And another: 'Members were charmed by Low's genial philosophy . . .' Was this Party solidarity? Or had I been good and not known it? Anyway, putting everything at its lowest, I could not have been as bad as I thought I had been. And if that were so, I had learned the first thing one should know about public speaking: what goes on inside a speaker, the inner ferment of emotions, is of no account whatever so long as he can keep a bland exterior.

A propos of that, I remember many years later than the time of which I am writing, listening to Lloyd George and Lord Moynihan, the eminent surgeon, comparing notes about their emotional disturbances.

Moynihan: '. . . And whenever I have to make a speech, I get a ball of ice three and three-quarter inches in diameter just over my navel.'

Lloyd George: 'What size did you say?'

Moynihan: 'Three and three-quarter inches.'

Lloyd George: 'Great Scott! Same size as mine!'

After the Lloyd George book and my performance at the N.L.C. I began to feel more at home. I became a regular attendant at a 'Wee Free' weekly lunch at the House of Commons organized by an extraordinarily energetic chap, Wedgwood Benn, where I renewed acquaintance with some of the people I had met at the Paisley by-election. The 'Wee Frees' though few were lively, and those meetings were jolly and gay, perhaps because of the absence of any feeling of impending responsibility. The group had no function but criticism, which, since it practically lived on loathing Lloyd George, was enough. In Wedgwood himself, Pringle (the original 'pringler'), Hogge and Kenworthy it possessed a quartette of political wasps unparalleled for velocity and manœuvre. The whole group when organized for debate constituted a commando as skilful in tripping up and throwing unwary Ministers on their back as one would wish to meet on a dark night. Donald Maclean, the Party leader, usually sat at the head of the table; sometimes the public monuments, Asquith, Grey or Simon, would turn up to tell us of the Great Future That Lay Before Us—or Behind Us, I forget which—at which winks would be exchanged; sometimes Samuel came to talk sense without humbug. We had our feasts of triumph, as on the arrival of a newly-elected 'Wee Free' member for Bodmin, one Isaac Foot. Once we were favoured by the presence of a good-looking dark young man with sleek brushed-back hair, prominent nose and a slight cast in his eye. He looked the company over appraisingly, listened to the quality of the conversation, offered little talk himself and did not come again. That was Oswald Mosley about to become a refugee from the Conservative Party, looking for a new home. He evidently found more promise in the Labour Party for he made his switch soon after . . . I found that House of Commons lunch a useful source for political gossip.

After a time, moving around as a journalist getting his bearings and NOT as another young man with his tongue hanging out after a glorious place in politics, I got around to meeting some people from the other two parties. The Labour Party seemed a peculiar concern. Echoes of past differences, including those about pacifists in the late war, hung heavily about it. A partnership of the Co-operative Movement, the Trade Union Congress and the Independent Labour Party Socialists and Fabians would naturally produce a healthy friction, but the hostility and suspicion of the 'workers' for the 'intellectuals' surprised me. The weakness of the Labour Party was that its brains thought of it as the party of morality and idealism, but its body did not feel that way at all and had the most material aims. Labour would not vote for Labour.

In the Parliament of 1920, Labour was only the fag-end of a party. It looked a pretty inadequate lot to take on Ll. G.'s clustered hosts. No militants. No leaders. Not that that mattered, since outside they didn't seem to be speaking to one another anyway. Ramsay MacDonald was reputed to have said he hated the Labour Party. Snowden had become sour and tiffy. Even Keir Hardie was losing interest.

The bright boys of the Party 'brains trust' appeared to gyrate around the Webbs, Sidney and Beatrice. Unfortunately for me I did not get far with the Webbs. At the time they disapproved of my fellow political cartoonist Will Dyson as a rebellious syndicalist and they evidently concluded that I, being also a cartoonist from Australia like Will, and a friend of his, must be similarly deplorable. At the other end of the stick, on Will's account also, I was outside the favour of one of the Party's chief pillars of Christian ethics, George Lansbury. George was then the editor of the *Herald*, Labour's newspaper, for which Will drew cartoons, and the two of them were constantly having rows because George objected to Will drawing capitalists as devils. Innocently I had introduced a devil or two into my own cartoons in the *Star*, and that settled me with George, to my regret.

Ll. G.'s clever move in taking some trade union leaders into his War Government (not to have a say in policy, as it turned out, but as hostages for the good behaviour of Labour) had produced some nice jealousy and back-biting behind the trade union scenes. The ground was trembling just then under Arthur Henderson. I had not been about long before people were taking me aside to explain the Henderson situation. Henderson, I was told, had been sacked unfairly from the Government for embarrassing it by attending a conference of the Second International at Stockholm while the war was yet unwon. Excluding the flesh-pot-loving Labour Ministers on the one hand and Ramsay and his pacifists on the other, this left him the one possible leader of the Party.

119

When at last I was presented to Henderson I thought him a perfect marvel of chesty, stiff pomposity. First impressions in that case were wrong.

Many years later, I was taking a cup of tea with 'Uncle Arthur' at Jack Straw's Castle on Hampstead Hill. He was approaching the end of his days, after long weary years as Foreign Secretary of sincere striving after world peace, stultified, frustrated but still chesty and unbent. 'If you had it all to do again, would you? Aren't you disappointed? Does it seem that all your efforts were worth while?' asked Low, ever the journalist. 'It isn't so much what one does as what one *tries* to do,' he replied. That, I thought, was a pretty good thing to say.

The Conservative Party had its 'intellectual' *v.* 'worker' trouble also, but with less obvious differentiation. To an Antipodean eye used to the comparatively exaggerated individualism of overseas M.P.s, the family resemblance among those in this sector of Westminster was somewhat confusing. At first there appeared to me to be almost a standard type, and I sometimes felt rather like the British Tommy in China who couldn't tell whether he had just seen a hundred Chinese or one Chinese a hundred times. They dressed alike, wore the same sort of ties, brushed their hair in the same style, walked and talked alike to an extent suggestive of the uniform product of a system. Which was just what most of them were, of course. This was the core of British public life, the public school–university man who had 'gone in' for politics as a career. The *élite* of the ruling class confident of its mission to rule, its members all understanding one another perfectly, laying down the conditions, setting the standards and in general making politics a game fit for gentlemen and Westminster 'the finest club in Europe.' And incidentally making it difficult for outsiders who did not come in by that door, by providing a smooth background against which these unfortunates might easily appear as misfits, impossible cranks or clever tricksters. Later, as time passed and I got my eye in, the units and groups of this *élite* separated themselves more and I observed that they pervaded all parties. I was told a story about how two brilliant young Oxford Union debaters, John Simon and F. E. Smith, had tossed a coin to decide which would become a Liberal and which a Tory. Probably in many cases the choice of party had been as fortuitous, though I had no doubt that many parliamentary seats came under the heading of family inheritance. In 1920 the Labour Party was somewhat less infiltrated than the others. If some far-seeing prophets felt the advent of Labour government to be inevitable one day, the general careerist view evidently was that the day was not yet so imminent as to risk one's shirt on it.

Ratiocinating these matters, I reflected further that I had been taking too much for granted. There were, it appeared, differences of emphasis as well as of essence about democracy. The aims of democracy overseas and in Britain were ostensibly the same regarding social and political equality and so on. Yet, as it seemed to me, the British article, while theoretically equalitarian, in practice had a great deal of paternalism about it. The English, the most influential element in British politics, while talking proudly of British independence and self-reliance, had elevated obedience —their opposite—to the highest of virtues. The Lords still had great weight in government. The Big Ones governed for the Little Ones. The middle classes identified popular rights with the privileges of the rich and the nobility. These arrangements seemed quite natural and proper to people of all classes who regarded themselves as sturdy democrats and talked of democracy as though it were something achieved. Here and there one met even people who, quite unconscious of being other than firm supporters of popular rights, held that the conduct of public affairs should be taken out of the hands of 'the politicians' and entrusted to 'business men'; or, much better, to the Royal Family, particularly to the Prince of Wales who was much admired at the time as 'Our Smiling Prince.'

It was not unnatural that when in the course of time a Labour Government actually did materialize with promise of change, some people should hail the event as a crisis of democracy and abandon morals and manners in attempting to obstruct the popular will. The upper and middle classes could hear the tumbrils in the streets. At this distance of time, their fright seems gently comic against the later experience of the modifying effects of responsibility, and of how conservative the Left can become in office.

At the end of twelve months, I did a little stocktaking. Seemingly I had done well enough, but there were some kicks as well as half-pence. Lord Northcliffe had let it be printed that in his opinion I was a failure; Hannen Swaffer, even then an ace columnist, had written that it would be better for everybody if I went back to Australia; and the *Sunday Times* had passed the doubtful compliment of devoting to me a leading article entitled POISONING THE WELLS.

I had been mistaken about the *Star*. It was very cleverly written for its readers. Surveying my own public and reflecting upon their receptivity, I estimated roughly that about sixty per cent took my stuff in their stride as funny drawings merely; about thirty per cent saw the main point more or less; and the remaining ten per cent saw the complete whole clearly. Satisfactory, considering that in some respects I had broken new ground technically and in idea content I had probably overstrained average 'awareness' now and then. It was bad that I had not had time to do anything properly. Always a blind dash. And, with a mass-circulation newspaper, always too many toes to tread on.

Once or twice I had noticed Henry Cadbury looking at me with a queer look, but I had been innocently unaware that I had offended until one day he took me out to lunch for a serious talk. I could not at first fathom what he was troubled about but at last it came out. I had drawn a cartoon showing the Supreme Council of the League, after having run out of suitable resorts for its interminable Peace Conferences—the South Pole, the Matterhorn, Niagara Falls, etc.—at last sitting down to a final session on a cloud, complete with wings, harps and haloes. Henry thought that this was in 'bad taste,' but why he could not say, beyond affirming, as a general proposition, that laughter was unseemly when associated with religious matters (i.e. the accoutrements of angels). I was astonished. Holding a different view, I could not take that lying down. I had to deplore the sweeping view that made no distinction between the crackling of thorns under a pot and the sweet music of happiness. Surely it depended on the nature of the laughter? One might separate singing from religion, because some singers made a raucous row. Was laughter itself wicked? As well ask if weeping be wicked. Were not the elements of humour as emotional as the elements of, say, grief, and as capable of selection and emphasis to express thoughts as worthy? Had I myself not just collaborated as a satirical illustrator with Canon Adderley in his volume *Old Seed on New Ground* re-telling certain of the Biblical parables in a modern setting, and had not *The Christian World* approved my 'biting satires on pretentious solemnities'? Was there no laughter in Heaven? For my own part, like Dean Inge, I could not ever conceive of God as a sour-puss. Further, I could not conceive of a Heaven at all without laughter. For without the perception of incongruity, which is the prime inspiration of laughter, how could there be any consciousness of harmony? When I get to Heaven, I told Henry, if there be any Heaven, and I get to it, I expect to continue as a caricaturist . . . Henry did not expect that. Anyway, he had no answer ready.

That my point of view was not shared universally, however,

was illustrated shortly after. Jack Hobbs, the famous cricketer, had touched a high point of his career in equalling Grace's batting record. I celebrated the event in a cartoon entitled RELATIVE IMPORTAÑCE depicting Hobbs as one of a row of statues of mixed celebrities, in which his towering figure overshadowed Adam, Julius Caesar, Charlie Chaplin, Mahomet, Columbus and Lloyd George. It was a piece of mere facetiousness, meaning nothing, but since the public interest in Hobbs was strong the *Star* gave it an importance it did not deserve by printing it twice the usual size.

It brought a large number of letters, eulogizing and applauding, which surprised me, and an indignantly worded protest which surprised me even more from the Ahmadiyya Moslem Mission, which deeply resented Mahomet being represented as competing with Hobbs, even of his being represented at all. The editor expressed his regrets at the unintentional offence and regarded the whole thing as settled. But no. Two weeks later cables from India described a movement in Calcutta 'exhorting Moslems to press for resolutions of protest against the Hobbs cartoon which shows a prophet among lesser celebrities. Meetings will be held in the mosques.'

An additional complication arose. Not only one prophet but two had been profaned because the Moslems reverence Adam also. Bitterness and fury were redoubled. To quote a Calcutta correspondent of the *Morning Post*: 'The cartoon has committed a serious offence, which had it taken place in this country, would almost certainly have led to bloodshed. What was obviously intended as a harmless joke has convulsed many Moslems to speechless rage . . . An Urdu poster has been widely circulated throughout the city, calling upon Moslems to give unmistakable proof of their love of Islam by asking the Government of India to compel the British Government to submit the editor of the newspaper in question to such an ear-twisting that it may be an object-lesson to other newspapers. The posters have resulted in meetings, resolutions and prayers.'

The British Government was unresponsive, for we heard no more. It is not without a twinge of regret that I reflect upon the loss to history of a picturesque scene on Tower Hill, with plenty of troops, policemen and drums, on the occasion of my unfortunate editor having his ears twisted on my behalf. When I was talking with Mahatma Gandhi some years later, he deplored the dearth of cartoonists in his country and suggested that the well-known appreciation of satire possessed by Indians might make it a

123

congenial place for me to spend some time professionally. I refrained from comment.

The whole incident showed how easily a thoughtless cartoonist can get into trouble. I had never thought seriously about Mahomet. How foolish of me. I was ashamed—not of drawing Mahomet in a cartoon, but of drawing him in a silly cartoon.

10

TIME was passing and I was not getting around enough. To do any good in London, I told myself, I had to know it inside out—the people and the places. That was not going to happen by accident. It had to be organized— and without delay.

I had brought to London my tattered copy of *The Parson and the Painter*, a reprint of light-hearted articles on rambles around the London of the eighteen-nineties illustrated by the great black-and-white artist Phil May. I had always meant to draw London like that one day. Here was the moment to combine a labour of love with a course of topographical education.

The idea was fresh then to London daily journalism but my editor was easily persuaded. The *Star* had one of the best humorous descriptive writers of the time in F. W. Thomas, who knew his London like a book. Together we sat down to toast in a cup of coffee the new partnership of Low AND I, whose business was to range London wild and free every Tuesday for a regular feature article. Judging by the accepted Fleet Street tests, circulation and imitation, the idea was a success from the start. Thomas was a bit of luck for me. We got on well. Low AND I had not so much the spirit of humour as of boyish glee. Those Tuesdays became a bright spot in my week.

We started my education tidily by seeing the New Year in on the steps of St. Paul's; thereafter proceeding, week by week, first, to a round of the commoner 'sights,' generally with the special facilities of press snoopers licensed to be caught up in any bizarre incident that might happen, as when we helped the Zoo to domicile a pink elephant and lent our moral support to an attempt to lay a ghost at Hampton Court Palace. The Tower, the Abbey, the Mint, the Zoo, Madame Tussaud's and so on; up the Monument, down the sewers, inside the clock-face of Big Ben and outside the roof of the weather offices, alongside the new 'wireless' mast of 2LO, Savoy Hill, underneath the warehouses of the Port of London. Up and down the old river by punt, steam and sail, not only past the ancient inns and the picturesque soap, glue and cheese factories which then fringed part of its shores, but returning later to enter the more sinister of them, one by one, with much importance to see what went on. We visited dutifully London's shrines and the places haunted by Johnson, Dickens and history. So as not to miss the common touch, we accompanied the populace on its holidays to Southend, Clacton, Brighton, and Margate, and in between whiles we gambolled with it at Hampstead Heath, waved beer mugs with it at the (old) 'Old Bull and Bush,' swam with it in Chiswick Baths, danced with it at Hammersmith Palais, skated with it at Holland Park, watched fights with it at the Ring, bowled with it at Denmark Hill, fished for tiddlers in and sailed model yachts with it on the Serpentine, played tennis at Battersea Park and argued sedition with it at Hyde Park Corner, while noting out of the corner of an eye the tail-end of the days when the rich oppressors really did ride horses in Rotten Row.

Virgil Thomas saw to it that his docile Dante missed no London occasion, from the Lord Mayor's Show to Beating the Bounds of the Liberty and Manor of the Savoy, W.C.2, complete with Beadle in bowler hat assisted by the choir-boys of Royal Chapel. When there was nothing on in our London proper, we took in anything within reach, such as Kissing Day at Hungerford, Shakespeare's birthday at Stratford, Henley Regatta or the Eton Wall Game. We embraced all the institutional entertainments and shows such as the Military Tournament, the Chelsea Arts Ball, the Horse, Cat, Dog, Motor, Business Equipment, Dairy and Poultry Shows (the latter a particularly memorable occasion because of Thomas's discovery of a way of conversing with cockerels by making peep-peep noises through the stem of his pipe); we encouraged Suzanne Lenglen at Wimbledon and Jack Hobbs did not lack our support at Lord's; we supervised the Boat Race, Ascot and the Derby, the latter from both the Royal Enclosure and the Gypsy encampments, and we accompanied for a respectable distance the Brighton Walk. (Dog racing had not then been invented.)

Culture was not neglected. Among those enjoying two shillings-worth at the Proms squatting on the hot-water pipes at the old Queen's Hall listening to Siegfried having a devil of a time per favour of S'r'enry Wood in his prime, were Thomas and Low.

We attended the Albert Hall and the Royal Academy, by both front and back doors, and took stock with patient cheerfulness of all the Museums and Art Galleries, one after another, mummies, manuscripts, meubles and mumbo-jumbo, including the underground workings of the British Museum Reading Room and what happens when you ask for a book. We sat for a lecture at London University; and, under the careful supervision of experts, planted bulbs in Hyde Park.

The face of London hotel and restaurant life has changed since 1921, but eating was as important then as it is now. We gave it our attention in all its various practices. Perched on high stools we ate counter-lunch with City men at Throgmorton Street, we dined with livery at Mansion House, shared sandwiches with the birds on the Embankment, gulped oysters at Scott's, ate ye famous Puddynge at the Cheshire Cheese, and roast beef at Simpson's, and 'did' ourselves expensively at the fashionable hotels and restaurants and cheaply at coffee stalls, finishing with dominoes at the Café Royal. Going more deeply into the subject we visited the kitchens of the Savoy and the Ritz to view the culinary processes. With cumulated interest we sought the sources of supply and distribution and began a comprehensive tour of the principal markets. The butchers at Smithfield obligingly laid the mysteries of their bloody trade bare for us, and Covent Garden showed its green fingers in the grisly light of dawn.

By this time we were occasionally being recognized, which was perhaps not surprising, since our ramblings were being 'plugged' week by week in the *Star* with its half-million circulation, and the portraits of ourselves I put into my drawings had of their own accord evolved into something vaguely recognizable. Public acclaim is all very well in its right place, but in its wrong place it can be an embarrassment. What happened at Billingsgate, for instance. As Thomas told it in the paper:

. . . That fish-porter had a keen and penetrating eye, and halfway through my catechism he stopped and glanced across at the distant sketchbook. For a few seconds he gazed at the artist who was looking round for a bolt-hole. Then he recognized the eyebrows, and 'Hi!' he said, 'Ain't that Low?'

I nodded and touched wood. One never knows in Billingsgate.

'And I suppose you're I,' said the fish-porter. Then he turned and called to a colleague.

'Here, Sandy! Here's Low and I come to draw our pictures! Bill! George! Jim! Here's Low and I. Run and find old Smiler and get his face in the paper . . .'

127

I was kept drawing portraits for an hour.

From Billingsgate to Covent Garden; thence by easy stages, naturally enough, to Petticoat Lane, the New Cut, the Caledonian Market, Sotheby's and Christie's, and off to buy a pony at Barnet Fair.

Let it not be thought that our pilgrimages were exclusively vulgar. Our records include a fashionable wedding, the divorce court, a garden party and the flower show; and there was an occasion when we were mixed up with a Royal Drawing Room. Thomas was an exceedingly resourceful chap.

Show business, of course. We covered the night spots, the cabarets, the famous theatres, gallery, stalls and dressing-rooms, first and last nights. We 'helped' George Robey to rehearse a Christmas pantomime; got ourselves involved with a ballet behind the scenes at the Coliseum; penetrated, under the wing of Lilian Baylis herself, every nook of the (old) Old Vic; and chewed meat pies with Tod Slaughter in Sweeney Todd's cellar at the 'Elephant and Castle.'

Even the pictures. They were silent in those days, although the 'silence' was not so noticeable at the Stoll, the biggest cinema of the time, where they had the most complete sound-effects installation in the business. Let Thomas report on our contact with a phenomenon familiar in the early 'twenties but now long dead and never to return:

> We went up a long ladder into the flies. There, in a little booby-hutch, was a weird contraption something like a type-writer, fitted with innumerable labelled switches. Behind this one sat pushing buttons and turning on heavy seas, simooms and siroccos as the screen demanded. With nimble fingers one loosed earthquake and eclipse, one rode the whirlwind and directed the storm. Down in the orchestra we found a long row of weird gadgets that looked like a lot of old dustbins and the entrails of a Ford; syrens for out-going steamers, bells for fire-engines, arrangements for imitating the gallop of horses, the smashing of crockery, the song of the nightingale, the crackling of fires, the roar of cannons, thunder, express trains, tornadoes, disappointed lovers, rhinoceri, chipmunks, howitzers, volcanoes. Low fell in love with it at once. If he'd been left alone with this thing he'd have emptied the place and flooded Kingsway six feet deep.

That was a most enjoyable afternoon.

I learned about everyman's London from Thomas. I could not

have wished for a better guide. I owe him many experiences which, though singly some might appear unrelated and without practical value except as a day's work, together tot up to intimate familiarity with the popular social scene of the nineteen-twenties. Without his management I might never have known what it was like to get the holiday traffic away from Waterloo Station or the Christmas mail through at the General Post Office. Alone, would it ever have occurred to me to go looking for spring on Primrose Hill, or for fan-tan in Limehouse? Or to spend hours finding out how five million Easter buns were made?

Today I cannot walk far in any part of London without memories of 'Low and I.' If I cross Piccadilly I remember the night we interviewed pickpockets. If I stroll around the lake in St. James's Park I recall the day long ago when we helped the authorities to drain it. When passing the City of London Maternity Hospital I reflect that not even it had secrets from 'Low and I.'

After five years or so of that intensive education I could say I knew my London.

So much for the places. Now for the personalities. With Thomas I was forming a wide acquaintance with the key 'characters' of everyday London. There were few holes-in-the-wall where I did not know some Alf or Bill to give us the freedom of the town. But I was taking an unconscionable long time to become acquainted with people on the upper shelves. If the mountain won't come to Mahomet, Mahomet might at least suggest an appointment to call on the mountain. I remembered that in my youth when I was travelling around Australia with a sketchbook, I had never had any difficulty in getting to know everyone of consequence in a given town within a couple of months. Why not in London? The technique would not be identical, but applied. All I needed was a publishing idea as a professional justification for the effort: a practical end to which I could use the material collected.

As a boy I had been lost in admiration of the masterly series of 'portraits chargés' by Daumier—the best stuff ever in that line. I would have a go at something like that, pure essence of personality carefully distilled from close observation. The omens were inauspicious for such work in Britain, for the English are not quick to distinguish art from craftsmanship in their caricature, and they look at caricatural studies of personality as they look at the symbolic 'likenesses' of politicians in newspaper cartoons, seeing only that the cartoons illustrate ideas and the caricatural studies do not, and therefore presumably must be of less importance. Nevertheless I would try a set of portraits. None of that clever superficial stuff 'in a few brilliant lines.' None of that easy exaggeration of physical peculiarities merely. I would aim at carrying each subject a stage or two further towards fuller and more rounded representation. This time I would go to infinite trouble. No time limit. Deep observation. Minute perception. Analysis and synthesis of character. Then, if no one would publish my finished drawings, I would do so myself.

Listing fifty names of the most distinguished men of the time, writers, artists, scientists, philosophers (it is surprising how easy it was to think of fifty in those days), I wrote to each of them expressing my wish to draw him in the Daumier manner. I sent out the letters in batches of three as seemed opportune.

How should a votary approach the gods of his being, until now only dimly discerned through the enchantment of distance, at last miraculously accessible to mere mortal? With circumspection, of course. Respect, reverence? Treading softly, speaking only when spoken to? Modestly bearing a lily to lay at their colossal feet?

Certainly not lining them up, waving them one by one to a chair with 'You're next!' and polishing 'em off like an iconographic Sweeney Todd. But needs must when zest rules the operation. My plan was effective, but it had its drawbacks. One was that it went a long way towards impairing the enjoyment I had as a reader in the literature of my time. It is a mistake to be acquainted with one's author. He has a way of popping up between the reader and the book.

Another disadvantage was that it sometimes subjected me to mortification. I was not yet sufficiently used to the ways of the English to carry the job through smoothly. Coming from a lifetime spent in an equalitarian society, my approach was naturally too informal, my speech too direct. I was, in short, inclined to be friendly to everybody right away, without decent preamble of the mutual circlings and sniffings customary among the English of that time. The consequences were not always happy with the more reserved of my subjects. These first encounters of 1921–25 therefore did not immediately transport me into the cosy intimacy of exclusive circles. Some, indeed, inspired mutual repulsion, and I never met the sitters again. Some meant nothing more than civil assent to civil request, ending, at best, in civil acquaintance. A few of my sitters became friends. In general, over thirty-five years it was inevitable that I got to know most of them much better.

Professionally speaking everything went well. I had only two refusals: John Galsworthy, who, I discovered later, had a constitutional aversion to caricature, which he thought malicious; and Rudyard Kipling, who had been grievously offended by a caricature of himself by Max Beerbohm twenty years before. Otherwise I found my 'raw material' sufficiently co-operative.

As I had planned, my method for these drawings was painstaking. I took an extraordinary amount of trouble to sense as much as I could of my man. In the case of those who had some public life in London, I would stalk them for weeks, even months, at meetings, public functions, private parties, in their clubs, anywhere they might be, just looking. Sometimes I waited for them in the street or ate at the next table to them at restaurants. My miniature sketchbook was always up my sleeve. Usually by the time I was ready for a sitting I had the essence of what I needed and only required a check-up. Doing the job in this thorough way took a long time, but piecing together my notes was great enjoyment. Allowing for my other activities, it was five years before I had my series ready to show. It was published in 1926.

The old stagers were richest in visual character, possibly because with them it had had time to develop. A. E. W. Mason with his monocle and his supercilious nose and chin, and Anthony Hope Hawkins with his rich dramatic voice just like a 'cello, were both complete characters who might have walked out of *The Four Feathers* and *The Prisoner of Zenda* respectively. Unfortunately my meeting with Hawkins was ruined by tactlessness.

'You know who he is?' said the mutual friend to me as he introduced us. (What a thing to say!)

'Certainly! What's worrying me is whether he knows who *I* am,' says I. (Damn! Can you beat that! These cocky sayings will bust out of me when I'm feeling good.)

I was interested to find how far the persons of authors could have been deduced from their works. Walter de la Mare, certainly. Just like it. Completely. As I had anticipated, A. A. Milne was a gentle, likeable man set in a neat and pleasant domestic interior, just what the father of Christopher Robin should be. Sir James Barrie, on the other hand, was not at all fey, and I got the impression that his public whimsicalities were all carefully thought up. Conan Doyle could have been Dr. Watson, of course, but never Sherlock Holmes. Hugh Walpole had the physical frame for

Rogue Herries, but there was a shy sensitive chap inside it. Thomas Burke looked like a solicitor who had never seen Limehouse except from the top of a bus. I was astonished one day when my bell rang, the door opened and in walked Joseph Conrad in the flesh, a small man like Captain Kettle, heavy-shouldered with delicate extremities, wearing purple socks. I had expected a sixfooter—why I don't know.

Somerset Maugham wore a black velvet jacket, no waistcoat. I noted on my sketch that he had glittering eyes in tanned skin, an Arnold Bennett stammer and a curl of the nostril suggesting the presence of an unpleasant odour. He was a patient sitter and he put me at my ease by saying that he thought artists should not be expected to converse cleverly, since they express themselves in their own ways. So saying, he himself talked all the time, mainly about how sick he was of writing plays because of the limitations of the theatre as a medium. An interesting morning.

I found Edgar Wallace just like a character in one of his own thrillers, apparently churning out three novels at once, writing, speaking into a dictaphone and dictating to a young woman secretary, all in lumps, so to speak, first to one, then to another, then to another. 'Good Lord! Edgar,' I said (he had one of those personalities that encouraged Christian names at sight), 'don't you ever get them mixed? What if Jasper steals the wrong papers and Handsome Harry marries the villainess and lives happy ever after by mistake?' He took that seriously. 'I've got an elaborate system of checking,' he said. He was wearing a lurid dressing-gown. 'Do you always go about like that?' I asked. 'No,' he said, 'I thought you'd like me this way.' A man and a brother. The bookstalls were packed with Edgar Wallace novels at the time, and the spectacle of Edgar resplendent in evening attire at the Savoy was Success incarnate, so I could not resist asking him my pet question. 'What *is* success?' 'Oh, you strike a balance,' he said.

As I had expected, the humorists were personally not funny, but looked rather as though they were studying for the undertaking business. W. W. Jacobs was a sad worried-looking man not at all like a Wapping Old Stairs bargee. Pett Ridge was gloomy. Even P. G. Wodehouse, a cheerful big chap easy to get on with, was not funny in the sense of jokey, apart from his peculiar wish that I should draw him after he had just had drops for his eye treatment so that he would have impressively large and luminous pupils like Edgar Allan Poe.

When jesting is your business, you get it out of your system in working hours. It's the mouthpieces, the parrots who *repeat* the jokes, who are funny, hardly ever the owls who create them. The latter in their leisure are usually serious, given to solemn ratiocination. This significant truth was underlined for me once and for all by the case of Professor Stephen Leacock, the celebrated Canadian humorist. A hundred or so M.P.s and a handful of privileged strangers like myself assembled in wistful anticipation to welcome the Professor, universally acclaimed in the 1920's as a master humorist of his time, to luncheon at the House of Commons. The Professor arrived, there was handshaking, the company hurried through luncheon, unbuttoned its waistcoat and sat back to roar. The Professor, who was introduced in suitably witty terms, rose and delivered a one-hour slab of verbal suet on the Constitution relieved by only one laugh from end to end, and that was when the clock over the fireplace went wrong and emitted strange noises. 'Was that for me?' asked the Professor. (Loud laughter.)

I had not foreseen G. K. Chesterton and Hilaire Belloc accurately. I had always relished my Chester–Belloc, although some of their political ideas gave me a pain in the neck, so I looked forward to a closer view.

I had already peeked at them from afar. The occasion had been a public meeting at Chelsea Town Hall to expose the sale of honours and the corruption of the House of Lords. There was a full house, naturally, since there was in these subjects much matter for exposure. It did not see the light on that occasion. Nobody came down to cases and all the audience got was vague anti-semitism, which I found very irritating. First impressions of Chester–Belloc had been decidedly mixed. They had been satisfactory in picturesque character, disappointing in intellectual output.

When I met Chesterton privately a little later, he proved his repute as a genial soul and the best of company. Yet, as I listened to his effervescent conversation, I felt an echo of my first impression in a faint suspicion that there might be a recipe for this sort of brilliance; and that if language were not such an imperfect medium for expressing ideas, it would be much more difficult to evolve paradoxes. While we talked I was drawing him surreptitiously under my handkerchief. He saw me and appeared acutely unhappy. 'Don't do that, *please*,' he said. I tore up the sketch and put the book away. Amiability was resumed, but I was ashamed, partly for myself, that I had allowed zeal to outrun manners, and partly for him, that a man of his parts, a satirist

133

with pretensions to being a caricaturist himself, should be so tender.

Chesterton's characteristics were so well defined that I needed no further notes anyway. Both he and Belloc were exceedingly good to draw: Chesterton's ponderous body, draped rather than dressed in roomy grey lounge suit with pockets made shapeless by carrying things, supported by shy, nervous legs; starched choker collar surmounted by the face of Millais' *Bubbles* grown to the age of forty-five and disillusioned, but still keeping his curls and complexion. He had a nervous habit of twiddling his fingers when speaking in public. 'If someone stole Gilbert's left forefinger, he'd be speechless,' said a friend of his.

Belloc was made of different stuff. His normal expression was severe, testy, and he was inclined to change colour to a bluish-red under strong emotion. Whereas Chesterton, regarded geometrically, was circles and ellipses, Belloc was squares and right angles. Nuggety body, short arms and legs, dressed so roomily that when in full movement he created his own breeze, and flapped like a ship under sail.

I had three goes at my Belloc and it turned out to be the best portrait of that first series. He thought so too, and inscribed a copy 'The only true image of the writer in his age.' The fact disproves the fallacious notion that sympathy between artist and subject is of any account whatever in making a portrait, for although I greatly admired the Belloc who wrote *The Road to Rome, Mr. Clutterbuck's Election* and some others, during a good part of those days my professional politeness was sorely strained by his impregnable assumption that I must approve also his book *The Servile State*. In the first place I was unconvinced of the superiority of the Distributive State over the Capitalist or the Collective States as the guarantor of intellectual liberty—the fundamental liberty so far as I was concerned. I certainly did not believe that the transference of coal and the railways to public ownership must inevitably end in compulsory labour. Nor that the Employers' Liability Act and/or Lloyd George's Insurance Act established the Servile State. Belloc, I felt, took things too much to logical conclusions, and everybody knew that things never went to logical conclusions in this world. His whys and his whereases were impressive, but his wherefores were utterly unconvincing. (Forty years later the imponderables and the unpredictables seem to have gone against his prognostications.)

But how could I have argued with Hilaire Belloc? He was too obliging and I was too busy. As I tried to show in my drawing, I found him a bustling aggressive man with endearing qualities and hints of human weakness. When I dined in his company at the house of a publisher, someone after dinner placed a box of chocolates on the sofa beside him. He waxed characteristically didactic and contemptuous of certain of his literary contemporaries, and as he polished them off one after another, chocolate after chocolate disappeared until he almost emptied the box. At length he placed his hand on his stomach, crinkled his brow and

G. K. Chesterton

said: 'I am not well; I must go.' 'Dear me,' said our host, as he departed. 'Next time we will get a two-pound box and get him going on the House of Lords.'

Temperamentally Belloc was frequently inclined to be cross about something. From 1920 the something was H. G. Wells. Having made no secret of my own fervent admiration for Wells I never achieved terms of even superficial social friendliness with Chester–Belloc. When some years later I met them both again under the roof of a friend, I lay under a further disadvantage. Some cartoons of mine about Dr. Marie Stopes, birth control and Ireland had just been published and I was in flaring trouble with the Catholics. There was a distinct chill in the air.

I was more at ease with the artists, and I had an enjoyable yarn about everything under the sun with Orpen. Under the sun was right. His studio had a glass roof and there stood 'Bloody Bill' stripped to pants and undershirt, painting away in the glare. 'Light, old chap, light!' He had just finished a big portrait-assembling job for his historic group of the Versailles Conference, and he was very willing to pull out his sketchbooks and to show me some vitriolic skits of that same massive work done in between times to relieve his feelings, regaling me the while with intimate anecdotes.

I found Lavery sitting in a dark studio. I had always thought his portraits lacked light. The harmony of my visit was slightly marred by a remark which in certain moods I could have taken as insulting. 'It's a remarkable thing,' says he pleasantly, 'but I can't make a caricature.' He was, as I say, pleasant, but I was stung. 'What's remarkable about that?' I replied. 'What would you say if I said: "It's a remarkable thing, but I can't paint a portrait like that one on your easel?"' . . . Fortunately at this moment in walked the lovely Lady Lavery, looking just like an Irish postage stamp. 'Let us both make caricatures of my wife,' said Sir John brightly. I was so unequal to the test that his was better than mine. But then he had probably had more practice.

The day I called at Augustus John's studio the presence of a lively party put a crimp in my concentration, and when I sized up after I left I found I had done precious little drawing. All I could remember of John was one glaring eye and a wild smile.

The artists were easy, but the actors were hard because of their occupational tendency to impersonating themselves all the time. Their characters were already too overdrawn, so to speak. The actor turned impresario, C. B. Cochran, was an exception. Behind the over-genial theatrical front there was an elusive simplicity very interesting to go after. From some of my subjects I got nothing but the bare appearance. Paderewski, the pianist-statesman of Poland, for instance, was preoccupied and received me as though I were a photographer. My drawing of him was superficial and worthless. Marconi was nervous and would not talk. There were too many women pressing cups of tea on me to get any real talk about the Life to Come with Sir Oliver Lodge.

Sometimes my preliminary scoutings were enough and I had no need of a sitting. In other cases it seemed inadvisable to incur any obligation from a subject when my advance notes warned me that the portrait would certainly put a strain on his vanity. Had I, for instance, invited Lord Chief Justice Hewart to pose for the drawing of him I subsequently published, he would have been justified in resentment. Happy chance fixed things much better than I could have done, by bringing us together face to face without pre-arrangement in an otherwise empty Underground railway carriage travelling to Golders Green at one o'clock in the morning. I was thunderstruck when the Lord Chief Justice of England, short, portly, tailed and top-hatted, evidently fresh from a party, got in at Leicester Square to pose for me. He did not know it, of course, but he must have wondered what the fellow over the way was up to so industriously behind his newspaper.

Hewart was angered over the drawing, but less at me than at a bookseller in the vicinity of the Law Courts who, to satisfy some fancy of his own, starred the drawing outside his shop for months. Hewart forgave me when he found we were fellow-members of the Savage Club, which seemed to me a queer reason.

One of the first subjects I called on was Bernard Shaw. I remembered that he had sent me a kindly postcard about my Lloyd George book and I felt good.

Bernard Shaw in 1924

The iron fence across the top of his stairs at the Adelphi looked pretty formidable. I was an admirer of the great man and I had no doubt there were others, but surely this could not be necessary.

A solid-looking domestic showed me in. Shaw was lying on a settee, wearing fancy slippers, very pleased with himself, talking to Barry Jackson and another man about details of the production of his new play *Saint Joan*, but I did not pay much attention because I was more interested in our host. Peculiar high skull, jutting beard, small eyes, pinkish bulbous nose, small mouth with false-looking teeth. I walked about the room, which seemed to be well furnished with portraits of Bernard Shaw. On the table was a bust of Shaw by Rodin, not too good. All these works represented a cocky Shaw, the head standing erect on a straight spine. When the others left I hadn't been talking to him long before I began to suspect that he was really a shy man, that the cockiness was a defensive façade.

'Why does everyone represent you like that?' I asked, pointing to a Shaw on the wall that looked as though it might crow at any moment.

'That is my public character,' he answered.

'Even to Rodin?'

'Rodin saw me only for a couple of hours. He knew nothing about me.'

My opinion of Rodin fell a couple of points. That brought up a European sculptor who had made a majestic eight feet high marble Shaw some time before, but when it was finished nobody had known what to do with it. My suggestion that it might stand outside a tobacconist's shop holding a box of marble cigars was not very well received. I began to feel a bit cocky myself, which was nearly always unfortunate. 'Well, I'm going to try to get the modest Shaw,' I said.

That, as it happened, was the wrong thing to say, for it set a social juxtaposition for all subsequent encounters. From then on he was a bit wary of me as a potential mocker, and adjusted his manner accordingly. For the next year or two fate seemed to have arranged that I kept finding myself facing or sitting near Shaw at parties, luncheons and dinners, watching him giving trouble with his specially prepared vegetarian and egg dishes. I could never work it out that eggs were not life. One day I asked him about it and he abruptly changed the subject. It dawned on me then that he was sensitive to ridicule. I was struck all of a heap. Who could have imagined it? Shaw! That explained why I could never venture a light remark in his presence without getting something crusty back. Once, I recalled, when we were both in the company of some Soviet diplomatists, merry fellows, they passed around cigars. Feeling the conversation had been solemn long enough, I made a light pleasantry about the Russian revolution not being able to call itself a success until it produced a good cigar. Shaw shut me up rudely with: 'Until they stopped producing cigars at all, you mean.' O-ho, I says to myself, no one else is going to make a funny crack while you're about, hey? Experimentally I changed my tactics and adopted the character of a stooge, feeding him with opportunities to exhibit his own brilliance. All went much better. When I learned that lesson I had the vast enjoyment of listening to some priceless Shaw. That man was the second best talker I have ever heard, the first being Wells. But Shaw's brogue was easier to listen to than H.G.'s squeak.

It took me quite a while to learn Shaw. Altogether, reading

138

him over and considering him, noting his person for eighteen months, on and off, I made about fourteen drawings before I finished off the final one. Even then it turned out slightly cocky.

After two years I could be said to have made some progress towards settling into London professionally. Things were becoming more tolerable in my private social life also. We had found friends, we began to be invited out not only to political receptions but to parties and week-ends. Our area of amicable relations grew as circles enlarge when one drops a stone into a pool.

London, the Big City of teeming millions, was probably more impersonal, inhospitable and insensitive to the feelings of the overseas stranger in those days than it is today, thirty years later. But in its infinite variety was the assurance of at least an occasional responsive eye.

I, like most people, make friends mainly upon the response I find in people's eyes. A peculiar thing, the eye. In itself as expressionless an object as one could find—a white marble with a coloured spot surrounding a smaller black spot enlarging or diminishing. Yet see two of these simple objects in holes in a face, surmount them by contorting eyebrows and surround them with skin crinkling in accordance with obscure muscular tensions, and you have the window of the soul, the key to attraction and repulsion, love and hate. Eyes have a positive effect on me. Under some eyes I am tongue-tied, inarticulate, stupid. Other eyes unlock my tongue.

It was a happy event for me when I looked Robert Lynd and his wife Sylvia in the eyes, for jointly they had not only the Svengali power to evoke conversation so that everyone felt as clever a talker as anybody else; but, what naturally followed, the ability to provide a run of good company to appreciate it. Their quaint old house in Keats Grove, Hampstead, was in those early 'twenties when I needed it a friendly house at which I could always bank on pleasant meetings.

The long drooping Robert was a picturesque figure, corkscrew curl adrift over the brow of his thin face, chain-smoking, mumbling soothing Irish sounds into the depths of his shirt-front. Robert came from Belfast, Sylvia from Dublin, and they had no particular interest in politics except for Robert's passionate support of Sinn Fein.

Nevertheless Robert took pleasure in argument of the fanciful ranging kind about almost anything, especially current topics relating to civilization and the humanities. He was always on the

139

side of tolerance and his view always prevailed, which was rather remarkable since in discussion his voice was apt to fall steeply in confidential diminuendo until it became not merely unintelligible but nigh inaudible. I observed him closely for a space to find out how he convinced his opponents, and I came to the conclusion that he did it by over-agreement—by 'helping' the opposing party to inflate his own case and then in the softest of tones adding a 'supporting' sub-idea, still presumably agreed, which quietly exploded it. The process was perfectly painless and left everybody pleased and amiable, especially, of course, Robert, for he was always unwilling to give the offence even of flatly exposing another's error. Indeed, sometimes this tender consideration was just plain funny. Listen, as I did, to this:

Robert: 'I'm reading *Zadig*. I like to return to Voltaire.'
Friend: '*Zadig*'s not by Voltaire.'
Robert: 'Ah, that's just where you and I differ.'

Sylvia was a sweet fragile woman, delicately witty, a sympathetic hostess, except perhaps for the minor faults, if they were faults, that she knew too many poets and had too many ideas for playing games. If it hadn't been for the infernal games Sylvia loved to organize on this expertness of hers, their parties would have been perfect. Madeline didn't mind, for she enjoyed charades and 'panel' games; but guessing the names of poets I had never heard of from lines I could make neither head nor tail of was not my idea of joy, so whenever I saw Sylvia getting that games look in her eye, I used to make for the garden.

There were leprechauns at the bottom of the Lynds' garden. Irish geniuses ran in and out of the shadows in the dusk. I was not surprised one night to cannon into James Stephens sitting behind a bush, looking as though he had just hidden his crock of gold; on another, to find that I shared the moonlight with a strange, silent figure that turned out to be James Joyce. He had a sheet of paper pinned on his back by Sylvia, with a simply dreadful chunk of poetry to be guessed. An embarrassing situation, full of social risk. We stood together for ten minutes but we had nothing to say to one another. He had no interest in my work, and I had done my best with his *Ulysses* but it had got away from me.

I had the good fortune to meet one man with whom my humour clicked. Philip Guedalla and I differed considerably. His wit was immaculate, polished like himself; mine was natural and rough-edged. But we both saw each other's points and, moreover,

140

laughed at each other in the right place. Without doubt Philip was in his day the best after-dinner speaker in London. He was, of course, a past-master in the parodied quotation, the incongruous association, the esoteric pun and the other conventions understood by the educated Anglo-Saxon to be the forms of wit; but in addition to, and quite apart from all that stuff, he could be very funny. As someone else said, he made all other after-dinner speakers sound as though they had not yet had

Robert Lynd

dinner. 'Brilliant' is the one word which the British recognize as expressive of merit in the arts of satire, and 'brilliant' was the word he learned to abominate, because in the mouths of hostile critics it became a rebuke when he turned to his serious business in life, politics and the writing of history.

As befits one of the keenest wits of his generation, Philip was appreciative of wit in others. The stairway hall of his home was hung thick with the caricatures of Max Beerbohm, including many of Max's most indecorous items of Queen Victoria and Edward VII. We planned to do a book together—reconstructions of historical personages, ancient and mediæval, deduced from their remains—I employing my built-up portraiture method, he correlating a textual synthesis. It was one of Robert Lynd's ideas, and great were the three-cornered arguments as to whether Philip of Macedon was a fattish type, what Cesare Borgia looked like when the painters were not flattering him, what kind of a nose Akhnaton had and how far it was possible to guess the character and even the appearance of Cheops from the fact that he built the first pyramid. I do not suppose such a book would have sold and it would have been a vast labour of research and thought but it would have been a lovely job. One of my lasting regrets is that it came to nothing.

Another fairly constant visitor at the Lynds' in the nineteen-twenties was Humbert Wolfe, another chap who kept me rippling with laughter. It was Humbert's complaint that Robert used humorously to introduce him as 'Humbert Wolfe, the civil servant—does a bit o' poetry on the side,' instead of 'Humbert Wolfe, the poet—does a bit o' civil service on the side.' Humbert, feeling that he and his last book of poems had been insufficiently appreciated, put an anonymous advertisement in *The Times* offering five guineas for a copy of it. Persons who replied were told that they were too late and no copies actually changed hands at that price. But as the news of this advertised evidence of increased value spread, Humbert had the innocent pleasure of seeing himself regarded with greater and greater respect.

Down the years it is astonishing to note what a large number of our friends we Lows first met at the Lynds': The Jack Priestleys, the John Drinkwaters, the Philip Guedallas, Rose Macaulay, the Humbert Wolfes, the Victor Gollanczes, the Alan Thomases, the Ivor Browns, the Norman Collinses and all, and all. . . . Dear Robert and Sylvia. I never met anyone who knew them who did not hold them in affection.

Meantime, while I was discovering London and the Londoners, politics were moving and the scene changing. A treaty had been signed with the Irish, Bonar Law had retired ill, the Tories had had enough of Ll. G. and were busy intriguing him out of the premiership. But they were stuck for an alternative, because Austen Chamberlain and other prominent Tory leaders would not desert Ll. G. Suddenly Bonar Law returns revived. His absence had freed him of all ties to the Coalition. Presto! The Carlton Club meeting, Stanley Baldwin's speech, break-up of the Coalition Government. My double-headed Ass splits across the middle, each end going its separate way. Bonar Law comes into power with his 'Government of cabin-boys' and has it stamped with popular approval at a rather confused general election which follows.

In those days the candidate's election expenses were not as drastically curtailed as they are today, and a good deal of my 'paper'—cartoons in poster, pamphlet and handbill form—went out to the constituencies.

It was a sad election for the 'Wee Free' Liberals. When the numbers were counted they had fallen behind the Labourites and were now the smallest party in the House. An undignified wrangle went on about which party's leaders were entitled to sit on the Opposition front bench as the alternative Government. I was on my way to the Commons Press gallery to take a look at the new arrivals when I was buttonholed by Donald Maclean who told me Asquith wanted to see me. Momentarily I savoured a fantasy. How many bygone aspirants to high office had felt their hearts leap at the promise of those very words, I thought. But no, no— that was past and times had changed.

Maclean and I found the grand old man sitting, a monument of dignity, attended by his faithful Vivian Philipps. All he wanted was to muster and consolidate his party flock. He paid me compliments. 'You are the best propagandist in the country,'·said the old man. The three congratulated me in such terms that an outsider might have concluded that I personally had returned them to power. I was touched because I respected the old man and his kindness, and embarrassed because I saw they were all judging me by the label on my packet (*Daily News*, The Liberal Newspaper) and had not looked at my work closely enough to see that I was not their party cartoonist.

The election made unhappy changes in Coalition–Liberal circles also. Lloyd George and his friends, including some prominent Tory leaders who had disagreed with Baldwin, found themselves out in the cold with plenty of time to think. Life for them became less exclusive.

My wife and I were charmed to be invited by Ll. G. and his daughter Megan to dinner at the House. The other guests were Winston Churchill, Gwilym Lloyd George and his wife, and Oswald Mosley and Lady Cynthia, who sat transparently beautiful, quiet, almost mute. An interesting company.

Mosley, who was sitting next to my wife, said to her: 'Who's that chap with the eyebrows?'

'That's Low the cartoonist,' said my wife.

'This is going to be good,' said Mosley. But it wasn't, in his sense. It was as sweet as butterscotch. At about this time Ll. G. wanted to be editor of *The Times* and he was curious about conditions and personalities in journalism. He pumped me a bit about the Cadbury Press, but otherwise we talked about Australia, cauliflower apples, the weather and cinema stars—about everything, in fact, except political cartoons and double-headed Asses. On this, the first time I had seen Ll. G. close up, I liked him very much and we had a most enjoyable evening with no casualties.

II

So this was the Welsh Wizard. The best-hated statesman of his time, as well as the best loved. The former I had good reason to know; every time I made a pointed cartoon against him, it brought batches of approving letters from all the haters—canalized the hate, so to speak. So much so that at times I had a feeling of performing some peculiar form of service in connection with the Department of Public Health. I did not, of course, hate Ll. G. myself. As a cartoonist I had recently done a fair amount of denigration of our host's policies and attitudes, and as usual the stoopids had explained that to one another as evidence of hate. I can without compunction, regardless of affections and loyalties, symbolize a mistaken idea in the person of the individual that promotes it and hold both up to contempt. But I can't be bothered hating and I am sure personal hatred is not the right inspiration for critical satire. In my experience the best pieces of scorn are conceived in detachment.

So far as I was concerned, having made my little contribution to the bringing down of the Coalition Government, I was by no means willing to assist in putting an end to the usefulness of a political genius. As for Ll. G., he had a little collection of originals of what he thought were my best efforts, including his favourite, YOU'RE NEXT! which showed the out-of-work Versailles veterans Clemenceau, Wilson, Orlando and Venizelos as a deputation of unemployed under his Downing Street window. I had promised him at the time that if ever there were a sequel in which his likeness was added to the others he should have that, too, and I was working on it. In return he had sent me, perhaps for inspiration, an outsize photograph of himself 3 feet high which he autographed across the hat, just for a change.

Looking at Ll. G. pink and hilarious, head thrown back,

A note of Lloyd George

generous mouth open to its fullest extent, shouting with laughter at one of his own jokes (at my expense, by the way—not a very good one either), I thought I could see how it was that his haters hated him. He must have been poison to the old-school-tie brigade, coming to the House an 'outsider,' bright, energetic, irrepressible, ruthless, mastering with ease the complicated House of Commons procedure, applying all the Celtic tricks in the bag, with a talent for intrigue that only occasionally got away from him. Dash it, they would say, the feller was no gentleman. 'Clever, y' know' (with a leer, meaning a dashed sight too clever). 'Intelligent—but not *intellectual*' (meaning not like us fellows with the fat faces). Over and over again the corpse of the Marconi scandal was exhumed for my enlightenment. Not once but a dozen times I was told the story about how the Prime Minister of Britain couldn't find Esthonia on the map at the Versailles Conference. And of course I heard about how in 1918, when the war situation was pretty desperate, he had toyed with the idea of a reconciliation between the junkers of Germany and those of Britain by cutting up Russia and expanding both empires at the expense of the Russians, which was as damnable an idea as I had ever heard of. But I always discounted, then and now, the tales of Ll. G.'s black wickedness, even from his ex-colleagues of Asquith's Cabinet when they led me aside to tell me between clenched teeth of his turpitude. In most cases, looking at the speaker, I concluded that what he meant was that Ll. G. had been one too many for him and had not played the political game according to what he, the speaker, thought were the rules.

I could readily understand the resentment of the younger generation of Liberal politicians against the one who had crabbed their Party chances; but that could not account for the older generation chewing their lips whenever the name of Lloyd George came up. It surprised me, for instance, years later, that in the presence of an almost invisible stranger like myself, the bare mention of his old colleague could send Reginald McKenna into an acid character sketch illustrated with a lifelike imitation of Ll. G. teetering at the Prime Minister's door in August 1914, at the last moment undecided about whether he would come into the war or not.

Ll. G. had changed and expanded his character down the three years of his premiership and was now dressing himself as his conception of a Universal Prime Minister. He had found himself a most original hat, had cultivated an Asquithian hair-do, and wore a neat grey tails suit and a pair of pince-nez hanging around his neck by a black silk ribbon. This was emphatically not the Radical Ll. G. I had pictured bringing in the famous Budget of 1909, but the whole effect was extremely endearing in its way. I always had the greatest difficulty in making Ll. G. sinister in a cartoon. Every time I drew him, however critical the comment, I had to be careful or he would spring off the drawing-board a lovable cherubic little chap. I found the only effective way of putting him definitely in the wrong in a cartoon was by misplacing this quality in sardonic incongruity—by surrounding the comedian with tragedy.

Sitting opposite me was Winston Churchill. This was the first time I had seen him, too, at close quarters.

He belongs to that sandy type which cannot be rendered properly in black lines. His eyes, blue, bulbous and heavy-lidded, would be impossible. The best one could do with them would be an approximation. At this time all the political cartoonists were using the approximation worked out by E. T. Reed, the *Punch* caricaturist, who was feeling a bit disgruntled about the plagiarism. 'That fellow,' Reed complained to me about a colleague, 'he's a thief. He stole my Winston's eye.'

I already knew about Churchill. Who hadn't? Born in the inner circle, but combining with that long start exceptional abilities; determined to be a big noise; broke from Tory Party to Liberal Party when young to find opportunity; Sydney Street; the Admiralty; The Man Who Had the Navy Ready . . . and so on. A democrat? An upholder of Democracy? Um—ah—yes . . . when he was leading it. Impatient with it when he was not. Consequently not naturally a good politician, but astute from experience. As might be expected from his origins and tempera-

146

ment, inwardly contemptuous
of the 'common man' when
the 'common man' sought to
interfere in his (the 'common
man's') own government; but
bearing with the need to
appear sympathetic and com-
pliant to the popular will. In
those days, whenever I heard
Churchill's dramatic periods
about democracy, I felt inclined
to say: 'Please define.' His defi-

Winston Churchill in 1929

nition, I felt, would be something like 'government of the people,
for the people, by benevolent and paternal ruling-class chaps
like me.' Remembering him as one of the most energetic mis-
educators of public opinion in the early nineteen-twenties,
when his dislike of political onrushes from below took him
within hail of fascism, when the rabbits of the T.U.C. were
held up as Russian bears and the idea of a Labour Government
was alleged to mean the enthronement of bolshevism at
Westminster, I could never accept him as a democrat in the
Lincolnian sense. Winston's characteristics were confidence in
himself and love of his country. His defence of England was
always against threatening foreigners rather than against threatening 'isms or 'ologies, which did not worry him, since he was
sure he would eventually turn up leading the winner. A high
sense of the dramatic; a talent for self-advertisement; and to cap
all, imagination and guts.

Churchill was witty and easy to talk to until I said that the
Australians were an independent people who could not be
expected to follow Britain without question. They were, in the
case of new wars, for instance, not to be taken for granted, but
would follow their own judgment. His eyes bulged a little, his face
seemed to rise and hang in the heavens and he ended the subject
with a piece of rhetoric to which there could be no reply. The
conversation turned to Art. An enforced political 'rest' had
turned his interest to a new hobby, painting; and the Laverys, I
heard, were giving him hints. His ideas of how I worked were
fantastic. He thought I made a drawing in half an hour, and I
had some trouble in explaining that it would take longer than
that to put the lines down on paper in disorder, without trying to
draw at all. But for all that he had a genuine appreciation of
quality in caricatural draughtsmanship. He flattered me by

recalling some of my old cartoons which I had thought forgotten. Once on another and later occasion he made me blush by advancing across a roomful of people with pencil and paper, ostentatiously pretending to make a sketch of *me*. For all his playfulness I find that I wrote at the time of these first impressions: 'Churchill is one of the few men I have met who even in the flesh give me the impression of genius. Shaw is another. It is amusing to know that each thinks the other is much overrated.'

Such meetings, besides being socially agreeable, were, of course, very useful professionally in helping me to take the measure of events. With some experience behind me I had decided that in cartoons for my new environment the light-hearted approach was the most effective to domestic affairs. But in foreign affairs at least two sets of happenings suggested a need for stronger treatment.

The world was still weltering in the aftermath of the war, complicated by the detachment of the United States and the consequent apprehensions of France. Questions of whether the course of world history would have been different had the United States not put the financial screw on Britain, causing Britain to put the screw on France, causing France to put the screw on Germany, must remain in the columns of political guesses headed IF. Had it ever been the policy of the victorious Allies to conciliate Germany and build up her liberal forces to a position of strength as the best guarantee against future wars? Was it now their policy to throw the new German democracy on its back and sit on its head?

The news grew daily more fantastic as so-called 'realists' in places of national power conducted their experiments in extracting blood from stones and picking coal with bayonets. In the slow degeneration of European relationships British 'realism,' which had been for concilation to Germany but above all for friendship to France, could not hold a candle to French 'realism,' but the British Foreign Office was not in a position to protest very loudly when Poincaré took charge of the Versailles Peace and its enforcement. It was hinted to me, however, that individual voices could, and I did, with a series of rather violent half-pages.

How to win a cheap reputation as an oracle. One did not have to possess second sight to know that when French and Belgian armies entered the Ruhr, an unknown Hitler would stir. My cartoons INTO THE ARMS OF THE ENEMY (showing Poincaré driving back the new German democracy at the point of a bayonet into

INTO THE ARMS OF THE ENEMY (1922)

the hands of totalitarianism) and THE VULTURES (depicting the
Weimar Government weakened, as the junkers and industrial
bosses grew strong enough to pick out its eyes) were sadly sound
anticipations. It was the threatened disruption of Franco-British
co-operation that seemed to me to ask for a bit of what might be
called surgical cartooning; so I filled some space with heavy
symbolic figures against backgrounds of desolate ruin juxtaposed
to the figure of a fat little Frenchman labelled 'Poinc': 'Poinc'
holding up the rebuilding of Europe (THEY SHALL NOT PASS!),
ordering the British allies to clear out ('THE WAR WAS "OUR"
AFFAIR, THE PEACE IS "MY" AFFAIR'), invoking the past and forbidding the future. All of these, by a happy chain of friendly hands,
went regularly to be passed under Poincaré's nose on top of the
other press-cuttings expressive of British public opinion. The
French Prime Minister wasn't going to get the wrong impression
if I could help it.

There is no one more romantic than your political so-called
'realist.' To him the idea of a concourse of sober statesmen from
all parts of the world meeting to settle international differences in
a peaceful and businesslike manner seems a dangerous absurdity.
On the other hand, the idea of a fat man in a black shirt waving
a revolver in one hand and a bottle of castor-oil in the other and

149

screaming threats of war at the rest of humanity seems eminently sensible. From the very first the League of Nations had its detractors and weakeners. When Mussolini took Corfu and defied the League, it was possible to estimate the power of these 'realists.' It looked for a moment as though Britain and France, the masters of League policy, would stand with the small nations against the revival of force and keep Caesar down to life-size.

I evidently thought so, judging from my cartoon of Mussolini surveying the potential opposition with trepidation, and fearing he hadn't brought 'enough castor-oil to go round.' But the 'realists' won and the League decided to hear nothing, see nothing, say nothing. Mussolini got away with it and the first chapter was written in his book of Success.

Reactions to the advent of the Duce had been curious. Leaving international morality and descending to mere national interest, it was highly improbable that an ambitious dictator in the Mediterranean could ever be friendly towards Britain or France. But there were considerations more important than that, apparently. The spectacle of the Duce so masterfully beating up his Liberal and Socialist opponents was one that could not fail to evoke admiration in some Anglo-Saxon breasts. A British Fascist Party grew up overnight; and the *Daily Mail*, then Britain's biggest popular newspaper, approved it. With some zest I added the first Lord Rothermere, its proprietor, to my cast of cartoon characters. He made up well in a black shirt helping to stoke the fires of class hatred. Lord R. was much incensed and complained bitterly. 'Dog doesn't eat dog. It isn't done,' said one of his Fleet Street men, as though he were giving me a moral adage instead of a thieves' wisecrack. 'You forget, old boy,' I replied, 'I'm a moa.'

Bonar Law's battle-cry to rally his followers at the general election just past was 'Tranquillity'—which seemed a queer slogan for a nation that was trying to pull itself together after a destructive war. 'Awake! Arise!' would have been more appropriate. I was moved as a cartoonist to symbolize this 'Tranquillity' in the person of the Prime Minister himself always in his pyjamas, conducting the affairs of the nation half asleep from bed.

Bonar Law struck me as a man without outstanding physical characteristics. I had heard all about his past liveliness, but in 1922 he was a subdued personality difficult to draw. For the election he had been represented as recovered from his illness. But it soon became painfully evident that he no longer had the reserves of strength needed for the office of Prime Minister. I was in full swing with a series of cartoons entitled ADVENTURES OF BONAR IN SLUMBERLAND when a political know-all told me the P.M. was having a bad time just then with insomnia. Rather unfortunate. I shut down on the series. I was considerably surprised a week or so later to receive a fan-mail from insomniacs far and near asking for me. I learned that the P.M. himself had found them diverting. One cartoon which showed Bonar in a mobile bed drawn by galloping nightmares gave pleasure to the venerable Lord Rosebery, who used to rise in the night and drive about in his brougham to induce sleep.

Here was a peculiar thing, an example of the inconsequential in life. One drew some pretty obvious political cartoons, and one found oneself suddenly in contact with a lot of people united by a common interest which had nothing to do with politics or cartoons—How to Get to Sleep. The interest of finding so many active insomniacs led me to enter into correspondence with some of them. I had just begun a new round of sleeplessness myself.

I had been a bad sleeper ever since the Melbourne City Council (may my darkest curse wither its entrails) started to tear up the rails of the tramways by night outside my bedroom window on Collins Street. Punctured by drillings and hammerings on iron, my sleep grew nightly less and more broken, and one night I had no sleep at all. I worried about it, which was the worst thing I could have done because I kept myself awake next night trying so hard to go to sleep. One night—two nights. Nobody seemed to think it was anything that could not be cured by a cup of hot milk. Three nights. By this time the operations had moved up the road almost out of earshot, but that made no difference. The silence was as bad. Four nights. I grew desperate and afraid I was going mad. I met a comforting chap who told me it was nothing. We all slept too much, anyway. He knew a man who hadn't slept for three years. It would do me good to keep awake for a week. Sharpen me up. Didn't I feel sharper already? (Yes, perhaps . . . a bit . . .) Very well then. Let's have a large rum and we'll *both* stay awake. . . . We both fell asleep.

With the burden shared by this true friend, nature let up and I resumed orderly repose. Until the next time. At times of too great activity of mind or not enough, I continued subject to sleeplessness. I tried lying still, pretending to be unconscious; reading; counting up to a million and down from a million; getting up and working; placing something hot at the feet and something cold at the feet; singing silently (this was a good one);

lying spreadeagled on the floor (strangely soothing); long walks at 3 a.m.; and most other methods of inducing slumber. There was the awful night when I took the advice of some ass and wooed Morpheus with the aid of two large bottles of stout. Operation Stout was not a success. But that was the night a mouse got into the piano.

Ah! Those miserable occasions early in my affliction when in despair I threw on my clothes over my pyjamas, banged the front door in the hope of waking everybody else in the street, made my way in the dark through some park or other to trudge along the banks of the Yarra river spouting Shakespeare at the dawn. Damn the dawn! How I hated it!

I found Shakespeare comforting on these outings. I used to leave a small volume about ready to stick in my pocket as I went. Tragic, bitter, self-pitying passages went well. The melancholy Jaques was made for it. But my favourite was Hamlet and the Ghost. Had anyone been about at such an hour in such a spot, I must have looked a strange figure—wild-eyed, dishevelled, lolloping through the half-light, warning in sepulchral tone: 'M a r k . . . m a a a r k . . .'

The first ten years of insomnia were the hardest. I had learned by then that sleep is a habit, both in time and duration, and a habit which can be modified to suit individual requirements. Everybody else could go to bed at ten or eleven o'clock and sleep eight hours, but was that any reason why *I* should do so if it did not suit me? The Lows were always nightbirds. Whatever time I got up, I was never properly awake—that is to say, all cylinders working—until noon. I could discipline my machinery to grind out its job passably well, adequate hack-work, before that; but it was not until between four o'clock and midnight that my brain worked most efficiently with the rapid clickety-click of idea and associated ideas. Fresh thoughts came easiest at the end of the day when the body was tired and the mind could ramble. Most inconvenient. Just how things should *not* be, because if the machinery winds up it has to wind down again before it can sleep. I attempted to answer that by making my time of sleep variable and adjustable to circumstances. The outside world was not always sympathetic. I turned up one day at the *Star* office yawning my head off. 'Sorry. Been up all day.' Thus began a legend that I was a small-hours roisterer.

It was years before I got to the root of the matter. My trouble was a failure of confidence. A doubt deep inside me as to whether I could sleep. I could not reason this doubt out of myself. Proof was required. It was not until I had run into this patch of insomnia in London that I had the luck to meet a sensible Australian doctor. He prescribed three soporifics, mild, medium and knock-out, to be taken as necessity demanded. With these I dosed myself for a week back into regular habits. Ever since then a bottle and a pillbox rest on my bedside table, the last thing I see before I switch off the light. The mere sight of them is enough. Looking at them I am comforted, I know all is under control and I drop off into sweet refreshing slumber. And when I read articles in the newspapers about dangerous bedside drugs, I smile a knowing smile.

It was overwork that had revived my insomnia in 1922. Fortunately family changes gave me a good excuse for an inter-ruption. My father had put the Empire emigration plan into reverse and returned the entire Low family (with the exception of one brother left in Australia) from New Zealand back to Britain. Now he was impatient to revisit the scenes of his youth after forty years' absence, and I could take a short holiday with a light heart to help him rediscover Scotland.

My father grew steadily more Scottish as we travelled North-wards. By the time we had reached Carnoustie, the cradle of our ancestors, he was the Scotchest man there. 'Whit way is the auld schoolhoose?' he asked a passer-by in the broadest Dundese. Puzzled look. 'Oh, you mean the old school,' said the passer-by in faultless English. 'First to the right . . .' etc.

My father's old school was still there. Small, deserted, dirty, with broken windows. We found the wee hoose that was his birthplace derelict, roofless. Alas, I was sad to see Dad's dismay. For evermore this scene would mar those sweet revisits to the past which comfort the aged in their decline. The man who said: 'Never go back' was right. We turned away dismally to visit the new up-to-date construction that overlaid Dad's youth, on the way passing troops of the fashionable golfers from the South, damn their eyes. Never go back.

The present was good enough for me. I was discovering the joys of married life and the rhythm and harmony of a London suburban routine for the first time in my life. Could anyone be happier than I? What delight lay in the simple pleasures of gardening, of wrestling with my dog, of searching for nicodum-phians and crackadalians with my tiny daughters, of endlessly quoting Romeo to my beautiful wife. This was a supremely glad time in my life, despite a fiend within me that constantly urged me to expand and spread, that incited me to impossible tests—to paint, to carve, to sculpt, to write, to make speeches, to play tennis and golf, at both of which games I was, and always remained, an utter fool.

This fiend sometimes became a problem. The rigid self-discipline I had imposed upon myself as a youth would not relax. I gave myself no rest. I worked hard even when there was no immediate point in it, sitting up half the night making improvements in a drawing which would surely never be apparent to anyone but myself. I had a period of overwork which induced a run of deep depressions. The agony of trying to incubate light-hearted ideas for cartoons was intolerable. By experiment I evolved my own cure. Low's Infallible Remedy for Depression: retire to quiet room, lock door, draw blinds, tightly bandage eyes and chin, lie down on back, fold hands on chest, clear mind, remain completely and stiffly still for twenty minutes imagining you are buried under six feet of wet earth. Then get up, go to a lively restaurant and have a good dinner. After that if the world hasn't taken on a new interest and you aren't glad to be alive, I'll eat my hat.

Although in cash terms I was a proved success, for my pay had doubled since I had begun in London, I was considerably dissatisfied with my work. My principal interest was still in drawing, and I intended to keep it that way, but I was getting too much mixed up with politics. Confound it, I was an artist who drew politics, not a politician who drew pictures. Public affairs were the raw material for my drawing and I had no wish to 'get on' in politics. Although I sought famous people for professional reasons, I did not long to trail around in their glory. The physical needs of the Low family were simple, so we had enough money. Over and above all was my vital necessity to draw, and if I were not having the fun of trying to do that as well as I could, I was not having fun at all. Now and again I had profound misgivings about the wisdom of my having got mixed up with newspapers at all. Then I was acutely unhappy.

No newspaper man gave a damn about Art; nor many newspaper readers either, apparently. A newspaper was a vehicle for circulating ideas. It was all ideas. When somebody said 'That was a good cartoon,' he meant it was a good idea. He probably did not know what a cartoon was apart from the idea it expressed. That was an attitude that irritated me profoundly. When, for instance, a friendly soul came up to me one day and said, 'That's a good cartoon of yours in today's paper,' I asked, 'What's good about it?'

154

'Oh, why, about Baldwin mending a tank with a hairpin . . .'

'Oh, you mean the idea. You're telling me it's a good gag. Well, never mind that. We both know enough about psychology to be aware that you probably like the gag only because it flatters your own prejudices, so when you think you are patting me on the back you are really only patting yourself on the back. Why should I feel satisfaction about that? Let's leave the gag out of it and tell me about the cartoon.'

'Why, what else is there?'

Was that why I sat up half the night fretting to get the right simper, frown or smirk on Baldwin's face? Was that the average response to the exercise of mind and imagination involved in playing with line values, as a musician plays with notes on the piano, to produce effects of farce, fantasy or tragedy? Was that why I strained my ingenuity inventing ways of drawing things that are undrawable, like an invisible man, say, or a couple of isosceles triangles having a fight, or a man chasing a dog on the blind side of a wall? Or why I strove to express emotions in familiar visual terms, to create—create was the word—pictorial symbols, for ideas that have no shape nor substance, like Freedom, War, Peace, Labour, Slump, Prosperity, Europe, Britain, and so on? To anyone who could ask, 'What else is there?' I could reply, 'Why, the cartoon. Are the details nicely composed so that the eye slides easily to the full meaning? Has the drawing the appropriate blend of fantasy and realism to insinuate the satire? Does the wit of its caricature suggest sound judgment of essentials? Do the portraits of the people depicted suggest insight into character? Does the performance fit the intention—not too laboured to defeat the spontaneity, not so facile as to be insignificant? Is it, in short, a good cartoon, or just another plate of hash?'

When the sciolists protested to me that cartooning couldn't be an art, I bade them tell that to Brueghel, Callot, Hogarth, Gillray, Rowlandson, Daumier. Art does not reside in the materials nor the subject-matter. It resides in the artist. A great artist drawing a boot on a wall with a piece of charred stick can make great art. Equally a hack could use the most expensive materials on the most majestic subject-matter and his work still be rubbish. Cartooning can be an art if the cartoonist is an artist; but equally, if the man is not an artist, his cartoons will have no artistry, however witty his ideas.

Certain it was that I maintained this passionately. If I hadn't been possessed by the idea that there were fascinating new possibilities lying in every blank sheet of paper, I should not have

155

spent my life trying to be an artist. Had I found it to be merely a craft, I should have given it up long before as a boring business and gone in for something lively like stockbroking. I was like the pastrycook who believed that there weren't any arts worth considering except architecture and pastry-making, and considered that pastry-making came first. I was a caricaturist and I believed that caricature was the most important of arts, if only because it clearly involved to a greater extent than any other the exercise of the two principles fundamental to all art in whatever medium of expression—selection and emphasis.

That was not to claim every scribbled sketch in the papers as a work of art. Far from it. In this mood one considered the highest performance, not the making of artless ideographs in rigid, almost official symbols, which abounded as a reaction from the over-representationalism of thirty or forty years before. I certainly did not set up as an artist your cartoonist who went out to piece together commonly accepted conventions to explain a jest, the jest being the main thing, graphic originality or individuality being restricted to improvisation and adaptation. But I *did* certainly insist that he who set out to capture the character of life as it struck him, and to whom illustration even of a jest was an excuse to present a good piece of observed life in appropriate atmosphere, was an artist. It was the difference between one who thought artistry unnecessary and even hampering, and one who thought it essential.

The fact that all cartoonists used conventions in one sense (what about my own double-headed Ass?) did not affect the point. There was a distinction to be drawn between graphic conventions like fixed recipes for drawing a leg, a hand, a tree and so on, and idea-conventions like John Bull, The Russian Bear, etc., which have to be drawn afresh with every use.

It irked me that what seemed to me plain common sense so often seemed to others just high-falutin' tommyrot that didn't mean a thing so long as the cartoon raised a laugh. A funny idea in indifferent pictorial terms was all they wanted. A writer or a talker would have scorned another writer or talker who had no grammar and used a narrow range of clichés to express himself. Yet when they wrote or talked about caricatures or cartoons they seemed unconscious of the equivalent weakness in my medium. The superior importance of the raw subject matter over the pictorial means of expression was so arrogantly assumed that no one bothered even to consider the nature of cartooning—much less that of caricature. There was, in fact, a contempt for the art of it.

No doubt one day someone would invent a typewriter with the face, hand, body and the other linear conventions in place of the letters of the alphabet, to be whanged out in all their permutations. Then the Philistines could make 'cartoons' for themselves. 'Every man his own "cartoonist." '

The unending arguments about presentation, space and position in the paper became wearing. Eternal vigilance palled. I had foreseen the possibilities of personal crisis about all this, so, as an insurance, I had begun to develop some footholds in quarters where I could place some better drawing: *Punch*, *The Graphic* and elsewhere.

The *portraits chargés* I had been working on so long were now coming up to the final stage. I had Robert Lynd introduce me to Clifford Sharp, the editor of *The New Statesman*, and I offered them to him for a first publication at a small fee on condition he spent real money on giving them top quality reproduction. He agreed to do them as offset plate-stamped loose supplements. How fortunate I was to find in John Roberts, the manager of *The New Statesman*, a man of enthusiasm who shared my determination to get the job done well. He dredged London to find the best paper, the best blockmakers, the best printers, and we both hung over them critically as they did the job. And they did the the job and it was good.

12

THE political wheels had been turning. Taking the end-of-Coalition election of 1922 as just a trial spin, 1924 was my first British general election. I put other things aside and threw myself into it. The *Star* worked closely with Liberal headquarters and we arranged that I would make at least one poster per day for reproduction into bills, postcards and leaflets up and down the country. I had this field practically to myself. It was probably the last election poster campaign in Britain. The limitations on candidates' expenses since then have made such features impossible on a nation-wide scale.

There were comings and goings, briefing luncheons, smoke-filled rooms, hole-and-corner plannings. Abstract principles were of less account than party strategy to these business men of politics; but I found something to admire in the efficiency with which constituencies could be graphed and results forecast fairly accurately.

Stanley Baldwin was virtually an unknown personality to the public, and he was handicapped by the jealousies and resentments of many of his followers who did not relish being put to the trouble of another election so soon. The Tory managers had not yet built him up as a 'character' except for a hint that he smoked an honest cherrywood pipe and wore an honest bowler hat. He overdid the 'I-am-just-a-plain-ordinary-man' routine almost to the point of getting lost in the crowd. The election issues were still trade depression and unemployment. Baldwin had an idea for a sovereign remedy—tariffs; but his right-wing diehard supporters placed more reliance upon identifying the Labour Party with bolshevism and throwing a scare into the electorate than upon their leader's involved calculations upon the possible benefits of imperial preference. The unattached self-styled 'first-class brains,'

Churchill, Birkenhead and Rothermere, banked upon the Red Peril cry and the appeal to snobbery, 'Labour Unfit to Rule.'

The grounds of controversy suited me well enough. I had never been one of those who thought of the tariff issue in ethical terms. Free trade or protection seemed to me to involve questions of expediency, not of absolute principles. I had advocated tariffs in Australia, free trade in Britain. The conditions were vastly different. Australia had a small population, could feed itself, was struggling to establish certain 'strategic' industries. Britain had a large population, couldn't feed itself, was heavily industrialized. For Britain, the conditions for prosperous free trade still existed just around the corner.

In this election the question narrowed down to an argument about the price of tinned fish. The logical evolution to absurdity which is the essence of caricatural symbolism made it almost inevitable that I should represent Baldwin and his friends first as herrings, then as sardines and finally as the Tinned Tadpole Government. In my contributions to the debate I gave enough hard knocks to warrant getting some back. Some rough things were said about my 'brutality' and 'coarseness' especially in the constituency of Epping where thousands of my handbills flooded the place. The Tory candidate, Winston Churchill, made no complaint, however. I was amused and charmed one morning to have a friendly letter from him wanting to buy an original drawing.

Out went Baldwin, an event I celebrated with a cartoon entitled THE MOURNING AFTER—a funeral procession headed by Garvin, editor of the *Observer*, Baldwin's most candid friend, playing on a tuba 'The Funeral March of a Tinned Salmon.'

In came Ramsay MacDonald and the first Labour Government.

My first cartoons of MacDonald were altogether too optimistic. He would swim the Channel to deal with Poincaré. He would destroy the barricade which Lloyd George had had built across Downing Street to keep off Irish assassins. He would settle the wages question, the unemployment question. He would restore healthy trade relations with the Soviet Union.

Under the conditions, there was no chance, of course, of a free run for socialist legislation. The first Labour Government took on the job for the administrative experience. They were dependent on the Liberals for a majority in Parliament and they aimed at winning over Liberal votes to Labour in the country.

Some modification of policies was expected. But what was not expected was that when Labour Ministers achieved office they should turn into quite different persons. They even changed in appearance. The significant politics of MacDonald's first term as Prime Minister were that he cut his hair, trimmed his moustache, assumed a tail-coat and was seen in a tall shiny silk hat, symbol for a generation past of the hated capitalist.

These happenings translated by me into terms of caricature were seen by my customers merely as a deplorable lapse into tasteless personality on my part. But the change in Ramsay's dress had in reality a deep symbolic significance. Continuity was to be observed. Sleep soundly in your beds, O Middle Classes. The harbingers of change, the party of revolution, might have defeated the aristos, but the angle of approach to the future would remain unchanged.

If the Labour leaders thought that going on their Sunday-best behaviour would do them any good they were mistaken. The anti-Labour tacticians laid their plans accordingly. When the election figures had been announced there had been a sizeable move by stoopids of the Tory Party tail to resist the popular will. They held that the King should press Baldwin and Asquith to co-operate in 'keeping Labour out.' That shrewdest of tacticians, Lord Beaverbrook, knew a game worth two of that. His newspaper, the *Daily Express*, gained credit by suddenly demanding 'fair play for Labour.' Beware the Greeks. A carpet was laid into 10 Downing Street for the Right Honourable J. Ramsay MacDonald, M.P. Thereupon the executioners proceeded at leisure to build a fire under Ramsay's coat-tails and sat down with the match to wait.

Labour Ministers hardly had time to get measured for their gold-braided Court suits when they were out again. Their innocuous sojourn ended after a general election which I distinguish from other elections as The Disgraceful Election. Popular elections have never been completely free from chicanery, of course, but this one was exceptional. There were issues—unemployment, for instance, and trade. There were legitimate secondary issues—whether or not Russia should be afforded an export loan to stimulate trade ('The Russian Loan'); whether or not it was public policy to prosecute for sedition an ex-soldier who had had both his legs practically blown off in the war ('The Campbell Case'); whether the Prime Minister ought to accept from a private friend (a biscuit manufacturer who subsequently turned up quite honourably in the honours list) the use of a motor-car to carry him around on the nation's business (since the nation did not then supply one), or whether he should travel by bus or under-ground like anybody else ('The Biscuits Car Question').

160

In the event these issues were distorted, pulped, and attached as appendix to a mysterious document subsequently held by many creditable persons to be a forgery, and the election was fought on 'red' panic ('The Zinoviev Letter').

I had watched the manœuvres with curiosity which turned to dismay at the raw debauching of the democratic process. Was this the way things were done in Britain? This callous exploitation of the common ignorance? This treachery to the common cause of enlightenment? I retired to utter ten thousand maledictions in private and remained a space to reflect. It was evident that in the defence of democracy, so far as I was concerned there could be no quarter against such unscrupulous villainy. The crude contempt for the masses was accurately judged. The mob had no chance to use its brains against the deliberate fomenting of a stampede. Mr. Baldwin, now reunited to his erstwhile caustic critics, was returned with an adequate majority. His predecessor, Ramsay MacDonald, had assumed the government under conditions which forbad the policies he had affirmed were essential for British recovery. Stanley Baldwin now took over, pledged not to apply the policies *he* had affirmed were essential to British recovery. Same mountain, different mouse. One had exchanged Ramsay Baldwin for Stanley MacDonald, so to speak.

It should be said, greatly to Baldwin's credit, that he was disgusted with the venomous tactics of his supporters, especially since, *sub rosa*, his personal friendship with Ramsay had already begun. Ramsay celebrated the change of government by presenting him with a couple of my original drawings on the event as a sweetener. I was glad of it and added my compliments. One of the best features of our democracy is that one may leave one's politics in the cloak-room for a moment.

In the interim of opposition, Baldwin and his managers had been building up his personality. From a comparative nonentity he had now become a rounded, recognizable character—honest, plain man, literary associations but not too clever, homely of face, pint o' beer, pipe, pigs. Farmer John Bull in person, in fact.

Statesmen must advertise. Indeed it is vital to the working of our modern democracy that the persons of political leaders be readily identifiable. Cartoonists and caricaturists have their use in creating or embellishing tags of identity, a fact which is not lost on astute politicians. Winston Churchill, for an obvious instance, deliberately advertised himself in his early political days by wearing a succession of unusual hats, and in later years, by always carrying an outsize cigar, foibles which were eagerly used and improved upon by the cartoonists, with his open encouragement. Since the inspiration of these tags is frequently poetic imagination, political analogy or plain prejudice, they are to be accepted as faithful reflections of truth with as much reserve as one accepts the pictures on seed-packets. More often than not they are clues to the possibilities rather than the probabilities of the subject's character. Gladstone never really wore the huge collars in Harry Furniss's caricatures. J. H. Thomas did not invariably wear the dress-suit I drew for him. Neither are the creations of 'subjects' themselves any more reliable when they become their own publicists along these lines. The early Churchill wore normal hats when the photographers were not around; and in his later years it was noticeable to keen eyes that his public cigars were smoked never more than about one inch. Likewise all those within range knew well enough that the pipe-and-pig-loving Farmer Baldwin was a businessman in the steel industry who probably couldn't tell one pig from another, and by the brown tint on his right forefinger probably smoked cigarettes in private.

My personal contacts with the Tory Party were slight until I became acquainted with two of its most improbable members. Of all Government departments engaged in holding off the imaginary British Communist revolution, the Home Office had to be the busiest office and the Home Secretary the busiest body. Sir William Joynson-Hicks ('Jix' for short) was a spectacular success as 'red'-hunter. He was in his element rushing the police around to seize sinister documents (including on one occasion a copy of the Holy Bible) from some branch of the then insignificant Communist party. Most of the time he seemed to me, of all Baldwin's men, the most intolerant, narrow-minded and dictatorial of anti-democrats. Week by week, I derided his moments of triumph. While the Conservative popular Press splashed dramatic stories of the raid of ARCOS, the offices of the flabbergasted Russian trade delegation, to seize their 'intelligence' files about British Life and Character, I had him, over the title THE EMPIRE SAVED, in the midst of a rushing forest of police, personally bringing in the prisoner, a miserable little pup. I made him the subject of a metamorphosis from bloodhound to long-eared ass. I drew him distorted with rage, speeding parting deportees from Britain's shores with 'Clear out! The Government can drive the country to communism without your assistance.'

162

I thought Jix's throwing out the Russians was not the right way to go about things, and that we would have to go to all the trouble of getting them back again; which, of course, we had. Even had the delegation been composed exclusively of dangerous professional spies instead of merely including two or three bungling amateurs, it would still have been a singularly uncunning proceeding. According to the accepted technique of spy-handling, one deals with the other fellow's

Sir William Joynson-Hicks

spies by keeping an eye on them without their knowing it, not by driving them out of sight.

I regretted, too, Jix's attempts to censor morals. He was a Home Secretary, not a governess. In 1927 a public enquiry into a case relating to the state of morals in Hyde Park gave occasion for a cartoon entitled THE JIX FAMILY IN CONFERENCE, which represented the enquiry being conducted exclusively by members of the Home Secretary's family. There was a vacant spot in one corner, so I filled it up with a cat also bearing the family likeness.

A letter arrived from Jix:

'Dear Low,

If ever that cat has kittens, send me one. I'm sure it would be an uncommonly good mouser . . .'

followed by an invitation to come along to the Home Office if ever I wanted to bring my portrait of the writer up to date.

Jix's vanity and giggling goodwill were irresistible. I abhorred his politics but I liked him and he liked me. There he was at the Home Office with a heap of reproductions of my bloodhound cartoons of himself on his writing-table, obviously put there for my benefit (how transparently naïve!). I could see he had groomed himself for my visit, expecting me to make it a 'sitting.' The man evidently *liked* sitting for his portrait. I fell in with his inclination and gave him the 'works'—running the gamut of his expressions so that I could note the play of his facial muscles; getting him up and walking him up and down the room so that I could note his peculiarities of dress and posture. He posed, first miming a speech for me, and then frozen with great dignity. Jix was a joy to draw, with his small lined face with the tiny snub nose. I had come primed by some of my writing friends with a few sensible comments on his egregious efforts to censor literature, to slip in if opportunity arose. But what could be done with a chap who insisted that the object of respectable men of letters in writing adult novels was 'L.S.D., which letters might stand for "Let's Sell Dirt" '? On this occasion the business of the nation waited while we both enjoyed a happy interlude, and the old Home Office echoed to unaccustomed mirth.

Jix was a queer mixture. He had a real feeling for political democracy, evidenced, for instance, in his gallant championship of the extension of the vote to women of 21. But at the same time his attitude to the electorate was that of a nagging hen, self-appointed to supervise the community for its own good.

I met him often after that, always with enjoyment. For years we exchanged Christmas presents regularly, I a little drawing, he a box of cigars: 'With best wishes from your devoted assassin, Low': 'With all good wishes from your most loyal victim, Jix.'

'It is in most men's power to be agreeable,' said Swift, probably warning his subconscious self to be on its guard when he kept company with the persons who were the raw material of his satire. For what would happen to the art of the satirist, or the caricaturist, who surrendered to the personal charms of his raw material? Must affection emasculate ridicule, corrupt invective?

Despite all our friendliness, neither Jix nor I thought it unnatural that I continued to mock him politically whenever he seemed to need it. I cannot flatter myself that it made the slightest difference to him, except superficially in one connection. When the elaborate portrait arising from that first 'sitting' at last appeared in print, it displayed him in Napoleonic attitude, dressed in the full glory of his habitual outfit as the Compleat Statesman, Victorian vintage, with choker collar and silk-faced frock-coat. A fortnight later—sensation in the House (Oh! Oh! . . . Hear, hear!) when a transformed Jix entered in a gay new brown lounge suit in the latest style, with tinted handkerchief, gay buttonhole posy and all. The Victorian statesman had vanished for ever. A footnote was added to history.

When in the fullness of time Jix died I gloomed for a man who, if mistaken, was at the same time honest and could be gay.

It had been an odd amity. Odd, too, was the personal harmony I found in another unlikely subject, Austen Chamberlain. The very apotheosis of English starchy stiffness, I had thought. A mutual friend had arranged an interview. It was just after the Locarno Pact and the Foreign Secretary was said to be in a good mood. Half-way down the spacious room at the Foreign Office was a table upon which rested the silk hat and the yellow gloves. In the distance stood what I thought at first was a statue.

'I have been asking myself how I should receive you,' it said, showing minute signs of life.

'Well then, don't receive me at all. Pretend I am not here,' I said.

'Must I wear my monocle? I cannot see to read with it very well . . .'

'Yes, you should wear your monocle.' It was a valuable tag of identity so far as I was concerned. Whereupon Sir Austen sat down and went on with his shuffling of papers, all the time troubled with short-sighted monocle and acutely nervous, shaky-handed, at my peering. I tried to put him through the drill necessary to my purpose. Too much on guard against 'liberties.' Stiff as a poker. For heaven's sake break down, I shouted silently. I exercised all the technique I knew. I charmed and I provoked. No good. Only when I talked about his father did he melt a little. After all my trouble, I left with only his shell.

Some weeks later I found myself placed next to him at a Savage Club concert. In the free-and-easy atmosphere he loosened up. We talked of everything, beginning with Art and ending with the Meaning of Life. Some of his remarks were so out of character that I was astonished. When one of the performers cracked a joke, very decorous, at his expense, he laughed heartily. This was a different Austen, so much so that I remarked on it. 'I had you pretty wrong the other day,' I said. 'I thought you were sensitive about being drawn. I had no idea you were so—ah—understanding.' This seemed to please him no end. He protested that if he had ever had any sensitiveness about his appearance it had faded when he saw himself on the films. Was horrified. Saw a lean, stiff, shirty person appear on the screen delivering the commentary upon the King George V Jubilee film. Said to wife: 'Great heavens, is that me?' Thought the sight of people's real appearance to themselves must first produce disquiet followed by an adjustment of their inner selves. Here, I said to myself, we have a genial soul trying to escape an uncongenial character imposed on him by public life. 'It is the pattern,' I said. 'All foreign secretaries look like that. If you will permit me I could suggest an improvement. You should smile more.' Thereafter, whenever

Sir Austen Chamberlain

I encountered Austen Chamberlain, the Savage Club version was always at hand (except on one occasion which I shall narrate in its proper place).

As encouragement I ran him in the paper for a while as a human chap with a smiling mouthful of teeth. I heard that the Foreign Office considered the original solemn version was better for business, but after all the Foreign Office is not everybody.

In the comparative inactivity of politics, opportunities occurred to improve my acquaintance with Ramsay MacDonald. On our first meeting he had been still suffering from the disillusion of Lloyd George's coupon election. Ramsay, having lost his Labour friends (who blamed his confused attitude to the first world war for their failure), retired into a corner to take a quiet think. His confidence in democracy had suffered a severe blow. He no longer—if he had ever—believed that the voice of the people was the voice of God. He well knew there was no equality of intellect. Painful associations had fomented a barely concealed hatred and contempt for those who went about buttering up the ignorant telling them that knowledge was unnecessary, feeling was enough; that leadership was unnecessary and would 'wither away' and that the nincompoop would inherit the earth.

Then there had been more than one function at which he had used my presence as excuse for humorous relief and left-handed compliments in speeches. We came to be well enough acquainted for me to be placed upon his list for occasional hospitality at the House of Commons. So, for example, to lunch on a spring day in 1926.

This was one of the days when Ramsay and his associates were out of sorts with one another. The leader was never one to hide his scorn for a colleague who, in his opinion, merited it; and naturally, the feeling, when sufficiently apparent, was apt to be heartily reciprocated. This was a bad day, it seemed. He had asked three other people to lunch but they did not turn up. As we went along the corridor to the dining-room we intercepted three others but they excused themselves. Finally we collected McNeil Weir, his grey-faced P.P.S., to make it a threesome, but he left after the fish course, leaving us alone. Weir's presence had given me a vague discomfort anyway, for I sensed that he disliked the Prime Minister. Ramsay had the atmosphere of loneliness and I was drawn with sympathy. Ramsay alone was simple and communicative. While we were talking one

Ramsay MacDonald

of his recent Cabinet Ministers came and spoke into his ear. As he went I said: 'A hot tip?'

'Straight from the ass's mouth,' said Ramsay while the visitor was still in earshot.

The conversation soon got around to how nobody was any good. The trouble was not with the people outside but more particularly with the members of the Party themselves. The Party could sweep the country at the next election were it not for the Party. 'I have a hard team to handle—terribly hard—they are my masters,' he said, fiercely chewing a mouthful of roast lamb as though it were a Clydeside left-winger.

What should a cartoonist talk about to a Prime Minister? I thought it useful to bring up a few stock leading questions disguised as light conversation.

Q. What did he mean by socialism?

A. It was a spirit rather than a programme.

Q. Did he . . . perhaps . . . I don't suppose . . . maybe . . . favour nationalization of the means of . . . etc. etc.?

A. Only when and where it was necessary.

Q. Not in order to further a constructive plan for industry?

A. We must build on the past.

Q. Well, then, has the Labour Party an innovating future or a reforming future?

A. We must develop innovations as they accord with our past.

I liked not the words 'develop' or 'accord.' To my mind Britain needed a much bolder approach. I gathered that the development and the accord might take time. This wasn't socialism, this was Liberal reform.

I took a good look at him sitting there. He was certainly a fine figure of a man with his square face, deep-set brown eyes alternatively kind and tortured, and wavy white hair. (He told me that when at Balmoral Queen Mary had congratulated him on his 'shingle.') Responsibility had left its mark on the romantic rhetorician that had entranced me at Paisley. He had become the very model of a front bench Liberal Minister. He would have looked at home sitting between Gladstone and Morley. I remembered that he had started his political career as a would-be Radical candidate. Why then was he the object of such hatred and suspicion among the 'working-class' trade union supporters of the Labour Party who were so evidently Radical reformers themselves? Coming from the equalitarian societies of Australia and New Zealand, it had always surprised me that the British Labour Party had ever managed to convince itself it was socialistic. The Webbs and the Fabians must have been very persuasive. Perhaps the spleen against MacDonald was just because he was the only possible leader.

The conversation rambled into homely channels, about a tree I had promised to design for him so that he could turn a damp patch on his dining-room wall into a mural design; and then came back to his party difficulties. He confided that his secret desire was to return to authorship and write a novel about 'all this' 'from the top.' My professional nose scented an opportunity.

'Great! Why not?'

'Because it would be the end of me *here*.'

'Well, leave it to be published when you're dead.'

'But then I couldn't see the fireworks.'

Nevertheless the occasion ended with serious talk about the possibility of his writing his life and my illustrating it, his own idea (with a little prompting from me). That would have been a grand book. Alas, the nearest we got to it was when McNeil Weir—the same grey-faced third party at that lunch—wrote it for him two or three years after his death. *The Tragedy of Ramsay MacDonald* was a bitter book copiously illustrated by reproductions of my cartoons, giving the effect of a collaboration. An error of judgment on my part in assenting too readily to a suggestion misunderstood. Too late to protest. This was not the kind of book I had wanted to do about Ramsay MacDonald.

In 1926 Baldwin's efforts to fit the post-war generation into a pre-war suit of clothes by main force were still not succeeding. Seams were splitting and patches giving way, exposing distressed areas of the national economy. The most notable achievement of the time was the so-called General Strike.

To see this event in its frame it must be recalled that one of the worst spots in the British economy was the coal-mining industry. A Royal Commission on Coal in 1919 had recommended nationalization. The diehards of the Tory Party, whose support was necessary to Baldwin, sidestepped this suggested interference with private enterprise. Had not their friends the mine-owners the only sensible formula for restoring prosperity to the industry —i.e. longer hours, shorter wages, no minimum wage and (to prevent any ganging up of 'agitators' who did not like it) no national agreements?

The miners objected. Their standard of living was already pitifully low. They had been the most obstinate champions of nationalization. The mine-owners, seizing their optimum moment, posted lock-out notices and declared they would not re-employ the men unless they agreed in advance to wage cuts. The entire trade union movement began to line up in sympathy with the miners. The Baldwin Government, smelling trouble, persuaded the mine-owners to hold off with a subsidy.

But nine months later it was announced the subsidy would end. The whole situation came up again—but with differences. Preparations were complete, the coal bins full. The miners asked Baldwin to interfere again, but the Prime Minister had become deaf in that ear. What to do?

The situation for months had bristled with opportunities for the trade union leaders to display their talents for strategy and tactics. But there were deep differences between right and left wings as to ultimate aims, and eventually, alas, as though to demonstrate that the faith of the 'worker' is no substitute for the

169

cunning of the 'intellectual' in political generalship, simplicity and guilelessness walked, with patched-up 'Solidarity' banners flying, into the trap. With ominous creakings the General Council of the Trade Union Congress came together and decided to strike.

The strike had not a hope. The trade union leaders had no experience of such a venture on this scale. Their case had not been well publicized. They had made no preparations, had no plans. On the other hand the Government had manœuvred the situation nicely. They had been signing up young men for 'emergency services' from six months before. The greater part of public opinion and the resources of the nation were behind them. The trade unions were now where their opponents had wanted them, in position to be given a holy drubbing. To the eye of a cynical observer, it looked like a competent piece of 'fixing.' In an atmosphere electric with impending doom, Jix took the air to declaim that the Government 'might almost say they were a Committee of Public Safety,' conjuring up a picture of steadfast lion-hearts guarding the menaced nation from an onrush of bloodthirsty *sans-culottes*. Had the menaced nation seen, as I had just seen, the batch of scared trade union rabbits scuttering up Downing Street, hats in hands, to implore the Prime Minister to make the mine-owners negotiate, they would have appreciated Jix's egregious absurdity. It was too much for me, and I drew a cartoon which scandalized hysterical readers who had been emoting themselves into the belief that this pathetic farce was the beginning of a revolution and that Ernie Bevin and Jimmy Thomas were the British equivalent of Lenin and Trotsky.

THE COMMITTEE OF PUBLIC SAFETY displayed Baldwin, Churchill, Jix and Birkenhead sitting around their council table, dressed in the picturesque French modes of the Robespierre period, waiting for the hour of crisis. Each face has a tinge of satisfaction, save that of Baldwin, who listens anxiously with earphones to a cat's whisker radio; proclamation on the wall, coal reports on the floor; the taxpayer trying on the guillotine for size; two tailcoated civil servants loyally mounting guard over the milk supply. An unsubtle jeer.

'That was a wicked cartoon, Low,' said Lord Beaverbrook, who had evidently been reading his own newspaper.

At zero hour the General Strike fell dead.

I had considered myself, coming from Australia, a seasoned hand in rough and tough politics, but the whole affair shocked me. This and The Disgraceful Election before it left me aghast at the revelation of how hypocritical were the 'decencies' of

British political life, how bitter the class-hatred from the top, how unscrupulous could be the 'gentlemen of England,' how crude the prejudices of the middle classes that would never take the trouble to learn the realities of their corporate life until their own selfish individual interests were touched. Most of all I was disgusted at the whole clutter of jealousies, sordid ambitions and idiotic suspicion of 'brains' that hampered trade union and Labour Party relations and had led to this ludicrous fiasco. At such time one is apt to forget the small minority of noble selfless idealists who leaven the whole and redeem the British character.

It seemed to me that the opportunity for building a better, juster and more stable Britain afforded by the weakening of obstructive vested interests had now finally slipped down the drain. The inevitable would come about the hard way, as usual.

Five years later on I sat at Transport House talking to Ernie Bevin about the actors in this bad show. He put it all down to Winston Churchill, then Chancellor of Exchequer, for returning the country to the gold standard without warning and throwing the whole wage structure out of gear (though Ernie didn't mention that at the time). Bevin had been the dynamic organizer of the welter of suspicious factions into unity. But he couldn't organize the miners. They wouldn't stay organized. He had had no confidence in the idea of a general strike himself. His own big idea was to build up the T.U.C. to the point when such a thing would be unnecessary.

'They couldn't do that to *me*.' '*I* could never accept that.' The frequent use of 'I' and 'me' was characteristic of Ernie's conversation. Such a vital and forceful man just naturally came to identify the whole Labour movement with himself. (I heard that Ernie was the original of the story of the massive figure coming around the corner with the light behind him that so impressed a foreign visitor that he stopped in affright ejaculating '*Mon Dieu!*' 'No,' said Ernie and passed on.)

He flashed a small black eye with spleen when Jimmy Thomas's name came up. 'As soon as Jimmy showed his nose around the door I could see he had done it to me.' Thomas, it seemed, was the culprit, not for having got them into it but for having ignominiously got them out of it. A couple of weeks later I happened along at the N.U.R. office and talked to Thomas on the same subject. He evaded my hints with manifest embarrassment. But for all that, it seemed to me he was the only sensible one in the bunch.

One lesson, at any rate, was rubbed into the trade unions. It is less trouble to go through the door than to push the walls down. Revolutionary strikes don't mix with political democracy. Faith without brains doesn't get you very far in politics. After that, the unions paid more attention to getting their representatives into Parliament and making proper use of their political powers.

These happenings gave my cartoons a sharper edge. In the hour of crisis Baldwin had made through the loud speaker his famous 'Can't You Trust Me?' speech, and with this as a general theme I followed faithfully the implementation of the trust as events unfolded. True, whether the miners trusted the Prime Minister or not subsequently became almost irrelevant, for he could do nothing with his party diehards or the coal- and mine-owners. In due course the shining hour of victory was improved by the passage of measures designed to weaken the link between the unions and the Labour Party. The miners went back with their problems unsolved, and bitterness grew in the pits for which succeeding generations have had to pay through the nose. But continuity was preserved . . . and there was plenty of sweet singing in the London gutters by parties of abandoned miners heralding the collapse of 1931.

13

A T about this time I was having the same old fight about space with the *Star*. It was proposed that the size of my cartoons in the paper be cut below what I knew to be the essential minimum. I was unable to convince my writer colleagues that reducing the size of a picture was not like, in the case of writing, setting up an article in smaller type, but more like removing from the article all adjectives and adverbs. I could not go on drawing without satisfaction in the published results of my labours. Claustrophobia set in. Desperate, I thought of Beaverbrook.

Three years before he had offered to double my salary if I left the *Star* and joined his *Evening Standard*. I had refused, for I thought I already had the essentials of well-being (except for this vexation about space), my tastes were simple and I was wary of getting myself used to soft living. I had no particular yearning for any increase of influence that might go with association with Lord B., although I was interested in life and in politics as an important part of it. How could I hope to explain an attitude of mind like that to such a business 'realist'? Paradoxically, it would have to be done in terms of money and purely material self-interest. So long as money was the measure of value I would have to demand stiff terms to show I was valuable to myself, and maintain that I couldn't be valuable to him also unless I had large space, good reproduction and a completely free hand. The proposition might seem a little peculiar, but Beaverbrook was a peculiar man.

To the eye of a stranger, the First World War had left the English with their social codes, customs and conventions preserved, if visibly destined for change. The respect for institutions remained, reinforced by traditional loyalty to family, class, sect, party, leader and monarchy. To the English this loyalty, so far as public practice was concerned, was sufficiently demonstrated by conformity to custom.

Beaverbrook did not fit this frame at all. He dislocated the pattern, ruptured the continuity, pushed traditions and institutions around. His loyalty was placed where and when, in his arbitrary judgment, at any given time, it was deserved. He certainly did not conform to anything. He was nobody but himself.

A man like that had ready-made enemies. The disturbance of the peace, the upsetting of the status quo, always has an unnatural and wicked air to the weaklings who feel safe only when clinging tooth and nail to their preconceived ideas, unable to move. Beaverbrook would have had his opponents even had his nonconformity been passive. But it was in fact challenging. He was one of those uncomfortable things to have about the house, a merger.

Two simple ideas underlaid the success story of his young self, Max Aitken, in Canadian business: mergers and the exploitation of new values arising therefrom. His subsequent story in British politics had run on the same lines. His main political operations had been all mergers, achieved or attempted, of people, parties and/or policies: the coalition of Lloyd George and Bonar Law/Carson in 1916; the absorption of the Liberal Party into the Tory Party, which had been his parliamentary tactic ever since the Labour Party grew to government size; the mixture of protection and free trade he called 'Empire Free Trade'; the combination of paternalism and popular reform he thought was democracy . . .

He was a born merger. His natural gifts of persuasion developed to a high point of genius as he learned from practical experience the science of Adequate Preparation and the art of Charm. The reconciliation of irreconcilables, the mixture of oil and water, presented to him not insuperable difficulties but interesting possibilities—even probabilities. The enjoyment of his big talent led the business man to become an artist attempting things for their own sakes, seeing how far he could go, exercising for a lark. He went around merging for the fun of it, bringing opposites together in incongruous circumstances. Innocent guests to his board found themselves seated next to their deadly enemies with their host, a glint in his eye, taking scientific observations. This amiable and, indeed, in some respects, highly praiseworthy foible accounted for his reputation as a whimsical mischief-maker. It accounted even for his wish to have me on his paper.

174

'If ever Max gets to Heaven, he won't last long,' said H. G. Wells to me one night as we left Stornoway House after Beaverbrook had been holding forth on John Knox. 'He will be chucked out for trying to pull off a merger between Heaven and Hell . . . after having secured a controlling interest in key subsidiary companies in both places, of course.'

I had heard all about his doings before my time, the success story, the mergers, the cement, the affinity with Bonar Law; of how he had unmade Asquith and made Lloyd George; and of how, after making a mistake and finding himself cast away in the House of Lords, he had fallen almost inadvertently into the newspaper business and was on the way to making the moribund old *Daily Express* into not only a great business success, but a kind of alternative government.

From then on it had become possible to keep an eye on him for myself. There had been other proprietors of popular newspapers who openly used them for exerting their personal power. Northcliffe, for instance. But Beaverbrook was unique in that he was also skilled in dialectic, the 1–2–3 clickety-click of exposition, and a political expert, with the uninhibited approach of the overseas mind separated by two generations from local orthodoxy. Gad, sir, what could be done with a 'Conservative' who thought nothing of trampling a herd of Canadian cattle (politically speaking) over his own party leaders and then blithely resisted the efforts of the Carlton Club either to make him resign or to itself resign from him? It would have taken a blacksmith to fix a party label on such a man even in 1920. The bitter rage of right-wing Tories was not at all assuaged by his explanation that he did not oppose the Government but only the men in it. In the face of their obtuseness and unreason, Beaverbrook gave himself the key of the Street and had his Independence Day. 'The normal attitude of the Press towards politicians must be one of complete independence,' he declared. 'Fleet Street dealt with Downing Street on independent and equal terms.' Thereafter his independence grew to be so important that he felt he had to justify himself whenever he found himself in agreement with anybody.

The mortification of his critics was that, like it or not, he was not always wrong. Indeed, gad, sir, Lord Beaverbrook was often right. He opposed Churchill's futile anti-Bolshevik crusade in 1920; and the Black-and-Tans in Ireland. After the First World War he came out for increased taxation on war profiteers. He opposed Ll. G.'s pro-Greek policy, and as though by arrangement with Lord B., the Greeks turned round and fled back in confusion to the coast with the Turks behind them. He went to Berlin on a financial quiz and reported unfavourably on the mark. The mark promptly collapsed.

It was all rather like the story told about Father Divine, the American negro evangelist, who, when the police court judge who decided against him dropped dead the next day, turned up his eyes and said: 'Ah hated to do it.'

He was right about Britain's thankless Zionist role in Palestine; about the Curzon-or-Baldwin-for-Prime-Minister question; and about Baldwin's futile policy of prosperity-through-wage-cuts. He was frequently right.

But the successes of his judgment pointed his failure. For although, when taken separately, they might seem to be the outcome of oracular prophecy and realistic vision, taken together they were revealed as the day-to-day, year-to-year haphazard expedients and shifts forwarding the consistent Beaverbrook ideals: at home, a place safe for capitalism in which the workers work and the capitalists capitalize; and abroad, British withdrawal from 'foreign entanglements' to within a closed Empire. Empire Free Trade, the policy calculated to realize the latter aim, and the *sine qua non* of Beaverbrookism, was never successful. For a very simple reason. Neither Britain, nor the Dominions, nor the Empire, nor the Commonwealth wanted it. Even the staff of the *Daily Express* didn't want it. Nobody wanted it—except Lord Beaverbrook. Little B-peep's overdue ewe-lamb never came home wagging its tail behind it.

Beaverbrook reduced political dining to a fine art. An invitation to dinner at Beaverbrook's, as I pointed out in one of my cartoons at the time, was apt to be considered by the invitees with the care of Romans considering invitations from the Borgias. The important stages of his political manœuvring were usually done to the music of mastication at his 'little suburban villa,' the Vineyard, or his comfortable country house, Cherkley, at Leatherhead. Sometimes his 'subjects' became aware of this and tried to counter by inviting *him* to *their* tables; but Lord Beaverbrook was too well aware of the advantages of playing on the home ground. Winston tried to spike his guns before introducing his budget by inviting him to lunch at Chartwell, but Lord B. declined. Ll. G. craftily tried to rope him in to breakfast at Downing Street, but unsuccessfully.

The best evidence of the high motives behind this hospitality was that the host obviously enjoyed it hugely. As much could not always be said of all the guests, hardly ever of those outside looking in. His masterpiece, the famous series of meals in 1916 which culminated in Lloyd George finding the Prime Minister-ship on his plate, had elements of tragedy as well as of comedy— but that was an historic occasion. Normally the emotional com-bination was rather astonishment and exasperation. Lord Curzon, the Foreign Secretary, for instance, could hardly appreciate the call of duty that prompted Lord B. to get the Prime Minister down to his beautiful home at Leatherhead and very nearly sell him the idea of sending him, Lord B., as British plenipotentiary to negotiate a deal with Mustapha Kemal . . . Bonar Law, Birkenhead and Churchill couldn't have been too pleased when at a week-end party they were working up to the point of imparting to him Lloyd George's letter to the Sinn Feiners (ssh, strictly confidential!) to have Beaverbrook come back by imparting to them (also in the strictest confidence) the Sinn Feiners' reply, which he had written for them himself at the suggestion of Tim Healy. (Which was true enough. The Irishmen, doughty fighters against the British as enemies, needed advice in the formalities of intercourse with the British as diplomats and through the agency of Tim Healy had got it from Lord B.)

There were the cosy parties of the early 'twenties when enough soured ex-Coalition Ministers passed through the Beaverbrook dining-room to form a government in exile: Churchill, dis-gruntled because God had created Baldwin; Beaver himself, dis-gruntled because of the poor look-out for imperial preference; and the others . . . jovially passing the acid clockwise around the table and exchanging side-splitting plans for blowing up prime ministers.

There was the black day when the company must have gnashed its teeth through napery, crockery, cutlery and all. Winston, the darling of the disgruntled as the advocate of economy, lower taxes and down with Baldwin's American debt settlement, had, with the energetic help of the Beaverbrook and Rothermere Presses, given the Tory Party machine a bad shake at a by-election. Its leaders capitulated, presented him with a safe seat, and what he wanted, the position of Chancellor of the Exchequer—at last! Whereupon he swallowed hard and ditched Lords B. and R. and the dinner circle by doing the very reverse of their expectations.

With all these prima donnas flying about, Montague, Ll. G., Winston, F.E., Worthy-Evans and Co., the famous 'genius for political friendship' involved keeping a date-pad to be sure when one shook the hand of A and turned the back on B, and vice versa.

It was in connection with two minor instances of these culinary manœuvres that I had my first professional relations with Beaverbrook. A large delegation of editors from the Dominions had come to London and Beaverbrook took the opportunity to stage a lavish dinner for them, and invited Lloyd George to make the speech of the evening, in the belief and hope that, in the empire atmosphere, some compromising reference to imperial preference might be conjured out of him. Beaverbrook invited me by letter to design the menu card. Whether my design, an innocuous piece of work representing an infinite variety of Ll. G,s, one capering on a plate before each editor, raised or lowered the harmony of the occasion, the political purpose of the occasion did not come off, for Ll. G. was too fly. He slid all around imperial preference without mentioning it once.

Then Beaverbrook had the inspiration of having me paint a mural panorama of caricatures of his friends to go around his dining-room. I couldn't work up enthusiasm for the idea. I thought it would drive him nuts. He got someone else to do it, but by the time it was finished he had fallen out with so many of the individuals depicted that it never went up.

The picturesque side of this olla podrida, as much as its public importance, had impressed me as a political cartoonist, and some months earlier I had begun to introduce Beaverbrook into my cartoons in the *Star*. He was not a ready-made subject for caricature. Large head, boyish face, full cheeks, wide forehead, unruly hair, small nose with peculiar curve, wide grin belied by sharp light eye, slight small figure, short neck, high shoulders, neat extremities, hairy hands, undistinguished dark blue suit. The whole thing lay in the wide grin belied by the sharp eye. It was some time before I could make anything at all out of this outfit, but in the end I built up a version which was not so much like him as like the kind of man he was, if you know what I mean, and started him off. The relationship between art and nature is sometimes very curious. The one imitates the other and, strangely enough, vice versa. As my Beaverbrook grew, with my increasing familiarity with its original, a closer likeness to him, *he* grew more like *it*. When at last I got to know him well enough to persuade him to 'sit' for me in comparative stillness for a few moments (something of an ordeal for everybody,

178

with telephones going incessantly, people rushing in and out with documents, and the gracious presence of Lady Beaverbrook peeping over my shoulder), I found the characteristics fallen into linear place and the circle practically squared.

His first appearance in my cartoons was entitled BABE IN THE WOOD, and showed Stanley Baldwin as the babe lost in tariff reform and highly apprehensive about the intentions of wicked uncles Beaverbrook and Rothermere.

Troubles between these three had been coming to the boil for a long time. Beaverbrook had plenty of grounds for annoyance. In the first place Baldwin had got all the credit for upsetting the Coalition Government, whereas he, Beaverbrook, thought *he* had done it. Again, Baldwin let the Prime Minister, Bonar Law, Beaverbrook's most bosom friend, in for the disadvantageous American debt settlement, which Beaverbrook found it difficult to scuttle without scuttling also Bonar Law. Then, on top of that, when Bonar Law retired and Baldwin, as the new Prime Minister, headed for the Protection Election, tossing imperial preference (Beaverbrook's political pet) aside like a soiled glove, all without word of explanation or apology to Lord B. . . . this was the last straw. Especially when Lord B. remembered that he had practically given young Baldwin his start in life by recommending him to Bonar Law as parliamentary secretary in Coalition days.

As Law's most faithful friend in life and after, Beaverbrook had appointed himself Law's political executor to dispose of assets like the Conservative majority, which he regarded as Law's personal political property. In this light, Baldwin's action appeared to be desecration, larceny and wilful sabotage, and Beaverbrook not only said so in the *Daily Express*, but had Rothermere saying so in the *Daily Mail*, too. (Lord B. was always ready to agree with his business and political rivals when he could persuade them that they agreed with him.) All, read the public, was being lost. Baldwin was forcing the Conservative Party to commit suicide.

Baldwin did not take it in good part and wounding words were bellowed from the housetops in a notorious 'interview' in which he was reported to have said he wouldn't have Beaverbrook or Rothermere in his house. Since few people in Fleet Street knew whether Baldwin's house was desirable or attractive, no one could measure the depth of longing frustrated in the two newspaper Barons, but 'them was fightin' words.' Newspapers outside of the Beaverbrook–Rothermere family tacitly agreed that if there were not a vendetta, there ought to be. Thereupon, on behalf of both parties to the dispute, all expostulations were brushed aside and

THE PLOT PRESS

they declared a vendetta to be in existence and began accordingly to print heavy articles on The Function of the Press in Society, The Responsibilities of Criticism, and so on. Lord B. himself, goaded beyond endurance despite his proclaimed imperviousness to criticism, weighed in with a booklet, price one shilling, giving a version leaving Caesar's wife cold for sheer purity and chastity, which he pushed to a mass sale with all the energy of his machine.

All this was made for a cartoonist. It was, in fact, comic strip stuff. I tried one or two cartoons developing the two press lords along from the wicked uncles in BABE IN THE WOOD into the 'Plot Press', two mischievous conspirators in mock-sinister cloaks and hats. The figures, fat Rother and little Beaver, were such 'naturals' to draw and the newspaper public gave them such popularity that in no time I found myself running a series dealing with their dark doings. Various incidents and accidents turned up by grinning fate in succeeding months tended to support and confirm the lightsome fancy. There were, among other things, a misplaced document supplied to Lord Birkenhead by Beaverbrook's *Sunday Express* which bedevilled a debate in the Lords upon the delicate Greek situation; and a mysterious trip by Beaverbrook to Palestine which left the nation wondering what was going to happen next. The Plot Press became one of my major properties and a regular feature of the *Star*.

Rothermere, who was very sensitive to criticism of himself, hated it. Not so Beaverbrook. He asked me to dinner.

I was slightly perturbed when this invitation arrived. I received my directions to meet His Lordship's car in an alley off Fleet Street. It was a dark conspiratorial night. The car was a long black shape. An obsequious shadow edged me into its black depths. Wait . . . wait . . . wait . . . a smaller livelier shadow jumps in quickly—away we go—my hand is grasped. Thereupon the invisible companion fired a cross-examination of questions. 'You're Low?' asks a gravel voice. 'Yes.' Couldn't see him. 'You're a New Zealander?' 'Yes.' 'How old are you? Are you married? Do you drink? . . .' (Well, I'm blowed! Who does this bloke think he is?) I told him as much as I thought was good for him.

We arrived, but I could not see where because of the darkness. Within, the suburban villa proved to be a commodious place with fourteen rooms. He hurried through a door leaving me high and dry in the passage. 'Come in, Low,' and I pushed open the door, then halted by an unexpected vision of his Lordship in his underclothing. Ho, I said to myself, the new technique, eh? (I had heard other guests of his Lordship report having had their reserve broken down by the test of having unexpectedly to bear the sight of their host naked, changing into his dinner things). Dressed, we repaired to a brightly lit long room where a joyous company of about twenty were in the middle of what could only be described as a baronial repast. Bright eyes and merry laughter. Lovely ladies with Valentine Castlerosse, pink with geniality, champagne glass in hand, at the end of the table, the centre piece. The scene was a ready-made cartoon. So this is how the rich live, I reflected. To think I am sitting, probably in the very chair in which prime ministers got their marching orders, statesmen cut one another's throats, the downfall of governments was arranged. Lord Beaverbrook proved an excellent host and I enjoyed my dinner tremendously.

'What will you drink, Low?' roared his Lordship from ten people away in imperial tones suggesting unlimited cellars.

'I would like a nice cup of tea,' I answered with somewhat damp colonial bravado.

A momentary hush fell on the company . . .

After dinner a piece of the wall miraculously fell away at one end of the room, a screen descended at the other and we had a cinema. In 1924 this was unheard-of luxury. I settled down to to enjoy Felix the Cat, but his Lordship drew me aside. He fixed me with a steady calculating eye and I put on my best Simple Simon look. (Here it comes.) The proposition was that I should leave the *Star* and draw cartoons for the *Evening Standard* at double my salary, whatever it was. Flabbergasted, I made refusing noises. 'What do you want?' he asked. In the circumstances, I could not start explaining that what I wanted was happiness, not a plenitude of purchasable pleasures. Besides, it might have seemed irrelevant. So I passed the question off.

He was persistent. To close the subject I said I wished to take the advice of my friends H. G. Wells and Arnold Bennett. He cordially agreed, and I decided not to trouble either, because I knew Lord B. would immediately telephone both and fix their approval beforehand. Which was exactly what he did do.

During the next three years I dodged delicately without rupturing the amicable relations thus begun—no easy matter, considering that he shouted this offer of his at me whenever we met, regardless of whoever was present. Beaverbrook was unused to taking no for an answer. It got about in Fleet Street and I had a lot of free advice from mutual friends who felt it their duty to protect a helpless artist from the Prince of Darkness. It would have surprised Lord Beaverbrook (or would it, after all?) to know what some people thought of him.

Came the day when through a third party I agreed to discuss a contract. The negotiations were no more protracted than those for an international treaty, but not much less. The crucial clause, which I drew up myself, was unequivocal:

'POLICY: It is agreed that you are to have complete freedom in the selection and treatment of subject-matter for your cartoons and in the expression therein of the policies in which you believe.'

It was an unprecedented arrangement. No one else on the paper had such a contract. Indeed I heard later that no one else on the paper had a contract at all.

Negotiations ended when I called on Lord Beaverbrook one morning at noon, finding him sitting up in bed, a plaintive figure like Camille, reading the Bible. He had promised me four half-pages a week, but I wanted precise guarantees about presentation. 'Dammit, Low,' said Lord B. 'Do you want to edit the paper, too?'

The signing was an odd ceremonial. By invitation, I presented myself with two of his executives at his Lordship's comparatively magnificent office on the top floor of the old *Daily Express* office, the one with the three-cornered view of St. Paul's, the bookshelves full of classics and the four electric fires. At first I couldn't see him at all, though I heard his words of welcome, punctuated by sighs. There he was, lying on the flat of his back on the carpet behind the grand piano, practising breathing exercises. 'Glad to . . . euffff . . . have you with us, Low . . . euffff . . .' He remained supine so long that I began to wonder whether he would get up, or whether I was expected to lie down too. Finally he arose and we completed the business and wetted our whistles. He reached for a telephone and rang up Arnold Bennett. 'I win,' he said. I felt vaguely disappointed in myself.

I spent sleepless nights before making my debut on the *Evening Standard*. What had I let myself in for?

The technical conditions promised to be grand, but I felt I was sticking my innermost self into the lion's mouth. The *Evening Standard* advertised my coming lavishly. No one took seriously the announcements that I was to express independent views. That was a novel idea, except for an occasional series of signed articles by some big name. Free and regular expression by the staff cartoonist was unheard of and incredible. Newspaper comments made it only too depressingly evident that in the general view I had sold out to the highest bidder. Friends began to give me peculiar looks. I became suddenly popular with strangers who pumped my hand with sickening congratulations and assurances that, after all, prostitution was quite respectable if the pay were high enough.

In my perturbation I grew exaggeratedly defensive. To the smooth friendliness of my associates-to-be I returned boorish rudeness. I determined to see that the crucial clause in my contract was observed to the letter or bust. Any jiggery-pokery and I would wreck the joint.

14

THE *Evening Standard* had a smaller circulation than the *Star*, but it was a West End sale among the upper middle-classes. The Tory clubman's evening paper.

Remarkable how newspaper-reading publics live in water-tight compartments, unaware of what goes on next door. To the mass of *Star* readers it was as though I had vanished without trace. To that of *Evening Standard* readers, as though I had been discovered, without past, by Lord Beaverbrook.

My first week was experimental as I felt out the possibilities of the new conditions and the receptivity of the new public. The blocks were good, the printing was better and the regular half-page space gave me scope. I started off with a cartoon displaying characters and symbols and personalities. It went well. I followed with one about taxation in a mythological analogy, to test the level of cultural awareness. A flop. The *Evening Standard* public was not up to Sin Baldwin and Devil MacDonald wrestling for the body of Alcestis Taxpayer. Then I tried broad farce. Not much response. Finally a political cartoon in the conventional form with personal portraits and a moral. That seemed to fit.

I do not know what precisely I had expected from the readers of the *Evening Standard*. A more educated audience, perhaps, more alert to symbolism and analogy. A party Conservative outlook, of course. A slightly higher level of appreciation of the nature of politics as a conflict of ideas rather than of parties and personalities, maybe?

I was not long in doubt. Almost immediately a copious correspondence began to pour into the office. At first the ratio of con to pro was about 75 to 25, but on a second wind enough pros turned up for the figures to break fairly even, which was not bad, because all newspaper people know that readers who like you don't write, whereas those who don't do. 'What shall we do with all this corre- spondence?' says the editor, worried. 'Print it!' says the master-mind. (By Jove, I thought, that is really clever! My estimate of Beaverbrook went steeply up.) After that the *Evening Standard* published the cream of the letters intermittently and at such length as the circumstances of the day demanded. After all, the management had an investment to protect and publicize. I played up and answered back in both cartoons and prose. Hard words, not to mention splenetic insults, were exchanged. The correspondence grew and grew, rows over the cartoons

The Right Hon. Dress- Suit, M.P., wearing his Jimmy Thomas

became one of the features of the *Evening Standard*, the outside world became aware of a piquant situation. Something new. London sat up and began to take notice.

So far as a general understanding went, it was a complicating factor that in the nature of my technique I used individuals to symbolize policies and attitudes. The more simple-minded of my new readers were very apt to see merely the surface indignity and to complain violently of 'vulgar personality.' There was much acrimony, for instance, when I used the frequency with which J. H. Thomas appeared hobnobbing with lords arrayed in full evening-dress to continue from the *Star* his 'run' as 'The Right Hon. Dress-suit, M.P., wearing his Jimmy Thomas'—a symbol of the new respectability of the Labour Party. To these critics under the impression that Caricature and Comic Art were one and the same thing, the symbolic boiling-down of a phase of political movement into this caricature seemed to be only a coarse libel on Thomas's sartorial beauty. There was talk of 'hitting below the belt.' My own loyal defenders sprang to the rescue and controversy raged for a space about where exactly Jimmy wore his belt: inside his hat or around his ankles.

Again, because he had been the obvious type of that political school which professed supercilious contempt for the Labour Party as 'unfit to govern,' and because he had never attempted to conceal his own possession of superior brains, I rechristened Lord Birkenhead 'Lord Burstinghead.' A first-class conflict arose immediately between my friends and his friends who demanded, seriously and quite regardless of the point, that I substitute 'Bestinhead.'

Usually the originals were not as sensitive about these attentions as were their admirers and followers. Some, on the contrary, were even pleased. Thomas was a friendly soul and I saw him often.

'I will hand you down to posterity, Jimmy,' I said to him.

'You don't 'and me down to posterity, David; you 'ound me down,' says he. While my mail was filled with angry letters from readers accusing me of gross assault on Thomas's dignity, there were very few cartoons about him that were not followed by an appreciative note next morning to 'dear David' from 'J.T.' The dress-suit, by the way, passed into the common currency, and was soon being used by other political cartoonists.

Lord Birkenhead, on the other hand, showed some resentment, which was rather odd, considering that he himself was a master of invective who did not scruple to deliver the most bitter and cutting wit at anybody's expense. He gave Beaverbrook a beautiful photograph of himself to pass on to me as a guide to his own personal configuration, from which might be deduced a considerable susceptibility to flattery.

'Why doesn't Low caricature himself?' asked an angry correspondent. Thus invited I did so, and thereafter I appeared fairly regularly in my own cartoons in a kind of 'Common-Man' capacity. The representation was, I must confess, not strictly approximate, even caricaturally. Pursuing a theory that small men most easily engage the affections of the public, I diminished my real size and recreated myself as a sad little Charlie Chaplin kind of character for public use.

The correspondence continued until at length it became accepted as normal, and was referred to in the *Evening Standard* office as 'Low's heavenly choir.' Besides having its value as a direct poll on reader-interest, it was instructive as to the difficulty of communicating ideas. Speech, an etymologist friend of mine used to tell me, is, as compared with pictures, an imperfect means of conveying thought because a word is 'loaded' with extraneous idea associations, whereas a line can have none and can express purely. He overlooked that just as a letter can express nothing until it is included in a word, a line, merely, can express nothing until it is shaped into a form—and that a form also can be 'loaded.' When the form expresses allegory, analogy, pictorial metaphor, when it conveys its meaning indirectly by a sideways approach or in terms of similarity to another idea, it may indeed be 'loaded', it may be highly explosive. I had some trouble then, as I have always had before and since, in accustoming my spectators, especially those with literal minds, to the individual peculiarities of my imagery. There was the man who protested angrily against my double-headed Ass of Coalition days, maintaining that there could be no such animal. There was the occasion when I drew a cartoon severely criticizing the design of the then new memorial to Nurse Cavell and was insulted by Sir Ian Hamilton at Claridge's, the old war-horse being under the impression that I had criticized Nurse Cavell.

I had considerable trouble also with people who were so accustomed to the innocuous humour of the time that any comment that was not banal seemed to them to be an intrusion, if not a deliberate outrage. Many correspondents of this kind wrote much of my 'bad taste.' But since they usually began by making villainous puns on my name I did not take them very seriously as arbiters of taste.

A comparatively innocent cartoon of mine about the Navy was a case in point. The Admiralty had issued a statement that, as a result of an enquiry held at Malta into certain disciplinary matters, three senior officers of *Royal Oak* had been suspended from duty by the Commander-in-Chief of the Mediterranean station. A report that a rear-admiral had struck his flag was confirmed. At the subsequent courts-martial which were followed closely by the startled nation, it appeared that the trouble had grown out of a series of differences between the Admiral and the officers of his flagship, and especially one about the kind of music played at a dance on board. The Admiral, it was alleged, had said in a loud and heated manner: 'I don't think I ever heard such a bloody awful noise in my life'; had called the bandmaster a bastard, and was only mollified when a jazz band was substituted. My cartoon, a harmless enough piece of fun entitled SYNCOPATED DISCIPLINE RECITAL ON THE 'ROYAL OAK' showed the court-martial proceeding along jazz band lines with the three Admirals at the drums, the chief witness giving his evidence on a trombone, officers in attendance accompanying on the saxophone, banjo, etc. It seemed to me to be a gentle jest, but it appeared I was mistaken. In no time it was the talk of the town. Sitting at lunch with a friend at Groom's Coffee House in Fleet Street, I was surprised to hear the people at the table on my left discussing the cartoon. Then I became aware that those at the table on my right were discussing it too. Next day when I called at the office there was a really amazing mound of letters with the features-editor and two assistants trying to sort it. 'It's up to you to help us,' says he. What a fuss! All the retired admirals in the country seemed to have taken a day off to fire broadsides. 'Execrable,' 'Blackguardly insult,' 'Foul filth,' 'Aptly named Low,' 'How long . . .' etc. I got a bit bored with reading other people's letters so I sat down and wrote one myself and slipped it in for publication:

> Sir,
> I am disgusted with some of the letters you print concerning the cartoons of my nephew Low. It astounds me that you should sell the *Evening Standard* to such people. I have advised my nephew (a more gentlemanly lad never lived) to stop drawing cartoons for your paper until you promise not to let these persons have *Evening Standards*. It is perfectly disgusting. Gad, sir, I wish I were 75 years younger.
>
> HORATIO LOW,
> (Hon. Lieut.-Col. of the Golders Green Fire Brigade)
> Golders Green, N.W.11.

I was touched when next day somebody sent a bunch of flowers and expressions of sympathy to my 'uncle.' Criticism settled down, so to speak, to a howling gale with seas rising to sixty feet on the port bow and top-mizzen-mast blown away before tailing down to a sinister swell.

It was perhaps too much of a good thing that shortly afterwards, again inadvertently, I touched another wider and even more sensitive section of opinion on the raw. The offence was a cartoon referring to difficulties which a famous writer on the subject of birth control had experienced with censorship in the Irish Free State. The cartoon was entitled ATTEMPTED REVOLUTION IN DUBLIN—*Capture of Desperate Person Found to be in Possession of Complete Set of Marie Stopes*. It represented President Cosgrave squeezed between two portly Roman Catholic bishops in a large official car heading a procession of a tight-lipped Censor on a white horse and an armed escort for the wretched malefactor, the latter's wife and ten children bringing up the rear. The onlooking crowd was composed of traditional Irish types of archaic burlesque with button noses, long upper lips and upside-down short cutty pipes.

I should have known well enough from my own family connections and from experience in Australian politics that Irish wit is largely a myth, that the Irish are a mystical people,

Detail of *Attempted Revolution in Dublin*

and that the sense of proportion which governs the perception of humour does not, with them, cover cherished hopes, fears and beliefs.

This cartoon had no particular axe to grind. It was, in fact, just a bit of fun about a topic of public interest. True, birth control was then rather less openly discussed than it is today; and no doubt my rooted dislike of the censorship of opinion and my disinclination to accept without protest the subservience of any democratic government to ecclesiastical authority both peeped through. But I was not prepared for the hullabaloo that followed. Judging from the volume of protests that poured into the *Standard* office, the Brannigans, the O'Flahertys and the Macnamaras appeared to be rising as one man against me. It was not necessary for me to take part, for the Dooleys, the Hooleys and the O'Tooles flocked to my defence.

Moral coat-tails flew and verbal shillelaghs whirled. Violent and coarse abuse boiled through post and telephone. I learned that the files of my past cartoons were being gone over with a tooth-comb for indecencies, presumably in the hope of finding something to prove my personal worthlessness. *The Catholic Herald* lashed itself to fury about 'advocates of the obscenities of birth control endeavouring to introduce into the homes of the country the devices used by prostitutes in carrying out their trade,' which was perhaps overdoing it a little. 'This sort of filth flung at the Irish Free State, and the Catholic Church and the Irish people generally . . . the Lows and the Beaverbrooks' (poor innocent Max) 'defame, denounce, calumniate and jeer at the Irish people . . .' 'The most important aspect,' said the *Catholic Times*, heavily elevating the occasion to national level, 'is the discourtesy shown to a member of the Commonwealth of Nations.' It seemed as as though the whole Roman Catholic community wanted my blood.

Still turning the other cheek, I devoted another cartoon to depicting myself ON TRIAL BEFORE THE DUBLIN OGPU—*Accused Makes Full Confession* with the following text:

The trial took place today before Judges Hooligan, Harrigan and Flanagan, of Old Low, charged with having drawn a cartoon entitled REVOLUTION IN DUBLIN showing the alleged arrest by alleged Free State authorities of an alleged Irishman, alleged to be in possession of a complete set of Marie Stopes. Accused, who wept bitterly, confessed that said cartoon was propaganda designed to 'sabotage' the Free State and named Mr. Stalin, M. Briand and President Hoover as in the plot.

Cross-examined by Crown Prosecutor Dooley, accused admitted that President Cosgrave never in his life sat, as depicted, in a car with two bishops. It would be foul libel to say that President Cosgrave sat anywhere with two bishops.

He withdrew unreservedly the chief implication that Free State authorities would discourage their citizens from possessing copies of 'listed' books; and he agreed that the Censorship was an advertising organization aiming at the sale and distribution of such 'listed' books through the Free State. Accused was sentenced to death amid howls of applause.

That should have ended the matter. But it did not. This, alas, was a story 'to be continued.'

I grew sick of being a target. I didn't mind political disagreement but it was evident that a lot of people were confused not only about the art of caricature, but about the function of the satirist in society. So I took time off to write a good long article putting everybody right. The *Evening Standard* starred it up and when the foreign newscuttings came in I was flattered to find it had a world-wide audience.

Fundamentally, I explained, the misunderstanding between myself and my critics was that they had the Wrong Idea. They lumped humour, wit and satire together without discernment, and taking the least common element of innocuous fun as the standard, found wit with a controversial point maladjusted or 'in bad taste.' Naturally they looked to me for amusement and their conception of 'good taste.' And sometimes found neither. Amusement was only an occasional by-product of wit or satire. Some master-wits had been notably solemn fellows and much wit or satire, including some of my own, was not intended to be funny at all. 'Mere amusement,' said Swift, 'is the happiness of those who cannot think.'

Other critics who *did* recognize the quality of satire took the view that a satirist should defer to the finer feelings of his readers and respect widely-held beliefs. According to them there were definite limitations to the subject-matter suitable for caricatures, or 'cartoons,' which it was the satirist's social duty to observe. Another misapprehension. I explained that whatever might be the duty of a satirist, it certainly could not be to reflect, confirm or pander to popular beliefs. Rather the opposite, for it was popular beliefs themselves that were frequently the aptest material for the healthiest satire. Popular beliefs were all too often popular prejudices and were nearly always founded upon undue respect or reverence for someone or something. The very essence of satire was disrespect and irreverence.

To the imputation that this disrespect and irreverence must be informed by malice, the obvious answer was that malice was an attribute of the individual, not of the form of expression. To the charge of malice and 'vulgarity' levelled at myself, I took as a standard of comparison the works of Gillray, Rowlandson and company, who were generally agreed to be the old masters of Caricature, with copious examples of their works: the celebrities of their time in the most ridiculous aspects and sometimes in the most indecent situations, unpleasantly fat people over-eating themselves or embracing their loathsome lady-loves. THE UNION CLUB, for example, which showed the prominent statesmen all drunk under the table; Gillray's picture of the reigning monarch lying in a tousled bed surrounded by bottles; and his scandalous versions of Pitt, Fox and the Broad-bottomed Ministry.

Gillray, Rowlandson and company worked for their day, not for ours. Times had changed. It may be debatable whether the swing away from 'coarseness' in early Victorian times represented a victory for true refinement or for sycophancy and hypocrisy, but certainly the spirit of graphic satire in England had weakened. The traditions of caricature had declined. It put on kid gloves, it sprayed its chest with lavender. It modified itself to such an extent that it almost ceased to be. The very name 'caricature' was dropped in favour of a nice new one, 'cartoon.'

The circumspect 'cartoons' of John Leech and Tenniel were a sign of the times; so also were the respectful 'pencillings' of Dicky Doyle. Artists concerned themselves with producing mildly humorous jests suitable for the family circle. 'Cartooning' was not so much satirical comment as humorous reporting. England had undoubtedly excellent humorous draughtsmen, but, in comparison with their opposite numbers in France and Germany, they had little to say.

From these degenerate practices had been deduced an etiquette of 'cartooning.' With considerable illogicality it was assumed by my critics in 1930 that there was a code of good behaviour for 'cartoonists,' to depart from which was to be unworthy of the supposed traditions of a completely misapprehended art.

I elbowed aside as undeserving of reasoned reply those of my critics who asserted that all caricature was ugliness without purpose. To those in whose view the caricature of the persons of public men was insulting and cruel, I pointed out that in reality the modern caricaturist was almost exaggeratedly considerate of the feelings of his subjects when real physical deformity or defect was concerned. Lord Irwin, for instance, had only one arm, but when caricatured he was given two. Snowden, again, walked with a limp on two sticks, but you would never have known it from his caricatures.

To others in whose opinion the personal appearance of great men was public property, their faces being regarded as component parts of the social or political scenery, but who held that, on the other hand, the personal habits of these great men were their own private and domestic concern, I demonstrated their strange wrong-headedness. People have to wear the faces that God has given them, and of all things these least deserve public scorn, while their habits are matters of choice, rightly deserving judgment and correction. The case of, say, J. H. Thomas's dress-suit, which had caused such protests, was an example. If to draw Thomas's dress-suit was bad, then how much worse was it to draw Thomas

192

himself within it. The public, however, was amenable to education in these matters. It was becoming recognized that the private lives and habits of statesmen were of the utmost importance to a democratic community.

Some people took the view that, while caricature and cartooning might be harmlessly amusing in general, there were analogies upon which it was objectionable for the artist to base his satire. Certain works of art, for instance, were invested with almost sacred qualities in their simple minds, demonstrating once again the common disposition to confuse the material with the spiritual. A cartoon based on that bathetic masterpiece in paint by Luke Fildes, *The Doctor*, seemed to be a sneer at infant mortality. A protest against Epstein's carved *Rima* of the bird sanctuary became a hymn of hate against the dicky-birds. . . . And yet the great Michelangelo himself is suspected of having literally given his enemies hell by placing their portraits in conspicuous positions in his picture *The Day of Judgment*, in which the nethermost place was reserved for a particular friend of his, a certain evilly-disposed cardinal. Leonardo da Vinci's forcible drawings of angels were said to preserve in many respects the features of the critics of his flying machine.

But it is in connection with subject-matter, as distinguished from treatment, analogy, and incidental personal portraiture, that a cartoonist (to give him henceforth the now universally accepted appellation) had to walk most delicately to avoid reproof. There were many subjects upon which the touch of the cartoonist was pronounced deplorable. Royalty or the institution of monarchy for example. If caricature had been exclusively a destructive art, no doubt that view would have been justified. But it was obvious that if the institution of monarchy were to survive in Britain after it had decayed elsewhere, it would be because the British people were aware of its weakness no less than of its strength. It was no matter for congratulation that a faint-hearted Press could not risk printing even the best works of great cartoonists on the subject. I could not regard that as a triumph of loyalty, but only of sycophancy.

The subjects of religion and the Church were thought unsuitable for the touch of the cartoonist. Yet in the Middle Ages caricature had been closely associated with the Church, and was, like the other arts, applied almost exclusively to the uses of the Church. The devil was the most frequent figure and the horrors of improper behaviour the most frequent subject of caricature. Observe the gargoyles, and the little carved compositions on the walls of mediæval churches.

If the satirist of 1930 refrained from laying pen upon monarchical or spiritual affairs, it should not be because his touch might appear unseemly, but because these affairs did not in these times obtrude into public business. But the same could not have been said of those more mundane institutions by which our daily life was ordered, and for which he, the satirist, in common with his fellows, bore the responsibility. It was his job to keep these institutions under constant examination.

The implied obligations of citizenship; the tendencies of society—with special reference to the causes which produce them and the probable consequences thereof; national and international relations; the sober use and the dangerous abuse of patriotic feeling; law and order; the public service; birth control; spiritualism; the Navy, the Army; the Press. . . . These were matters of real importance for inspiring subjects for the satirist. It was folly to say that all or any of these were 'untouchable' because there were strong differences of opinion about them. Truth and the Good remained unimpaired by ridicule. Only humbug died.

The appreciation of satire was a heavenly attribute which all did not possess to the same degree. That Gillray's caricatures could not appear in a newspaper of 1930 was no matter for regret. But, on the other hand, there was no reason why our national pictorial satire of the day should have been spiritless and tame. The average Englishman was not spiritless and tame. A caricature or cartoon of the true genre, while pleasing some, must at times displease others. It was too much to expect that when performing his function conscientiously a cartoonist could please everybody. The measure of a cartoonist's real success, therefore, should be not only how much approval he excited, but also how much disapproval. I was consoled, I wrote, when I thought of the people who troubled to tell me that they were disgusted with my cartoons. I bore them no ill-will. One day I proposed to form a Disgusted-with-Low League and to invite them to a smoking-concert at the Albert Hall.

15

THERE had been much fuss among *Evening Standard* readers about the matter and the manner of my work; but the main bone of contention was, of course, its political direction.

We cannot all be politicians even if we wanted to be, which most of us do not. The ideal of a thinking democracy is still a long way off. At its present stage of development, when people have not yet learned to use their own brains, many depend upon their newspapers to tell them what to believe about the passing world. Once confirmed in this dependence, which both relieves them of the bother of individual ratiocination and comforts them with the feeling that somebody has everything in hand, they have no wish to be reminded (especially in terms of satire) that there might be two sides to the question. The nightmare of uncertainty raises its head. Chasms yawn.

In a Conservative newspaper one expected to find Conservative cartoonists. As time passed and it became evident that I was not a Conservative cartoonist, the circumstance took on the appearance of a betrayal. Betrayal by whom? By Lord Beaverbrook, of course. This was a question which ranged beyond mere letters from readers. This was news itself. What lay behind the introduction of a wooden horse into the Tory Troy?

Motives were sought and the various deep thinkers came up with answers according to their occupational complexities. My apprehensions about Beaverbrook had been groundless and I was gratified to find that the alleged prince of darkness was scrupulous in observing my charter of independence, and even defended it against his friends. That was something to say when one considered that very soon he was being accused by his right-wing Tory critics of 'blackguardly bolshevism' for having opened his pages to me at all. Even sober foreign newspapers like the *New York Times* were scenting plots and writing, on my account, of his 'swing to the Left.'

> Lord Beaverbrook, according to gossip . . . was prepared to put himself and his newspapers at the disposal of Mr. Lloyd George if the latter would accept certain proposals. . . . These rumours started with an announcement that a certain very popular cartoonist who was working for a Liberal paper, had joined the staff of Lord Beaverbrook's *Evening Standard*, a Conservative organ. . . .

The *Manchester Guardian* thought the innocent explanation was that Lord B. had no particular party policy at all:

> . . . as can be seen from the fact that Mr. Low the caricaturist of the Radical *Star* has recently transferred his services to Lord Beaverbrook's Conservative *Evening Standard* with no apparent change in his political bias except to serve up Tory politicians with a more tartaric sauce.

The *Manchester Guardian* was not quite so sure a few days later. Maybe Lord B. *was* changing his party:

> . . . These rumours also declare that this newspaper magnate is moving with a Left-turn . . . and colour is given to this by the recent cartoons in the *Evening Standard* which are quite unsympathetic to the present Government—indeed, go as far as anything the caricaturist had done in his *Star* days.

Damn it! I said to myself. For a world always yawping so much about the freedom of its Press, the idea of one man's independence seems to take a lot of swallowing.

The most widely-held opinion, however, was that of a number of lesser journals which had it rather confusedly that Lord B. aimed at Downing Street and had hired me

(*a*) to stop my satirizing his efforts to become Prime Minister;
(*b*) to advertise, popularize and aid him to become Prime Minister.

In vain did Lord B. refute these speculations and inventions:

> . . . the case of Low's caricatures. My views as a shareholder in any newspaper are that its columns ought to be free and open to the expression of opinion by men and women of distinction. I should no more be in favour of excluding such

work because I disagreed with the opinions contained in it than I would countenance the colouring of news to suit preconceived ideas.

At least part of this declaration of journalistic ethics had been admirably acted upon so far as I was concerned; but this affirmation, awaiting the experiences of subsequent years, would have aroused no admiration in the *Morning Post* of 1929. Nettled by an observation of mine that what it called 'Mr. Baldwin's wholesome leadership' meant leadership into some hole, it shot me bang at his Lordship's brisket:

> There was the *Evening Standard* which week by week published cartoons whose whole intention was to hold up the Conservative leaders to ridicule and contempt with a malicious mockery not equalled in modern times. They were the work of a brilliantly gifted artist, whose political sympathies were amply revealed during his connection with the Radical Press, from which Lord Beaverbrook enlisted him; and it is sufficient criticism of the cartoons in the *Evening Standard* to say that their artist made no capitulation at all of his political sympathies. Nothing so inimical appeared in the Radical or Labour Press as the poison which Lord Beaverbrook thus purveyed.

Beaverbrook did not always laugh in the right place at my cartoons, and some galled him, but in the twenty-three years of my association with his newspapers I can recall only one cartoon being left unprinted because of a disagreement over its political content—a spirited effort about the situation in Greece in 1945 which was blocked at the request of Churchill the Prime Minister in what he held to be the interests of Western democracy. There were, however, about a couple of dozen left out for other reasons: because of unhappy chance turning my analogies into pointless insult, as for instance when a scoop photograph of King George V on the deck of his flagship to review the Fleet was found to be going to press facing a cartoon of Colonel Blimp doing exactly the same thing, but analogically, in quite a different connection; because of sudden illness of a politician figuring in the cartoon; because of the tears of Lord Rothermere at seeing himself caricatured, which made an impossible situation for Lord Beaverbrook since R. had helped B. to finance the purchase of the *Evening Standard*; or because the entire situation had changed between the time of drawing the cartoon and its going to press.

There was a facetious little whimsy in which I celebrated the opening of the London season by a set of drawings of my dog, Musso, being presented at Court curtseying, with veils, feathers, pearls, bouquet and all among the débutantes. I did their Majesties the justice of drawing them, with democratic restraint, as real people, not waxworks. My nervous editor feared for his head and when I wasn't looking sent his most diplomatic lieutenant with the drawing along to Buckingham Palace for approval before printing it. I knew nothing of what was going on until it was relayed to me through a network of smooth voices that Queen Mary was greatly diverted by Mr. Low's extremely amusing drawings, loved my dog, but asked me to consider that in Britain we did not put the monarchy into cartoons. There was room on that point for argument, but I was already disarmed and pink with compliments.

As a 'subject' himself, Beaverbrook was uncomplaining, which was just as well since his political importance made it necessary for me to draw him frequently. The more simple-minded readers, those who see in political cartoons only the comicality and do not understand the politics, no doubt summed up the situation as one in which some cheeky employee had somehow got himself into a position in which he could rag his boss and was out to see how far he could go. But the fact was that I drew Beaverbrook only when his political activities warranted it.

He never protested, partly because he had a genuine sense of fun and didn't care a damn; partly because he was aware of the popular advertisement accruing to a personality much cartooned, well or ill. (Besides being a Nero and a Napoleon he was also a bit of a Narcissus); partly because of the reputation it gave him as a large-minded newspaper-proprietor who gave everybody on his staff freedom to say anything; partly because it sold papers; and, perhaps, partly because I had a contract.

The *Morning Post*'s strictures to which I have referred, printed as part of an 'inquest' on the Tory defeat at the general elections of 1929, were in fact misplaced. Baldwin had given many opportunities for satire. In the country's parlous position, his party slogan '*Safety First*' could not but inspire cartoons of his Government meeting the crisis by getting under the table; and his encouragement to farmers to solve their problems by growing more broccoli would naturally set any caricaturist examining a broccoli to see if in its intricate features there could be found any resemblance to the facial lineaments of Baldwin himself. I had certainly criticized the Baldwin Government, but not unfairly, mainly for its failure to produce a policy to deal effectively with the rapidly worsening unemployment situation; but then I had criticized both of the other parties for the same reason. The uniform helplessness with which all three established parties confronted a situation which was degenerating day by day towards danger level had, in fact, created somewhat unsatisfactory conditions for a cartoonist. One needs one's contrasts. One can be *against* something, but to be effective one must also be *for* something. So I decided to fill the vacuum by creating on paper a brand-new party—the Low Party, with a policy of hollow mockery pointed at the futility and frustration of what appeared to be the common national policy, as things were going. The Low Party issued its Manifesto:

> Low has consented to stand for Parliament and confidently asks for the support of those who agree with Mr. Baldwin about MacDonald and Lloyd George, of those who agree with Mr. MacDonald about Baldwin and Lloyd George, and of those who agree with Mr. Lloyd George about MacDonald and Baldwin.

The Low Party presented some samples of its unemployment policy, which it guaranteed was more to the point than that of the three other parties: the reconstruction of roads, also rooting 'em up and reconstructing 'em again and again; pink motor-bikes for bosses to ride up and down the roads while waiting for orders which didn't come; factories for cutting up brown paper and pieces of string to tie up said orders if necessary; the issue of a large number of free passes to somewhere else; the institution of a national 'Hope-for-the-best' Week; and more of the same kind.

Although I had not intended the Low Party to be taken as other than a device for comment, its reception grew astonishingly real. What had been a joke suddenly became serious. Opportunity and imagination met and outsiders began to clothe it with their own ideas. It was evident that large numbers of the electors were so deeply disturbed at the way things were going and at the inabilities of the established parties that they snatched even at the shadow of a straw. Enquiries began to roll in, and a movement began to group itself around me with the object of sponsoring my parliamentary candidature at the elections as an Independent. I had some difficulty in extricating myself when it was announced that a public meeting would be held to nominate me. Beaverbrook thought I should go on. Wells thought not. The putative candidate decided to refrain from attendance, so I don't know what happened. I made use of the Low Party up to the elections and then wrung its neck quickly with a sigh of relief.

There had been some disturbance of my social relationships on leaving the *Star* for the *Evening Standard*, naturally enough; but there were a few curious retacions I had not expected. I lost some friends. The demonstrated actuality of my independence gave no joy to some who had talked much to me about the freedom of the Press. It spoilt their arguments. It was like throwing a spanner into their works. Some whom I had come to regard as familiars sheered away with a queer look as though there were something fishy about one who had so disappointed expectations of mishap.

Keyed up to the responsibility and constant vigilance attached to playing a lone hand in what I still felt to be hostile company, I gloomed sourly on the distinction between those who appreciated the reality of freedom and those to whom liberty was merely a good talking-point.

There was, however, the other side of the penny. The malevolence of some of my critics had created an opposite benevolence in others, so that I had, on paper, for the moment, a large and growing body of goodwill to rely on. An evidence of this was the numbers of correspondents who wished to help me with their suggestions for cartoons.

The fabrication of cartoon ideas with meaning intelligible and readily appreciated from one end of the country to the other, reasonably up to the minute in subject and as fresh as may be in treatment, is an expert affair. A cartoonist who is worth his salt and in the swing is rarely worried by a lack of ideas. It is the selection that takes time—choosing one that will be alive on publication. My well-meaning correspondents could not know that. Of the numberless suggestions they sent to me, only half of one per cent were of any practical value; and even that half of one I had to avoid, because the use of an idea from a total stranger could very easily result in embarrassing copyright complications.

Most of the time these contributed ideas seemed to be distinctly reminiscent. Plentiful among them were whiskered old stagers about Prime Ministers walking tightropes marked 'Crisis,' and Ships of State heading for rocks inscribed 'Disaster.' Whenever a Cabinet Minister resigned a dozen correspondents, with memories of Tenniel's classic cartoon of the 1880's, suggested 'Dropping the Pilot.' I received 'On, Stanley, On' suggestions about once a week when Stanley Baldwin became a political leader. When

Budget day came round I always had plenty of well-meaning people writing to say: 'I cannot draw, but I have a good idea for a cartoon—the Chancellor of the Exchequer riding in a *taxi*.' The gratuitous adviser of one cartoonist friend of mine had octopuses on the brain as cartoon analogies. Protection, unemployment, communism, capitalism, the Catholic Church—all appeared in his one-track imagination as octopuses with spreading tentacles. My poor friend, seeing him approach, used to mumur bitterly: 'Damn! Another octopus,' and leave hurriedly.

On the credit side, too, my relations with the *Evening Standard* managers and editors became most cordial. Much to everybody's surprise, the fuss had increased circulation. And my salary had been underwritten by subletting reproduction rights of my cartoons to twelve provincial newspapers.

Much advertised up and down the country like a new toothpaste, and an object of some public curiosity, I found new doors began to open. Invitations from the most unlikely people to dinners, receptions and country week-ends began to arrive. Here was quite a different world from that of my *Star* days. The upper-income-bracket, obviously. In pursuit of experience we accepted the most promising of these. We began to lead a busy social life. On threadbare excuses I found myself lured into contacts with persons I had never heard of before. The horizon constantly widened. Several people 'took us up' but dropped us like a hot potato when they found I was a prickly fellow, not the dinner-table wit they had probably expected.

We were invited to dinner on a slight acquaintance by a pleasant chap to meet a Distinguished Lady. By the time we had got to the fish course I gathered the Distinguished Lady (who proved very amiable) was the intimate of a Very Important Personage Indeed, and I became aware that I was being put through a process of examination as a preliminary to future possibilities. I chilled and the evening was a fiasco.

Again, apropos of nothing, I found myself at dinner with three millionaires. We did ourselves extremely well. It was a miserable affair and cured me of any lingering doubt that happiness might reside in the possession of great wealth. Poor chaps, if ever there were three who had lost their way, they had.

Here and there I felt the shutters go up when I came along. I was a public eye and a reputed scoffer—worse, one of those left-wing people. On the other hand I found more than I had expected of jolly and congenial company. But moving in this champagne atmosphere in my white tie and tails I was restrained by the tight-lipped caution of my Scottish forefathers from high living and close social entanglements. Not along that road lay the happy but precarious life I saw for myself. Long ago I had decided that the two traps most dangerous to artists of any kind were material success, the wish for easy living undermining the wish to do good work; and the pleasuring of friends, the effort to meet the standards of others rather than one's own.

Although I became more smooth and agile in small talk, although I learned to dissemble, to flatter and to adopt the protective colouring that would enable me unobtrusively to survey this new jungle of honeyed amiability, my social encounters were not invariably attended by honour. There were callow bounders of both sexes who assumed with cool impudence that I could be used to further their private interests. Some of the overtures were so crude as to be laughable. A society hostess offered me a handsome fee to attend one of her parties. One brash fellow approached me to know how much I would take to put him in a cartoon. He wanted the advertisement. 'If you will repeat your proposition before George, there, so that I may be protected from your denial that you ever made it,' I said, 'I will put you in the paper offering to pay me to put you in the paper. And it won't cost you a bean—only your dignity.'

He looked at me with a fish-eye and turned away. Later he told a friend of mine that I was a bit of a cad.

It has been said often enough that without leisured classes able to interest themselves in higher things the world could never have developed in culture and the arts. Certainly I found here and there civilized individuals who gave some truth to an otherwise questionable statement. Lords, after all, are not always lords for nothing. Pondered wisdom sometimes issues from plush easy-chairs. A certain detachment of view may be gained by sitting in the middle of a hundred-thousand-acre estate.

In the 'thirties, however, the most notable feature of what remained of the 'privileged classes' was certainly neither culture, art, nor philosophy. Here and there I encountered the survival of an arrogance which was almost ferocious. I understood why Britain had lost the American colonies. I understood for the first time why so many of my own grandparents' generation had chosen to pack up and go to live somewhere else. Looking at and conversing amiably with some of these respected relics I felt that not very far under their skins was the brutal stupidity that, even in 1930, could regard human beings as property and quite naturally identified the public interest with the sanctity of their own purely private interests—those disagreeing being, *prima facie*, treasonable dogs. All my life overseas I had taken for granted a general assent among the British to the ideals of democracy. It was something new to me to find people who strongly disapproved those ideals, and would, if they could, have reversed engines back to the eighteenth century.

It was interesting to me, with New Zealand eyes, to note the obstinacy of class-consciousness, and the depth of the political cleavages. But apart from the evidence afforded by these survivals, I could only surmise what the 'upper classes' had been like before the war. Many of the children of the pre-war rich had been left financially high and dry by the First World War and many of their children had sensibly gone to work. A new generation of 'nobs' had arisen. Baldwin in the early 'twenties had described its parliamentary representation as 'hard-faced men who looked as though they had done well out of the war.' They had also swamped 'Society.' The gaiety was rowdier than I had expected. There was more rudeness and more grab. One could pick those who had the tradition of graceful living behind them from the jostling of the more recently elevated, over-playing their parts.

Gradually I became aware of a top layer of our social system peopled by the successful, or about-to-be-successful. In this company if one were a success, it hardly mattered what one was a success *at*. This was the Ambition Exchange in which members openly but in the most amiable manner made use of one another. Obviously they were trained for it. This was the cruder aspect of a salient in the British way of life. The parents sent their children to the 'right' schools to make 'useful' companionships; their mentors taught them the art of choosing friends with an eye to future material advantage, with or without congeniality, and the business system completed the process by teaming them up for mutual profit; the final product being modern primitive man, the single-track self-seeker, perpetually on the make. This, it appeared, was the business of life, and here they were all trying to climb up on one another's shoulders. To the hopefuls of the well-to-do classes from which the bulk of this layer appeared to be drawn, this 'you-scratch-my-back-and-I'll-scratch-yours' spirit seemed the most natural and right thing in the world. But to me, a lone stranger plonked down in its midst, an outsider from an equalitarian society accustomed to being loved or unloved for himself, it seemed degraded in its cynicism.

'Outsider' was the word. Even in 1930 there remained the lively vestiges of an exclusive system in which not to be of 'us' was to be *declassé*, with decided disadvantages. My own auspices were convincing, otherwise I surely would not have been moving freely in this vast club of which the management committee, the already successful, the people in the top jobs—church, law, medicine, industry, finance, diplomacy, politics (Left as well as Right)—seemed all, if not actually related, at least to have been at school with one another, and naturally striving to keep the plums in the family.

On and off this level I got to know more politicians of both sides on more conversational terms.

On the face of it one would not say the attitude of political caricaturists was one of admiration or even goodwill. The traditional terms of their expression are perhaps better adapted to censure than to praise. Admiration is for the poets. A satirist perverted to hero-worship becomes pathetic and sickening. His approval can best be expressed by leaving its object alone.

Yet it need not be assumed that a caricaturist is unaware of the facts of life.

When at an early age I began to take a real interest in current problems and their solutions, I soon dropped the glib assumption that the mere existence of the miseries of mankind proved politicians to be a crowd of fools and skunks. Having made the rough distinction between statesmen as the designers, and politicians as the fabricators, of policy, I learned to adjust my expectations accordingly. With more understanding I tried to put myself in their respective places and I began to appreciate the difference between carping and criticism. It became clear that there must be, after all, many good men in politics out to do their best within the limits of their own ability. The motives that impelled men into public life were not necessarily sordid, but, on the contrary, could be, and often were, noble.

Having observed that, I noted also, on the other hand, that there were the attitudinizers, more concerned with their own emotional release than with any real concern for the common weal; the calculating careerists looking for power and the lush life; the yearners baying the moon; the obsoletes who had long ago lost their score-cards; and the plain stoopids who approached every problem with an open mouth.

Searching for common attributes among my political acquaintances, I was struck by what appeared to be occupational characteristics. The first was vanity. Politicians in a democratic system must be vain. How could it be otherwise? A candidate without a good opinion of himself could hardly command the respect of electors. And doubt would be justified. Lack of self-confidence is no sound qualification for leadership, however attractive a façade of humility in a well-established monument might be to sentimental voters.

The desire for importance moves everybody—high and low. In politics more than in any other calling it may be seen at work, not merely among the hopelessly unimportant and insignificant, but, since it feeds on success, in the highest places. In this life there are no advantages without their attendant disadvantages. As a consequence, many politicians are quite ready to save the country, not so many to help someone else to save it.

Another characteristic of politicians was charm. Politicians were nearly always likeable personally. Indeed, they went to some trouble to make themselves likeable, for in a political democracy an engaging personality was essential to success in public life. Since I am one of those people who socially can do no other than meet a friendly approach with friendliness (even though professionally I could never allow my personal predilections to take the chill off cold objectivity), I found I liked most of the politicians I met, although there were some who for various reasons did not return the compliment.

I joined clubs and had the freedom of others; and I was on nodding terms with *maîtres d'hôtel*, *chefs*, house managers and doormen everywhere.

In a determination to overcome my inner fearfulness of public speaking, I accepted, for a time, all invitations to make speeches; and at length, through pain and suffering, achieved a passable fluency, which led me into a variety of pleasant social, professional, commercial and even industrial occasions. One speech led to another and I became a regular attendant at the Omar Khayyām, the Titmarsh, The Odd Volumes and other dinner clubs which had as their *raison d'être* the airing of the eloquence of members.

Of the strange characters I collected at these now somewhat old-fashioned institutions, two made marks on my tablets of memory as particularly congenial—Rupert Gould, who subsequently gained fame on the radio 'brains trust' as the expert on sea-serpents; and A. J. A. Symons, who could be described only as a builder of castles in the air. These two, dissimilar in all else, were alike in their ability 'to talk the hind-leg off a pot. Rupert was unique in that he had an incredible memory. I once heard him repeat from memory a magazine article of 2,000 words without a single error; and I enjoyed nothing better than to be buttonholed by him in Whitehall and used as audience for a session of tall tales. . . . A.J. was a self-made man if ever there was one, and even if the character he built for himself was too brittle to endure, the fact did not lessen the regard of those who knew his more obvious qualities. I think of him only as the man with whom I had the longest-winded argument in my life. It was about the Nature of Beauty and beginning with a preamble occupying an entire midnight walk from Piccadilly to Hampstead, continued intermittently and sporadically for about six months. A.J. took the line that beauty was fitness for purpose—a good motor-car or a good lawn-mower, for instance, was beautiful. I held that beauty lay in character. A.J. was disinclined to admit that there could be any lines of beauty in the abstract, but finally plumped for symmetry. I felt that the lines of beauty lay in asymmetry, in bumps and bulges, and brought forth Rodin and Meunier to shame the Greeks. We could not agree on the proposition that beauty lay in the eye of the beholder; but agreed that sex made it difficult to come to an absolute judgment since a man would always think a woman more beautiful than a cow, and a bull would always think a cow more beautiful than a woman. . . . We had a grand airing.

This was the decade of vast parties. Of all the parties, Beaverbrook's took the cake for variety. Bankers, diplomats, peers, writers, artists, tycoons, film stars, Tories, Liberals and Socialists, Cabinet Ministers and trades union leaders. I met there so many rising lights in politics of both the left- and the right-wings framed in cigars and champagne that I began to think Lord B. represented a stage in the political neophyte's education. On one big night the Right Hon. Dress-Suit M.P. himself, Jimmy Thomas, stood at the top of the stairs audibly identifying for me new arrivals as they ascended. 'Look! Here are two bloody dukes. Watch that one. Always does the wrong thing.' As if to provide apt illustration the duke indicated promptly knocked over a vase.

Garden parties on the cropped lawns of stately homes; studio bottle parties where the crush was so great that one had to move out into the street to lift one's elbow; music parties, fancy-dress parties, folk-dance and ballet parties, sporting nights-out at the fight with Harry Preston. Anything less than a hundred guests to a plain party was a quiet evening at home. As confirmed guests we took our turn—bought a new and larger home and gave some parties ourselves which shook our quiet suburb.

By the end of the 1920's I felt I knew my London and most of the people in it.

16

INSPIRATION is a promiscuous jade, not caring how many she picks up on a bright night. Frequently two cartoonists thinking along the same lines get the same idea for the same occasion. That was how I met Bernard Partridge. Similar analogies had occurred to both of us and we had each drawn virtually the same cartoon. He wrote to explain the time-lag of his method to prove that the 'plagiarism' was inadvertent—as if I did not know it. The incident ended in our taking one another to luncheon with his friend and 'junior' colleague Leonard Raven Hill as host.

That was a red letter day for me. I had awe for them both, particularly for Partridge, the last of the cartoonists of the Victorian grand manner. After all, poets, prophets and princes were all very well, but this was the great B.P. himself, an idol of my boyhood. His knighthood troubled me, for I could not think that critics or commentators ostensibly of satirical temper on public affairs should accept, like other men, the insignia of trammelling loyalties. A fool may conceive the satirist to have no purpose beyond throwing over-ripe tomatoes at passers-by; but viewed on the highest plane of responsibility, his duty must be to humanity as a whole, not to groups, institutions or individuals. No conscientious satirist could be a 'King's man,' with the implied restriction.

Partridge had begun life as an actor, one of Beerbohm Tree's boys, and rather let you know it. A handsome man of much dignity, reserved at first. Raven Hill, an amiable fussy chap, fond of his food, was responsive. Both were ultra-conservative, even reactionary, I thought. I was the colonial radical. Our different angles on life came out when we exchanged ideas about our calling. I have never enjoyed a 'shop' talk so much, especially when it ranged to the traditional mythology.

Partridge, as the inheritor of the Tenniel tradition in *Punch*,

208

specialized in cartoons dealing with national occasions, such as laying laurel wreaths on the tombs of dead statesmen (THE NATION MOURNS), congratulating epic sportsmen (WELL DONE, SIR!), extending the helping hand in disasters (BRITAIN'S SYMPATHY), etc., in which he represented the Anglo-Saxon people by *Britannia*, a massive matron moulded according to the Graeco-Roman idea of beauty.

I had a point of view about this.

The personification of the higher abstractions as beautiful females was a convention handed down from our unsophisticated forefathers. To put it mildly, they overdid it. To them *Justice*, recognized in these later times as a stern cold unfeminine virtue (unlike *Mercy*, *Hope*, *Love*, etc.), was rather absurdly a woman; as also was *Liberty*, the most virile of human ambitions; and *Peace*, the business of strong men, still impersonated by that futile maiden carrying the allegedly peaceful but actually rather quarrelsome bird, the dove.

The idea of representing nations in this way was not new, of course, with *Britannia*, though one suspected that the beautiful females of other modern nations were but imitators, *Colombia*, *Germania*, *Marianne* or her degenerate equivalent *La Belle France*, and the whole bourgeois boiling lot of them.

Through these figures could be discerned the dead past in which the influence of women was such that man ascribed to the feminine mystery the divine qualities. Both sexes now knew better, but the *Britannia* family lived on, still adequately expressing the conception of dignity, national and international, which died last century. Could it be that the modern woman of 1930, smart and independent, regarded herself as related even remotely to these female tanks? Could it be that the citizen of 1930 in national emergency liked to be told that he was behaving like a perfect lady?

Both Partridge and Raven Hill rose in defence. Why should cartoonists lay aside signs and symbols which their public had been educated down the ages to accept as symbolic of certain ideas? I had to admit that in making cartoons for newspapers and periodicals it was necessary to make a generous compromise with the average receptivity, and that a cartoonist could not afford to be independent of the values and associations already accepted.

But, I asked, on the other hand, what are cartoonists for? If, in their more conscientious moments, perceiving how far signs and symbols constitute the mental stock-in-trade of the average man, they sometimes reflect that as symbol-makers possibly they have

209

a responsibility, certainly it would seem to involve keeping themselves abreast of the times.

Look at *John Bull*, invented in 1712, personification of the English people and/or the average Englishman, and *Uncle Sam*, 1775, his counterpart for the United States of America—two more figures in the gallery of classic cartoon symbolism then still in current use. No doubt the *John Bull* pictorially developed with obscene disrespect and popular success by James Gillray and contemporary cartoonists of the eighteenth century was fairly representative of a type of Englishman which was numerous and assertive at that time. No doubt, also, *Uncle Sam* was once more or less a truthful portrait of the dominant American type. But, leaving on one side their obsolete dress, it might be difficult to find less truthful representatives of the average citizens of Britain and the United States of America in our time than respectively this obese, smug, side-whiskered country squire, and this lanky long-haired, goat-bearded farmer. What were these agricultural left-overs doing monopolizing the masquerade as Britain and the United States in these industrial days? Was this the machine age or wasn't it?

The male representatives of the average in other countries were not always so distinctly personified. But when in the middle of the last century cheaper and easier photomechanical reproduction encouraged the spread of cartoons throughout journalism, Anglo-Saxon cartoonists, spurred by necessity, invented rubber-stamps for the foreigners in keeping with what was outstanding about them at the time.

Then were created the Conventional Frenchman, comprising all the peculiarities of French appearance and character that impressed themselves upon the Anglo-Saxon mind at about the time of Napoleon III—waxed beard and moustache, shiny funnel-shaped hat, waisted frock-coat and fixed explanatory gesture of the hands; and the Conventional German, fat, water-fall moustache *à la* Bismarck, spectacles, peaked cap, jug of beer and large bowl pipe.

In defiance of the march of events, these moth-eaten creations still cropped up in cartoons for the world of 1930. The Conventional Chinese still wore his long-abolished pig-tail: the Conventional Turk continued to wear his banned fez, and the Conventional Russian continued to appear as a middle-aged nihilist with whiskers, leading a Russian bear and carrying a smoking bomb of antique model.

There had been a war. France and Germany of 1930 were far

from being your dandy Alphonse and your fat Fritz. And there had been revolutions. Whatever your political philosophy may be, the representative Russian of 1930 was a clean-shaven young man wearing overalls smeared with oil and carrying a large spanner. The *Russian Bear* was a tractor; and the bomb a machine-gun around the corner.

Mention of the *Russian Bear* led us to the Sacred Animals. In Partridge's view the people who were responsible for 'lifting' from ancient heraldry a lion as a symbol of the indomitable spirit of the British nation had a good idea. The *British Lion*, we all three agreed, certainly had his points as a cartoon 'property.' With his waving mane and his tufted tail he could be made to look very striking, crouching in dignified anger or glaring nobly at nothing. He made what they called 'powerful' cartoons. But apart from this purely aesthetic consideration, there seemed no justification for continuing to libel the British people by likening it to this unworthy creature, notoriously a loud roarer but a cruel and cowardly beast, only bold when facing something weaker than itself. Nor to a *Bulldog*, either—a snuffling, dribbling creature, the most uncomely of the entire canine species, with, as its most remarkable feature, an unmanageable jaw. Raven Hill objected that it had always been part of the recognized technique of warfare to seek to terrify enemies by making ugly faces and big noises. If some primitive urge impelled us still to try to identify ourselves publicly with some fearsome beast, he was all for it.

And the Birds. Many nations, from the Hittites and the Persians downwards, have favoured *Eagles*. Almost it would seem that at some time there must have been a rush on a job line of *Eagles* at the Olympian pet-shop. The United States got an *Eagle*. Germany got an *Eagle*. Imperial Austria, Imperial Russia, going for quantity, got two-headed *Eagles*. Italy got a Roman *Eagle*. Poor France, arriving late, got a *Rooster*.

One could understand a certain low type of patriot revelling in visions of his patria swooping and soaring about. It would not have occurred to him, for instance, that his *Eagle* is a bird of prey. What would a decent American think if you walked up to him and said: 'When I look at you I am reminded of a bird of prey?' He would be peeved. And rightly.

New models were required for a world in which as science annihilates time and space, with its speed machines, its sound machines, its vision machines, it is annihilating also regional peculiarity. Unfortunately for the cartoonists the same kinds of suit and felt hat were now worn in New York, London, Moscow, Paris, Berlin, Tokio, Istanbul, Pekin, Stockholm and Addis Ababa; and it looked as though it were becoming both untrue and unprofitable any more to represent peoples as being essentially different one from another, save in function and usefulness.

A bleak prospect for cartoonists. It was difficult to mature new symbols in such a world; but it became evident that to perpetuate the old ones was to perpetuate confusion.

'A symbol always stimulates the intellect,' said Emerson in a weak moment. Well and good, if it were a symbol of living thought; but symbols which have outlived their significance yet still persisted as habits of thought did not stimulate but only drugged the intellect.

I remember that meeting with my two eminent fellow-cartoonists as one of the genuinely delightful spots in my life. We disagreed frequently and emphatically, we each consumed two helpings of roast duck and we parted friends.

If Partridge was the most representational of draughtsmen, Max Beerbohm was the least.

It was in the twilight of a soft summer evening dining on a roof in Lincoln's Inn that I first made the acquaintance of Max. Ellis Roberts, the literary critic, arranged it for us three and our wives.

The *chiaroscuro* is just right. First act. Curtain. Dinner-table set against back-drop of the quiet trees dim-lit by last rays of the sun, with thin new moon thrown in as a decoration. Enter our hero, immaculate in evening dress with topper and carnation, drawling a *bon mot*. But no! Our hero is already there, but so quiet of presence that at first he escapes the eye. A sad face, a small middle-aged figure of fine-pointed extremities and sharp perception.

I recognized immediately the occupational characteristic of the caricaturist. The slight detachment produced by habitually trying to do two things at once—concentrate on the particular while expanding to the general.

The scene was set for Wit. But I don't remember that anyone said a memorable thing all night. I had feared he might be like his public legend—dandified, exquisite, ultra-fastidious and scintillating with dreary Edwardian wisecracks. But no, we began almost immediately to talk about how to draw a brick wall over the way.

Many years had rolled since as a very little boy I had come across a funny picture of Oom Paul Kruger signed microscopically

'Max.' It was so simply drawn as to seem to have something in common with my own artless attempts. Since that distant day I had learned that there are more ways than one of rendering individual character. Max never could *draw* in the accepted sense of expressing himself in polished classical draughtsmanship, and therefore his quality of innocent discovery emerged in terms of childlike freshness. In my opinion, although a 'free' technique like Max's permitted to an unlimited degree the artistic 'catch-as-catch-can' involved in all-round representation, the results could not have the depth of solid caricatural drawing based on reality of form. Max was too modest to do more than register doubt on the point.

'It must be awful to be a slave to skill,' said he, shuddering delicately.

Like Phil May, who laboured so successfully to eliminate the appearance of effort that hundreds of imitators jumped to the disastrous conclusion that the way to make drawings was to 'dash them off,' Max so avoided academic form that his imitators came to believe that all that was needed to become a caricaturist was not to be able to draw. Their mistake.

Max had the disadvantages, as well as the advantages, of his qualities. His wit was sometimes so cultured in derivation and so local in application as to make his caricatures almost private. And his collections sometimes had the air of having been designed for a small exclusive clientele. Caricatures of gentlemen, for gentlemen, by a gentleman. When Satire walked hand in hand with 'Society,' as it used to do when Max held his exhibitions, the danger of the patronage was that one was encouraged to be not only a gentleman (which, of course, every caricaturist should be), but also a 'gentleman' (which, of course, no caricaturist should be). Looking at me sadly, Max agreed that this was a Peril.

This first meeting ended. Others confirmed the impression of an unassuming man, free from envy and malice.

Long before I met Walt Disney over H. G. Wells's lunch-table in the early 'thirties, I had been an admiring fan of his. He turned out to be a modest young man in a loud check suit. To my disappointment he shied off art talk, except to tell me that many of his film-cartoon creations were built up from sound first. *Donald Duck*, for instance, arose from the discovery that one of his office staff could imitate a duck. The hen prima donna suggested itself when he found a singer who could sing like a hen clucking. Disney found an interest in London listening to the orators at Marble Arch, astonishing to a visitor from America where all 'dangerous radicals' are put in gaol. Politically he seemed rather naïve—thought pensions sapped initiative and enterprise.

After *Fantasia* and *Bambi* I grew enthusiastic to the point of expressing my opinion in print and on the radio that he, as the outstanding representative of his kind, might prove to be the most significant figure in graphic art since Leonardo da Vinci. (Loud sneers from the numbskulls who couldn't see beyond *Mickey Mouse*, and who wouldn't put aside the music and the noise, forget 'film-cartoons' and consider just moving drawings.)

The burden of my lay was this:

The man Leonardo was an adventurous mind, fond of wheels, an engineer. As an artist he was an innovator constantly experimenting, one of the first to go after painting round instead of flat, so that he produced an effect, new in his time, of the figures standing out from the background. Leonardo added to the scope of expression, extended the power to give depth of atmosphere. His philosophy was that will was the energy of life. He was all for energy. Muscular movement and the dynamics of anatomy were favourite studies of his. The sketches for his famous equestrian bronze of Francesco Sforza show that he worked out that horse in a whole range of movement, galloping, rearing up, and still. Just like the drafts for what we call a 'film-cartoon.' Although Leonardo omitted to invent the cinema for himself and therefore had not its possibilities to play with, he was more than a bit of a cartoonist in our modern sense. Ordinary shapes bored him. He was no caricaturist, but he liked strange blobs, angles and burlesque outlines, and he often drew allegorical sketches, moral and social satires and fables.

As to the other one, Disney. The first moving drawings made for screen projection by Emile Cohl in 1908 were elementary. They moved. That was as much as you could say. There followed a procession, mostly of Americans, up to *Felix the Cat*. With Sullivan, in 1924, it was evident that the collective fertility in original tricks of draughtsmanship and novel mechanical devices had enabled the whole art-form to be advanced a couple of miles or so. The movement, improving slowly, had up till then been confined to the simplest actions from the easiest angles, in profile mostly, tiresome in repetition. Sullivan's animation was not yet subtle, but it was 'all-round.' His figures moved, sometimes a bit painfully, from all angles and they had the beginnings of perspective and individual character. Then along comes Disney.

214

Pat Sullivan and his predecessors were, so to speak, penny comic. Disney organized the experts and with specialized animators, better draughtsmen, colour, and multiplication of the number of drawings per foot soon pushed the art first to twopenny comic, and then to threepenny. Then, by gosh! he made it sixpenny—no, shilling! His feature films, *Snow-white*, *Pinoccio*, *Fantasia* and *Bambi* (I leave out *Dumbo*, which was a sixpenny holiday) were each an advance upon the last in artistry and extension of range. They reveal a growing understanding of the meaning of observed movement and therefore greatly increased powers of creating imagined movement. If one compared the play of human expression in the face of Snow-white with that in the faces of the Centaurettes in *Fantasia* one could mark the striking improvement. Subtlety was now possible.

Now there was the point. It was perfectly clear donkeys years ago that graphic art, hit by the mechanical age, needed a new idea. Heaven knows it hadn't had one since somebody 2,000 years ago thought of painting pictures to frame and hang on the wall as a change from carpets and tapestries. The improving quality of facsimile reproduction probably meant sooner or later a consequent reassertion of *real* values in art as opposed to rarity and other sham commercial values. The painting of pictures to hang on walls threatened to become an increasingly precarious profession except for the few best artists. Admire the new 'schools' and 'movements' as much as you liked or as much as they deserved, their merits were irrelevant here. All the cubes, abstracts and surrealists' ironmongery hadn't really saved the situation.

It was perfectly clear also that as the machinery for representing movement improved some intelligent lad would drop to it that the new idea was here—that the means were present for opening a new and exciting vista of possibility in graphic Art (with a capital A). In our time your conventional artist who wished to represent the beauty and character of, say, a woman or a landscape looked for the emotional elements of shape and colour in the subject, and, following principles of selection and emphasis, put them down in clarified form. But the woman moved with charm, the trees bent in the breeze. There were emotional elements in the movements to be discovered, selected, emphasized and represented in heightened form, also. Why not?

What would Leonardo have been up to if he were alive in 1935? I asked. He would have been in his back room inventing simplifications of animating processes and projection devices.

It was ten years or so before I saw Disney again, this time visiting London with his brother Roy. We (Walt, Roy, some interested cinema chaps and I) sat in plush chairs complete with drinks and cigars discussing production and distribution like executive industrialists. The finance of film-cartoons was not as good as I had imagined. They were hired out at only a small rent and it always took eighteen months before Walt got his money back on one—before he 'made a nickel.' He employed two hundred artists and up till then had never had a strike.

Sad to relate, when the opportunity offered Walt and I hadn't much to say to one another. The subject of politics was obviously out. Walt complained that some interfering people accused him of moving towards 'social awareness' and he denied it vigorously. It was pretty plain Walt didn't want to talk about Art, either. *Fantasia* had not been box-office. I gathered it was thought to be bad for his business to have it said he was an arty fancy-pants with any ideas beyond fairy-tale level. Out with all the long-hair stuff.

'Don't you like to draw?' I asked, looking at his long, thickish fingers.

Walt looked puzzled.

'He doesn't draw. He just thinks up ideas and compositions. He hasn't had a pen in his hand for six months,' said Roy. 'He isn't an artist. He's a visualizer.'

It was my turn to look puzzled.

'Does big outlines, and the boys do the rest.'

There seemed no more to say on that point so we changed the subject. These were the business men of art. When one talked of 'Disney' one talked of a factory. That the factory was the most significant thing in graphic art since Leonardo da Vinci I still had no shadow of doubt. All it needed now was its Leonardo. I looked closely at Disney. A friendly man, not putting on airs, not trying to be funny all the time. A massive enough achievement for two or three lifetimes. But how the devil could a man resist having a crack at the big pot when he had such a glorious chance?

Life was not all politics, social struggle and newspaper dead-lines. Amid the hectic preliminaries for the fateful nineteen-thirties I enjoyed meeting artists who in my earlier days had been to me only shining names. Great was the delight of talking 'shop' with Bruce Bairnsfather, Edmund Dulac and even of smiling and smiling and smiling at Louis Raemakers (since I could not speak Dutch).

When the Japanese delegates came over for the Naval Conference, Ippei Okamoto, the most celebrated political caricaturist in Tokyo, came with them. I was delighted when Ippei, accompanied with two dead-pan Japanese diplomats, called on me with scrupulous politeness. Ippei was a happy chap, speaking a little English. We drew one another, each of us thinking he had done a good job and the other a pretty bad one. I cultivated Ippei's society, wishing to get the Japanese viewpoint. I was telling him and his friends what their political ideas should be when I noticed him looking at me, inhaling at a queer angle.

'What's the matter?' I asked. 'Do I smell?'

'Yes,' he said.

'Badly?'

'Not badly. Like cold mutton. All English people smell like cold mutton.'

'Well, is that so? That's strange. You smell to me like clear soup, sharp and appetizing, I assure you.' I took a good lungful. We discussed racial smells at some length. One of the attendant protectors took a shorthand note.

Ippei was quietly humorous in his Japanese way and we took to one another at once. When I got him alone for a few minutes I had to ask him the first prize question as one cartoonist to another.

'What happens when you want to make a caricature of the Emperor?' He made no reply but drew the edge of his hand across his throat, making a noise like a saw.

I remembered this when I met Boris Efimov, the political cartoonist of Moscow *Isvestia*, who shared with Deni of *Pravda* the highest popularity in Russian caricature. He got 6,000 roubles a month, in contrast to the paltry 1,500 or so received by Stalin.

'What are the conditions of your employment?' I asked him.

'I do what I like,' said Efimov.

'Do you ever criticize the regime?'

'It is unthinkable,' said Efimov gravely. Perhaps his style was a little cramped by the fact that our interpreting was being done by the Soviet Chief Censor.

17

WHEN my contract with the *Evening Standard* came up
for renewal I did what was expected of me in my
assumed character of tough business man and found
myself sailing into the five-figure income bracket
without any particular hankering on my part. By this time I had
extraordinary means of estimating the growth of public interest,
goodwill and popular celebrity. My mail was absurdly large. We
were surfeited with invitations. At Christmas the postman had
arrived at my house loaded with gifts from people I hardly knew
or didn't know at all—two cases of champagne, five boxes of
cigars, hams, a side of mutton, even articles of clothing. I had
been in the moving pictures and on the radio. I had had at least
two impersonators, one of whom was wanted by the police. One
evening Madeline and I were sitting with some friends at the
theatre watching a musical play when the Duncan Sisters howled
my name across the footlights, plugged me with gags and held up
the show until I rose bathed in limelight, and bowed to the
audience to terrific applause. Even more remarkable evidence of
ubiquitousness was that a letter arrived safely to me addressed
simply 'Low'—nothing more. This, surely, amounted to fame. I
reflected on the tale of the man whose ambition was to become
important enough to have a tablet bearing his name put on his
birth-place after his death. He died and his ghost returned to see.
From a distance—yes—there it was! The tablet! Coming closer
he read it: 'To Let.'

Above all, I was in the waxworks.

I spent two interesting mornings with old John Tussaud
learning how to make a waxwork. When I got to his studio the
model (he hated to have his models called 'waxworks') was well
under way, he having built it up from my photograph. It made

me vaguely uneasy, but then waxworks always have done that to me from a child. Their sinister stillness and their unresponsive eyes scare my subconscious.

I told the old man that in the Exhibition as it was before the fire I had had to make a drawing of the Chamber of Horrors, and overcoming my repulsion had spent three hours of a winter's day virtually alone in that horrible place. To get my best angle of view I had had to lean between Burke and Hare. That night I did not sleep a wink. Personally I think it was the emanations from the authentic clothes worn by the models that undid me.

There was no denying that getting into the waxworks denoted a measure of fame, however transient.

As I left after my sitting I met a friend of mine, a film producer. He told me he was at work on a picture that required a wax effigy and had come to Tussaud's to collect a cast-off.

'Who did they give you?' I asked.

'Keir Hardie,' he answered.

Sic transit . . .

As my social circle broadened at home, it lengthened abroad, which was unexpected. A rash of articles about the revival of caricature in Britain broke out in the foreign Press, literally from China to Peru, accompanied from time to time by reprints of my cartoons as evidence. It was an unprecedented honour for me when the *New York Times* and other American newspapers spread over five columns of their leader pages some of my pacifying cartoons about Anglo-American relations. That was a kicking and yelling subject even in those days, and, as one grown up in dominion conditions which were in effect a compromise between the ways of life of both countries, I had felt it to be my special province. When I drew a cartoon called 100% AMERICAN HISTORY, including the Ku Klux Klan, the Sacco–Vanzetti case, and other less wholesome features of American life, it was a novelty to find an editor in Texas retorting tartly that, anyway, American children, unlike British children, had shirts to their backs. He had evidently heard of our 'distressed areas.' It was an even greater honour a few weeks later to be offered a contract by one of the largest newspaper chains in the United States. I typed out the freedom clause in my Beaverbrook agreement and sent it to the management asking if they would agree to it. 'We would not wish anyone to join our newspapers who thought he would not be happy with us,' replied the editor, evasively. 'I should be perfectly happy. The question is, would you?' I answered, keeping to the point. There was no reply. Beaverbrooks don't grow on trees.

Among these American exchanges occurred an important event which had a considerable effect on my future. To the *New York American* in 1928 was wirelessed one of my cartoons across the Atlantic. The cartoon itself was not much—something about an abortive Franco-British naval pact—but it was the first newspaper cartoon to be sent overseas by radio. Technically the result was appalling, but I was struck by the wonderful possibilities of the new transmission. Would it ever be feasible to sit in London drawing cartoons for circulation over a world network? I put the idea away on ice for later consideration.

On the whole my reception in America, even when I was critical, was friendly. I had a little trouble with the French Press about a cartoon in which I characterized the behaviour of Laval and Briand as resembling, politically speaking, that of gangsters. I had amiable comment and fairly regular reprintings in Germany, Scandinavia and Central Europe. A few cartoons filtered through to the Italian Press, but the choice was too obviously designed to fit the wrong policy to be pleasing.

The affairs of India came into my cartoons a lot in the late nineteen-twenties and early 'thirties. The personalities engaged tempted attention on their picturesqueness alone and Churchill supplied enough vehement opposition to the idea of Indian self-government to invite pertinent comment. To the harsh wranglings which brought the break between Baldwin and Churchill I contributed a string of cartoons which directly and indirectly, by ridiculing their diehard opponents, supported Baldwin and Hoare and their Government of India Bill. As a result I came in for some of the anger flying about. Churchill wrote me off (in his book *Thoughts and Adventures*, 1932) as a 'green-eyed young Antipodean radical . . . particularly mischievous . . . Low's pencil is not only not servile. It is essentially mutinous. You cannot bridle the wild ass of the desert, still less prohibit its natural hee-haw.' According to Churchill I delighted to 'gibe at the British Empire' and was 'all for retreat in India'—which was pretty rich, since by birth, growth and viewpoint I was considerably more representative of the Empire than he was, and probably more advanced too, so far as India and the Commonwealth were concerned.

During the India Conference of 1931 Mahatma Gandhi came to town. I found him at the House of Commons explaining his views to an all-party meeting of M.P.s. Gandhi was evidently a voluble talker, difficult to get him to subside when answering questions. His son, a round-faced youth, and Miss Slade stood on one side modestly, speechless. He received me with loud laughter as though I were a very funny friend of the family. He was waving the evening paper about with a cartoon of mine on the meeting of Gandhi and Windhi (my name-play for Winston). Mouth a wide gap with three teeth on each side lower jaw. On this encouragement I invited myself around to his abode to see him more privately.

At the Knightsbridge flat, conducted into presence by Gandhi junior. Found Gandhi squatting on floor near fire, spinning-wheel on right, little brown head with short grey hair peeping elfishly out of copious home-spun blanket—large hands and feet—skin warm and pleasant to touch—all very welcoming. He was the richest piece of character I had seen for many a long day. He was surrounded by Indian friends sitting on chairs in a semicircle. 'Shall we draw apart?' says he. We did.

My attitude was that of the artist, not the news-hawk. I was not out after political secrets but to get the flavour of the human being. I foresaw, however, that he would expect me to ask him questions, so I had designed some the night before, woolly enough to get him going without demanding too much reply from me or distracting my attention from my own particular kind of observation. All the same I found his talk so much a part of himself that I had to make some notes. I opened:

'I have come to observe your shadow, not to ask questions.' (That was a good one!) 'But I should like to hear from your own lips whether the national spirit you are fostering in India is likely to draw your people closer to the Western peoples or to separate the two even more.'

That covered a lot of ground and started him off nicely. I knew the answers, which were that two peoples cannot draw together, but rather otherwise, while one is subject to the other; and that his 'national spirit' aimed at putting a free India in such a condition that she could draw as close to the Western peoples as was good for her and vice versa, etc. etc. From there we passed to desirable forms of association between India and Britain, tossing 'provincial autonomy,' 'self-government,' 'central responsibility,' 'limited dominion status,' 'gradual dominion status' and 'commonwealth fiscal union' about like garments at a bargain counter. Gandhi saw too many Churchills about; he feared straitjackets and he wanted no British cut of government for India. He particularly objected to the words 'imperial' and 'empire' as having a 'conquering' significance. To keep the pot

Gandhi

boiling and with an eye-and-a-half on the picturesque I suggested that he might solve that problem by accepting the commission of Governor-General himself. The mental picture of a cocked hat crowning his native homeliness was irresistible.

I had heard most of this before, but it sounded fresh coming from the Mahatma himself, eye to eye, his face close to mine, breathing a perfume of goat's-milk over me as he talked animatedly. A future India mostly agricultural, returned to village communities and peasant crafts in the old Indian tradition, sounded natural and wholesome. Industrialization, by comparison, sounded perverse and miserable. Highly industrialized peoples like the United States, for instance, were surely marching to disaster. The British working people, even before they were touched by their future problems, did not live as well as the workers in South Africa . . . etc. etc. We got around to the subject of clothes.

'I myself habitually make use of many Western ways,' said Gandhi, looking anything but Western. 'But habits and customs depend on locality. I myself wear a simple loincloth in India. Here I have to wear all this stuff. Look at your clothes. No good for India. Homes for moths. Those curtains. Dust collectors. "Draw closer," you say. Why don't *you* wear a loincloth? Chairs are not an improvement upon sitting on the floor. Why doesn't everyone sit on the floor? There is much in Western culture that is good for India— but vice versa. By the interchange of ideas and the absorption of what is good by both, will they draw together in hearts.'

'Let us turn from petty politics to the wider subject of living,' I said. 'Tell me how to live.'

Exposing three of his teeth in a happy chuckle, Gandhi gave me his blue-print: 'Have no possessions and want none. No trivial ambitions to win admiration, wealth or power. Do what you do because you think it right, seeking nothing else, not even the personal gratification that would accompany the achievement of your purpose. In simplicity, directness and strength, such a man could never be defeated.'

Unanswerable. I had asked for it and I had got it. I unlocked myself from the squatting posture and turned to go.

'Do you want also to interview my go-o-oat, Mr. Lo-o-o-ow?' twinkled Mr. G., as he resumed his place at the fire, lean legs falling into their impossible position with a click. Now from the distant years I reflect on the successful exponent of passive resistance, with his genius for exploiting a situation. Would he have succeeded in other circumstances? With other people than the British? Maybe not. The British had had a sturdy band of moralists keeping the exploiters up to the responsibilities and aims of empire long before Gandhi appeared. The people had grown a conscience about India by the nineteen-thirties. Moreover, the old imperialism was wearing out, and change had to come about. Gandhi happened to be in the right place at the right time, like many other great men, when the necessities converged and the opportunity offered. No derogation of his greatness in that. On the contrary. One has to have what it takes. Gandhi was patently a good man, and endearing, with a penetrating quality of happy benevolence. It would have been easy to pursue perfection in his company.

Nehru, whom I met a little later, impressed me strongly, too, but in a different way. An Indian Cripps, blend of idealism and practicality, far more political talent than Gandhi, but less inner sunshine.

It wasn't long before I was attending diplomatic functions and inside the embassies. Naturally I was most readily received by the representatives of countries who found in my cartoons some hint of sympathy to the policies being followed by their governments. My opposition to fascism barred Italy. I had been constantly advocating resumption of trade with Soviet Russia, believing in the good old principle of keeping people from fighting by making them mutually profitable. That made me *persona grata* to the Russians, when, through my amiable colleague Bruce Lockhart, I met a few of them in 1931.

In the early 'thirties the Soviet Union was still the experiment, not yet the highly polished centre of an empire. Its representatives were eager and wore chips on their shoulders. Members of an embassy were not where they were for fun, but to work for their countries, and I was never fool enough to forget it. But over and above that, their merits as human beings could be appreciated.

223

I had met Krassin when he had come over in 1920 to negotiate the first trade treaty, but only for a word; and after him several lesser officials. With only one could I ever talk politics, and then inconclusively, as a sceptic might discuss Genesis with a fundamentalist. (That particular chap turned up ten years later in Berlin as one of the elastic boys who fixed up the preliminaries of the Soviet–Nazi treaty with Ribbentrop.) There was a procession of charming fellows passing through the Soviet Embassy in those days. Ambassador Sokolnikov, who always looked like Banquoski's ghost, had a sort of sad humour. His account of the exile's return journey from Siberia was rich. According to him (and he had had the experience) in pre-revolutionary days the blundering incompetence of the Czarist police was such that there was a regular return traffic with fixed routes, code sign-posts, aid stations and all, and prisoners were no sooner billeted in their huts up north than they were preparing to escape back again to the south as soon as the snow permitted. By Sokolnikov's account one walked into some chap in Moscow who should by rights have been in Siberia, and one just said: 'Hello, Joe! Back again?' The unexpected, told with such authenticity and plausibility, made me laugh so much that I spilt my Russian champagne into the Ambassador's lap. That was a memorable party. Most of the company were recalled to Russia during the purge and I never saw them again. Sokolnikov was sent to Siberia.

When Litvinov came to town for a few days he impressed me as a likeable snuffling old chap with a good sense of humour who enjoyed nothing so much as putting his opponents on toast with an unexpected turn of argument. It was pleasant to see his big face perspiring and his big stomach shaking with Russian mirth. The company had been talking about a surprising production of gold in Russia during the year.

'What does a self-contained socialist economy want gold for? What are you going to do with it?' asks innocent Low.

'Make public lavatories out of it,' says Litvinov.

When Litvinov rose at the League of Nations to proclaim the great truth that the way to bring about disarmament was for everybody to disarm, there was a tinge of affection mixed in with the general exasperation of his fellow delegates. When Molotov said much the same thing at much greater length in pontifical periods at the United Nations twenty years later, there was plain exasperation.

In the early 'thirties Anglo-Soviet relations were on the upgrade again and the Russians were encouraging visitors to the U.S.S.R. The suggestion came up that I should be the Soviet Government's guest on a round tour. I couldn't see myself going alone, so I attached myself to a party of writers which was just leaving. Many of them I already knew — Kingsley Martin, Hamilton Fyfe, Francis Yeats-Brown, Robert Fraser and others.

Litvinov

I hurriedly packed toilet equipment and rushed for the boat to the New Civilization.

I need not have hurried. Russians, I discovered, always take their time. After interminable farewells to well-wishers and a couple of tiresome stops in mid-Baltic while the engineer did something mysterious to the engines, we arrived.

18

In those days of 1932 conditions in Soviet Russia were somewhat less rigid than they became later. The story told in
London was that the people were miserable, that the plans
for reconstruction were a failure but that visitors to Russia
saw only what Stalin wished them to see. I wasn't surprised to
find none of this was entirely true. It always aggravates me to
know why people have to spoil a good case by childish and
irrelevant misrepresentation. The case of a good Western democrat
against communism (or, to be precise, the Russian practice of
communism) is that it makes liberty the price of efficiency. For
material ends it demands the curtailment of freedom of opinion
and expression, regiments thought and thereby limits the growth
of the mind. Is that not enough to move a man? No, not for some
people, apparently. They have to be moved by instances of
bestiality, of less importance comparatively, and more easily
inspiring the needless exaggeration and invention which defeat
their own object in the long run.

Like any government with its guests, our hosts wanted to show
us the creditable things rather than the discreditable, but we had
no difficulty in seeing what we wanted to see—when we knew
what we wanted to see and could get around the language
difficulty. That didn't worry me because what I was interested
in was the Russians and how they liked living in order. Particularly the young ones. Oddly enough the typical Russian was
young. Leningrad, Moscow, Nizhni, Kharkov, Kiev were full of
boys and girls of eighteen or so. (Where were the old?) Millions
and millions of shortish square people. The typical Russian was
clean-shaven. Some fellows shaved their heads even, and went
about with naked polls, outraging beauty with their likeness to
worn billiard-balls. Wide simple faces. I felt sure that if I shouted

'Freedom of the Mind!' nobody would know what I was talking about. The new generation was not sinister-looking and, in defiance of all the known facts about the food situation, didn't seem to be starving. Whatever the dead ones had thought, the live ones seemed cheerful, running about to their various jobs and stopping on street corners to pass the time of day, just like you or me. It was hot, mind you, undervest-and-pants weather, and therefore shortcomings in clothing and boots were not specially noticeable.

That was the proletariat, of course. Where was the peasant? Everybody knew that the Five Year Plan was being built, so to speak, on the stomach of the peasant. If you wanted to meet the peasant you had to go to a railway station, where you literally stumbled over him lying about in heaps, surrounded by all his chattels, waiting for the train to take him to somewhere else. One of the results of the revolution was that it had aroused in the peasant a desire to travel. On the Volga boat as I looked down from the upper deck on the sprawling mass of travelling peasants sleeping or chewing sun-flower seeds below, I observed that they did not look happy. But then they did not look unhappy either. They just looked blank. 'What can you do with 140 millions of those?' said a fellow passenger. 'Give 'em the vote?' I, a lifelong believer in democracy, maintained a dignified silence. (Question for private reflection: by how much and for how long might it be tolerable to impose order and restrict the individual liberty of a backward people to enable it to catch up?)

All visitors to Russia had, of course, to absorb what they called 'cultural background,' which meant a gay whirl of museums, public monuments, and parks. The parks of culture and rest were soothing. A troop of naked sunburned kids romped under the trees, and the proletariat spent its 'sixth day' sleeping, boating, bathing and playing games on the beach. I inspected the interior of one of the rest houses, once the gilded mansion of a golosh-king. Under the large portrait of the former mistress, a dainty beauty, lay a worker in an iron bedstead reading a novel. Subject for a drawing.

I mixed with the holiday crowd at Peterhof, and I disliked intensely the loud speaker attached to the front gate delivering lectures. I was reprimanded for mishandling the Tsar's photograph album at Detskoye Seloe. These public properties are well looked after. I visited Lenin's apartment at Smolny and, in a moment of rebellion against museums, outraged the attendant by sitting down on Lenin's sacred wire mattress. I was rudely prevented by a soldier from sketching in the precincts of the Kremlin. I 'did' an Anti-God Box, a hut filled with propaganda against religion. It was more anti-clerical than anti-God—and dull. There were many churches left, so I went to one of them, too. Fairly full, much better 'produced' than the Anti-God Box. The Bolsheviks didn't stop you, they just said you shouldn't. But then they said you shouldn't get drunk, either, and I saw drunks.

This religious question was very interesting. The first time I saw a Lenin Corner, with a big black bust of Lenin looking out of a nook of red draperies, flanked by two aspidistras, and illuminated by red lights, I was taken aback. But after seeing more, and after treading solemnly in the daily procession to the mausoleum in Kremlin Square—(take your hats off! No horseplay here!) to inspect the embalmed Lenin himself, I understood. Simple hearts yearned for a personal symbol.

With Kingsley Martin I went to the Suksharevski Market, where people supplemented their rations by purchase in the open. This was the seamy side. A kind of Caledonian Market of oddments of food and clothing, dirty and crowded. An old woman with a cake of home-made soap, another with a lump of sausage in a bit of newspaper, an old man with a pair of worn slippers. A greasy person tried to sell me a fish. It was an extremely dead fish, and he wanted as much for it in British currency as would buy me a good dinner at the Savoy. 'No, tovarish,' I said, 'I will stand for almost anything, but I will *not* become the owner of that fish.'

I went to a court presided over by a competent damsel, not without sex appeal, who had, I was told, power to inflict sentences up to ten years. It was all very homely and there were no policemen. And I visited a gaol in Moscow which was practically run by the prisoners themselves. Inmates who made themselves a nuisance were voted cads by their fellows and sent to coventry —just like a West End club. There was in those days no talk of slave-labour camps.

I inspected hospitals and examined babies; I was impressed by the incredibly vast enterprise of Dnieprostroi; and I met a number of Americans. American engineers seemed to be popular and helpful thereabouts. I slept in one of the new workers' flats there one night under the impression that it was an hotel.

Factories? Yes, I visited factories—lots of 'em. Good, bad and indifferent. There was the confusion at Nizhni; but there were the smooth Amo works and the clock-work Shelmastroi. I saw over a collective farm, a state farm and a communal farm.

VISITOR TO SOVIET RUSSIA (1932)
'I, as usual, had merged myself in the scenery by wearing a Russian blouse.'

228A

Good and bad. We had long solemn talks about all kinds of subjects with all kinds of important persons. It was too early to generalize about the Five-Year Plan at that stage.

I had never travelled with a mixed body of 'intellectuals' before. In some ways my companions were as interesting as Russia. Fair-minded, trained observers as most of them were, it was difficult to be starkly objective about a subject surrounded by years of passionate controversy. One could see on one side the subtle struggle against accepting too easily, on the other against rejecting too easily. One of us, finding a bolt lying on the road, deduced that all Russian machinery fell to pieces; when through manifest incompetence our boat arrived at Astrakhan at black midnight, another insisted that this was designed so that we should not see the defective local tramway; another, on the other hand, noted with enthusiasm the advance in transport production evidenced in a vast assembly of motor vans, dismissing as a detail of no consequence that they had no wheels.

We were a happy band, apart from one small rift in our domestic lute. It was hot rocketing about from farm to factory in the Ukraine, and the company had let itself go a bit sartorially. I, as usual, had merged myself in the scenery by wearing a Russian blouse. Kingsley Martin wore a rambler outfit. The only really creditable chap was Francis Yeats-Brown, who appeared always, whether facing a steam-hammer or a wheat silo, as though he had stepped out of Bond Street. The rest of the company looked as though it were on holiday in a fishing village. 'Damn it!' said Fyfe (a peppery chap when vexed), 'We are ambassadors! What will the Russians think?'

I poked about a bit by myself in the back alleys of Moscow. By night it appeared to be orderly and well kept. Clean streets, no cadgers, no prostitutes. It reminded me of Sunday in New York minus Broadway. Although my Russian speech was limited to 'Please,' 'Thank you,' and 'Give me a cup of tea, comrade,' one could do a lot by waving one's arms about and drawing ideographs. I found the inhabitants friendly and interested.

In a shady spot at the bottom of the garden at the Foreign Office I found a gnomish person who looked as though he should have been sitting on a mushroom. This was Radek, then the Soviet Press chief and supreme boss of propaganda. He spoke English fluently, and after he had buttered me up telling me how good and important I was, and I had buttered him up telling him how important and good he was, he proved to be a lively entertaining chap by no means uncritical of his colleagues. When

229

Radek

we were joined by Ivy Litvinov there was some graceful sarcasm flying about. It felt just like home.

The lady was called away and I was left with Radek. We talked of propaganda, the techniques of persuasion, emphasis and diminution, the comparative effectiveness of statement and parable, soothing expression and exciting expression, shock or tickle in the use of words and images. It came to this: it all depends upon the receptivity of the audience. You have to stay within its range of pick-up, otherwise you are talking to yourself.

'Now, that's where pictures have an advantage,' said he.

'Not really,' I said. 'Much the same limitations. All right if you stick to trite simplicity and traditional symbolic forms. But if you want to extend and bring your picture-language up to date, it's an educational job of labelling and impressing new associations—reiteration and repetition.'

'I always look at the cartoons in a newspaper first,' he said. 'They tell me how things are. Your medium is no good for plain statement, but it is ideal for creating prejudice.'

'Sounds immoral,' said I, knowing better.

'Oh, no,' he said. 'That depends on the aim of the prejudice.'

'Supposing your aim is to weaken prejudice and provoke people to use their own brains?' Someone spirited him away and our pleasant talk ended in the air.

No doubt the widespread illiteracy, the slowness of building an adequate education system, and official urgency to help along public understanding accounted for the plentiful use of cartoons in historical, instructional and social establishments. The Bolsheviks certainly seemed cartoon-minded. The Revolutionary Museums in Moscow and Leningrad had every stage of the popular progress copiously illustrated with cartoons. The clubs and meeting halls had their cartoons representing Lenin urging on workers, or Stalin pointing meaningly to some factory or other. Go into a hospital and ask questions about infant mortality, and

230

ten to one an official would produce cartoons of a babe lying on a tomb to illuminate his statistics. Go outside and you would find on each side of the front door cartoons showing the evils of dirtiness or carelessness. Cartoons preaching temperance or service adorned hoardings along the public highway, in the style of our Western advertising posters. Here and there cartoons on canvas streamers stretched across the road or from end to end of a building. The parks of culture and rest had the best current cartoons on international politics reproduced in colour six feet high and mounted on trees. As a variation there were caricatures in the round, large dummy comic figures of reprehensible foreigners like Austen Chamberlain and Poincaré, standing about under the foliage and in the open spaces for the dogs to sniff at.

The public appetite for pictorial satire was revealed in the wall newspapers, feature of all apartment-houses, business offices, factories and clubs. The wall cartoons ranged from light criticism of local affairs to serious subjects crowded rather painfully with symbolism. Just to be friendly I myself contributed a ponderous work to a wall newspaper, containing one symbolic representation of Lenin, one symbolic rising sun, six symbolic peasants' dwellings, five symbolic ships and one symbolic grain elevator. Nobody knew what it meant, but it gave great satisfaction.

The free use of public ridicule as a social corrective was a feature of Bolshevik Russia in 1932. It was difficult for Boris, who turned up tight for work yesterday, or for Olga, who had been loafing on the job latterly, to resist the point of large colour cartoons fixed above their machines, representing them respectively as a sot and a slut; or for Ivan, who allowed his flat at the apartment-house to get into an insanitary condition, to ignore a drawing of a filthy hog posted beside his front door. The High Authorities, recognizing the inestimable value of this medium of public opinion (except, of course, so far as they themselves might be the object of adverse attention), encouraged and assisted it by issuing ready-made coloured posters of, say, the Camel or the Tortoise, commonly accepted symbols in Russia of stupidity and sluggishness, with convenient blank space for filling in name or names, to be publicly presented with loud jeers to deserving persons or departments. Other posters of the like kind applied to bad temper, speculation and loose morals. Their presentation was an unenviable distinction.

The position in the Soviet world of the more sedate pictorial arts was interesting. The régime took proper care of art treasures, old masters and new, but all that belonged to the past, they said.

231

No more 'studies,' no more 'scenes.' Art for art's sake be blowed. In 1932 artists who were more concerned with technical virtuosity than idea content had a thin time. They painted what they liked, but there were few customers. The biggest buyers of pictures at that time were the workers' clubs and government bodies, central and local, which all had every-picture-tells-a-story tastes. 'Let art bear some relation to the life of the people.' If you must paint landscapes, paint them with collective farms. If you must paint nudes, paint them working a tractor. 'Do us a hundred yards of art showing the success of the Five Year Plan, or the heroism of the Red Army.'

On our return journey across the Ukraine to the frontier railway station of Shepatovka we were gone over thoroughly by Russian customs officials. Standing alongside an ominous heap of books, photographs and undeveloped films confiscated from a group of Bavarian students our train had picked up on the way, a fat inspector solemnly inspected my two sketchbooks. He grew more and more glum as he turned the pages. He came to a rough note I had made of some Red Army soldiers singing. Naturally they were in uniform. This was something he understood. Military spy-work. The sketchbooks could not be allowed to leave Russia, but must be sent to Moscow for examination. When I told him I was a guest of the Soviet Government he just shook his head, intimating pretty clearly that he had heard that tale before.

By a bit of good luck, Hamilton Fyfe saw a man in a uniform, obviously high up in the service since he was doing nothing. He seemed only mildly impressed by the threat that the whole British Press would be filled with the incident and *The Times* would make it a front-page story; somewhat more moved by the argument that such treatment of a guest of the Soviet Government would not improve his chances of promotion. Matters grew serious. The train whistled. I was desperate and threw a little temperament around. The wheels began to move, the whole wrangle moving at the top of its voice with them along the platform . . . The official's nerve broke, he thrust the sketchbooks at me and I scrambled aboard. It was a near thing. I wore the sketchbooks beneath my undershirt for the rest of the journey.

Parting from my companions I broke the return journey at Berlin. I wished to take a look at the Germans. My obscure little hotel was clean and comfortable, but otherwise the experience was depressing. I had never seen so many prostitutes, male and female, at one time as in the Kurfurstendam. Coming from orderly Moscow, some parts of Berlin appeared to be corrupt and out of hand. There was a tense, desperate air about the faces, although one could escape, of course, into one of the expensive restaurants if one had the money.

It was evident something was brewing. Every now and then there were scowling young men in raincoats and leggings. (The Nazis had just evaded the law against private-army uniforms by all wearing identical raincoats.) I went to a political meeting and although I could not follow what was said the temperature of expression was violent in the extreme. A few months later Hitler was in power.

My Russian tour made two changes in my personal appearance which became permanent tags of identity. The bright Ukrainian sunshine had troubled my eyes, which had always been more comfortable in shadow. In Germany I bought a continental wide-brimmed hat to shade them. Coming down the Volga several of us grew beards for a lark. As time passed one after another of my companions became horrified at their reflections and shaved. I did not, and when I returned to London, my Leninesque appearance so entranced my family that I kept my beard for eight years.

Travel broadens the mind, undoubtedly. I decided that since I was expressing myself so freely about world opinion, world reactions, world menaces and so on, it was high time I saw this world. After that my newspaper contracts arranged for periodical breaks for travel abroad. During the succeeding years up to the Hitler war I covered Europe from Finland west and southward, part of Northern Africa and both North and South Americas, getting the general hang of things, on the way visiting political institutions and making a hit-and-run personal contact with a mixed assortment of the prominent political figures of the time.

After Eastern democracy I had to survey Western democracy. Public enterprise planned and controlled by party oligarchy for the working classes, contrasted with private enterprise, restrained and safeguarded by representatives elected by a majority vote of all classes. Collective order versus individual liberty.

I got around to the United States in 1936 when things were settling down after the slump years. We approached via South America in a passage full of argument with South Americans about Spain, and punctuated by explosions. A sea-fight in the port of Lisbon, two Spanish Franco gunboats in mutiny trying to run the gauntlet of river-bank batteries to reach a government port; remains of recent revolutions in Santos and Lima; a bomb against the British at Buenos Aires; and more remains of another revolution at Havana.

The United States seemed remarkably peaceful by comparison. This was my second visit, I having crossed from San Francisco to New York by easy stages in 1919 on my way to London. I found some previous floating impressions confirmed. Such as, for instance, that American newspapers, movies and radio did their people a disservice by representing American life as sensational, so that when a visitor arrived and saw calm and order he thought it was phoney. I was surprised when I rambled by midnight around big American cities to find them so well behaved. Probably the average amount of sin went on behind closed doors, but I felt that American vice was over-publicized. So was the crookedness of American public men. One should not leave it to be taken for granted that there were good Americans.

In the United States I kept forgetting I was not an American. Naturally. My native land was 'new' too, and its early settlers had met pioneering conditions not so very unlike those their kind had met in America. The ways and social atmosphere of American small towns resembled those I had grown up with. I had had to learn the English but I felt I knew most about Americans to start with.

Being, therefore, by nature a sort of honorary American, I had no difficulty in talking freely to anybody. There were, of course, plenty of obvious things to argue about in our (American) way-of-life, things an Englishman would have found hard to understand. The way Americans had material success mixed up with virtue, for instance. If 'successful,' you were good in America. If a 'failure' it must have been because you were wanting in diligence or character—which amounted practically to sin . . . This Englishman would certainly have approved the American idea of the family as the social basis; but he would have disapproved the tendency to herd, to live in one another's pockets . . . Arising out of that, this Englishman might have thought that for a people that talked so much of individualism and private enterprise, there was not enough tolerance of individual eccentricity. Where life was lived pretty publicly and everybody had his nose in everybody else's business, the very friendliness of American life made the dissenter more conspicuous. If the country club and the business community were mobilized against one, life could have been as intolerable as it might have been for the official misfit in Soviet Russia. Decidedly he would have been sure there was more individualism among the supposedly class-ridden English. He would have ended by having grave doubts as to whether Americans really understood democracy.

There were Americans and Americans, and I did not meet enough of them on this occasion to write a book on The Mind of a Nation. But I found the everyday ordinary Americans I did meet ill-informed and irresponsible about politics outside their own local affairs. Few had a truly national, much less a world view. I became almost frightened at some of the nonsense talked about Russia, Italy, Germany, Spain, Britain and what we people overseas had come to call The Situation. Few appeared to think that Hitler was any business of theirs.

Here, it struck me, was the weakness of Western democracy. Unlike the Eastern version which demanded only subservience, it demanded a measure of intelligent interest and comprehension on the part of its members. Otherwise it became a hollow fraud, and its members a pushover for the first dominating personality that undertook to do their thinking for them. Even the power to change leaders, when exercised by those who have to substitute emotion for reason and prejudice for knowledge, is no guarantee of its survival.

I was still pursuing this theme when I came to New York and found two pertinent exhibitions of current methods of debauching the mass mind, different but oddly similar.

New Yorkers told you with pride that they were hard-boiled. Well, they might have been boiled, but I should not have called them hard. Try to boil a marshmallow and you will get my meaning. On the contrary, I concluded that they were sentimental, loving emotion for its own sake.

There were at the time, besides a pending presidential election, at least four popular irruptions of a religio-political-economic nature. The most important was that being raised by the celebrated priest, Father Coughlin, a radio phenomenon who, I was told, had reached a position of national influence. I listened to his vehement diatribe against President Roosevelt, and other persons and things, but the precise substance of his objections eluded me. Parts of the Press had evidently been cruel to him, so Father had included them also in his list of anathema.

I found that he was staying at my hotel, having arrived earlier with a fuss that blocked the traffic, so I paid him a visit. The interview was a bit jerky. He was changing his shirt at the time.

'What of the Press?' I asked this short, plump glowering person.

'Our degraded Press has its tail in the gutter,' he replied, eyeing me suspiciously.

'And what of the Radio?' I pursued.

'Come to my meeting tonight,' he answered.

I went. 'Is this Father Coughlin's meeting?' I asked the taxi-driver.

'Sure. Look at their faces,' he said.

A full house was in process of being worked up to emotional heights by a cornet playing *When Irish Eyes are Smiling*. A pretty cutie handed me two flags to wave and sold me a song entitled *Father Coughlin is Coming*. Then, to loud applause and waving of flags, a company of young men in grey uniforms with shiny helmets and drums arrived, followed later by Father Coughlin himself, illuminated by two spotlights, popping up in a red plush pulpit decorated with flags and six microphones.

The applause, ably guided and swollen by the drums whenever it weakened, lasted for ten minutes by the clock. Father Coughlin then delivered an address during which he contradicted himself so often and so vehemently that I thought his lower jaw would drop off.

Mosley, in Britain, did it much better. Coughlin made two inartistic touches which Mosley would have scorned. He often tipped to the audience the right place to applaud by pointing to the 'mikes' and clapping himself: and, after rising in his peroration to bawling ferocity, he suddenly consulted his wrist-watch, grasped a 'mike,' assumed a soothing announcer's voice and said into it, 'That concludes the broadcast from the Hippodrome, New York. Father Coughlin will be on the air next Saturday through the Mutual System.'

Pretty raw. But decidedly a popular success.

A more satisfying evening I spent looking up Father Divine. Father Divine was 'de Lawd' of *Green Pastures* come to life. Hailed by 2,000,000 negroes as God himself, Father Divine had a chain of establishments known as 'heavens,' miraculously financed and dispensing free chicken dinners to his followers. As I approached the headquarters in Harlem the noise could be heard a block away.

I edged through the squeeze of coloured brothers into the hall, which had a capacity of 500 but was holding 700. The air was thick. A streamer saying *Father Divine is Dean of The Universe* floated across the narrow platform at one end, and several crudely lettered texts saying *Thank You, Father*, and *Father Divine is God*, tastefully illuminated in gold paint, hung on the wall.

Everybody was crooning, not to say howling, a monotonous, interminable rhythm of *Oh, Thank You Father, For All You've Done for Me*, clapping hands and dancing from the knees. When 700 strong people all dance up and down together the floor dances with them, so I, therefore, under protest, found myself dancing up and down too, but calmly and with dignity.

An obliging angel, very like a distinguished Fleet Street journalist, but of course much darker, steered me past a drum and a banjo to the platform, where he took my name. 'I have come all the way from London, England, to hear Father Divine,' I explained. A tall, thin, coloured man next to us was overcome by his feelings and broke into a wild spasmodic dance, like the reflex actions of a chicken with its neck wrung. The singing stopped at last, and a lady started to testify, interrupted by occasional blasts of 'Wonderful!' 'He's Gahd!' and yells of just plain emotion. 'Yoo-hoo! Faa-ther!' squeaked a female voice at one-minute intervals.

My angel took me down one floor to the Banqueting Hall. There I found a long horse-shoe table, at the curve of which was Father's upholstered chair, with spoons, knives and forks radiating from it. The inner space was chock-a-block with coal-black mammies, tight-packed as sardines crooning endlessly; and along the sides were small tables at which mixed company feasted on chicken, stopping now and then, with mouth full, to shout, 'He's Gahd!' 'Peace.'

Suddenly a frightful hullaballoo upstairs. My angel turned to me shining with excitement. 'He's come! Gahd's come!'

'Hooray!' I said, just to be sociable.

We stampeded with about 200 others out and up a fire-escape back to the floor above, where through a small door we bulged on to the back of the platform.

237

There he was. A short, broad, coffee-coloured person in a brown suit and sporting tie, sitting benevolently regarding his frenzied flock. Someone introduced me, saying that I was a visitor from London, England, come to hear him speak.

Father rose with a peculiar glint in his eye and announced in a voice that needed oiling that he had not intended to speak, but there were visitors present who had come to hear him speak and so he was speaking, and since such could only eventuate upon a reciprocationing basis, he would now like to hear the visitors speak and the visitors would now speak. (Ear-splitting applause, during which Mr. Low of London, England, retreated down the fire-escape covered in confusion.)

Opinions may differ as to the secondary qualities required in a President of the United States, but undoubtedly the first is personality. I went to a dinner of Democrats where Franklin Roosevelt's magnificent voice (magnificent is the right word—it was magnified ten times life-size), coming from a big black box, completely stole the whole show from the local orators.

I had to sample this presence for myself at first hand, so I slipped a sketchbook into my pocket and went to Washington. At the same time I wished to add some authenticity to my portraits of the United States Executive, so first I kept a series of appointments made by a friend of mine with members of the Roosevelt administration. Secretary of the Treasury Morgenthau had the funniest stories. Talking over people, I told him Americans should not make the mistake of thinking Neville Chamberlain was a coward. Far from it. He once saved a girl from drowning. 'Morgy' thought this was a gag. 'Did he get his pants wet?' he said.

I enjoyed most my morning with Secretary of State Cordell Hull, who was kind and fatherly. I had respected Hull from afar, and as he sat for me, with his sad eyes, lean expressive mouth and aquiline profile, answering my questions in his soft accent, my respect deepened into confidence. At length, by arrangement with Steve Early, helped with a handful of letters from mutual friends in Britain, I came to Mr. President. In real life he did not disappoint.

European dictators affected the cheap dodge of sitting afar off in the corners of large rooms, so that callers had to walk over an acre of carpet, shrinking progressively at every step; but President Roosevelt's room at the White House was not big, and in four or five steps you were on top of him—or rather he was on top of you,

MT. PRESIDENT

President Roosevelt

for at close range he put himself over with tremendous effect.
Six feet two inches and broad, he sat against the curved window
with an inconspicuous Stars-and-stripes over it, and his desk
seemed too small for him.

He was a bad sitter. From the waist up alive and on the move
all the time, ruffling his hair, throwing his arms about, twisting
his body, turning his face to the ceiling, laughing too much,
either opening his mouth or distorting its shape by wedging
his cigarette-holder too far to the side. He might have been
a swell President, but he didn't know how to pose for his
portrait.

Beyond the formal routine of agreeable noises to visiting
foreigners and a few personal tit-bits about people we both knew
in London, talk with Roosevelt was short and unimportant.
But it was enough to give me his aura and to fix his personality
in my private panorama of the times. When, six years later, in
the middle of World War II, his friend Harry Hopkins brought me
compliments from Mr. President with a request for an original
drawing of a cartoon he had liked, I sent him also that drawing
I had made at that first encounter, for full measure.

I stayed for one of his Press conferences. That was Mr. President
as the Great Guy. He seemed to know everybody by his first
name and it was all very jolly.

'Well, boys, what are we discussing today? Not politics, I hope,' he says.

Q. 'How's the campaign going, Mr. President?'
A. 'Travelling about is costing me a lot for laundry, Fred.'
Q. 'What are the odds, Mr. President?'
A. 'I've got my bet locked in the safe with the result, Harry.'

(This, I felt, was not how Mr. Baldwin would do it. But I found myself wishing it were.)

19

COMING to the fateful 'thirties, I must sketch briefly my own viewpoint. Of the various systems of order yet tried, I saw democracy, with all its lamentable imperfections, as having the best blend of stability and dignity. Democracy, that is to say, in the Lincolnian sense of government of the people, for the people, by the people through elected representatives; rather than in the Eastern sense of government of the people for some of the people by fortuitous leaders. And if there had to be a choice, as some held, of priorities between political democracy (the right to lift up one's voice and utter one's opinions) and economic democracy (the right to an adequate share in the ownership and production of the common wealth), for one at the expense of the other, I placed political democracy before economic democracy; because, wishing both, I could imagine the second proceeding from the first, but not the first proceeding from the second—indeed I feared that the suppression of the first would eventually be the end of the second, too. Here, it appeared to me, was the rub. With freedom of expression there was democracy, without it there was no democracy. That was fundamental. I believed that the progress of mankind (in which also I believed) was quickened by the free exchange and clash of ideas. It followed that, to me, the most important freedom was the freedom to think and to express the thought. To aid the thinking, the first priority of good government was education, universal and uninhibited, to the end of producing the Community of Informed and Responsible Citizens.

That put me solidly up against the impatient ones who took the view that earthly paradise could be reached much sooner if people were made to shut up and do what they were told; the paternal ones who assumed they were born to do the thinking for everybody else; the self-appointed 'leaders' who sought to restrict the full intellectual development of their 'followers', supposing that by so doing they would increase the latter's efficiency or spiritual well-being.

I believed in freedom. But I knew that freedom was, in an absolute sense, impossible; that it was relative, a constantly changing balance, its application adjusting to circumstances. No freedom to drive on the wrong side of the road, or to set up a private police force, to establish a glue factory in Hyde Park or even to walk naked up and down Regent Street. No freedom to crab other people's freedom, no freedom for the strong to impose their will on the weak; nor even for large majorities to sit on little minorities without due consideration. On the other hand, no freedom for little minorities to frustrate large majorities. I could contemplate with equanimity reconstruction or revolution so long as it were done by democratic process, with freedom of expression intact to help redress manifest injustice. I did not delude myself into believing that many people actually prized freedom, and would not actually prefer comfortable slavery, if it were called something else and they had a generous and kind master. But I believed it to be of the utmost importance that the door be kept open wide for those that did prize it, so that they might be the guardians of opportunity for the others.

In 'foreign affairs' and on questions of peace and war I took the world view. My views were pacific but not pacifist. To my mind it was the first duty of statesmanship to keep people from biting one another. I was enthusiastically for the reduction by agreement of national armaments to a bare minimum, and for the open settlement of international disputes through the League of Nations. The boundaries and interests of peoples in 1930 were far from just, but to dissuade nations from abandoning negotiations and using war as an instrument of policy I looked to the use of collective economic and financial pressure, backed if necessary by a collective or international armed force. If moral and material standards had to be protected from brigands I approved efficient police and defence forces. Under the inexorable pressure of Man's own fertility and ingenuity, I favoured evolution towards a world order along federal lines, strictly preserving local cultures. Local nationalisms, on the other hand, seemed to me to represent a system visibly growing obsolete. Meanwhile, therefore, I did not object to 'unions' and 'spheres of influence.' But no distorted or unnatural influence imposed with a club; certainly no forcible domination of a separate people by a 'master race' for its own profit.

242

'PHEW! THAT'S A NASTY LEAK. THANK GOODNESS IT'S NOT AT OUR END OF THE BOAT' (1932)

This comment on the world depression of 1929–32 was reprinted all over the world and was probably my most widely circulated cartoon

243

That brought me into collision with romantic nationalists, the 'my-country-right-or-wrong' people and believers in race superiority.

The early 'thirties were full of tumult, and there was plenty of material for a political cartoonist. The world slump and long unemployment, the collapse of European finances and economies were all happening. The second world war was cooking, quietly, in far-off China where the Japanese militarists were presenting the League with its first major challenge by seizing Manchuria. The disarmament conference was failing, the carefully drawn pacts to outlaw war were melting away.

I was too busy drawing my cartoons of statesmen falling off precipices, warlords using the League as a doormat, and wolves apologizing to sheep for not being able to restrain their (the sheep's) savage impulses, to attend to the domestic politics of Germany. But at last crisis grew to crescendo and political convulsions culminated in the rise to power of Hitler and the Nazi Party.

After the war everybody had wanted Peace everlasting ('This frightful tragedy must never happen again'); but war was not to be abolished just by throwing one's rifle into a ditch and walking off the battlefield. Peace had to be organized.

There was no doubt about the attitude of the British. They were heartily sick of war and they wanted to try out the possibilities of the new League of Nations. The first step was to hold a disarmament conference. Party leaders vied with one another in advocating disarmament. So much so that the British could hardly tolerate even the idea of contributing to a collective police force. They certainly balked at the risks of a new alliance with France to lessen her feeling of insecurity that made her so unwilling to disarm; and they shied away from the chances of conflict in applying collective economic pressure against Japan. Apart from ethics, the British had an economy wave and they wanted to save money. Of their own accord they did some drastic disarming of themselves in advance.

Time passed and ideals began to decay. The idealists gave ground before the self-styled 'practical' man. On the one hand, the derogation of the League and its collective ideas accelerated. The League, it was said, was a ferment of mischief-making, with its protests and interference. A waste of money, too. Collective security, it was said, was a trap. As for the men of peace, it was said, they were the dangerous ones, starry-eyed cissies that loved every country but their own.

Detail of *The Rehabilitation of Mars* (1929)

On the other, the uniting value of a strong national spirit was discovered anew. The re-establishment of the respectability of war began. One heard more of the nobility and less of the tragedy of the late world war; more of glory than of blood and mud. Sombre naked war literature, plays and films as typified in, say, *All Quiet on the Western Front, Journey's End, Sergeant Grischa*, 'tarnished British heroism.' Any tendency to consider the late war as sordid was 'an indignity to the spirit of our dead.' (It is worthy of note that precisely the same views were being vigorously spread by the new political party in Germany, the Nazis.)

The trend had gone fairly far in 1929 when Lloyd George commented publicly that ten years had left in Britain only a glamorous memory of the war. No Englishman, he went on, had written even approximate truth about it. That had remained for veterans of other nations. 'A quarter of the daily Press of London seem to have undertaken to prove Lloyd George right,' said the *New York Herald-Tribune*. 'They seem to be riding a wave of reaction against realistic war stories—and at least by implication against the correlated peace campaigning.' Various instances of

245

romantic treatment were given, mostly in the Kipling tradition of 'the thin red line of 'eroes.' Ponderous organs of conservative tradition came to the defence of war as fought by Englishmen. Popular newspapers printed side-splitting tales from the trenches to show that it had even its funny side.

This was a drift of feeling which invited an astringent cartoon, so I made one, THE REHABILITATION OF MARS. It showed, against a shop full of unromantic war books, a bemedalled donkey leading a procession of two beefy military figures bearing shoulder-high a burlesque classical God of War powdering his nose, accompanied by a red-faced would-to-god gent and a boy selling newspapers billing 'Jokes about the late good-humoured war,' followed by a mixed crowd of foolish-faced persons carrying banners with captions signifying their opinions that war was gentlemanly and sporting, neither so bloody nor so muddy as had been reported.

That did it. My heavenly choir of critics broke out into the liveliest reaction on record. All the anti-disarmers seemed to be readers of the *Evening Standard*.

Perhaps the cumulative effect of previous cartoons much more direct in debunking the romance of war had brought irritation to the boil over this one. The point of THE REHABILITATION was simple enough, and I had underlined its specific application to the prevailing fashion in war-books in an explanatory caption. Sometimes, however, the impact of a picture on an overheated mind produces a myopic condition in which the meaning, clear at a lower temperature, becomes completely obscured by emotional associations. 'A Low insult to the King's Uniform.' 'This black-guardly suggestion of the madness of all patriots who did their duty in the war . . .' The imagination of one writer went so far as to identify the medals on the donkey's breast with a separate denunciation on account of each one. My careful explanation that the donkey symbolized, not ex-Service men, 'but the movement towards the glorification of war as war . . . [which] to my mind is the sort of tendency that is suitably represented in cartoons as asinine,' was ignored. Many of the published interpretations and descriptions were so twisted and grotesquely unlike my original as to be unrecognizable. One correspondent with more wit than was usual among my hostile chorus summed up the adverse view on a postcard:

'You are so Low you would have to go to
hell in a balloon.'

After eight years of wrangling about the French Security–German Equality question, the Disarmament Conference met and it became evident that nobody was going to disarm much. The world had changed. Japan was eating up China and Hitler had taken over Germany. The emphasis moved from disarmament towards the idea of collective security. In Britain all three political parties agreed that British one-sided disarmament had gone far enough.

British public opinion was virtually united about stopping disarming. It was not until *re*-armament came up that trouble began. Doubtless all would have been well had public opinion been convinced that the 'National' Government was unequivocally devoted to League principles and collective security. Some of its leaders undoubtedly were, but powerful groups among their supporters as undoubtedly were not. There was anxiety, especially on the Left, about where such a government might get to with a double policy of rearmament and conciliation to the dictators, especially since this was the very policy the anti-League elements had been demanding for years.

The emergence of Mussolini had given the men of force (as opposed to the men of persuasion) encouragement and cohesion, as much for his castor-oil methods of dealing with his politicians at home as for his strong-arm treatment of the League. Here was the man of force triumphant. With his aggressive deportment, his shout and his rolling eye, what an impressive contrast to the futile mumblings of the League, the delays of the democracies. To the child-minds obviously Il Duce was patriotism, devotion to country, efficiency, order incarnate. A Strong Hand at the Helm. Pity we didn't have one like him here, old boy.

The British Fascist Party (playfully known by the meaningful initials the B.F.s) was comparatively insignificant until Mosley took over its leadership. Mosley was young, energetic, capable and an excellent speaker. Since I had met him in 1925 he had graduated from close friendship with MacDonald to a job in the second Labour Government; but he had become disgusted with the evasions over unemployment and had resigned to start a party of his own. Unfortunately at the succeeding general election he fell ill with influenza and his party-in-embryo, deprived of his brilliant talents, was wiped out. Mosley was too ambitious to retire into obscurity. Looking around for a 'vehicle' he united himself to the B.F., rechristened 'the Blackshirts,' and acquired almost automatically the encouragement of Britain's then biggest daily newspaper, the *Daily Mail*, which was more than willing to extend its admiration for the Italian original to the local imitation. That was a fateful influenza germ.

By the time Hitler came along in 1933 there was in Britain a fairly active minority of men of force complete with powerful Press support and the beginnings of a private army.

It was not surprising that in these moving circumstances my own post-bag from hostile students of my cartoons in the *Evening Standard* picked up again, ranging from the discursive ('As a business man I feel it my duty to ask whether Low's cartoon is calculated to improve our relations with Germany') to the inarticulate (my own cartoons sent back to me with 'Liar' or 'Lowest of the Low' scrawled across them) and including my own particular regular panel of castigators: from Lord Alfred Douglas who peppered the *Evening Standard* with letters about me so violently insulting as to defeat their writer's offensive purpose and cause only amusement, to Lucy Houston, 'Lucy' to all, who continually assaulted me with 'poems' of calypso quality written in mauve ink, following up any one which she thought might have been too strong with a box of cigars to mitigate the hurt. She liked her picture in the paper. I had not yet invented Colonel Blimp, but Lucy was his premature female counterpart. When I told her she had no policy at all—just Rule-Britannia-and-Damn the-Details—she was delighted and adopted what I had intended as a rebuke for the slogan of the poor old *Saturday Review*, which in its old age had become her property. And there was also a demented female who identified herself with *Joan Bull*, a figure I had created to represent the modern British young woman. Whenever I put Joan in the paper she wrote threatening to sue me for libel. To her, the dictators appeared in the light only of avengers of her fancied wrong, very properly advancing to wipe me off the face of the earth.

Evidence on the whole confirmed the presence of more fans for the older established firm of Mussolini and Fascism than for Hitler and Nazism. And at first defence of the latter came not from Nazis but from dupes of Nazis, usually upbraiding me in terms of pseudo-morality for my lack of generosity, trust and pacific spirit. People who had been coy about shaking hands with German democracy now appeared in the role of peace-makers, all for forgiving and forgetting, ready to clasp the hands of Nazi leaders as fellow-soldiers. One respected general actually collected the German drums 'taken as souvenirs' by the British in the First World War and restored them with great ceremonial as a token of comradeship. No one had thought of doing that to the

Detail of *It Worked at the Reichstag—why not here?* (1933) which caused my cartoons to be banned from Germany

Weimar Government. A retired diplomat wrote to tell me he knew for certain that Hitler was not anti-Jewish at all, that the libellous story that he was so had been put about by villainous Jews who were anti-Hitler. Some, obsessed by propriety, took umbrage at my drawing Hitler at all, because Hitler had just made himself Head of State and it was disrespectful to put Heads of States in cartoons; and others were more moved by the insult of my having in one cartoon carelessly drawn the swastika the wrong way up than by the tragic miseries of the Jews which were its subject-matter.

Although I did not realize it at the time, my cartoons against Hitlerism began in 1923. One of my general themes then was that if the victorious democracies carried on as though German democrats were as much the world's enemies as German junkers, and if they did not foster and strengthen the new Weimar Government instead of driving it to collapse, the wrong Germans must inevitably regain power. The point of the contention was sharpened by the Hitler–Ludendorff 'Putsch' of 1923, which followed the French march into the Ruhr and inspired a cartoon, PLENTY OF ROOM, in which I drew a militaristic figure (resembling the better-known Ludendorff rather than the comparatively obscure Hitler) regaining standing room on the prostrate German people.

As the Weimar Government, despite the efforts of Stresemann and Brüning, withered from discouragement and the field-marshals returned, the outside world began to hear more of the new force in the Brown House at Munich, and in 1930 I began to draw Hitler himself. Bruce Lockhart, the foreign correspondent, returning from Germany after interviewing the Führer, told me that Hitler was an artist, that he was interested in my cartoons and would appreciate the gift of a few originals to hang around the Brown House. I passed on a couple as from one artist to another. It was not clear then, as it was later, that he erroneously supposed my attitude to be anti-democratic because my comments frequently satirized politicians and parties. His mistake.

Hitler lost little time in suppressing all opposition and reorganizing Germany on totalitarian lines. He made no secret of his intentions to disintegrate the world order in which Germany, being deficient in raw materials, was dependent upon friendly collaboration with other nations, and to produce by territorial and political expansion a Greater Germany which would have absolute freedom of political action. In other words, his aim was German dominion over Europe.

I never could believe that Hitler was a certifiable lunatic, as H. G. Wells did, nor even a mere windbag. When I saw how cunningly he had deployed his party men in the key jobs in his first coalition Government, I was pretty sure he was neither. I saw a lot of the artist in Hitler. His political conceptions were the artist's conceptions, seen in shapes, laid on in wide sweeps, errors painted out and details left until later, the bold approach and no fumbling. Essentially a simple mind, uncomplicated by pity. The clever-clever political analysts were deep-thinking the inner meaning of his words, imparting their own complexity of mind to the object of their attentions and writing about Hitler as though he were an inexplicable enigma. I assumed he would do just as he said and made my comment accordingly, earning for myself a cheap reputation as a prophet of remarkable insight when

Detail of *The Girls He Left Behind Him* (1935), which caused my
cartoons to be banned from Italy

now and then I got in a cartoon about an event well before
it happened.

To instruct myself I laid in a stock of the best works I could
get on Communism, Fascism and Nazism and gave myself an
intensive course of comparative ideologies. About six months
later I had for my pains a wall of my studio divided into four
compartments (I had added Liberal Democracy) within which I
entered for future reference, neatly typed by my secretary Jean, the
philosophical fundamentals and working principles of each system.
Although both Nazi and fascist systems were nebulous and their
principles unstable by comparison with those of communism and
liberal democracy, my wall was vastly illuminating.

As befitted the attempted accomplishment of such momentous
aims, from then on much of my space in the newspaper was
devoted to following closely the development of Hitler's plan.
The sheer brazen audacity of it was intensely interesting. It
logically involved the destruction of all existing institutions
upholding international law and order. It attacked the League

251

of Nations on the favourable ground that it could not bring about a general disarmament, yet it would not allow Germany to rearm. He denounced the disarmament clauses of the Versailles Treaty, and withdrew Germany from the League with warmth of expression designed to burn up, metaphorically, the whole Geneva edifice. This thought I translated into a picture of Hitler attempting to set fire to the League buildings, over the title IT WORKED AT THE REICHSTAG—WHY NOT HERE? The allusion was to the destruction of the Reichstag by fire in Berlin some weeks before, which there were good grounds for believing had been arranged by the Nazi leaders to provide an excuse for accusing and eliminating their political opponents.

The effect was immediate. The *Evening Standard* and all papers printing my cartoons were officially banned from Germany.

Things were not going too placidly for me in Italy either. I was soon to be banned there too.

By the time Hitler arose, Mussolini had become accepted as a feature of the Mediterranean scenery and was taking part, like any respectable advanced liberal, in League of Nations affairs, disarmament conferences, peace conferences, security conferences, and even conferences to 'contain' the possible new menace Hitler. But if Hitler, newly in power, needed time to consolidate, Mussolini was established and still possessed by his ambitions to resurrect the Roman Empire. His capacity for action was limited only by Italy's lack of sure resources for the raw materials without which a modern warrior state could never challenge the Mediterranean power of France and Britain. Abyssinia had these raw materials. Many years before the League had existed international agreements had admitted Italy's claim to 'special interests' there, but she had never been able to assert them. Adventures had to be carefully calculated. Why not take advantage of the prevailing suspicion, anxiety and failure of international co-operation, especially since Prime Minister Laval of France had just tipped him the wink? To hell with the League. He invaded Abyssinia.

A conscientious cartoonist could not but record, within the terms of his peculiar medium of expression, the sequence of tortuous shifts of diplomacy that led up to and followed the act. From time to time I had drawn Mussolini as a bully or as a buffoon. Such cartoons as that rarely got under his skin, of course. They could be taken easily as examples of conventional 'democratic' wit in the accepted terms of caricature. Besides, propaganda depicting dictators as wicked inhuman monsters did them little harm among the sheepish masses, either within or without their

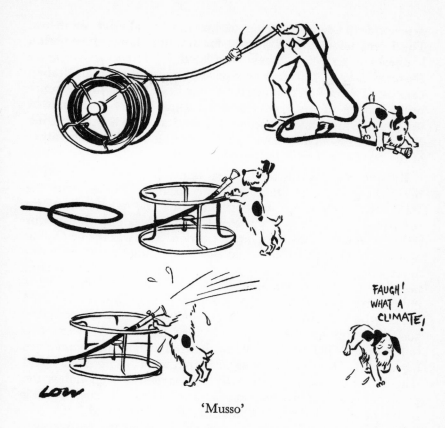

FAUGH! WHAT A CLIMATE!

'Musso'

domain. Very often the opposite. No dictator was ever incon-
venienced or even displeased by pictures showing his terrible
exercise of power or his terrible person stalking through blood and
mud. That may be even good for business. But it is damaging to
have the idea propagated that he is a fool, especially if the idea
takes root among his own people.

Actually it was a cartoon about Mussolini's precarious
dependence on Hitler's sympathy that the Rome censor found
unsuitable for Italian eyes. The drawing was entitled THE GIRLS
HE LEFT BEHIND HIM and contained the suggestion that Hitler
wanted Mussolini involved in the Abyssinian gamble so that
he, Hitler, would then be free to appropriate Austria, which
would have brought him altogether too close to Italy for comfort.
The suggestion (which was completely justified in due course)
was too harmful just then to the Duce's personal legend.

After that, under the ban, the occasional appearance of my
cartoons in the Italian Press stopped, except sometimes for their

253

description in news despatches accompanied by abusive comments. The Rome newspaper *Il Travere*, for instance, flattered me with a banner caption which, freely translated, read: *Our Answer to the Degraded Low of the 'Evening Standard'* printed over an Italian cartoon of John Bull floundering in the Suez Canal, the reference being to one of my own published some time before entitled SUEZCIDE, which hadn't been seen in Italy anyway, depicting Mussolini in Roman armour tremulously testing the temperature of the Suez Canal with his big toe.

Rebuke became ridiculous when one day I received a call at the *Evening Standard* office from an excited attaché from the Italian Embassy about my dog. This dog was my trusty studio companion. One day I christened him Mussolini—Musso for short—and introduced him into a cartoon. This was the beginning of a long and popular career in the Press. Judge of my astonishment when my visitor conveyed the regrets of the entire Italian people at the desecration of this exalted surname, and requested— nay, demanded—that in the interests of international concord the dog be rechristened. I pointed out that there were probably 500 Mussolinis in the Rome telephone book. There were two in London. Which was he talking about? Further, the coincidence by which Il Duce and my dog answered to the same name could not, I opined, be fairly met by the suggested step unless the principle were carried further and applied also to dogs bearing names of other celebrated Romans such as Caesar and Nero.

To this there was no reply, and after talking the matter over with my dog we decided to let the matter drop. I was too busy. I had on my hands the preparation of a new up-to-the-minute comic strip, a series in slapstick farce about two dictatorial characters, *Hit & Muss*.

In Britain uncertainty and confusion blotted the next page of political history. On the Left the pacifist masses, which had rightly clamoured for a British lead at the Disarmament Conference, from force of habit kept on clamouring for disarmament even after the conference was palpably dead, but now coupled that demand with others for a British lead to collective security and immediate economic sanctions against Italy, the aggressor. On the Right, there were Tories who deplored the League and all its works, and demanded a closer integration of the Empire, with rearmament to defend it in an uneasy world; and Tories who either admired or feared the dictators and thought a deal might be made with them to the detriment of the 'reds' and required rearmament to create a bargaining position. Finally there were

Old Sealed Lips

the 'Geneva Guards' of all parties who upheld the League and favoured sufficient rearmament to back up its decisions.

This was for me as a cartoonist my Collective-security-with-teeth-in-it Period. A difficult time, lining up rearguard actions to defend the League with its enemies' guns while the Labour Party forces under the pacifist leader Lansbury were off tilting at windmills on the left. Throughout the uneasy body politic there was a pretty general feeling that the rearmament, if any, should be conditional upon a clarifying of the Government's foreign policy, since there existed some doubt about which cause was eventually to have the indirect benefit of the proposed British arms. A sudden and extreme rise in temperature over a masterpiece of Russian clumsiness, the arrest and trial of British engineers as alleged spies, hinted at the possibility at least that we might as easily finish on the side of the Right as on that of the Left.

Personification of the prevailing confusion and the difficulty of readjustment to changing conditions was the Prime Minister, Stanley Baldwin, then about to face the general election of 1935. Torn by a wish to lose neither the favour of the pacifist masses nor the chance one day, with a change of wind, to begin a programme of rearmament, Baldwin could not bring himself to trust the people with the full facts of the national position.

255

'My lips are sealed,' he said. Whereupon I labelled him OLD SEALED LIPS and drew him regularly with gum-tape across his mouth. The nickname spread and I heard that his staff used it at Downing Street.

When at last in 1935 the Prime Minister did decide to let the electorate into his confidence, the Lips were not even then unsealed enough to give more than warning mumbles. But his party was returned with a large majority and he was enabled to get on with his rearmament programme.

The Parliament of 1931 had been elected in a stampede and, apart from the paramount financial issue, had been unrepresentative and out of touch with the people. Its successor, that of 1935, was, on the evidence, representative of a people not so much misled as mystery-led. Perhaps, therefore, the Prime Minister could thank himself in some measure for the disunity of the nation behind him.

I had dealt faithfully in cartoons with Baldwin's animadversions, but he had taken it in good part, 'Old Sealed Lips' and all, and when we met he was always friendly. M.P.s had often told me of how he sat apart in the House of Commons smoking-room crustily repelling would-be conversationalists. They explained to me that this was a defensive attitude from years before against slights from some of the venomously witty Old Guard of his own party. Two things suggested that there might be something in the idea that the past still sat heavily on his chest. Whenever he complimented me on some cartoon it would be one that showed some old opponents in an unflattering light; and although I found him a man without much small talk, he could be induced without much pressing to talk about his beginnings.

According to his own account, Baldwin intended his Carlton Club speech in 1923 as a political retirement, because he thought Lloyd George was a wicked man and he wanted no more to do with him. But when Bonar Law, who had grown an affection for him as private secretary and brief-case carrier, arose and said he agreed with him, the die was cast. He earned not only the reversion to the premiership but the envy and animosity of most of the Tory leaders. Pity the poor Prime-Minister-by-accident.

As a cartoonist favouring the Opposition, I did not know whether to be flattered or otherwise to get the impression that my efforts, far from disturbing the harmony, had sometimes even been useful to him, by enabling him to show the more obtuse of his Cabinet colleagues what they looked like from outside. Apart from the personal attachment which he had grown for Ramsay

STEPPING STONES TO GLORY (1936)

Hitler had reoccupied the Rhineland without resistance from the Western democracies

257

MacDonald, the 'National'-Labour partnership suited him well, not only to provide a bi-party camouflage for a moderate conservative policy, but also to hold back the Tory wild men who pestered him to use his advantage and come out as extreme anti-socialist.

Baldwin was by no means tough enough to please some of his critics. Relations within his party were rather sore. He was telling me the caricaturable points of some of his own Cabinet colleagues when I said: 'Hi! Hi! You shouldn't help me, Prime Minister. I've just been blackballed from a West End club by some of your friends for poking fun at *you*.' 'Probably you ought to be congratulated,' he said. 'Tell me what club and I'll propose you again myself.'

Certainly the Prime Minister had a worrying job. The Americans were still sore because they thought the British had let them down by not following Stimson's line against Japan. The Japanese were taking advantage of this disunity to build up a naval preponderance for themselves in the Pacific. Laval, for the French, thought the British had double-crossed France by making independently the new Anglo-German treaty allowing Germany a navy, and he was leaning over backwards to make a private deal with Mussolini, whereby Mussolini would agree to become an 'anti-Nazi' if Britain and France would agree to remain passive while he bagged Abyssinia. Eden and Simon had gone to ask Hitler please not to arm so much and Hitler had replied by showing them his huge air force.

One night in 1935 after a dinner of the Parliamentary Press Gallery at which he was the guest, we—Madeline and I—sat down with the Prime Minister for some talk. I had decorated the menu with a drawing I knew he would like. It represented him as an early eighteenth-century farmer character smoking a long churchwarden, with a pig asleep under his chair. He loved it. He had been playing that gag about simple farmer Baldwin with his pipe and pigs so long that he almost came to believe it himself.

I had some difficulty, as always with sandy-lashed people, in looking him square in the eye, especially since he had a slight squint.

The Prime Minister was distinctly sorry for himself. The Japanese were deep into China; the Hoare–Laval Pact had burst, the oily let-down of economic sanctions was in progress; the Berlin–Rome Axis was formed; and now—Spain. On top of it all, his own party was full of intriguers out to force his resignation. That last made him sick, almost ready to quit.

THE 'OPEN DOOR' POLICY IN CHINA (1934)

We did not talk of these matters, of course, but passed only the amiable pleasantries, veiled hints and bits of 'background' proper to meetings of political caricaturists and prime ministers on social occasions. But when he asked me what I had in the paper next day, I told him I was thinking of drawing him as Caesar surrounded by half a dozen Brutuses. Leaning over and dropping his voice he said, 'Low, of all the deaths a man can die, there is none worse than being talked to death by a lot of bloody fools.'

In Spain clashes which had begun over the passage of radical land reforms and anti-clerical laws had culminated in an Army revolt against the democratic Government. General Franco, military commander in Spanish Morocco, being unable to find enough Spaniards to help him, transported Foreign Legion and Moorish troops across the Straits to the mainland under the protection of Italian airplanes. Nazi aircraft joined them three days later, and it was common knowledge that the revolt had been organized and equipped by the Axis Powers.

The immediate reaction of the British people to all this was, as might have been expected, sympathetic towards the Government and hostile towards the Army fascists. The liberal-democratic feelings of the people rose spontaneously, in fact, to a high pitch of moral indignation. There were, however, honest British democrats who were also members of the Roman Catholic Church. These soon found themselves caught on the horns of a dilemma.

Naturally the Church placed religion first and politics second, the survival of democracy, British or otherwise, being of secondary importance to the survival of the Church. Naturally, too, the Church thought of the government which sought to curtail its traditional powers in Catholic Spain as evil and next door to, if not actually, communist. The Church had always been able to come to terms with dictatorship or democracy, but never with communism (probably because communism is itself a religion, and an exclusive religion like the Church). The Church therefore identified itself unhesitatingly with the interests of Franco.

But beyond the labels 'Catholic,' 'Fascist' and 'Communist' could be clearly seen the strategic realities of the situation—the preparations, open and brazen, to weaken and destroy the Anglo-French domination of the Mediterranean, a step forward to Mussolini's dream of empire and Hitler's world conquest. Magic words and ideological slogans might fly hither and thither, but whatever one's views, it was glaringly obvious that it was not communism that was the immediate danger. It was fascism.

The whole situation soon bristled with wry humour. My versions of General Franco presenting Moorish mercenaries and Foreign Legion riff-raff as 'the true Spaniards'; reflecting that it might be necessary to wipe out the Spanish people to 'save' Spain; and receiving complaints from the Moors that his conduct of war was un-Christian, brought reassuring evidence that in favouring the Government I was reflecting the common feelings about Spain. But there was also a steady supply of curses among the compliments. A fair-sized tide of confused rebuke from far and near, printed and spoken, narrowed down finally to the simple proposition that since my cartoons about the dictators were likely to anger them, I should cease to draw them. I disagreed, of course. This was just my old friend 'Disgusted' from the correspondence columns, aggravated, multiplied and reinforced. No doubt the dictators detested criticism of any kind. To concede them dignity would be fatal.

It is possible, however, to miss even the glaringly obvious if one shuts one's eyes tight. Uneasiness of spirit doubtless accounted for the exaggerated resentment from this quarter which met those who took the part of the Government of Spain against Franco. My own efforts to keep to the point, which, as I saw it, was the threat to democracy, were vigorous but perhaps no more vigorous than those of many writers, but cartoons were a more direct medium with a wider appeal, since pictures speak even to the illiterate. So I soon became a focus for attack. My telephone rang all day long and my post-box was crammed with insulting postcards.

Amateur abuse, most of it. I have said earlier that it takes an expert to insult a satirist. If you say his work is 'not funny,' he can retort that it is not intended to be funny; 'inaccurate,' he can show that it is allegorical; 'obscene,' you must produce a modicum of evidence or risk leaving the impression that not he, but you, have the dirty mind. To say it is 'subversive' might suggest more promising grounds for damage (I heard that my private life was sifted to see if I could be proved to be an alien named Loewe) for this is an adjective, like 'patriotic,' charged with emotion, requiring no evidence for hot-heads but the say-so. But to be effective its users must be reasonably above suspicion themselves. In this case my attackers were the champions of General Franco, and by implication also of his active assistants Hitler and Mussolini, who were obviously engaged in, to say the least, un-British activities.

261

Finally, after I had drawn a heavily serious cartoon, IN RETREAT, depicting the British Empire in a line of refugees toiling away from a smoky horizon, rebukes boiled down tamely to concern with the untimeliness and peril of commenting upon foreign affairs, particularly on dictators and their doings in 'comical cartoons.' This met completely the views of those whose fixed conception of a cartoonist was of a clown in whose efforts to amuse coherence and direction were misplaced. My alleged comicality was accordingly exaggerated to the requirements of the argument and deplored.

Things came to a pass when Father Francis Woodlock, the Jesuit priest of a fashionable Farm Street church, preached in favour of a temporary censorship of the Press, particularly of disrespectful newspaper caricatures about sensitive dictators. The Catholic Press followed this up, naming me as the reprehensible example. With the soft jest to turn away wrath, I cooked up a burlesque announcement in the *Evening Standard* appointing Father Woodlock my Diplomatic Adviser on cartoons about dictators, and promising that in future he would act personally as model for all drawings of Mussolini, thus ensuring calmer international relations. This I illustrated with a genial little sketch of both of us at work in my studio.

Whether it was the sensitivity to the unfavourable climate produced by his sermon or just a determination to 'get' me, this made everything much worse. The Father's friends, finding an extended arm and a bent knee in my little sketch of him, professed to interpret these (no doubt after considerable strain) as a fascist salute and a goose-step, and, as such, a foul imputation. The Catholic Press broke out into a front-page rash of quite superfluous indignation at this representation of him as 'a slavish admirer of the dictators.' The Father himself was more astute. Taking me up on my announcement of his 'new job' as my 'diplomatic adviser,' he went into effect right away with a good big piece of diplomatic advice: Lay off the dictators.

Too many sturdy champions were just bursting with views both pro and con on the principle involved in that suggestion. From that point the argument extended beyond me, over the hills and far away.

I continued for some weeks to involve Father Woodlock as my 'assistant' in slapstick cartoon adventures about censorship, but a year elapsed before I actually met him. That was nearly a turbulent occasion also. It was at one of Foyle's literary luncheons and I was the chairman. On one side of me I had Professor

J. B. S. Haldane, burly outspoken Left-winger, on my right emaciated, bird-like Father Woodlock. Haldane spoke of the danger to Britain of a Germany in control of aerodromes in northern Spain and chided people who had worked to secure a victory for Franco, 'one of whom is sitting within a few yards of me.' That stung Woodlock to sharp interruption, and for a boiling minute the whole thing threatened to degenerate into an old-fashioned barney across my defenceless chest. In between times the Father and I had a pleasant conversation, under the basilisk eye of dear old Dean Inge across the way disapproving us both, about the difference between religion and loyalty to ecclesiastical institutions. The worst of me is that I cannot help being friendly to my opponents.

Frustration over the failure of the Disarmament Conference, the weak acceptance of Hitler's rearmament and the let-down of economic sanctions against Mussolini's war had left British common sense with a hangover. The adjustment of ideas to a world in which the cruel brutality of war was still possible, even probable, was difficult for people who had taken for granted that it had been abolished with the setting up of the League of Nations. Peace was not to be ensured merely by being peaceful. Nor, for the matter of that, by being inefficiently warlike. The collective organization of peace had been unrealistic—not taking sufficiently into account the fallibility of statesmen, the ancient traditions of statecraft, the duplicity of scoundrels and the primitive emotions of peoples. There was a rush of impulsive youth to join the International Brigade at Madrid, expecting optimistically to meet a solution in direct action. Faced with the need of an attitude to a choice, real once again, between resistance and subjection, individuals searched their souls. Besides virtue, there were some curious finds.

20

FROM 1934 the supermen of Nazi propaganda had begun to sow confusion among their intended victims by standing truth on its head. The inversion of long-accepted meanings of political key-words was in full swing. The Nazi 'dictators,' it seemed, were the real 'democrats.' What we had been accustomed to think of as 'slavery' was, in reality, 'freedom,' and vice versa; Hitler, with a revolver in each hand, was the apostle of 'peace'; while any democracy that protested was a 'warmonger.' This simple trick of changing around the labels on the bottles was painfully effective. Uncertainty prevailed.

It so happened that the editor of the *Evening Standard* had just placed at my disposal a whole page in the Saturday issue for a weekly topical budget of small local cartoons. It was a big job, unprecedented in its line in London newspaper journalism, and I needed a few regular features to fill it. I decided to invent a 'character' typifying the current disposition to mixed-up thinking, to having it both ways, to dogmatic doubleness, to paradox and plain self-contradiction. This sort of thing:

> 'We need better relations between Capital and Labour. If the trades unions won't accept our terms, crush 'em.'
> 'What the country wants is more economy. Our fellows should fight Russia and China and damn the expense.'
> 'Look at those foreign agitators sapping the Constitution! We need a dictator like Mussolini.'

Here, almost ready-made, I thought, was the essence of laughter as Hazlitt described it; 'the incongruous, the disconnecting one idea from another, or the jostling of one feeling from another.' Emerson had said: 'The essence of all jokes, of all comedy, seems to be an honest or well-intentioned halfness . . . The balking of the intellect, the frustrated expectation, the break of continuity in the intellect, is comedy . . .'

I was taking a Turkish bath, ruminating on a name for my 'character' . . . Goodle, Boak, Snood, Glimmer, Blimp . . . BLIMP! . . . Lord Blimp, Bishop Blimp, Dr. Blimp, Mr. Blimp . . . when I overheard conversation coming from two pink sweating chaps of military bearing close by. They were telling one another that what Japan did in the Pacific was no business of Britain. In the newspapers that morning some colonel or other had written to protest against the mechanization of cavalry, and insisting that even if horses had to go, the uniform and trappings must remain inviolate and troops must continue to wear their spurs in the tanks. Ha! I thought. The attitude of mind! The perfect *chiaroscuro*! *Colonel* Blimp, of course!

It began as almost a formula: Colonel Blimp and I at the Turkish bath performing our ablutions or exercising, he uttering to me a blatantly self-contradictory aphorism. It continued in that form with a few exceptions until a war shortage of paper ended my topical budget six years later. As a cartoon character he ran quietly for twelve months, and then suddenly he 'took the town' and was everywhere. His subsequent progress was so astonishing as to warrant narration here as an object-lesson in what can happen to a symbol.

It may have been that in 1934 the exaggerations of caricature were being outdone by the realities of the time, that truth defied burlesque and that people really were thinking as Blimp did, without suspecting that anything was amiss: or perhaps people were trying to deceive themselves without making a very good job of it, and resented any disturbance to their efforts. Certainly a great number of complaining people missed the point of Colonel Blimp from the start. And having done so, they imposed upon the Colonel a point of view, indifferent to the plain evidence that in his very nature he had, for himself, at least *two* points of view, mixed. To them his cancellations-out and self-contradictions appeared in the light of destructive attacks on hard-held beliefs and institutions, especially those of a military nature, since the fellow was a colonel.

Here objections became more precisely occupational. Although Colonel Blimp's comments rarely had anything to do with military affairs, and were almost exclusively political, the prefix 'Colonel' fixed his supposed significance for inelastic minds. The Spanish War and subsequent events began to give rise to references to

Colonel Blimp in the debates of the House of Commons as a symbol of military incompetence. When Sir Thomas Inskip, the Minister of Defence, rose to deny indignantly that he was 'associated with a number of respectable Colonel Blimps'; when Mr. Hore-Belisha, the Minister of War, took pains to announce that after a dust-up at the War Office Colonel Blimp was now dead; when Mr. (later Lord) Pethick-Lawrence warned the Government that 'if they wanted to carry the country with them in the war effort they must set about abolishing blimpery'; and when Sir Stafford Cripps, the Leader of the House, replied by promising the 'early funeral of the late and unlamented Colonel Blimp'—that particular misapprehension was confirmed.

For years after I first introduced Colonel Blimp to public life, his character, habits and outlooks were defined, denounced and defended by publicists, philosophers and politicians the world over, amply demonstrating the variety of ways in which one may be misapprehended. To begin with, on the slender evidence of his appearance in a London newspaper, nearly everyone assumed him and his qualities to be exclusively British. *The Times*, London, wrote: 'Blimp stands for that inertia in British policy which drives the quick-witted to distraction . . .' The *New York Times* wrote: 'Colonel Blimp is the symbol of all that's dull and stupid in British life . . .' J. B. Priestley wanted him kept in Britain, where he could not harm Anglo-American relations: 'When I read quotations from the American Press [about "British Blimps"] . . . leave the Blimps to us over here, I say.' But 'Blimp is not a result of the iniquity of mankind but a symbol of tradition,' said a paper in Shanghai, seeing a wider horizon.

The Universal English Dictionary summed up Blimp as plain reactionary in its entry: 'Colonel Blimp. Figure in cartoons by Low caricaturing an extreme die-hard type of outlook.' 'The cost of Blimp is too high,' said a paper in Peru with the same idea. 'To be a colonel, after all, is not exclusive evidence that one's a blot,' sang A. P. Herbert, taking a narrow view of Blimp as representing a vendetta against colonels. Harold Nicolson went to the other extreme and opined that he was 'a vast excuse for deriding authority and justifying disobedience.' To Arnold Lunn, though, he represented, more modestly, an assault on 'England's feudal and aristocratic tradition.' Percy Wyndham Lewis, on the other hand, wrote him down as part of a Press plot to foment international discord and mass murder.

Views differed considerably, but at first they fell into roughly two categories:

(*a*) That Blimp was a destructive representation of something bad and therefore to be approved; and

(*b*) That he was a malicious misrepresentation of something good, and therefore to be disapproved.

Col BLIMP PERSPIRES WISDOM

Gad, sir, Mr. Lansbury is right. The League of Nations should insist on peace — except, of course, in the event of war.

I duly appreciated the friendly intent of (*a*) and was exasperated by (*b*), but one feature common to both often amazed me. That was the facility with which Blimp acquired purely fictitious backgrounds to fit the romantic requirements of an argument. Complete strangers in large numbers wrote passionately to tell me of his honourable war record. 'Is it fair to ridicule men like Colonel Blimp, without whose steadfast courage we should never have won the war?' was a frequent type of comment. I learned of his supreme sacrifice: 'The comfort and security we enjoy rests, as it always has done, on the bones of dead Blimps—Blimps who lacked the cleverness to see that patriotism and loyalty were humbug but fortunately did not lack the fidelity and courage to die for us' . . . wrote Arthur Bryant in the *Illustrated London News*; and of how he had rushed to join the Home Guard: 'Those early veterans [of the Home Guard] included a much-abused, much-derided individual, "Colonel Blimp",' wrote the author of *It All Happened Before*, who also gave details of the good company Blimp kept: 'Any professional soldier, sailor or airman above the age of forty and approximate rank of major was liable to qualify for the opprobrious name of Blimp if he gave up the inaction of retirement to offer himself for duty once more . . . men like Wavell, Alexander and Montgomery . . . all could have been dismissed contemptuously as Blimps.' Another know-all told me about Blimp's sons in the Royal Air Force. It got about that I had founded Blimp upon the late Field-Marshal Lord Roberts, which showed what a disgusting fellow I was, to make fun of a dead man who couldn't answer back.

Col. BLIMP'S NEW DEAL

Gad, sir, Hitler was right. We should absorb our Unemployed by starting them building concentration camps to lock themselves in.

Obliging writers in the newspapers provided him with complete life stories. From Australia, no less, I learned that he was 'well-connected' in the country, that he had been to a good public school and thence to Sandhurst, that he held a command in the Indian Army, that he now lived in South Kensington and that he married the second daughter of the Bishop of Bath and Wells. An M.P., Sir Herbert Williams, wrote to me to tell me that Blimp believed in racial equality. I replied saying that he had authorized me to say it was a black lie. Sir Herbert wouldn't accept that and said that he *knew* Blimp's mind on the subject.

My brain began to reel. Blimp was bolting. Had I invented this buffoon or did he really exist? Was he a creature of my imagination, his qualities of mind, his peculiarities of appearance touched in according to my fleeting whim? If so, who but I had the authority to create his home life? What right had others to tell *me* his source, who or what Blimp was? Was there someone of the same name actually living somewhere hidden away, whom I had unwittingly traduced? Worse, were there *several* Colonel Blimps, all traduced? Two old gentlemen whom I had never seen had vaguely threatened to bring libel suits against me, each claiming to be the original Colonel Blimp. Were there others?

Time rolled on. Out of all this mist of wild nonsense a new, third, category appeared:

(c) That Blimp was a misrepresentation of something good, which was intended to be destructive, but backfired on the artist because the misrepresentation only proved the goodness.

Lord Elton, a typical exponent, solemnly deplored my treatment of Blimp as a subversive 'attack upon the military virtues . . . loyalty, courage, endurance, discipline.' His Lordship produced the evidence of some quotations from Blimp to support his contention, but it transpired that he had come by these quotations through cutting some Blimp-isms in halves, printing only the half that suited his argument. For instance, Blimp saying: 'Gad, sir, Winston is right. We must have more armaments,' was quite a different thing from Blimp saying:

> 'Gad, sir, Winston is right. We must have more armaments, not only to uphold international law, but to protect ourselves from justice and right.'

I was incensed at the cool butchery of my performance and I protested in letters to

the Press; but I did not succeed in convincing his Lordship that when one cuts a confusion of ideas in halves one gets more than one end. When his Lordship produced a further quotation, a whole one this time, and a departure from the usual Blimp form:

> 'Gad, sir, Lord Castlebosh is right. We must not neglect chemical warfare. The future of civilization may depend upon our making a worse smell than the enemy'

to prove, to his own satisfaction at least, that I had been the ass and Blimp the wise one, I retired from the correspondence, mortified by this exposure of my misguided oracularity.

Another interesting example of the same attitude of mind, but in the political field, was afforded when the Central Office of the Conservative Party collected a dossier about Colonel Blimp and myself, under the impression that for their party interest it was necessary to prove that Blimp was right and Low was wrong. A Conservative Party exhibition was held, for which the promoters mounted and exhibited clippings of my Blimp drawings, complete with confused dicta, and faced them with photographs of Conservative leaders with specimen statesmanlike utterances, to prove that the libel had been foul and there was no real identity between the two groups. To me the whole thing was a singularly futile proceeding, since I had never at any time given Blimp a party label. But evidently to others there existed at least a large doubt.

Gad. sir.
Lord Bunk
is right. The
Govt. are going
over the edge
of an abyss
and the
nation must
march solidly
behind them.

Col.
BLIMP'S
LEAD

The incident reminded me of the prank cruel small boys used to play on their simpler kind by egging them on to shout repeatedly what was alleged to be the Siamese war-cry: 'O wa ta na Siam!' Say it quickly several times and you get the idea.

Like other cartoonists, I knew very well from experience that the success or failure (in a popular sense) of a cartoon depended not only upon the merits of its execution, but also upon the receptivity of the beholder. I worked upon the assumption that half the effect of a cartoon was contributed by the fellow that looked at it; so I, for my part, tried to evoke associations of ideas which would bring him to see it my way. But I was appalled sometimes at the revelation of what went on inside the heads of my customer-collaborators. The inventor of a symbol may tolerate its misinterpretations, but to endure censure for them was too much to be borne. When it was affirmed that Blimp was right and Low was wrong, I was tempted to argue on both public and personal grounds; for here, it seemed to me, was the justification and enthronement of disorder; and here also was the impugning of my own judgment, for I had deliberately contrived the disorder. I turned from the drawing-board to the typewriter and flew into print to clear the air.

Was Blimp right? Was Low wrong? I had contended that Colonel Blimp had been conceived and sustained by me as a symbol of stupidity; not of colonels, nor of stupid colonels in particular; not of Authority, nor especially of stupid Authority; not exclusively of the Right nor the Left; for stupidity had no frontiers, domestic or foreign.

Boy! Bring me the records!

The files showed that Colonel Blimp up to the date of my article had made 260 odd appearances, the subject-matter of his reflections dividing up as follows:

Military virtues (and vices) ..	..	7
Feudal-aristocratic tradition	..	3

Gad, sir, the Maharajah of Kapootle is right. There must be no monkeying with the liberty of Indians to do what they're dashed well told.

PUKKA SAHIB BLIMP

If we permitted ourselves to employ the unscrupulous deductive methods of some hostile critics to straighten out the asinine twist into a positive conclusion, it seemed that Blimp, though he usually contradicted himself, was no enthusiast for democracy ('The only way to teach people self-respect is to treat 'em like the curs they are').
He was impatient of the common people and their complaints ('To give the unemployed enough to eat is to sap their sturdy British independence'). His remedy for social unrest was less education, so that people could not read about slumps.

He was an extreme isolationist, disliking foreigners (which included Jews, Irish, Scots, Welsh, and people from the Colonies and Dominions); a man of violence, approving war, *per se*. It was good for the physique ('Bayonets bring the best out of a man—and it stays out'); and for the spirit ('Wars are necessary —otherwise how can heroes defend their countries?'). He had no use for the League of Nations ('Too many foreigners') nor for international efforts to prevent wars ('Shut up Geneva, so that people may make war in peace').

In particular he objected to any economic reorganization of world resources involving changes in the *status quo* ('Never shall we yield our colonies, even if we have to buy a geography and find out where the blooming things are').

He whooped for rearmament while a chance of constructing peace remained to be sabotaged. The arms were not for defence of any ideal or 'way-of-life,' but to protect the overseas investments of his friends. Blimp believed in the production of these arms by private enterprise strictly according to the rules of profit ('We must not stop our arms factories from supplying the enemy, or they might not supply us and then what sort of wars would we have?').

When the dictators menace came along, Blimp didn't recognize it. To him, China, Abyssinia, Spain and Czechoslovakia seemed

271

SHOWER BY Col. BLIMP.

Gad, sir, Lucy Houston is right. The only way to deal with these agitators is to shoot 'em all down and then make 'em work.

to be just dirty smacks at the 'dashed reds.' He excused the aggressors ('The Japanese are only killing the Chinese to save them from their enemies'), ('How can we expect Mussolini to behave decently if we object to his dropping gas-bombs?'), ('Hitler only needs arms so that he can declare peace on the rest of the world'); he objected to the use of economic means to cramp their style ('We can't declare a boycott of Japanese goods because then how could Japan pay innocent business men for the raw material to make their bombs'). He was all for appeasement ('There's only one way to stop these bullying aggressors—find out what they want us to do and then do it').

Even when it became obvious that the British would have to fight he obstructed collective resistance, especially with Russia ('Before we can allow Russia to protect the British Empire we must insist on her restoring the capitalist system').

I was supposed, by inference and under the same kind of reasoning, to deny Blimp's dicta, to represent his opposition. (I was responsible for Blimp's side, too, of course. But that could pass.) Very well. That made me a sturdy democrat, considerate of the condition of the common people; for more education; for international co-operation; holding war, *per se*, as bad; for the League of Nations and united efforts to build a sane international system; for economic reorganization of world resources to that end; for piping down national arms while hope of constructive peace remained; for nationalization of arms production, for mechanization and up-to-date equipment; for collective defence with other States against war-mongers; against the dictators, when they came along; for cramping them early with an economic stranglehold; against appeasement; and, when Hitler showed his hand plainly, for collective resistance, especially with Russia. Well, that suited me. I rested my case.

I undertook that analysis more as an exercise in clarification than with any idea of converting the heathen. Having got it out of my system, I found, with a faint dismay, that I had gone far to get Blimp out, too. I had other fish to fry and my interest in him was diminishing. With all creations of his kind, personifications, synthetic types and symbols of abstractions, there comes a time when they must look after themselves. I could not go on keeping Blimp in line for ever. I still controlled by copyright his commercial exploitation, and I still emphatically denied the personal discredit of his misinterpretations, but otherwise he could live his own life, like John Bull, Britannia, Ally Sloper, Old Bill and the other myths.

When Michael Powell proposed to make a film epic about him, and Emeric Pressburger, his script-writer partner, spun his tale of *The Life and Death of Colonel Blimp* into my fascinated ear, I was too dazed with admiration of Emeric's phenomenal power of story-telling (he left Scheherazade standing) to find any reason for not agreeing. I woke up in time, however, to make two stipulations: that Blimp had to be proved a fool in the end, and that they, Powell and Pressburger, took all the responsibility. I enlarged my experience of life watching from a privileged position behind the camera the solid work of building up my simple symbol into a super-colossal two-and-a-half hour feature film. Amazing chaps, both blending social ideas with entertainment in their own medium for their own public. A different blend, a different medium and a different public from mine. I did not interfere. The product emerged at last as an extremely sentimental film about a glamorous old colonel whose romantic attachments nearly—but not quite—obscured the conclusion that if Britain followed his out-of-date ideas in modern war, we should all be blown to blazes. In the cinema, I am sentimental and I like films about romantic attachments, so at the première I sat in an obscure seat with a large cigar and enjoyed it.

Why not? I did not hate Blimp. I hated stupidity, but I would have had a bilious life of it had I hated all people that were stupid. Furthermore, my original conception of Blimp had been as a corrective of stupidity in general, not exclusively of that in hateful people, and it seemed to me useful to drop a hint that even nice people can be fools. This view, I was pained to find, was not shared by some of my erstwhile good friends and supporters, to whom the Blimp film was an outrage against their simple belief that, in political or social fantasy, hateful ideas must always be represented by hateful characters.

'Blimp de-Blimped,' 'Attempt to whitewash Blimp,' 'Blimp's answer to Low,' 'Low's pot-bellied tyrant rehabilitated' were sample expressions of this view in the Press. 'O Low! O Low!

What induced you to offer up your character . . . to be made unrecognizable under a thick coating of technicolor sugar, to be laughed at, loved and made piteous as just a dear sentimental doddering old fool?' wailed the *New Statesman and Nation*. Such innocence of the more subtle forms of persuasion seemed to me to be itself apt material for a few ripe Blimpisms.

Other eyes saw a different significance. Under the heading *Blimp Film Must NOT Go Abroad*, the *Daily Mail* waxed indignant at a 'gross travesty' of 'British officers as stupid, complacent, self-satisfied and ridiculous . . .' It appeared that the depiction of Blimp as a fine fellow, in keeping with the expectations of those who thought of him as a fine fellow, had had a double-edged merit in that, in their eyes, it imparted a greater verisimilitude to the whole, stupidity and all. 'We cannot afford,' said the *Daily Mail*, 'to put out a burlesque figure like this screen version of Colonel Blimp to go round the world as a personification of the regular British officer.'

Churchill, the Prime Minister, was at the first night with Eden, his Privy Seal, and, I heard, formed some pretty definite ideas about it. According to my *Evening Standard* friends, he talked to his colleagues in the Cabinet and to Whitehall officials. Then almost every Government department sent delegations to view the film and give their impressions. Then six high-ups made the decision that it would not be advisable to let the film go out as representing the British Army.

Some months passed before everybody cooled down.

Nobody need have worried. The film got at last to the United States but on the way its Blimpish content had apparently communicated itself to its entrepreneurs. The poster publicity in New York showed Colonel Blimp (by an irrelevant association with a popular character regularly appearing on the cover of the magazine *Esquire*) as a lecherous old bounder leering at leggy females. That made me wince rather more than the unauthorized use in the Moscow Press by my old friend Boris Efimov, the Russian cartoonist, of Blimp as the personification of British delay in forming a second front in World War II. The latter was at least in character.

Blimp's life as a film star and a season on the stage in a revue sketch did not affect his life with me. For the rest of World War II he cropped up intermittently in *Evening Standard* war cartoons, in which, naturally, his connection with military affairs tended to elbow aside his other aspects. I could never be quite sure, when I entered a room where there were army officers, whether I was going to find friendly smiles or bloodshot glares. There were some awkward moments socially.

A memorable one occurred when my old friend Edward Thompson, the poet and novelist, arranged a meeting for me with Lord Wavell. The Field-Marshal was about to set out for India to become Viceroy. When I arrived at his flat I sensed a vague hostility in the atmosphere. I observed that I was not to be accorded the courtesy of privacy; another visitor was present, and I soon was frozen out of a conversation which became very technical on military matters. In time the talk switched to the irresponsibility of the Press in its comments on army matters and I found myself, to my surprise, faced by a Field-Marshal with a distinctly unfriendly eye, being bawled out about Colonel Blimp and his alleged part in this wrongdoing. I got sick of this. I seethed with repressed indignation. I said, icily: 'Sir, you are misinformed. Colonel Blimp is not a military, but a political symbol. Only about two per cent of his aphorisms are concerned with military affairs and those ridiculed your own critics. The only thing military about Colonel Blimp is his title.' There was an awkward silence. The other visitor wound up his business and went, leaving me looking for my hat. The Field-Marshal said: 'Aren't you going to draw me?' I said: 'Thank you, it is unnecessary. I will remember all I need about this afternoon,' and left.

After such an unpromising opening one would hardly expect subsequent cordiality. But there was a happy ending to this story. Some weeks later I was pleasantly surprised to receive out of the blue a long and friendly letter from Wavell at Delhi about features of Indian life and affairs which he considered might interest me as an artist. Evidently the old man had thought again and concluded he had been unjust. I replied in kind. The correspondence left a fragrant memory.

When World War II ended there was just as much mental muddle in the world, perhaps even more than before; but Blimp as a character had become too identified with the pre-war and war years to fit easily into the post-war chapter. I could never have overtaken his military legend. Sometimes, when, twenty years after his invention, I come across his name in a newspaper spelt as an ordinary word without a capital letter and used as a synonym for military or administrative incompetence, I wonder how he might have turned out if in that Turkish bath of 1934 I had chosen to christen him Dr. Blimp, or Bishop Blimp, using the same aphorisms, without the alteration of a single comma.

Would I have been struck off the register by the British Medical Council for infamous professional conduct? . . . Would I have been excommunicated for subverting the Established Church?

Perhaps not. After all, it was a great and good Archbishop of Canterbury, William Temple, who said that it was not the ape or the tiger in man that he feared; it was the donkey.

21

T
HE bannings of my cartoons in Germany and Italy cut
both ways. Although they nipped in the bud my sparse
circulation inside the German Reich and Italy, the advertisement did me more good than harm elsewhere, for
reprintings in foreign newspapers began to increase and went on
until I had quite a respectable regular syndication throughout
non-totalitarian Europe and Asia.

German Foreign Office documents published after the war
revealed how the Nazis took criticism by the British Press in the
pre-war years. They complained repeatedly to Lord Halifax, then
Foreign Secretary. The German Ambassador in London, Dr. von
Dirksen, in drafting a telegram to his immediate boss, Ribbentrop,
on insults to the Führer in the British Press,* recalls that:

> On the occasion of his [Lord Halifax's] visit to Berlin he had
> had a serious talk with Minister Göbbels on this subject . . .
> On his return to England he [Lord Halifax] had done his best
> to prevent excesses in the Press; he had had discussions with
> two well-known cartoonists, one of them the notorious Low,
> and with a number of eminent representatives of the Press, and
> had tried to bring influence to bear on them. He had been
> successful up to a point.

> It was extremely regrettable that numerous lapses were again
> to be noted in recent months . . . Lord Halifax promised to do
> everything possible to prevent such insults to the Führer in the
> future.

Thereby hangs a tale.

* *Documents on German Foreign Policy, 1918–1945*, from the archives of the German
Foreign Ministry, Series 'D,' Volume 4. 'The Aftermath of Munich,' October 1938–
March 1939.

Towards the close of 1937 Lord Halifax visited Germany, ostensibly to see the International Hunting Exhibition in Berlin but mainly to talk to Hitler and advance the prospects of keeping the peace in Europe.

On his return he met Brigadier (then Captain) Michael Wardell, chairman of the *Evening Standard*, and spoke of the intense bitterness among the Nazi bosses over attacks on them in the British Press. Halifax said Hitler and the others were particularly sensitive to my cartoons. Every Low cartoon attacking Hitler was taken to the Führer at once—and he blew up.

Wardell suggested that Lord Halifax should tell me these things personally. Halifax agreed. The meeting took the form of a lunch at Wardell's flat in Albion Gate, where we three had a pleasant and interesting luncheon.

Lord Halifax described the Nazi point of view, explaining that, partly because they had no long tradition of government, the Nazis were unable to take press criticism calmly. He drew verbally a pretty picture of Göbbels raging over a selection of my cartoons laid out in a row on a table. He said the fury and bitterness caused by the *Evening Standard* cartoons was 'out of all proportion to the motive which prompted their publication.'

Lord Halifax, I knew, was a good man, an upright man. He looked worried and I felt respect and warm sympathy for one who was sincerely striving for peace under the most discouraging circumstances. At the same time, although I did not say it, I felt in my bones that Lord Halifax was not quite the right person to deal successfully with persons whose conceptions of goodness and uprightness were the opposite of his own.

I said something about my having a duty, too, like any other journalist in a democracy whose work had an educative element, to present faithfully the substance of what was happening. I added that although I could understand that the Nazis might find criticism mighty inconvenient, I had difficulty in believing they were so volatile that politeness would cause them to modify their plans. 'Do I understand you to say that you would find it easier to promote peace if my cartoons did not irritate the Nazi leaders personally?' I asked, finally.

'Yes,' he replied.

We left it at that, and sitting on Wardell's roof-garden we looked at Hyde Park below and talked about the weather.

I had my private sources of information, British and American correspondents travelling to and fro between Britain and Germany, Webb Miller, John Gunther, Raymond Daniel, Ed. Keene and

others to tell me how Lord Halifax was being taken for a ride; I had just returned from Austria myself and had smelt something on the wind; and Hitler's last published Budget had given him away as being headed for war. But Lord Halifax, after all, was Foreign Secretary with all the strings in hand, and maybe I was wrong. Without relaxing the critical note, I played it in a less personal key. I dropped Mussolini and Hitler and to take their place invented *Muzzler*, a composite character fusing well-known features of both dictators without being identifiable as either.

In Germany, Dr. Göbbels followed up his lead to Halifax by a dissertation on humour wherein he told his fellow-countrymen at what they might laugh. He approved of jokes against Jews; communists (and even liberals) were, of course, fair game; but 'a joke,' says he, 'ceases to be a joke when it touches the holiest matters of the national state'—that is to say Hitler, Nazism, the racial state and presumably himself.

One of the most appalling things about those confused days was the sheep-like docility with which well-meaning people followed a lead up the garden path. One expected such brazen nonsense from Göbbels. But it was horrifying to read a little later in the *Church Times*:

> Good taste, one element of which is kindness, forbids joking concerning subjects which are held sacred by others . . . I doubt whether Low's cartoons make Mr. Chamberlain's appeasement path any easier.

A few weeks after my conversation with Halifax, Nazi troops entered Austria. Halifax was reputed to have been at first incredulous, then amazed. He *had* been taken for a ride. My restraint had been wasted—if indeed I had not by softening protest contributed my mite to a Nazi manœuvre to weaken Britain morally before this fresh outrage.

I considered that this let me out and I dropped my politeness.

Things got a bit mixed at times between me and the *Evening Standard*. On the main issues of the day, I believed it was One World, upheld the League and was for combined effort to defend peace by economic pressure and international force. Beaverbrook didn't believe it was One World, thought the League was meddlesome and that Britain should mind its own business and develop the Empire.

Cartoons and leading articles often flatly contradicted one another, scandalizing the worthy souls who saw it as a serious defect in Lord Beaverbrook that he be not one-eyed. Inevitably stories got around, when for some reason or other, a cold or a journey, I missed a cartoon, that I was undergoing 'discipline.' My friend Hannen Swaffer, the columnist, who had a watchful eye open for occasions when my cartoon should have appeared and didn't, was apt to draw conclusions at the top of his voice and headline his suspicions *Is Low Censored?*

Such vigilance would have been a useful safeguard for me had Lord Beaverbrook not been the sort of man he was. But the truth was that his attitude to my personal charter of freedom remained impeccable, and the misgivings I had had on joining his paper long had been forgotten. Often he disagreed with me profoundly and did not fail to say so. Cartoons of Hitler tripping up to glory on stairs formed by the spineless backs of democratic statesmen; and Hitler demanding with menaces to know what the same democratic statesmen would give him not to kick their pants for twenty-five years, hardly fitted the Beaverbrook line, but went into the paper without a word, except after publication. There was an occasion when I drew a doubt as to whether the inclusion of Japan in the Axis did not show the Hitler–Mussolini crusade against 'godless' Russia to be a fraud, and a telegram arrived from his Lordship in Canada to protest that the imputation was unfair, since Hitler had not declared himself against Christianity. But even after he visited Germany, where he succeeded in getting the *Daily Express* ban lifted but was told frankly that so long as he kept me as cartoonist the *Evening Standard* would be banned, there were no recriminations but instead a worried solicitude for my own safety. Fresh from Dr. Göbbels, and hearing of my occasional trips to Europe, Beaverbrook was full of dire warnings that to show my nose in Germany would be asking for an 'accident.'

The problem of free comment and personal relations had solved itself years before so far as we were concerned. How fortunate. Since the political scene would have been notably incomplete without his busy Lordship, I often had to draw him, and I never insulted him by pulling punches just because it was his newspaper. One misunderstanding chump said to me one day: 'How Beaver must hate you in his heart!' I did not mention that I had spent the previous afternoon in the greatest amity with Beaverbrook flying along the south coast in his new airplane.

I well remember the day because the sky was so blue, the airplane was so shiny and Beaverbrook was so proud of it. He kept urging me to buy one like it, but when I saw the petrol consumption I privately thought not. His chauffeur, who was also a pilot, took us up, so I made him the excuse, while we sat with a lot of maps figuring the course. 'I wouldn't like having a pilot,' I said. 'If I had one of these I'd want to handle it myself.' It turned out the machine had dual control, and Beaverbrook got in alongside his pilot to get the feel of the controls and show me how simple it was. Then it came to my turn to have a go. After smoothing along for a while, I felt my way out a bit, and the machine joggled slightly. I looked over my shoulder. It was the only time I ever saw Beaverbrook nervous. Next day I got a letter:

Lord Beaverbrook's Office,
43 Shoe Lane, E.C.4
July 28, 1937.

My dear Low,

 I have been thinking about the airplane . . . of course you must have a pilot. You should not attempt to drive the machine yourself. It is imperative that you should have a pilot . . .

Yours sincerely,
BEAVERBROOK

H. G. Wells was a friend of Beaverbrook's, and my own acquaintance with H.G. had ripened long before so I now saw more of him.

It had always been something to be on the Wells's visiting list, and the graceful hospitality of Jane brought us among some congenial people—the Will Rothensteins, the Richard Nevinsons, Richard Gregory, Denison Ross, J. B. S. Haldane, the Harold Laskis, the Frank Horrabins, George Catlin and Vera Brittain, the Julian Huxleys, as well as the occasional meteor from the open sky . . . Chaliapin, whose wonderful voice surged out of H.G.'s flat and filled Whitehall Court with delight at a memorable party. Apart from that, he sticks in my memory only as a boisterous, chesty, emotional chap whose talk I couldn't understand . . .

Boardman Robinson, the American cartoonist, who seemed mild and genial for one who, I had been told, had violent views. He was shocked when I said that John Reed, the American writer whose book *Ten Days that Shook the World* had made him a hero in Soviet Russia, struck me, when I met him in a Chicago cellar, as a bit of a gasbag . . . Walt Disney and many others.

These occasions, and others more private, were valuable for me mainly because they kindled H.G. to hold forth.

A stimulating and evocative talker is no remarkable phenomenon; but Wells had the rare ability to make himself clear, to make difficult ideas assimilable, to excite curiosity and to prompt enquiry. Willingness to dispense enlightenment does not always connote the power to do so, in our age of popular education. Through H.G., who seemed to me to be himself a symbol of this age, both produced by it and producing it, millions of my generation could glimpse for the first time the possible excitement and entertainment of history and science. He had little patience with those who talked and wrote only for their own esoteric kind, and to him the label 'journalist' was no term of belittlement; and though he himself was an artist, he came to have even less patience with virtuosity merely. The man of talents who used them without social purpose was like a motorist who ran his car in the garage and never ventured on the roads. He well knew that ignorance is the enemy. And to combat it, he was at one and the same time specialized and comprehensive, the genius and the ordinary, the bridge over which commoner men could struggle through their own confusion towards understanding of the affairs that rule their life and death. Scientist, novelist, sociologist, prophet—but primarily the co-ordinating link between all these and the ordinary man, who, without his like, must live forever in darkness of mind . . . I was an admiring audience.

H.G. was most effective in print, and more effective among a private company of half a dozen or so than at a public meeting. That was a trouble, because frequently he liked a public meeting, and he just hadn't the equipment. The vibrant baritone of his writing came out a peevish soprano in his speech. The handicap of a high-pitched voice that squeaked when he got wound up was easily imitated and ridiculed. 'If only he could change the needle, what that guy could be.'

When, after losing a contest for the Lord Rectorship of Glasgow University to Lord Birkenhead, he made another attempt on London University, I faithfully sat in the front row to hear him address the students. It was soon evident that we were in the

H. G. Wells and I exchange hats (1937)

presence of a mistake. They were listening to his voice, not to what he was saying. 'You shouldn't have come, David,' said he, mortified at my witnessing his bad show.

Conversation with H.G. called for more listening than speaking, but in its nature discouraged passivity. Disciple that I was, there were some things upon which I disagreed. I didn't believe in his scientific Samurai, for instance—the technical *élite* that, according to him, were to take over the future running of the world. I can remember only my own disapproval, 'I should have to be very careful indeed of your damned supermen with their damned oil-cans, H.G., arranging everything for us boobs whether we like it or not,' I said. 'I have use for socialism only so far as it helps us all to grow to our full stature mentally as well as physically, and I might have to stand Samurai, too, up to a point. But by God I would keep an eye on them . . .' I could never repose the sublime trust he did in scientists, who seemed to me a remarkably simple-minded set of people apart from their specialities.

We had a bit of a difference over a cartoon I drew of a little wee Hitler defying the universe standing on a big hand reaching out of the clouds. H.G. said it was the hand of God and I was fostering superstition. I, a bit sore, replied that I wasn't religious about not being religious, like some persons I knew.

Our discords were few and friendly, but enough to try H.G.'s patience and to make it clear that he could be sensitive to criticism. No one becomes completely impervious, I thought when I witnessed his irritation at a guest who repaid his week-end hospitality by printing an article entitled *The Failure of H. G. Wells*.

H.G. never talked to me about his attitude to sex or his widely-advertised love affairs, although of course I, like forty-seven million other people, knew all about them. I was probably not a sympathetic-looking prospect for such confidings. For one thing, as a New Zealander, in whose country women's rights had been accepted long before, doubtless I had insufficiently realized the infuriating stupidity about sex against which H.G. had ranged himself twenty years before. The assertion of principles by flaunting example is one thing. But an individual search, by trial and error, for perfection in the sexual act is another, narrowly personal, with nothing particularly admirable about it.

Then again, although I myself am incurably romantic in my approach to women, the actual means whereby the species is perpetuated always struck me as richly comic, and I cannot help laughing in the wrong places at Romeos who want to romanticize

H. G. Wells

their biological urges. When I hear poets striving to clothe life's jolliest but certainly most undignified act with beauty, and trying to show that in obeying the most carnal of impulses a human being is living poetry, I bust my sides. One could live poetry too, of course, in eating a pound of marshmallows, or smoking a box of cigars or drinking a bottle of whisky. Undoubtedly it is just as well that the machinery of reproduction provides such an enjoyable sideline, for if it did not, Lord knows what many people would think, plan and talk about. But I see nothing but childish humbug in trying to salvage dignity by confusing the ideas of 'love' and love. The two are as essentially different as taking and giving.

And there were other interests in life after all. There were times when, like the paperhanger in the funny story, 'If it's all the same to you, mum, I'd rather have a pint of beer.'

H.G. rather fancied himself as a drawer of 'picshuas' in delinquent-child style. Sometimes, when I seemed to be becoming a public scandal, I had a feeling that he thought I had a better medium for scoring off people than he had. He was always interested in what I was doing, but his suggestions for cartoons were generally unprintable. Writers cannot usually be of much help to artists, for makers of words and makers of pictures don't think along the same lines, both naturally adjust themselves to the limitations of their respective techniques and each makes a different balance of statement and suggestion. What may be a delicate hint in a picture, becomes a roaring assertion in words, and vice versa. But if the chances of happy collaboration are at least as rare as those of a happy marriage, there will always be plenty of optimistic attraction about both.

So H.G. wrote a novel which was in effect a political cartoon and had me decorate it with a series of political cartoons which were in effect illustrations. *Nash's Magazine* gave me eight double-page spreads and we ran off the serialization of *The Autocracy of Mr. Parham* in style. It was a lark, even if it did not quite come off.

I was accustomed to presenting living persons and situations in the exaggerative terms well understood and accepted as proper to the forms of political caricature. But in association with H.G., to whom as a novelist any comparable freedom was unusual, possibly deplorable, and therefore likely to attract libel suits, even my own freedom became risky. We both had to restrain, to tone down, to remove sting. There was an angry fuss when H.G. had to be stopped from making his characters identifiable as the editor of *The Spectator*, Curzon, Beaverbrook, Castlerosse, two well-known society women *et al.* I had to disguise the likenesses in my pictures into mere non-committal resemblances except in the cases of named headline politicians, and in one way or another H.G.'s publishers were saved a million pounds-worth of libel actions. Even so, questions arose here and there as to who was who, various nobodies gave themselves the credit of being H.G.'s originals, and *Time and Tide* started to build up a controversy which might have been inconvenient. H.G. swearing under his breath at the irony of life had to weigh in with crushing affirmation of his own innocuousness. Damn and blast it!

This combined operation proved not particularly happy but before long H.G. had another idea. I ran into C. B. Cochran at a dinner one night. 'How's the opera coming along?' he asks. 'Opera?' says I, hiding my puzzlement. 'Oh, fine, fine . . .' It appears that H.G. in an expansive mood had promised, he to write a kind of revue-comic-opera and I to do the décor with effects unspecified but new and remarkable. A grand idea, if only I had known what it was all about. All I could get from H.G. was that he had Cochran enthusiastic, that it was to be a great revue of a decadent world with Noah as the central figure, full of Wellsian politics and satire, and that the staging was to be in the style of ancient Greek comedy, with the actors wearing masks turning them into caricatures of living politicians and other nuisances. That was to be my department.

Cochran was properly sold on the general idea. I got a bit tired of dodging embarrassing enquiries about how we were getting on with it every time I met him. Something had to be done. So H.G. and I met one night at his flat in Chiltern Court, and after a hearty dinner we drew up easy chairs, one on each side of the fireplace, clean scribbling pad on knee, pencil in hand. We sat looking first expectantly, then angrily, at one another, waiting for the lightning of inspiration to strike. Nothing happened. The clock chimed twelve. I went home to bed and the subject was never mentioned again.

After Jane died, H.G. had moved to town, where I saw him

more frequently. Occasionally I trailed around after him as a sort of attendant shadow to his public as well as private occasions. We showed up in pomp to the première of the film based on his book *Things to Come*, and it was not all pleasure to sit next to H.G. sweating and cursing audibly at the mangling of his ideas, and afterwards to be mobbed by people with autograph-books as we scrambled into a taxi. H.G. perversely signed 'Low' so I signed 'H. G. Wells,' and we both sat back with easy consciences, feeling that if collecting autographs were anything like collecting stamps these 'errors' would inevitably become very valuable to their owners. One night when H.G. was in his most irritating mood we called on Beaverbrook. Lord B.'s political all-in-wrestling match with Baldwin was in full swing, and he sat alone at his fireside looking like Man-mountain Max in his corner waiting for the next round to tear his opponent apart. On his knee was a copy of next day's *Daily Express*, full of Peace, Prosperity, Liberty, Equality, Fraternity, Empire, Justice and Damn-foreign-entanglements— quite a sufficient body of doctrine to persuade Beaverbrook that he was politically active. 'Why don't you *do* something, Max?' shrilled H.G. 'A man like *you*, with your power! Why do you *waste* your opportunities?'

Lord B. looked taken aback. Shortly afterwards he began the Empire Crusade. I do not claim that there was any connection. I merely suggest that two and two make four.

Living in a flat, H.G. got less exercise, waxed plumper, and had to arrange for 'fitness.' I am no good at games. I make an appearance of contending, but I always lose, because I could never care a damn one way or the other. That made me in one respect at least an ideal contender with H.G., who always liked to win. So every Thursday morning for a while my wife and I were willing sacrifices at badminton to H.G. and a variable fourth, and great were the leaps and smashes and shouts of '*no!*'

H.G. was good, especially on his home ground, not so infallible away. I don't remember his ever losing at any game he had invented himself. But when Madeline and I organized a brand-new game ourselves at our house—'Pfff,' played with a ping-pong ball on a very wide table, four aside blowing their heads off— it was a different tale and he did not do so well. However unjustly he accused her of blowing offside, even fragile Sylvia Lynd could soundly beat him.

Some notable American writers came over during these disturbing times, probably to sample our latest crisis for themselves. My introduction to Sinclair 'Red' Lewis took place in Harold Laski's lavatory. He was not well and had had an exhausting day. 'Red, meet David Low,' says Harold. 'Glad to—' says Red and was immediately violently ill. Later we met again at another party but Red sat silent through the first two courses of dinner. Suddenly, without warning and apropos of nothing he rose to his full height and declaimed Chesterton's *Don John of Austria* from start to finish in loud ringing tones. It made the occasion, which up to then had been a bit formal.

There was something different about these Americans. Distinctly not in the English tradition. They reminded me of Australia. I was driving James Thurber home after a party, he was telling me about his own car and I asked him: 'Don't you find having only one good eye a bit of a disadvantage when driving?' 'Not much,' he said. Then the conversation got around to glass eyes and he told me of a chap who had had a special one made for himself with the American flag on it. When in company and afflicted by bibulous bores, he would turn aside, effect a rapid switch with his everyday regular model, and the bore would find himself withering under the impersonal glare of the Stars-and-Stripes. The effect usually was to reduce him to such teetering uncertainty as to his own condition that he reached for his cloak and retired.

By gum, I thought, blessed be the light of heart. If I were not me, I'd like to be this guy Thurber.

I was fortunate in having at this time unusually congenial associates in Fleet Street. Percy Cudlipp was that rare phenomenon, an editor who knew what a political cartoon was and how to present it. A writer himself, he had also intuitive grasp of pictorial expression combined with a naturally satiric wit. Unique in my experience of editors, Percy would have been a bit of luck for any cartoonist. He was made for me. We were, so to speak, on the same wave-length. With him ideas flowed. When we met for a mug of tea once a week, sparks flew.

Life was not all politics. I had resumed the *Low and I* line of articles about London from the old *Star* days, under a new title *Low & Terry*, with a new partner, Horace Thorogood. Horace was another bit of luck. Spending myself too long and too deeply about foreign politics, nature demanded relaxation. Horace had an abiding love of country walks, which meant that whatever our assignment, Limehouse, the Dog Show or a Piccadilly night club, we always approached it via Rickmansworth or Epping Forest after a leafy ramble and lunch at some old country pub.

That suited me well. Our Tuesday excursions came to be a weekly holiday to which I looked forward as occasions upon which I could be taking in instead of giving out, mixing pleasure with our business of 'covering' the social scene, not only at home, but sometimes abroad for a change.

Under the meekest of exteriors Horace had a John Bull heart. There was the nightmare occasion in Vienna upon which we had strayed in search of local colour into a tough night-spot and became involved in a dispute about the bill which it seemed to me could only end by both of us being tied in sacks and thrown down a trap-door into the Danube. Horace threatening four big brutes in indignant English was an inspiring sight—and successful, for we each got out in one piece, with the loss of only our hats.

Horace had the peculiar qualities which I found restful and congenial. A dry wit, not cynical, based upon a conception of essential decency, a willingness to argue interminably about fundamental principles, a liking for a good big cigar and the cinema. Our expeditions invariably ended with two seats in the front row, bang up against the screen because we liked to see the faces of the actors, and we found that position best for 'audience participation.' So were formed the habits and customs of an enduring friendship.

The cinema was an important adjunct of our association. At this time I had just discovered the uses of films as an anodyne, a precious aid to detachment and recuperation of the mind in that flat period after the end of an exhausting labour and before one is readjusted to face the world anew. Its value did not occur to me until one evening when I was too exhausted at the end of a gruelling ten-hour day to go straight home and had flopped into a news-theatre for a sit down. That was just what nature was calling for—a seat in the dark, a cigar, music, a picture of something going on that invited but did not demand attention, if one preferred to doze. So after that I went every night to a different cinema for one hour before dinner and derived great benefit thereby, in addition to becoming, in due course, perhaps the world's champion collector of film fragments, beginnings, middles and ends. This nightly dose of films for health purposes was additional to my weekly homage to the full art of the screen with Horace, because he was irritated at what he thought was an affront to all concerned in making the films. In his opinion, one should see beginning, middle and end in that sequence. In vain I protested that, considered quite apart from my physical needs, the effect of my way of film-viewing was more representative of real life, since in real life one is always barging into the middle of some story and leaving before the end to go home to dinner.

Suitable recreation was very necessary to me at this time, because I was certainly overworking. Acting on the principle that the way to cure a headache is to hit one's head with a hammer, I had embarked on a lovely new job in addition to my regular work. In the spring of 1925 I had spent a family holiday at Biarritz. The Prince of Wales was there, a beautiful piece of character in his golf-suit, getting persistently in my line of vision, set up invitingly as a model for me. As I played a round of golf with a friend right behind the Prince's foursome on the local links, a bright idea struck me. Why not use him as a peg upon which to hang a pageant of London life of the time, in all its variety, with all its personalities and characters? I planned it there and then, walking under the trees. But it was not until 1933 that I got to work on a series of twelve colour plates.

Unfortunately, when it came to the point, inspiration would have been cramped and publication impossible had the figures, especially the central figure, been too readily identifiable; so I had to tone down the likenesses and scramble the situations. As it turned out I disguised it all so well that it became almost completely unrecognizable and changed into something else, which wasn't the intention at all. Served me right. I had to abandon the original conception and pull the whole thing together again on somewhat different lines, giving it a backbone of Hogarthian morality and re-making the central character (who by now had nothing to do with the Prince) into someone coming into wealth and leading a life of fashion. Finally I called the series *The New Rake's Progress*. To my delight Rebecca West was persuaded to write a beautifully satiric commentary to go with it.

The New Rake's Progress was an enormous labour that kept me working early and late without holidays, but I enjoyed every minute of doing it. So much so that when a rich American offered me fifteen hundred pounds for the twelve originals. I could not bear the idea of their being stowed away in some private gallery so far away and I refused, and kept them for myself.

With this behind me, I ought to have been stimulated when there arose in 1936 the domestic crisis which culminated in the abdication of King Edward the Eighth. But in the intervening few years I had become too deeply interested in the development of affairs abroad to find this crisis inspiring. My contribution to the matter was only three or four cartoons about Baldwin's rebuff to Cupid, a midnight scene of mysterious figures getting away with the throne, crown and sceptre, and a romantic piece celebrating a new addition to the world's great love stories.

More than a century had passed since the ribald days when Gillray used to stop the traffic in Piccadilly with caricatures of the Royalties hanging in the print-shop windows. The evolution of the British monarchy from a political to a symbolic institution and a corresponding merging of the individual importance of royal personages in the idea itself, accounted for the change. In 1936, thanks to the carefully adjusted 'treatment' of the Press about the intimate private life of the Royal Family, the public knew nothing of discord until it was far advanced; and even then it watched the agonized comings and goings of Mr. Baldwin and the spiritual wrestlings of the Archbishop of Canterbury with sentimental interest but without anxiety, knowing that there was, if necessary, another and obviously model king around the corner. There was for me some personal disillusionment. I had not so far lost my overseas simplicity as to doubt that 'Our Smiling Prince' really had had the affection of the populace. I was slightly shocked to find it was only skin-deep. There was something revolting in the revelation of insincerity about 'demonstrations of love' for royal individuals which could be turned on and off like water from a tap, according to an official steer.

When editor Percy Cudlipp, with some idea of giving the paper a good shake, assigned Valentine Castlerosse, the liveliest social columnist of his generation, and me jointly to fill a page of the *Evening Standard* with whatever we could find, I was a little apprehensive. Expansive, exuberant and inexhaustibly cheerful, Castlerosse knew the idle rich from the inside. But he was a dislocating chap to work with. I arrived at 11 a.m. at the rendezvous, his club, to find him sitting in the front doorway watching the people passing the street from behind a bottle of champagne. He always began the day on champagne. 'Always start the day with champagne, Low. Good for the liver.' I dislike champagne. Think it a woman's drink.

'Come,' I said, 'let's go to the football match.'

'Football?' says he. 'What's that?'

At half-past three we were still lunching at the American Club arguing the point with a mixed batch of lords and Americans about an historic character called Old Parr who was buried at Westminster Abbey after having been convicted of rape at the age of ninety. It was getting late for the football.

'Let's go to Westminster Abbey, then,' I said.

We set out in his enormous car, one of the first—if not the first —to be fitted with a radio. Its blare of *You are My Heart's Delight* was much appreciated in traffic blocks. He occupied four-fifths of the back seat, I the other fifth, both of us sporting ten-inch cigars and for a whimsey wearing one another's hats. Altogether we were just right for Westminster Abbey.

We removed the hats respectfully and passed through panelled doorways into a chamber where sombrely dressed men of ascetic appearance were sitting around. But this was not the Abbey. We were at Ladbroke's, the bookmakers, listening in solemn silence to somebody with a voice suggestive of the dean of all denominations announcing the number of a hymn, retailing from a telephone the progress of the Cambridgeshire.

'Come on!' I said. 'The Abbey!'

'Ah! The Abbey!' said Castlerosse. 'Waiter! Champagne!'

Again we set out, the car playing The Love Call from *Rose-Marie*, and again we overshot the Abbey . . . This austere office with the formidable safe in the corner was, I gathered, the sanctum of Castlerosse's pet moneylender. That was a sad interlude. There was a depression in the money-lending business and Castlerosse promised to sow more wild oats in future. . . . The expedition finished up at half-past two in the morning sitting in Castlerosse's flat disputing vaguely about social justice.

'I must go home,' I said. 'Don't you ever work?'

'My dear Low,' he replied, 'don't be blasphemous.'

Long after he was dead I stood, alone and ruminating before the remains of his ancestral seat in Ireland, burnt out during the 'thrubbles.' Before me ruins and a mounting-stone, behind me whispering trees, under me the cobbled stones of a courtyard. I thought what a lovely sight it would be to see Castlerosse in armour riding up on a big white horse, calling out: 'Waiter! Champagne!' A likeable soul. How strange that this should be his environment.

22

I N times of real anxiety about public affairs, most people find
relief in signing and joining. The busier ones rush about
drawing up manifestoes, letters to the Press, petitions to
Parliament, etc., and forming 'Progressive Groups,' 'Peace
Fellowships,' 'People's Unions' and so on. The others sign and
join. Therein lies a temptation for the overwilling. I knew one
zealous chap who was known as the President of the Joiners'
Union because he joined everything.

I had been to a limited extent a signer but rarely a joiner.
It seemed to me that a public commentator should be unattached,
a being sitting apart, perched in the blue. I had never felt called
upon to join any party: I was positively uncomfortable in crowds,
and I felt no need to pump up my own enthusiasm with mass
emotion. Parties there had to be if aims were to be realized,
but my place was always on their flanks, doubting, careful lest
loyalty be perverted from the ideas to the organizations which
existed only to carry out the ideas. Being sceptical particularly
of ideology identified with the permanent success of one party
organization exclusively, I was unsympathetic to those whose
reaction to the brutalities of the Nazi Party and the Fascist Party
was to pop headlong into the Communist Party. If the ideas of
the first two were misconceived and fallacious, the communist
faith seemed to me to have obvious flaws both in diagnosis and
cure. No doubt the capitalist system had within itself the seeds of
its own disintegration, as the Marxists said; but so had all systems
—if they didn't burst new buds now and then. It was too simple to
imagine that capitalism had no adaptability whatever. I had my
doubts whether communism was the medicine at all for a political
equalitarian society, already highly industrialized, that could make
the necessary blend of individualism and socialism. I banked on

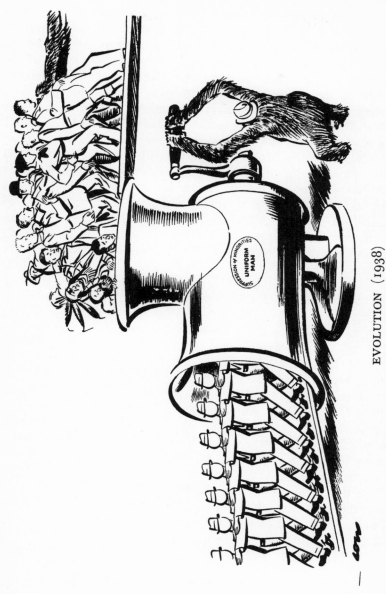

EVOLUTION (1938)

A protest against the trend towards uniformity and the discouragement of minorities

the British political genius for mixing oil and water. I thought H. G. Wells was right when he said: 'Someone should shave that fellow Marx.'

Under the menacing advance of fascism I came off my perch and relaxed my detachment to the extent of demonstrating sympathy with various anti-Nazi and anti-fascist groups. For a space I signed away at joint letters of protest, letters of indignation, letters of appeal, letters of admonition and 'awake-arise' letters, as one of them put it, 'for the purpose of planning the best immediate methods of arousing the various professions and the public at large to energetic action on behalf of world peace.' I was glad to be in the distinguished company of Epstein, John, Paul Nash, Henry Moore, Herbert Read, Eric Gill and others whose moral indignation was proof against cheap sneers about 'manifestos of long-haired intellectuals.' Someone had to record opposition to Göring's political trials, to the recognition of Mussolini's right to Abyssinia, to the bombing of civilians in Spain, even if the frequent appearance of the same block of names did rather give the impression of a divinely self-appointed body of Conscience.

If the first step to Public Life is writer's cramp, the second is platform-sitter's spine. When the oracles speak there always have to be a row of supporters behind them to sit with stiff dignity 'dressing' the platform. As a platform sitter I underwent my share of the occupational discomforts, but I met some fine people who looked as admirable from the rear as they no doubt did from the front. I was glad to form part of the background to Lord Robert Cecil, Gilbert Murray, Henry Nevinson, Norman Angell, Maynard Keynes. There were golden moments, too, as when one portly speaker, after a magnificent address, sat down on his glasses without the least sacrifice of dignity, or when Harold Laski lost his notes.

The third step is making the speech oneself. To platform-sit is one thing, to make the speech another. I had learned to make a bumbling after-dinner speech to a sympathetic company and to deliver a set address from a script; but I had not made more than two or three political platform speeches before I perceived that there was a big difference. The conditions of this kind of public speaking demanded a long and arduous apprenticeship, especially for me. My habits of thought and expression were against me. I could not think fluently without pondering now and then. My crushing rejoinders were too slow. The drawer feels and expresses himself in images. The talker thinks and expresses himself in words. The two are different exercises, and the two processes of mind involved tend to be, if not mutually exclusive, at least mutually obstructive. That kind of politics was not for me, I decided. To celebrate my retirement, I went on the platform for a swan-song, in the company of Stafford Cripps, Nye Bevan, J. B. Priestley, Victor Gollancz and others, at a bumper meeting of protest at the old Queen's Hall about the Government's supine attitude to foreign intervention in Spain. The meeting was packed to the ceiling and when the chairman called me up to speak the audience applauded for a solid five minutes. A new and warming experience . . . direct hot contact. . . . What a pity, I thought. . . . What am I doing here? . . . Not my line. . . . That had to be my final appearance as a political platform speaker.

Between these steps there were the exhibitionist interludes with a political undercurrent; in my case, chalk talks at the village schoolroom blackboard, draw-your-portrait stands at garden-parties-for-the-cause, and so on. There was one uproarious occasion when, ostensibly to raise money for a London hospital, I was publicly put on mock trial at the London School of Economics over a cartoon entitled NURSEMAIDS IN THE PARK. I was charged, under the Government's new and highly-contentious Incitement to Disaffection Bill, with seducing from his allegiance a young soldier, who turned out to be Kingsley Martin, editor of *The New Statesman and Nation*, in disguise. The court, including A. P. Herbert, Philip Guedalla and a brilliant 'bar,' succeeded in having me sentenced to transportation for life to the National Portrait Gallery.

The interludes were sometimes grim. At the hightide of Mosley's Blackshirt movement, when public opinion was being shocked by the brutality of his supporters against dissenters, and even against those who omitted at fascist meetings to 'salute the leader,' I became an 'observer' for a Society concerned with popular rights, for one night only, to attend a Mosley rally at the Albert Hall. I was one of several whose 'observations' were to form the substance of a report on the conduct of the meeting, to be sent to the Home Secretary.

I went. The meeting was most successful, the Albert Hall was filled. Sixty per cent of the audience looked like middle-class people who had come out of curiosity, with a backing of 30 per cent of honest British morons who had apparently decided that Mosley represented the British way of life, and 10 per cent of paid bruisers who would have bashed anyone for five shillings. Looking across I saw an acquaintance of mine, one who had prided himself on being an anti-socialist, clapping his hands off. What the infatuated ass thought he was doing there, goodness only knows.

The hall darkened, Mosley entered in full limelight with a bodyguard which trailed him along the full length of the hall between two lines of his 'troops' all with hands outstretched in salute, the bands playing crescendo, the audience (excepting me) saluting too. . . . Hooray! Hooray! Hail, the Leader! It occurred to me that what I had seen at the meetings of Father Coughlin and Father Divine in New York was not so un-British after all.

Mosley spoke effectively at great length. Delivery excellent, matter reckless. Interruptions began, but no dissenting voice got beyond half a dozen sentences before three or four bullies almost literally jumped on him, bashed him and lugged him out. Two such incidents happened near me. An honest-looking blue-eyed student type rose and shouted indignantly 'Hitler means war!' whereupon he was given the complete treatment. I took copious notes of this damnable outrage to British liberty and shook the dust of such brutal foolery from my feet.

That incident had a sequel. Soon after, an anti-fascist Exhibition at the Hampstead Library was burnt out by the Blackshirts. A meeting was called by the same Society to ginger the Home Secretary to action, and I accepted a seat on the platform. Looking over the company and officials of the convoking assembly . . . where have I seen that face before? . . . why, of course . . . our honest-looking, blue-eyed friend who had yelled and been dumped at the Mosley meeting. And there was another . . . and another beside him as large as life. Had our society been providing not only observers on that occasion, but also somebody to be observed? Or was it merely coincidence? The agent provocateur may be a perfectly justifiable performer in such active politics; and whether these chaps had been planted or not, they had certainly been mistreated. I may be naïve in preferring my object-lessons uncooked. All the same, I did not like it. My enthusiasm for the Society waned. It was evident that for a critic independence was the only thing.

Around the time when Mosley's Blackshirts were turning Olympia and the Albert Hall into bear-gardens, Madeline and I were dining one evening at the Harold Laski's with Stafford Cripps and his wife. The Home Secretary, Sir John Simon, had just said that the doings at the Albert Hall 'made his blood boil,' and I had drawn a policeman standing amid the battered casualties making tea from a kettle balanced on the pointed top of Simon's steaming head. When the conversation turned to what could be done to discourage this Blackshirt business, I suggested with Australian gaucherie that the believers in our democracy could adopt a shirt, too, and counter-demonstrate. Cripps snapped —yes, snapped—'I fail to see how it would be useful to do something which would not only be illegal but opposed to the democratic spirit.' I made no more facetious cracks that evening.

Mosley had begun as an imitator of Mussolini and neither of them had thought of using Jew-baiting until Hitler came along. But Hitler so identified Nazism with anti-semitism as to make it an article of faith for up-to-the-minute would-be dictators. The call of race-hate brought immediate results as a means of increasing and consolidating Mosley's following and once again anti-semitism became an active element in British politics.

Hating people because of their race was to me as childish as hating people because they had blue eyes or curly hair. In general I found Jews like anybody else, good, bad and indifferent. All the same, I decided, a spreading social movement was not to be dismissed without even a glance to see what it was made of. Although in my lifetime I had observed various forms of aberration, I had never looked closely at a race-hater. Choosing from among many anti-semitic importunings, I answered four correspondents who seemed comparatively rational, in terms calculated to draw out a more detailed exposition of charge and evidence. Nothing highbrow, just plain sense. Unfortunately, out of the resulting rather mad correspondence came little illumination. Plenty of individual instances, but nothing ethnological that was not sheer bunkum. Flat assertions to which the answers were so obvious that I did not trouble to make them.

One man who wrote to me in sedate terms, presenting a formidable indictment on notepaper with the heading of a very respectable club, I invited to tea at the National Liberal Club, to tell me quietly why the Jews were worse than other people. He proved to be a pretty ordinary-looking chap, bald, eyes disappearing into his head, glasses, a flat voice. Right away he began about the Protocols of Zion. 'Look,' I said, 'supposing we skip the old P.o.Z. One of your friends and I just cleared that one up. Tell me about the thousands of secret Jewish spies pouring into Britain.' He had already put me to a lot of trouble investigating a story he had sent me about the landing of two thousand Jews on given dates at Southampton. His brother had actually seen them disembark. The official view, however, was that it was six hundred Czechs and that this chap's brother not only couldn't count but evidently couldn't tell a Jew from a Slav. He gave me the story again with all the trimmings. 'Official records don't tally with your story,' I said. 'There are plenty of Jews in the Civil Service to doctor the records,' he replied. 'You think your brother would know a Jew when he saw one?' I asked. 'You can always tell them,' he said. 'Look,' I said, 'there are two Jews sitting in this room right now. Point 'em out to me.' He pointed out the Club's most distinguished Scotsman and a Welsh divine in mufti.

We passed to his sweeping assertion that Jews were bad citizens. 'Well, now, that should be capable of proof,' I said. 'Criminal records, I suppose. What have you got?' He passed that over and went on to tell me that 95 per cent of the brothels in Berlin were run by Jews. 'Now that's very interesting,' I said. 'So neat. From what police files did you get that figure?' 'You don't get figures like that from police files,' he replied. 'Well, where did you get them?' I asked. 'You have reliable friends who checked up? Am I to assume that you went around yourself?' He was insulted. 'I am not accustomed to having my word doubted,' says he, trembling. 'You are trying to convince me without evidence,' says I. 'I can't condemn a whole people on your say-so.' 'I could never convince *you*,' says he, "because you are a Jew.' His voice throbbed with passion. I looked into his eye and caught a glint of red madness. The poor chap was perfectly sincere. I had never seen so clear a case of preconceived idea colouring all associated thoughts.

From 1933 onward had come the pathetic procession of emigrés —mostly, in my world, artists, writers, musicians, politicians, from Germany, Austria, Czechoslavkia, Spain. . . . There was the sad little party at Stefan Zweig's. A dull winter's day, the flat was gloomy, the lighting was bad, too much heavy mahogany furniture. There were about twelve people present, all Austrians barring Thornton Wilder, the American novelist, and us two Lows. We took drinks and sandwiches and talked without laughter or smiles. Soon Stefan steered us all into an adjoining room where there stood—no, it couldn't be! Yes, it was!—a magic lantern pointing at a suspended sheet. For an hour Stefan and his daughter showed us a succession of portrait slides of people strange to Madeline and me, but evidently well known to the rest of the company. These, I gathered, were the familar figures of art and letters in their Vienna, now gone for ever. Tears fell, my own eyes were wet with sympathy. That was a sad evening.

Ernst Toller removed from his Berlin environment was a fish out of water; and obviously he was embarrassed for money. To overcome this difficulty he evolved a grandiose idea for a huge satirical film-cartoon which I was to do under his direction and inspiration. He explained at great length—about three hours, during which I could hardly get a word in edgeways. I have often marvelled how it is that otherwise intelligent people think there is nothing to know about the comic arts, that everybody knows about them naturally. In this case there were also the technical limitations. I had not the heart to tell Toller that to oblige him I should have to go out of business as a political cartoonist for at least two years, that his film would cost at least one-and-a-half-million dollars and when made would get no bookings in the United States.

The Czechs when they came were not so emotional. Beneš was a politician, perhaps too much of a politician for the dramatic circumstances. A company assembled to commiserate Beneš would quite naturally turn into an audience listening to his calm balanced 'inside story.' The only emotions he betrayed were some anger and some contempt. I found Jan Masaryk more to my liking, personally.

Outraged and evicted from his domains, now snubbed and ignored by the British Government that was seeking to please his despoiler Mussolini, the Emperor Haile Selassie of Ethiopia was a model of majesty even in the depths of adversity. At an assembly arranged for him to meet his sympathizers, someone had provided a small platform upon which he and the Empress sat regally on a level six inches above us ordinary people standing around drinking coffee and munching fancy cakes. The Empress was gracious, the Princess charming and the Ambassador talkative, but the Emperor said nothing to anybody, just looked at us with steady half-lidded eyes and curled nostrils. His thoughts were no doubt worth more than a penny.

It was a prank of the fates that placed Pablo de Azcarate, a kind and gentle scholar, as Ambassador of Spain, a country being torn to pieces by human wild animals. As the political temperature fell and fair-weather friends disappeared, the innate goodness of the man and his gracious wife grew so plain as to win the respect and affection of those that remained. It was painful to see him, spare, bespectacled and soft-voiced, striving to assemble the supporters of democratic Spain; and Negrin, more solidly-built and phlegmatic, the active politician, just arrived from Madrid after the fall of his Government, hopefully explaining his hopeless cause to a select company of listeners of which I was glad to be one. Hope deferred made the heart sick. Sadness brooded over the Spanish Embassy when one day near the end Madeline and I lunched alone with the Azcárates. 'What will you do now?' I asked. 'I will go and look at the sea,' he replied.

The dictators were pursuing a deliberate policy of wearing out opposition and they saw to it that the atmosphere of crisis continued on the boil. Peace or war, war or peace, was the subject littering all the channels of communication, especially public speaking.

When at a dinner of the Ruskin Society, in the middle of a speech which should have been devoted entirely to approving the humanities and describing the blessings of peace, I felt myself called upon to jar the proceedings by remarking that as things were going we could expect men to live together without murdering one another perhaps after another two Armageddons. Lady Snowden, a few places away, moaned. After dinner she invited my wife and me to visit Philip and herself in the country, no doubt to convert me from a suspected tendency to bellicosity. I had heard that Philip, now sitting an invalid in the country, had reverted to passionate pacifism.

Snowden was one of the generation of socialists whose historic purpose was to inspire—to create an atmosphere. A reformer, not a revolutionary. When it came to doing anything—finding ways and means—he always looked to me like a radical liberal, treating socialism as an attitude for the individual rather than as a public policy. Hence developments like the 'iron-jawed Chancellor' of financial orthodoxy when he was in office, the 'correctness' of his attitude in the financial crisis of 1931, and the conventional free-trader's indignation with which he flounced out of the National Government shortly after.

His house buried in the country was not hard to find, because of the Snowden system of marking the way with little Union Jack flags at every doubtful turning en route. Approaching by car it felt like completing some military manœuvre. At last we found him sitting in his Olde Englishe atmosphere like the Father of His Country. After luncheon (roast beef with Yorkshire pudding, apple pie), we conversed about peace and the state of the world. Almost immediately he got around to free trade, which seemed to me off the beam at that moment. Out of the corner of my eye

I saw on the wall the original of my cartoon CONFLICT OF CHINS—the Snowden chin jutting forward against the Mussolini chin at the Hague Reparations Conference in 1929. It was evident from a couple of leading answers that our host still thought of that occasion, when he had been John Bull triumphantly upholding Britain's rights against chiselling foreigners, as the apex of his career.

Snowden had been drafting a letter to the Cobden Club, and he read me pieces. His purport was that the idea of all the nations trying to ensure peace by impoverishing themselves in a competition of armaments was ridiculous foolishness. When our people realized this, he was sure they would stop it. He was shocked at the indifference of Parliament towards the taxpayers and the indifference of the taxpayers towards their own interests. He was dismayed at the piling up of the national debt. . . . It was clear that, however moral might be the basis of Snowden's pacifism, the really serious aspects of the current situation were to him financial.

When he wagged his finger at me and said I should do some educative cartoons about all this, I could only ask the old questions: what did we do if the other fellow wouldn't play? Ignore him? The last German financial statement released by Hitler had showed that the Nazis were scraping the barrel for their last remaining saleable assets and using them to acquire materials for unreproductive manufactures like tanks, planes and bombs. Would Hitler be impressed by the news that if he encouraged us to arm, he would put us all, himself included, in the Bankruptcy Court? On the other hand, I couldn't imagine Hitler being deterred from aggression by a thrifty victim who hadn't armed saying: 'Here, you can't touch me, I'm solvent.' Nor Genghis Khan, nor Attila, nor even Napoleon Bonaparte. What about Marx and the Marxists who positively hoped for the collapse of capitalism anyway? And what about Schacht's exploitation of Germany's bankruptcy? And his bright new ideas for basing his credit on fear instead of on wealth? And what about Keynes?

The conversation got nowhere. On these grounds I was unconvinced.

In restlessness of spirit I talked with all sorts of people, testing my own conclusions, which I disliked but could not avoid. I lent an ear to the ignoramuses who save themselves the trouble of thought by accepting the blanket explanation that all wars were caused solely by the black villainy of miscreant politicians.

I listened with some exasperation to non-resisters who implied, even sometimes stated, that their concern was not only with spiritual but also with physical preservation. It seemed to me that a religious pacifist who claimed that faith in his God was surest defence for body as well as for soul was presuming that his God's ideas of what was best for himself and his followers were the same as their own, which was more than a little arrogant. The Bible, it seemed to me, conveyed a contrary view. . . . I climbed the steps of St. Martin's Church to talk to Dick Sheppard, beloved pastor and good man. A pacifist, if ever there was one.

Is Life sacred? More than, say, Justice? What is Life worth without Justice? Can no distinction be drawn between offence and defence? Is resistance as reprehensible as aggression? . . . As well ask what would your human conception of justice be worth in a dead world? How can one kill to defend the principle of not killing? In such a case what becomes of the principle? He who, as they say, 'loves peace so much that he will fight for it' is a peace-lover only when the need for being otherwise is not apparent. True enough. Principles are of the inner self, indestructible save by the holder, not lost nor won in battle. . . . Yes, yes, but come down to earth. Is not this the personal attitude of one with no sense of responsibility for anyone but himself? You or I personally can be against killing anybody and war generally, but we couldn't dare, in 1937, to elevate our feeling into a principle to be operated on behalf of others as a public policy, leaving forty-six million people naked to the blast. What kind of leadership would it be for a Cabinet to issue a proclamation ordering the people, masses of which did not share its hopeful beliefs, not to mind being killed, and above all, not to be violent about it? . . . The principle is the foundation. If when built on solid foundation the building collapses the fault is in the superstructure. . . . Of course. Then should the hard-won opportunity to build something better be defended or abandoned? What can be done when a leader of millions deliberately decides to use war as an instrument of policy? Prepare to resist.

But there was more than one possibility that the answer might not have been acceptable as the national policy. A theoretical conclusion is one thing, practical politics another. Our semi-Nazi extremists of the Right were disposed to concession and co-operation; and the Labour Party was led by George Lansbury. The dear old chap was that rare thing, a Christian in politics, and under his guidance the Labour Party's policy on armaments had become far from clear or consistent. I did not get a chance of private conversation with old George when he returned from Germany in 1937, after going to see if Hitler was as black as he was painted, but I was one of a handful of friends to whom he gave his impressions. It was easy to see what had happened. To say they had pulled the wool over his eyes would have been an understatement. Rather the whole sheep.

'The trouble about old George is that he's so good he'll have us all in Heaven before our time,' said a plaintive M.P.

Some of my writing friends, I found, were writing books calling for peace because war was horrible. They did not say how this peace was to be secured. It was sure that if we made war there would not be peace; and if we surrendered in advance it would be highly improbable that British youth would escape military servitude to the conqueror.

Pamphlets, tracts and leaflets. Winnie the Pooh was left in the cloakroom while I talked over a lamb chop with A. A. Milne, a well-disposed man earnestly wishing for peace, about whether we could do yet another book, a joint affair, on how to stop the drift to war. But when we got down to brass tacks, it was distressingly evident that the initiative for peace lay with the dictators, not with the democracies.

Talks, talks, talks. Earnest talks with earnest people, combined into an impersonal stream of anxious searching for a Way.

No point in appealing to our people, nor the French, nor the Americans. They were if anything a bit too flocculently peaceful already. Then let us appeal to the German and the Italian people! . . . But how did you do that? Even if you could get to them, they were unreceptive in the power of a rigid mind-tyranny which had taught them to 'think with the blood,' not with the brains, that war was noble, they were the Herrenvolk and we were their push-over.

Can we not use cunning, then? Make a deal! Meet them half-way. Let us give Hitler Czechoslovakia on condition he stops right there and keeps the peace . . . Oh, yeah? You gave a whole nation, people like us, up to hell? You surrendered one of the most powerful strategic points in Europe with one of the most powerful armament centres, and you expected your opponent not to act upon the proof that it paid to be tough with you?

Well, deflect him! Steer his forces away from us. *Let* him attack Soviet Russia . . . overboard with morality, hey? The short way to make Hitler master of the world, hey? When the Nazis have defeated and integrated Russian power, how long did you think we could stand up?

All right, then, let's play it his way—go in with him, hoping to modify Nazi excesses as time passes. . . . Yes? Starting with a mass incineration of Jews in Hyde Park, perhaps, and an elimination camp for intellectual idealists like you, brother?

One acquaintance of mine returned from Germany and reported that a lot of rot had been talked about the Nazis living under a dictatorship. It was not really so bad.

'The point is—can one have an adverse opinion?'

'Yes, certainly! Of course!'

'What! Don't they put you in gaol if you disagree with the official view?'

'Utter nonsense! Of course not! They always reason with you first. . . .'

A note of exasperation crept into friendly discussion as the Spanish Civil War got under way and the outlook grew blacker.

A person trying to go in two opposite directions at once is one of the stock inspirations of satire. I lost some friends and aroused the wrath of the lamb with a couple of fairly mild cartoons, one of Dick Sheppard, George Lansbury and a representative of anti-war youth mounted on a white steed trying unsuccessfully to convince it with maps that it could go to Resistance-to-aggression and Opposition-to-risky-sanctions at one and the same time; the other, *Pmilb* (or *Blimp* in reverse) trying to balance himself on two diverging circus horses 'Anti-fascism' and 'Sitdown-pacifism.'

Too often my breakfast would be ruined by the arrival of some letter, like this one, referring to a cartoon about three 100 per cent pacifists affirming '*We Won't Fight Anybody*' to two butchers of the weak and destroyers of the peace, whose comment 'ANYBODY INCLUDES US, PAL' made the title:

> Mount Royal,
> W.1.
> 2/12/36.

Dear Low,

Three pacifists versus two butchers certainly provide a comic spectacle. But will you please in a future cartoon portray the alternative—i.e. three butchers with longer knives against two butchers. And in yet a third cartoon will you draw the result of the conflict between the three butchers (anti-fascist collective security) and the two butchers (fascist States). True, these results have already been set down by Callot and Goya;

304

but these artists had the misfortune to live before the age of mustard gas and bombers—so there is still plenty of scope for you.

Yours very sincerely,
ALDOUS HUXLEY.

After the taking of Austria, life became more strained. The luncheon parties of perturbed anti-fascists that were a feature of the early '30's (it seemed that in England nobody could discuss the End of the World except over food) increased in frequency and were supplemented by anxious drawings-together of like-minded writers, politicians and others concerned with public affairs, exchanging doubts and fears, uncertainties and determinations, brushing the dust off principles, stock-taking the ideas of a lifetime to see if they could possibly be mistaken, or if there were any sound argument overlooked that could absolve an honest mind from coming to unpalatable conclusions.

The subject was not to be avoided even on my morning walk across the heath to my Hampstead studio. In earlier days this walk had provided an interval for reflection usually uninterrupted, except for an occasional hang over the rails of the duck-pond talking shop with my friendly rival George Strube, the cartoonist of the *Daily Express*, who lived close by; or a stroll under the larches with the aged D. S. McColl, the critic poet. Now I kept running into the most unlikely people full of argument, like Cyril Joad.

The first time I met Joad was at a party. He came up to me and said: 'I'm Joad. Why don't you draw me?' That put me off him for a long time. But two men can't frequent Hampstead for ten years and not meet often, so at length we got to know one another better and finally I *did* draw him.

One day we walked through Hampstead talking about pacifism hotly. It was amazing how famous his broadcasting had made him. Walking with him was a royal progress, which was a bit of a nuisance on this occasion. We ended up on the steps of the Underground station, just as Joad was making his point. He would bank on passive resistance to defeat any dictator. 'Now, look here,' I said. 'Suppose I'm Hitler and I command you to get on with some job. You passively resist. I get you and fifty of your principal followers lined up over there before the people and I get a firing party and I have the lot of you shot. . . . No good, hey? Still someone resists? . . . All right, I line up another fifty and I have them shot, too . . . and another . . . and another. You

305

tell me I wouldn't break——' I was talking vehemently and perhaps I had been gesticulating a bit. Anyway, I noticed out of the corner of my eye that we had collected a small audience and it evidently was misunderstanding the position. Someone said: 'Who does he think he is? Ought to be locked up. Dirty Nazi!' Impossible to explain. The discussion was postponed; but soon after Joad abandoned his pacifism, so that settled it.

During these fateful years my own political position was no bed of roses. Through the 'twenties and early 'thirties I had been for cutting national armaments to the bone and depending for the defence of the international law and order upon collective security under the League, especially through the application of economic sanctions; when Mussolini's defiance over Abyssinia demonstrated the weakness of collective security I was for giving it an adequate backing of armaments, still under the League.

After 1936–37, when Hitler reoccupied the Rhineland and showed plainly his intentions, I was for additional increase of national armaments, and after Czechoslovakia in 1938 I rampaged for full rearmament and close association with Russia. The only other country that had the manpower to offset Germany, the United States, was deep in isolation and passing laws to forestall another entanglement in European wars.

Conventional enough as all that might seem, there was sufficient contentious matter in it to provide constant friction. For one thing I was a bit early in plumping for the Russians and that excited our considerable anti-bolshevik element. The League was anathema to our patriotic nationalists. Collective security and economic sanctions were bad for business. There were the backward thinkers of the Left who were moved by the very mention of arms to the most warlike anonymous letters; and there were always our fascist admirers of Mussolini and Hitler, to say nothing of those who (latterly) excused Franco on religious grounds.

The telephone rang all day and my correspondence grew violent. New elements introduced themselves—packets of filth, and threats. Signs of my growing political importance, no doubt. Gladstone said: 'Never reply.' I once heard Margaret Bondfield say that the hardest thing she knew was to sit silent when someone was traducing her.

When there was anything substantial in the letters, I wrote answers to them. But I posted my replies not at the Post Office but in a bottom drawer.

23

STANLEY BALDWIN, visibly aged by his arduous efforts as king-maker and pacificator, had finally retired to the country with an earldom and a mild persecution mania. Neville Chamberlain took over.

Fleet Street knew Mr. C. to be an honest, well-intentioned man, not a brilliant statesman, who had been developing fixed ideas that he had the answer to the dictator problem and that he was the man to carry it through. His recipe for improving things was friendly understanding, appeasement. The scene began to change. Goodbye to Foreign Secretary Eden and his stiffness to Mussolini in the Mediterranean; goodbye to Foreign Office head Vansittart whose resistance to the Nazis became inconvenient. Mr. C. would surround himself with men whose past and whose reputation would not irritate either of the dictators. Inskip became Minister of Defence to organize rearmament, apparently because he had never opened his mouth on the subject. Not Winston Churchill, who had opened his mouth too freely. Churchill's appointment would have distressed 'our friends in Italy and Germany.' Some ridicule was poured on the Churchill 'theatrical attitude' as opposed to the Chamberlain 'settled purpose of peace.'

The people sank back soothed with fair words. In Spain it had become comfortably clear that the British conscience need no longer fret because it was now too late to do anything. The whole situation had slumped into hypocrisy. Franco was well supplied, but for fear of falling foul of the dictators neither the United States nor Britain would sell arms to the Spanish Government, and the Non-Intervention Committee that was to have stopped shipments of arms to both sides in practice stopped them only to the Government. The pressure of cruel and bitter war on Madrid

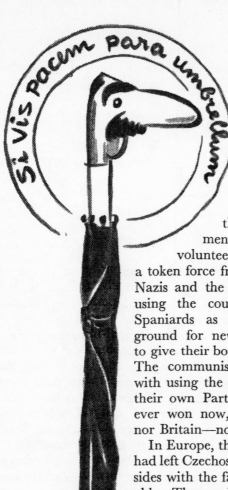

had edged out the statesmen and brought forward the extremists. The 'civil' war had become openly a war of ideologies with, on the one side, Franco's Falangists heavily reinforced by Italian fascists and German Nazis; against, on the other, the remnants of the Government armies, supplemented by volunteers from the democracies and a token force from communist Russia. The Nazis and the Italian fascists were openly using the countryside of the unhappy Spaniards as an experimental proving-ground for new weapons and as targets to give their bomber-pilots war experience. The communists were concerned mainly with using the circumstances to advantage their own Party strategy. Certainly whoever won now, it would not be France, nor Britain—nor Democracy.

In Europe, the Nazi possession of Austria had left Czechoslovakia hemmed in on three sides with the famous Skoda works vulnerable. Those who followed the course of events waited for Hitler's next move. It stuck out a mile where—and when—that would be.

St. James's Park was always my favourite park for a little quiet communion with ducks and pelicans. I used from time to time to see there Neville Chamberlain, looking rather like a bird himself, with his small head on long neck and unlidded eye (the glare but without the cruelty) and the inevitable umbrella tucked under the arm poking out behind, a kind of tail. The umbrella stuck in my mind. Chamberlain was the sort of Englishman who carried his umbrella everywhere. I was struck by its symbolic possibilities. Here could be a new symbol in the ancient tradition of ideographic picture-writing, like the palm for Peace, the clenched fist for Force, and the others. Keeps the rain off, shelters from the blast, can lean on it, poke with it, may be blown inside-out, might attract lightning. Perfect. After that I used the umbrella regularly as the symbol of Chamberlain Appeasement. Sometimes he carried it, sometimes it carried him.

Mr. C. would walk around the lake, sometimes with Sam Hoare, often with his wife. This morning it was Horace Wilson, the new 'appeasement' head of the Foreign Office. One could tell from the curve of their backs that all was not well. The new chapter of the Hitler Story was beginning. The man in Berlin was placing them squarely on the hot seat again. Czechoslovakia, according to plan. To stop him or not to stop him? Testing time of the 'appeasement' policy. Crisis.

While yet the newspapers were printing the success of Chamberlain's talk with Hitler at Godesberg, I was calling on Beaverbrook that morning to find him looking blue. 'It's all off,' he said. 'Hitler doesn't want any part of Chamberlain.' I went to Westminster to smell the wind. 'How will we get on with these fellows running it?' said a knowledgeable correspondent I met on the way, jerking his thumb in the direction of Whitehall. I listened to a little knot of M.P.s. 'He would have gone on his knees for a kind word from Hitler.' Then I went to see Hore-Belisha's sixteen A.A. guns being installed in Hyde Park. The tale was that half of them had no breech-blocks. From there I went and got out my car, drove to Selfridges, laid in a stock of mineral water, canned beef and hard biscuits and returned home to start digging a shelter. My next-door neighbour, who had read in his paper that Hitler had shaken hands cordially with Prime Minister Chamberlain, thought I was crazy.

That chapter ended with the tailpiece of Mr. C. alighting from his airplane waving a paper bearing Hitler's signature and uttering: 'Peace in Our Time.' It was very difficult to discuss the Chamberlain policy sensibly in those days. To his friends he was a saint, to his critics rather less. 'He wanted peace'—but so did we all. No one impugned his motives, but only his judgment. That his appeasement approach to Hitler was wrong was soon demonstrated, for the ink was hardly dry on the Munich agreement before the Führer was openly and noisily preparing his next step. But devotion to Mr. C. was so strong that his friends were unwilling to admit. it. Having committed themselves to a fairy-tale, they could not bring themselves to face cold reality. They were determined to wish appeasement into a success both as a

matter of loyalty to Mr. C. and to protect their political investment. There was, naturally, some defence of their position when
I struck discordant notes with a couple of cartoons on the brutal
truth: WHEN THE PIE WAS OPENED, with Mr. C. finding, not singing
blackbirds, but a dead dove in his Humble Pie; and MEIN KAMPF,
showing crippled Peace accompanied by a crestfallen Mr. C.
hobbling down the steps from the Nazi Chancellery. Such expression of doubt seemed almost indecent. Mr. C. inspired that kind
of personal loyalty.

Had Mr. C.'s appeasement policy succeeded, all would have
been well. His personality would have been well suited to the
role of constructive peacemaker. But it was as ill-suited to the
contrary role of determined defender. His qualities as a man of
peace made him a failure as a man of war. If the high price at
Munich had been to buy time, we had to get value. But there
was no urgency in the air to prepare to the utmost and quickly.
The vested interests adapted themselves at leisure. My sardonic
suggestion that the slogan *Business As Usual* be painted on our
factory roofs in foreign languages so that enemy airmen would
know we were keeping calm, was not kindly received. To irritate
into greater activity, I 'ran' for a while a pair of cartoon business
twins: *'Sno Use* and *Can't Be Done*. There were depressingly
frequent opportunities for their use.

There were dreadful weeks when the nation seemed to be
speeding at the rate of a mile per year. One day in the foyer of a
West End hotel a Cabinet Minister whom I knew fairly well—a
high-up in the councils of decision concerning these fateful topics
—so far relaxed his discretion as to ask me: 'How are we doing,
do you think? What do we look like?' Good God, I thought, he's
doubtful, too. Under my seeming nonchalance I was a bit aghast
and wondered how far this lack of confidence extended to his
colleagues in responsibility. Poor chaps, theirs was a tough job, to get
things moving against the mass of indecision, reluctance and plain
damned stupidity. Leslie Hore-Belisha, an old fellow-worker of mine
in the Beaverbrook newspapers, was a case in point. Because of
his energy and drive Chamberlain had made him Secretary for
War. After he had stung the military council with a spring-clean
of the War Office so much animosity was aroused among the
military poohbahs that even his own choice of Commander-in-
Chief advised him to disturb the generals no further. There were
more bitter passages and Hore-Belisha departed from his office
soon after the war began. The event was greeted in the military
back-rooms as though it were the Greatest Victory of the War.

Moving around fairly widely and keeping my eyes open, it seemed to me that apart from those 'realists' to whom the principles of democracy were expendable, and who thought Britain would actually benefit from partnership with Hitler, Mr. C. had the aid and encouragement of well-meaning people who still cherished the idea of striking a bargain—a present of some colonies in exchange for a quiet life. Mr. C.'s Cabinet contained a group of diehard imperialists to balance matters and keep him awake at nights.

It was a prolific time for intrigue and private 'shadow Cabinets,' country-house cabals and other extra-democratic activities. I was in the back row of some of them and was aware of others. Busy gentlemen unadvertised by the Press and unhampered by the wishes of the vulgar mob, scheming and planning, bringing influence to bear. 'What did you tell the P.M., Eustace?' . . . 'Did you put that analysis in the Chief's teapot, Percy? . . .' Unfortunately, noble family, public school education and a distinguished career were not necessarily the best qualifications for understanding such an outsize diversion from type as Hitler. The clever ones were quite often disastrously wrong. The inflated reports of Lindbergh, the American flier, on the immense superiority of Germany and the immense inferiority of Russia found attentive listeners. And when Ribbentrop came to town as Hitler's Ambassador, he seemed 'quite a nice fellow really,' despite his rather caddish trick of giving the Nazi salute to the King. (Thereafter he was 'Brickendrop' in my cartoons.)

Occasionally I met around Hampstead an interesting chap named Vladimir Poliakoff who sometimes passed on items of information. I was not the first in print on the subject of Lady Astor's parties at her country house Cliveden, at which 'Brickendrop' was a guest, because 'Polly' had already communicated this tit-bit to the editor of a mimeographed news-letter *The Week* who invented the label 'The Cliveden Set.' But my cartoons on the subject probably brought it before an audience that heard of it for the first time. They flashed around the world as news and produced a reaction that surprised me. I had made them deliberately farcical, not mordant. Nancy Astor's good, if at times rash, heart was well known. But the week-end meetings at her home of important non-parliamentary public figures, retired diplomats and distinguished ex-civil servants, no doubt for harmless week-ends but supposedly as a kind of private 'brains trust' to cook up appeasement deals, created morbid interest. The presence of Dawson, editor of *The Times*, and Bernard Shaw did not allay public uneasiness. *The Times* ('*The Temporiser*' to me now in cartoons showing Dawson reviewing his Correspondence Column in Printing House Square) had become the clarion-voice of Nazi appeasement; Shaw, to the consternation of his admirers, had applauded Mussolini as a practical socialist. That was the *old* man losing patience and wishing for action, even at the expense of principle. When I asked him what about freedom of expression under a fascist régime, he said airily that that would adjust itself.

On the other side of those exclusive front doors, apprehension gave birth to a whole litter of Things to Join, medals and buttons provided, crusades, leagues and unions, most of them futile. People were almost too eager to 'do something.'

'Come along to the committee room at Caxton Hall tonight,' said a busy friend of mine. 'Secret! A few of us—about a dozen— are going to discuss a military movement—Churchill's behind it, but doesn't want to appear—the *Hundred Thousand*.'

I went. So did a vast horde of others. Someone had blown the gaff and the building was crowded out, to the panic of the promoters who hadn't bargained for such support and had nothing to offer but good intentions. My memory of that night was of citizens stamping out of the hall whitefaced with indignation.

Such a fog of wishful thinking and self-deception descended on ruling circles that one could hardly see Whitehall. As it thickened, public confidence on both their power and will weakened and the people inevitably looked around for new infusions of strength. There had never been any doubt about the uncompromising and consistent attitude of Churchill and Eden. But up came that question of loyalty to Chamberlain. Churchill, lacking Eden's tact, had become Tory Hate No. 1. If you were for Chamberlain, you were against Churchill; for Churchill, you were against Chamberlain.

Murmuring grew to argument, much of it not too scrupulous. As might have been expected in such conditions, advocates of Churchill–Eden and opponents of appeasement soon found themselves labelled war-mongers and irresponsibles. So far as I was concerned Mr. Chamberlain himself set the example. Addressing the Newspaper Society's annual dinner he said that 'German Nazis have been particularly annoyed by criticisms in the British Press and especially by cartoons. The bitter cartoons of Low in the *Evening Standard* have been a frequent source of complaint.'

After that newspapers that didn't like me referred frequently to my 'bad-blood cartoons' and my 'bitterness.' Abuse grew hysterical. 'Low is the worst war-monger we have,' said a Left paper. 'Low, politically on the extreme Left, is regarded as the Prime Minister's most powerful enemy,' said a Right paper. (Phew!) When I carried out a commission to draw a series of large cartoons on the world situation for an American magazine, *Ken*, my old friend Beverley Baxter, who had reached the point of identifying loyalty to Chamberlain with patriotism, suspended amicable relations long enough to pillory me in an article entitled 'Slanderers of Britain' as one who had probably taken 'thirty pieces of silver to betray his country.' People I knew turned away and wouldn't talk to me. Complete strangers held me up in public places and *would* talk to me. My tobacconist refused to serve me. People wrote to me:

44 Bedford Square,
W.C.1.
22 April 1938.

Dear Mr. Low,

Were I not a *true* admirer of your art, and a friend, I would not write this letter—as *no* one is a good judge of those they dislike. But I thought your cartoon on Wed. (20th) *Evening Standard* both cruel and mischievous. I *know* the P.M.—do you? He is a man of iron courage, calm and resolution. If we were going to refer to the Bible, you should have quoted Christ's saying 'Love your enemies'—It is not as silly as it sounds. Neville is doing the *only* right, wise, thing, unless you want war. Hate, threats—which you can't carry out—and suspicion do not advance Peace, and if the P.M. fails we can *always* go back to the policy of the war-mongers—Winston and Co.

I think Neville has saved the world by his courage—and so do *much* cleverer people than

Yours in sincerity
MARGOT ASQUITH.

April 26, 1938.

Dear Lady Oxford,

Were I a bitter man, by this time I should be turned to acid by the way people jump to the conclusion that my works are all inspired by hatred. . . . Mr. Chamberlain may possess all the qualities you mention and his policy may be the best one under the circumstances, as you say. I hope so sincerely. But viewed from the historical standpoint I think the more notable

313

feature of recent happenings has been the final desertion of Abyssinia, Spain, and the whole League of Nations idea. My cartoon did no more than record that fact with, I think, some dignity and restraint. Were I a politician it might have seemed more expedient to forget all that side of it as soon as possible and applaud the Prime Minister's courage, as did many politicians whose hearts were torn with disappointment at the loss of so much. But I am not a politician. Within the limits of my peculiar medium I strive to be a recorder and here I was marking a turning-point in history. It is my misfortune that in doing so I seemed to have offended you so grievously.

Yours sincerely,
DAVID LOW.

I had no wish to get into Lady Oxford's bad books because I admired her. Away back in the early 'twenties I had been flattered to receive her notes, in wild pencilled calligraphy, complimenting me about my attacks upon people she did not like and suggesting quite impossible cartoons against Lloyd George. When I drew her husband, Asquith, she took umbrage on the ground that I made him look too fat. Few women have a real appreciation of caricature.

It was their daughter, Elizabeth Bibesco, a brilliant woman whose perpetual wit made my head swim, who introduced me into the famous Margot luncheon parties, once the cynosure of political talent. There were too many ghosts present for my liking. I had the feeling that if I sparkled in the wrong place, I might be rebuked by John Morley.

But all was well. The lady replied to my letter, thus:

44 Bedford Square,
W.C.1.
2nd May, 1938.

Dear Mr. Low,

I should have answered your letter *long* ago—for which I *apologize*—but I have been ill: I am well now. I never in my life thought any of your wonderful drawings were inspired by *personal* dislikes—nor have you 'offended' me. I am quite free from *personal* touchiness in politics and am certain that you have *no* political enemies. Your cartoons are a *delight* to everyone, as no man living can draw as well as you do. But I don't think we could have gone to war to protect a threatened race—Abyssinia, nor China. Nor indeed do I think we can fight for the Czechs.

314

But alas! I am a passionate Pacifist, and deplore the anti-peace policy of the present Liberal Party. What do the Liberal Party think that we shall gain by constantly censoring the government, and for *what*? pursuing a policy of Peace. The P.M. may *fail*—tho' he has not done badly up to now—in which case we can always return to Hate, Suspicion, and more threats, which we can't carry out.

Don't be angry with your Liberal admirer

MARGOT ASQUITH.

Sometimes I received gestures of goodwill and letters of encouragement:

Dec. 8th, 1937

To David Low, from one who is proud to be his fellow-countryman (or nearly so)

GILBERT MURRAY.

20 Maresfield Gardens,
London, N.W.3.
Nov. 12th, 1938.

A Jewish refugee from Vienna, a very old man personally unknown to you, cannot resist the impulse to tell you how much he admires your glorious art and your inexorable, unfailing criticism.

SIGMUND FREUD.

I was pleasantly surprised at the number of people who wanted to 'help' me. I was still essentially a lone hand, but bit by bit, without design, almost inadvertently, I had acquired a network of sources of information and 'background' which would have done credit to an expert spy. Though much of it was of the side-door variety, I became familiar with some mighty important front-doors, too.

My years of attendance at annual conferences, debates and demonstrations of all three Parties, with occasional looks-in at the plottings in their back-rooms, had given me a wide enough circle of acquaintance to enable me to keep a fitful finger on the national pulse. A newspaper office is as good a place as any for estimating the currents of public opinion, and the Fleet Street grape-vine is as rapid as any telegraph. My association with the Beaverbrook Press gave me a ready-made Right-wing interpretation of events, and I had become a director of the *New Statesman and Nation*, which kept me in touch with the view from the Left.

I benefited greatly from the fact that I had some close friends among the press correspondents always dashing backwards and forwards across Europe. Particularly I found the American 'specials' dependable usually for the up-to-the-minute inside stuff, imparted with candour and reality undiluted by local loyalties. In America, two of my books published there had reached the best-seller list and were much written about. Comments on the cartoons, as cartoons, were generous, but, perhaps more significant, the attitude they illustrated appeared to be widely approved by American public opinion. I promptly strengthened my American connections by accepting some commissions, both to draw cartoons and to write articles. I do not know whether I found, or was found by, a good friend in New York journalism, Lester Markel of the *New York Times*, but I do know that it was under his kindly encouragement I began to write fairly regularly. I kept this last activity quiet in London, because a delicate plant can get too much sun, and because it was a bit of a lark to be a cartoonist in one place and a writer in another.

I had drifted into leading a double life, spending half my time alone drawing or writing in a quiet room at Hampstead, no telephone, no messengers; and the other lunching, dining and talking with knowing birds, unimpeachable sources and chaps just back. I learned much of the inside doings of the Foreign Office, the State Department and the Quai d'Orsay; of who was who at the White House and the private habits and latest sayings of the President; and of what callers the Prime Minister had yesterday and what (probably) had passed between them. It was like having a front seat at a nightmare—interesting, frightening and exhausting.

I had not realized that I myself was 'hot' until one day when I was visiting, for a quite innocent purpose, a well-known politician and getting up to go, I saw his secretary open the door and cautiously look up and down the passage to make sure no one saw me leave the office.

I had acquired this personal 'heat,' I suspect, for a variety of reasons: a rumour that had got around that I knew more than I let on; John Gunther in his book *Inside Europe* had inflated my importance as an influence on British public opinion at the time, and the passage had been widely republished; and my wife and I were known to be friends of the Maiskys.

For years the British Government had played safe, to avoid 'offending' Hitler, by maintaining at best a frostily correct attitude towards Soviet Russia and its diplomatic representatives. Moscow's circumlocutory policy, to say nothing of its occasional blatant errors of judgment, had not helped matters. For long spells, when it was still a matter of doubt whether the West would make an accommodation with Hitler at the expense of the East, the Soviet Embassy had been a lonely island and its Ambassador a Robinson Crusoe. Ivan Maisky was a small plump man with bright black eyes, small moustaches and small chin-beard, who could be made by an unfriendly photographer to look sinister. But neither he nor his wife were in the least sinister. They were cordially likeable as human beings for their own sakes. Maisky had much wit and humour (including the ability to laugh heartily at himself) and we took to one another. He never tried to put one over on me, although frequently we had disputes especially about the import of some cartoon or other which he thought hadn't done his country justice. It was illuminating to me to have a Russian comment on passing events among the wild tales that flew about.

My wife and I were visitors to their house and they to ours. Our acquaintance weathered some difficult passages. An Ambassador must be the faithful servant of his Government, and neither his conduct nor his views on public matters even when expressed in private, could ever be as free and easy as those of a cartoonist like me, who sometimes forgot to dissemble and be tactful. There was, for instance, the occasion when Madame Maisky, a dear woman, took me aside and started to tell me with every appearance of horror what a thorough brute Tukachevsky had been. Taken by surprise at this, I exploded into loud laughter. Very rude. But it wasn't cheap laughter, just Homeric. I thought of the military wonder-boy who had been on show in the Embassy garden outside where we were sitting, only a few weeks before. He was in fatal trouble in Moscow because he had been found out trying to make an agreement with German officers. His timing had been wrong. . . . 'Oh, I say,' I gasped, 'Excuse me! I was just thinking how fortunate it is he isn't a *good* man— how inconvenient that would have been!' Madame looked pained. I could see she didn't understand me, which perhaps was just as well.

And there had been the Awful Moment, at a Beaverbrook party in the early 'thirties, when Maisky had asked me to introduce him to Sir Austen Chamberlain, and I innocently did so, not observing all the signs that Sir Austen definitely and positively did not wish to meet him. With the coldest of salutations the Chamberlain nose went up in the air and he turned away. Maisky's face was a study in Russian rage. 'Well, you asked me to,' I said.

At length someone wakened up to the thought that if the British wanted the Russians they had better be cultivated. The scene changed. Abruptly that house was crowded with a brilliant galaxy of military and diplomatic nobs and their social appendages. Even the Prime Minister himself came along in all his orders to celebrate in vodka the anniversary of the Bolshevik Revolution. He made an historic sight pretending to be at ease standing alongside Maisky. I caught Maisky's eye in passing and he gave me a barely perceptible wink.

My cartoons had for months been plugging co-operation with Soviet Russia. I had a strong feeling after Munich that if Hitler forced war, the Western democracies would need both Russia and America with them to survive, and this consideration eclipsed all minor spittings and growlings. The passage of events also influenced my outlook to some extent. Six 'key' cartoons, among dozens on this theme, both tell the story and illustrate the evolution of the viewpoint. THE WATCHING EYE reflected that Soviet Russia, although its Government had been the only one to signify readiness to carry out its obligations to Czechoslovakia, was excluded from negotiations in order to avoid 'offending' Hitler. SCRAP OF PAPER underlined the fact that Soviet Russia and China alone had stood out against the League's acceptance of Mussolini's conquest of Abyssinia. WHAT, NO CHAIR FOR ME? recorded that Soviet Russia had been ignored and snubbed at the Munich Conference. A PIECE MISSING, TOVARICH? illustrated the attempt of the Western nations to build a new defence wall without the man-power of Soviet Russia. SIT DOWN, the arrival, at long last, of a British emissary in Moscow to discuss an alliance, although the knowing ones in London feared that Soviet Russia had already lost confidence in France and Britain and was trying to 'hedge' its risks with the Nazis. IF THE BRITISH WON'T, MAYBE WE WILL was a forecast of the Nazi–Soviet Pact.

We knew the Maisky's sufficiently well to dispense with diplomatic courtesy when occasion demanded, as it did when, keeping a pre-arrangement, we lunched at the Embassy three days after the news broke of the Pact. The only other guest was Arthur Cummings of the *News Chronicle*. All started off smoothly, just as though the country our host represented had not just given the green light for a world war. Half-way through lunch I could stand it no longer, I forgot my manners, smacked the table and spoke my mind.

RENDEZVOUS (1939)

Arthur followed up in the same strain, but with more English reserve. There was plain speaking that day.

Hell, everything had gone wrong. Hitler had divided his opponents at last and was now in a position to dare all comers. Drama waxed inevitably to tragedy. Advertised months, years, beforehand, plainly warned long in advance, even as to time and place, the blow fell. Britain and France were dragged to war under such uninspiring and disadvantageous circumstances that it seemed hardly possible for them to win. What a situation! In gloomy wrath at missed opportunity and human stupidity I drew the bitterest cartoon of my life, RENDEZVOUS, the meeting of the 'Enemy of the people' with the 'Scum of the Earth' in the smoking ruins of Poland.

But no one who knew Maisky thought of blaming him or of doubting his desire for and belief in a closer association between Soviet Russia and Britain. The next time I called on them Maisky was engrossed in the building of a most magnificent air-raid shelter, full of gadgets, in his garden. He presented me with an inscribed copy of Tolstoy's *War and Peace*, and hinted, as broadly as a diplomat may hint, that all was not lost and things were not what they seemed. At which I was more comforted. When the Maiskys returned to Russia, they left behind them affectionate memories with a varied multitude of friends, from Winston Churchill downwards.

With the Maiskys ended a chapter. After them came Mr. Molotov's Young Men. A very different type in a very different world.

24

THE public had heard the Nazi voices rasping menacingly in a foreign tongue and Chamberlain's pained expostulations back. But not one in a hundred had a clear notion why the British had to go to war precisely at this point for Poland. Confusion. But if it was too complicated to say what the war was *for*, it was easy enough to say whom it was *against*. That was the Germans, at it a second time. Meanings and reasons seemed to have disappeared. Clear as were the ideologies and stark the issues, very few even of the 'educated classes' were not completely foolish about the essential principles of Nazism, Fascism, Communism, Democracy, however much they talked about the labels. We had a noble cause, but nobody seemed to know about it. In no time it all got confused with the usual extraneous trimmings of this war, that war, any war—atrocities, maiming of children, raping of nuns, shooting of escaping refugees, and so on.

'No use talking reason now,' said a thick-necked chap I knew, with, I fancied, a certain pleasure in telling me, 'we're at war; only one thing counts—that you win.'

'What!' I said. 'Another one of your damned football matches to settle nothing, end nothing? Where is our propaganda?'

Warned by what they had seen in the papers and the newsreels about bombing in Spain, householders collected their gas-masks and stirrup-pumps, filled their buckets and waited. We Lows already had a shelter left over from Munich-time. Its drawback was that it always contained a foot of water.

Nothing happened. Anti-climax. On the far side of Europe terrible events were going on. On the near side, our airplanes dropped leaflets on the enemy.

In the last hours of peace there had been a scurrying for places.

Almost overnight a vast bureaucracy erected itself around the function of 'telling the world.' Obviously the old-school-tie brotherhood had moved in. It surprised me to find how many bright lads of my own acquaintance all of a sudden turned up in jobs connected with censorship or information. Surprised, I say, because it had never occurred to me that they had had any particular fitness for such jobs.

It was proper that I should place my services at the Disposal of the Nation. One day a letter arrived for me within two sealed envelopes, one inside the other, very important looking. The utmost secrecy was imperative evidently. It was from someone I did not know inviting me to call on his chief. Duly I went to the inconspicuous address given, was passed through three doors by three different officials and into the presence of the Brain.

'Why, hullo, David!'

'Why, hullo, Valentine! What the ——!'

He turned out to be a friend of mine who could have rung me up on the telephone and saved himself some trouble. But in civilian life he was a thriller-writer, which perhaps accounted for the cloak-and-dagger approach. I had never suspected this genial chap of having any flair for propaganda, nor, indeed, any familiarity with the techniques of persuasion. His province, it appeared, was the leaflets dropped from our planes, and he wanted me to make some cartoons for them. I agreed with alacrity. He showed me a sample leaflet, a miniature newspaper. I looked at it, and then at him. Most of the contents, interest-pieces, statistics and jokes, were practically innocuous, salt for the main ideas. The Bavarian farmers upon whose heads this effort was to flutter, were to be subverted by being told that Hitler would take all their crops, that Hitler had sold them out to the Russians, that the Bolsheviks were coming! Refuse! Resist! Don't fight the French and British! In the circumstances of that time, with Hitler rampaging victorious, and the Russians practically hiding under the bed, the thing seemed to me childish.

'What do you think of it, David?'

I said mildly that it was one of the most foolish documents I had ever seen and that if young men were risking their necks to drop this tripe over Germany, someone should be arrested.

Was this our reply to the most efficient propaganda factory in history? Was this our counter to those devilishly clever Nazi leaflets that were rotting French morale and splitting the Allies? A good example lay on the table—the famous twin pictures leaflet, the first showing a British and a French soldier side by side poised to dive into the swimming-bath of blood, the British soldier saying 'Ready—One—Two—'; the second showing the French soldier splashing in up to his neck, the British soldier remaining where he was—'Three!' It was reported to have been uncomfortably effective. A potent discord-sower.

I had been told often enough that the British never had taken propaganda seriously, because they believed in themselves so much as to regard the rightness of their causes to be self-evident. Certainly, although they were fighting what was ostensibly a war of ideas, in striking contrast to the Nazis, the Russians, the French and the Americans they placed little value upon the presentation of their case to the enemy in cartoons.

Seething with frustration, I nevertheless made several drawings for the news-sheet. One was printed, a picture of a German soldier writing to his mother. I cannot believe it affected the course of the war.

On two other occasions I lent my aid to the authorities. There were the weeks when, under Ministry persuasion, I stopped producing my newspaper cartoons to tour the American camps in company with a visiting American journalist, making drawings that were to appear from one end of the United States to the other to sweeten Anglo-American relations. The authorities had omitted to make proper arrangements for publication, so none of the drawings ever saw the light.

Again, there was the little matter of the design of Churchill I made, also at the prompting of the Ministry, for a special Toby mug which was to be sold in vast quantities in the United States to help our special export drive—and, of course, to sweeten Anglo-American relations. There was much official correspondence, congratulations and admiration, until it came out that there were no orders for such a mug and no one proposed to make it.

It occurred to me that I was wasting my time trying to play ball with ineptness and futility. After that I minded my own business and conducted my own war.

There were still wide reprinting arrangements for my *Evening Standard* war cartoons in free Europe, the Americas and the Commonwealth. The *New York Times* gave me a good showing and I was now sending special stuff by radio regularly to *Collier's* in the United States. My fancy of twelve years before—a world issue beamed from London—took a step forward.

Sometimes at first the results, regarded as art, were dreadful. More like studies in ectoplasm than cartoons. Radio transmission,

I found, required a special adaptation of technique. Faces drawn in dark lines like that of Göbbels, for instance, travelled well, but I always had great difficulty in sending Hitler's eyes across. Unaccountably one or both would disappear on the way. Bad weather, too, caused freakish transmission. Sometimes a short dumpy Göring would encounter a thunderstorm en route and come out the other end a tall thin chap.

The problems involved gave me much trouble, not the least part of which was due to the need for me personally to have these drawings for America passed by the censorship. All would have been well, since this obviously dealt with opinion and not with military secrets, had it not been that I had the bad luck to encounter an examiner who didn't know about cartoons. Apparently I was a unique case, since nobody else wanted to send cartoons. He had no cartoon sense and would argue the point about details, suspecting any little piece of background to be a map of the coastal defences. To make matters worse the stupid oaf couldn't tell the difference between my cartoon versions of Göring and Mussolini, and, quite outside his line of duty, would inflict on me his pitiful ideas on the world situation and how undesirable it was to irritate Mussolini. At length I was rescued by an alert colleague and taken to the Chief Censor. He was an admiral, but a sympathetic admiral. After that a simple routine was established which lasted until the end of the war.

Moving around freely and keeping my eyes open in those early days of the war, two things were painfully evident: one, that in bringing the masses of the people to an attitude of defence the appeal to primitive passions was still more effective than that to moral indignation; and, two, that two generations of popular education had mitigated popular ignorance only to a limited degree and in limited areas. All the same, I was revolted by what appeared to me to be the assumption prevailing among ordinary people I talked to that ideologies and basic principles could be best left to a supposed body of experts vaguely known as 'they,' especially when there was so much evidence to suggest that 'they' must be far from sure themselves. True, we had got past the Symbolic stage of defending the Dear Old Flag, as though there was a shortage of flags, or the Dear Old Country, as though the country would disappear if somebody did not hold it down. And we no longer took literally the Mediaeval Approach, that the whole war was under way to frustrate personal enemies of His Majesty. But at the time a great deal of glib patter about

THE ANGELS OF PEACE DESCEND ON BELGIUM (1940)

the 'British way of life' was coming from people who suggested no very clear idea of what they meant. Except here and there in the tail of a political speech, or sandwiched away in a radio programme, nobody seemed to be making any particular effort either to correct past misconceptions or to educate youth in the practical differences between Democracy (or whatever he was to be called upon to defend) and Nazism (or whatever he was to be called upon to defeat).

One urgent need of the time, to my way of thinking, was a simple statement understandable to the meanest intelligence of what had led up to the war. There were many books written by clever chaps for clever chaps, but few of these would be read by the masses. It seemed to me a useful, even an essential part of our defence, that everybody should know what the war was about. I collected a hundred cartoons telling the story and knitted the sequence into a story with a terse commentary in words, and Allen Lane, one of the liveliest publishers in Britain, produced *Europe Since Versailles* as a Penguin book at sixpence. Its acceptability was proved immediately. In quick time it sold a quarter of a million copies.

These enterprises took up time. I had a pretty full day when to them were added part of the universal war chores: some clumsy drill, at which I found a rifle heavier than a brush; attending an ambulance class; and patrolling a couple of streets two nights a week with a stirrup-pump and a bucket of water, while also keeping close watch to see that enemy spies did not steal my little heap of sand.

Six months passed in a Maginot dream. Anti-climax and the distance of battle bred the idea that this was a 'phoney war,' that Hitler would be satisfied with Poland and all would be patched up. Armament crept on without any pressing sense of urgency. When voices rose proposing acceleration argument grew hot about Government interference with private rights. The Battle of Norway was a sharp reminder that the British, far from being equal to the test of modern war, had not even begun to think of it in the right terms.

Retreat, reverse, retreat. After turning out my cartoon for next day ('Only one position will never be evacuated—the position of the Chamberlain Government in Downing Street') I went to see how Parliament was taking it. In the peculiar half-light of the House of Commons, fantastic things were happening. Looking down out of my seat in the Press gallery, some people who had been just

LEBENSRAUM FOR THE CONQUERED (1940)

In occupied countries the removal of Jews and inconvenient minorities
to concentration camps was in progress

people now enlarged to historic size, others shrunk to vanishing
point. 'In the name of God . . . *GO*!' said a monument about ten
feet high that a few moments before had been little Leopold
Amery. Chamberlain sat yellow, glazed of eye, the picture of
personal tragedy. How different from the immaculate, confident
junior Minister I had seen enter the House in 1922. But now
Britain needed not a whistle but a trumpet. Churchill with the

music of Demosthenes's philippics in his back pocket was just right.

Everything wakened up when Hitler's armies opened battle on the west and displayed the woeful weakness of democracy's defences. Our war lords had forgotten motor-cycles. Under these dismal circumstances I discovered the acoustic properties of Hampstead Heath; the distant thunder of the guns could be heard distinctly from across the Channel as our British troops were pushed to the pocket of Dunkirk . . . As I walked daily across the Heath to my studio trying to focus and digest the news, I stopped and listened. I felt a heavy weight in my chest. Curious, 'a heart as heavy as lead' was literal truth, not poetic fancy.

After Dunkirk, Britain was, by all military reckoning, defeated. Obviously the Nazi programme would be to gain control of the air over the Channel and invade. Fortunately, as an earlier dictator is said to have remarked, the stupidity of the British is such that they never realize they are beaten until the occasion is past and a new one has arisen. I was amazed to note how few realized the size of the disaster, and how everyone appeared to think we had won some kind of a victory in getting so many men off the beaches. The coastal defences now being extended in such a hurry might have held off the ancient Romans, but we could no more have stopped a well-equipped and determined assault on the coast in 1941 than could the Nazis later have stopped the Allied invasion of Europe—if we had already lost the air. Fortunately we had not lost the air—yet. But nobody could know in advance that the R.A.F. would beat off the much advertised Luftwaffe. What had we before us?

The answer was not long delayed; nor the opportunity for the inhabitants of London to show what they were made of under one of the most searching ordeals of history. It was very heartening to have the rest of the world raving with admiration at one's fellow-citizens; as it was pleasant to have us all, for a change, admiring one another.

But for all the Churchill assurances at the microphone that this was Britain's 'finest hour'; and despite the firm resolve in my suburb (and there were many indications that it was representative) that the invaders would meet a desperate defence by the whole population with any weapons handy, it would have been over-romantic not to recognize that the chances were against us. Britain might be occupied and identified enemies of Nazism shot. I was reliably informed that my name stood high on the Gestapo list of those who would not enjoy a happy old age. (A report which was confirmed by official documents found in the Berlin head-quarters of the Reich Security Police after the war.) It struck me that, in the circumstances, and remembering the Nazi treatment of family hostages, I should take measures to deal with the safety of an aged mother and aunt, and a wife and two daughters. That necessitated a scurrying-about by car to Wales and the Midlands looking for suitable bolt-holes in which if necessary the identities of old ladies could be temporarily lost and their persons disappear in the crowd. I was glad the necessity to put this project into practice did not arise; for I was sure the removal of my two old ladies from their London home would have begun a new war. With my own family, I worked out simple plans for use if we were forced apart or scattered in some blind rush. We would have an annual rendezvous, pass-word and all, at the White Stone Pond, Hampstead, at 2 p.m. on Christmas Day. In one way I rather regretted that one never came off. The mental picture of Daddy toiling up the hill disguised in a large red beard was very tempting.

Having arranged tentatively to dispose more or less of my women I turned to lesser matters. I dug a deep hole in the garden, made a concrete box at the bottom of it in which I buried my intimate archives. I removed my files and records to a safety deposit. That was a mistake, for they were neatly blown up by one of the first bombs. Fortunately I had carefully hidden six parcels of duplicates with trusted friends in other parts of the country. In another place I buried a sizeable wad of currency in a sealed tin. Goodness knows what was the point of that, except that I thought it would be nice to know where there was some money, however much it might be depreciated in value by an occupying power. I figured that if I were on the run and hard pressed I might have a better chance to rob my hiding-spot than anywhere else.

It seems evident by all this that in times of peril I revert to the burrowing type, seeking security in holes in the ground. Many among my acquaintances and friends who were also known to be on the Gestapo list, had other ideas. I admired the foresight of one politician who, to guard against just such a situation, for months had been at work building himself a completely separate second identity in the Midlands. One or two took the situation with phlegm, leaving action to the inspiration of the last moment. Others showed agitation. One chap took me aside and wanted me to take one of his little poison capsules for use in an extremity. Another tentatively offered me the last seat in a launch bound for Canada ... I decided to stay put, partly because I had intense curiosity to see what would happen and partly because I knew two trusted friends who were cherishing an old printing-press which might conceivably do for an underground paper. With my much advertised small beard and heavy eyebrows I was too much of a marked man to disappear easily. Even as it was, strangers in the street and on trains and buses recognized me and approached me with: 'How's the war going, Mr. Low?' As priority measure, cursing Hitler and his whole brood, I shaved the beard.

Every Londoner has his snapshot memories of the 'blitz.' My own were a mixture of the trivial and the tragic. The hellish sky-effects of the burning in the East End mixed up with, say, the day early in the piece when Madeline and I were driving up Curzon Street and bombs began dropping close. 'Keep calm,' said the official what-to-do instructions for citizens in such circumstances. 'Park your car carefully out of the way, and proceed to the nearest shelter.' This we did. The shelter door was locked with a notice pinned on it: *Sleeping. Do not Disturb.* There was the night my own heavy oak front door flew in with a frightful crash. This was a family affair, it being the blast of the bomb that blew up the home of my mother and aunt a street away. Fortunately they were in my house, complete with dog and canary, at the time. The recollection of my tennis-court littered with rubble and rubbish that had been a home and familiar neighbours is mixed with another of two taxi-drivers pulled up arguing the right of way at a crossing in Bond Street, bombs falling all around. Odd details like travellers sitting in their trains in the dark staring at one another with cat's eyes; the statue of Charles the First buried in sandbags in Trafalgar Square; and a placard in a little shop which had had its front blown away, 'More open than ever'; the old lady dug out from under a collapsed building who, when asked "Ow are yer, Ma?' replied 'A bit shook.'

A vivid spot was left on my memory the night I went with Ellen Wilkinson, who was the Minister concerned, for a round tour of the London shelters during the blitz. It turned out to be one of the bad nights. The car with lights out had a lumpy passage through the black streets with an occasional bump of a bomb. We came at last to perhaps the biggest shelter of the lot, down by the docks. The idea was to see what could be done to improve matters. The interior was a perfect Hogarth, a vast cave, full of foggy shadows overhead, hordes of people ranging from the cheerful to the hysterical, not much organization yet, just camping out. All with complaints and demands. There were about half a dozen of the new double-decker beds, just arrived, and of course everybody wanted them. Little Ellen vanished in an importuning mob. I, in my black felt hat and overcoat, looking every inch an under-secretary, was left. Out came my notebook and, on behalf of the Government, I gave as many as possible a sympathetic hearing. I had some difficulty with a husky chap who demanded that I take immediate steps to mend a leak in the roof. 'Do it yourself,' I told him. 'This is no time to wait for others to keep the rain off you.' After registering legitimate complaints and adjudicating on the ownership of a disputed bed, I found Ellen again, passed in my recommendations, and closed my official career.

Some of the shelters in the West End were better. We found a good one in Regent Street where the company was playing snakes-and-ladders, and tea was being passed round, although up above the air was full of hot blasts, smoke and ashes as a stretch of Conduit Street was burning. Hell.

25

THE physical conditions for cartooning during the blasting of London were discouraging. At the beginning, when the old Town seemed defenceless and the suburbs longed for the bark of A.A. guns that didn't come, I would rise exhausted from the coma that passed for sleep in our one 'fortified' room (sandbags, beams and sheet-iron) huddled with the other nine members of my household. I would walk over the Heath, side-stepping the bombholes, to my studio with its large windows criss-crossed with adhesive strips of cellophane, optimistically intended to prevent my becoming a human pin-cushion if an 'incident' happened. One could hardly be expected to feel in form to produce wit or good design. But actually I found the discipline involved in drawing kept me on the rails and brought comparative repose. From lifetime habit the ratiocinative part of the process was usually over before I began to draw, and thereafter feeling took over and the part of me that fretted intellectually went off duty.

As winter drew on, light became a major difficulty. The supply of art materials shortened. I ran out of sable brushes until it occurred to me to make some quite good ones for myself out of my own hair, and then to draw with soft wooden toothpicks, which gave quite a good effect. Communications intermittently became uncertain. It was a question whether (a) my studio or (b) the editorial office would be still standing next morning. One night early in the blitz the *Evening Standard* office actually was bombed. In the flurry of moving over to an emergency set-up close by without missing an issue I was provoked to chip in a special cartoon with the requisite note of British phlegm, entitled BOMB SEVERELY DAMAGED IN SHOE LANE. In that 'incident' one of my original drawings was neatly pierced by a bomb fragment. The subject was peculiarly appropriate to the circumstance. It represented a British soldier with obstinate jaw defiantly making the thumbs-up sign to a grinning Nazi figure of Death. I wrote around the hole 'Thanks for the compliment—Low' and gave the original to Ernie Pyle, the American war correspondent.

To forestall accidents, for a time I worked several days ahead. Special drawings for some foreign papers frequently had a time-lag of six weeks between delivery and publication. Quite respectable feats of prophecy might seem to be required to calculate the probabilities so far in advance, but to journalists habituated to reflection upon the nature of man, the comparative significance of events and the inevitability of cause and effect, not quite so remarkable.

Superficially a cartoonist's range in time of war tends to narrow down to the one subject, but of course its ramifications are infinite. The constant reiteration of the points that the enemy was a fool and a blackguard, and that our brave boys would kick his pants, was already old-fashioned and a bore. The anguish which infused the great occasions imposed a pregnant simplicity on their interpretation. ALL BEHIND YOU, WINSTON; VERY WELL, ALONE; and HARVEST MOON, three of my widest known cartoons of the time practically drew themselves at white heat. On the level of plain illustration the everyday glimpses of the essential soundness of the ordinary people provided good material. This time, at least, the crowd was sticking together, not stampeding, every man for himself. The relief and satisfaction of knowing that the London public was riding the bombardment was reflected in my own cheerfulness, occasionally frivolity, in cartoons about our collective miseries.

But, man being imperfect, all was not noble. There was the ugly side. The rapid debasement of war aims; the degradation even of the V sign by cheap commercial hucksters; greedy cheats and their under-the-counter evasions of the food rationing; a perceptible decline in morality and a rapid increase in the ranks of 'tarts' and petty thieves, 'liberating' one another's small belongings; snatching of advantage by the cunning exploiters of need; little Hitlers exceeding their brief authority; the usual flocks of humbugs, hypocrites and incompetents that flourish like the green bay tree in the soil of war. All these and a sizeable Fifth Column of our local Nazis and Fascists, frustrated but hopeful; with, to put a top on it, a sprinkling of professional enemy agents. The harassed British Government settled the latter question by locking up all foreigners, foes and friends. One chap I knew, a Czech artist, went in with the rest. I was sure he wasn't a Nazi spy, so with the friendliest intent I applied to the Home Office for his release, and after the usual investigation got him out. To my surprise he was very angry. 'What did you want to interfere for?' says he. 'I was perfectly happy in concentration camp with my friends. We were just organizing a sports meeting.'

The military threads of the war itself were distressingly simple to follow as subject-matter. Not so the political. The months immediately preceding and after the opening of fighting had been disruptive of the political scene, especially that part of it concerned with Soviet Russia. The Berlin–Moscow Pact had rudely jarred the idealists back to reality. Socialists who had confused their creed with the practice of Russian Communism recoiled. Uncle Joe had sold the lambs up the river. The new revised 'line' was too phoney to satisfy any but the doped party man.

It was understandable that the Russians might have had fears of being left by the Western Powers to do all the fighting once the war had begun, and everybody knew that on a balance of dire risks Stalin had chosen to buy time at the expense of the West; but from the first it looked like a bargain that would eventually blow up in his face. It was understandable, too, that the Russians would wish to forestall Hitler at points where they were particularly vulnerable, in Finland and the Baltic States. But to occupy these places forthwith by methods indistinguishable from those of the Nazis became, to Western public opinion, equally immoral and reprehensible.

The Soviet 'line' screamed from the amplifiers (*Peace—Stop the Imperialist War*) was not quite the same as that whispered around in Fleet Street and Whitehall ('Leave it to Joe—he will outsmart Hitler at the right time'). Experience had taught me that physiognomy is a doubtful key to character, but looking at that forehead, that narrow eye, and the cut of that mouth under the moustache, I was depressed. I had never been an admirer of Stalin's brand of smartness.

The complexity of this situation from the cartoonist's point of view took a bit of straightening out. I had to condemn Soviet Russia's deals with Nazi Germany root and branch, on grounds both of morality and of expediency; and this I did in forthright manner beginning with RENDEZVOUS, and carrying on to UNDER NEW MANAGEMENT, Molotov borrowing the methods of Nazism to invade Finland.

Simultaneously I had to damp down the increasing pressure of

334

ALL BEHIND YOU, WINSTON (1940)

335

our local anti-Russians to push the Soviet Union finally into Hitler's arms. Their infantile strategy had always been to divert Hitler to the East, regardless of consequences; and when Russia attacked Finland there had been powerful influences at work to change the direction of the war.

I had acquired some goodwill among the communists and their followers by my comments on the Nazis, but this I lost overnight. Then I had acquired some goodwill among the anti-communists, because of my sarcasm at Stalin's expense, but this disappeared even quicker. At both ends of the political scale I was left with angry arguments. After the Nazi–Soviet pact I could never be convinced that the combination could stick, and I decided that where there was the slightest chance of it becoming unstuck, I would certainly not obstruct the process.

Privately I felt that we could never avoid defeat in the war without the help of both America *and* Russia. Unhappily few people take a cartoon as a link in a consecutive argument— today's instalment, to be continued tomorrow. To most the single picture stands alone and complete. My ambiguity confused the lambs whose idea of politics is to choose a side and stick to it. I had some difficult cartoons to draw before Hitler's own folly later simplified the situation by invading Russia.

Fortunately the signs and omens from the United States became propitious also. The back rooms behind the blackout had been welcoming more and more American faces. Wendell Wilkie, for instance, whom I was thunderstruck to see one night in a London pub being shown how to play darts by Herbert Morrison. A broad cheerful chap who made all the right sympathetic noises. And Harry Hopkins, who suddenly appeared from nowhere like a fairy godmother to arrange for virtually unlimited supplies under Lease-Lend. Harry, an elongated elf with a thinnish little face in a flat hat on the top of a voluminous greatcoat told us, with the kind of humour that the British like to think is American, that the real reason he had come to London was to get a night's sleep. I gathered from Harry that life in Washington was hell. Roosevelt got his best ideas in the middle of the night and always had to telephone his advisers out of their beds for immediate discussion.

Russia was not the only irritant. Alongside that there was the question of priorities. Our armies had been thrown out of Europe, and even Churchill was going around asking people what to do next. Hardly the moment to count unhatched chickens. A time

336

'VERY WELL, ALONE' (1940)

when it seemed more important to survive than to make conditions about it. I was not prepared for a row with H. G. Wells on the point. H.G., who had been getting more exasperated and exasperating in his seventies, had been concentrating on post-war construction.

> 13, Hanover Terrace,
> Regent's Park, N.W.1.
> June 20, 1941.

Dear David,

I note your attack on me in the *Evening Standard* and naturally I think it damned silly. Your poor wits have given way under the war strain and you have become a Gawd-saker. What the hell do you think will keep people fighting Nazidom if the outlook our own side offers is equally ambiguous and unattractive? Give me Göbbels any time if the choice is between his promise of a New World and the 'New World' of the Emperor Otto, Otto Strasser, Franco, the old English school-tie lot and a gang of syphilitic Poles which your heart seems to desire—with Hess thrown in. *Who has got hold of you, David?* Who's pumping stuff into your brain arteries?

Sorry to lose you, Low.

> Regretfully,
> H.G.

Probably he was surprised when I let fly back like a bear with a sore head:

> 3 Rodborough Road, N.W.11.
> June 24th, 1941.

Dear H.G.

Am I mortified!—to find myself in the bughouse with Otto, Franco, Strasser, Hess and a lot of syphilitic Poles. Lumme, that must have been a 'powerful' cartoon.

It was *not* an attack on *you*—unless your conscience identifies you (*I* never should) with those who play at New World planning not for stimulus but for anodyne. Would you take another look at the cartoon? It seems plain enough to me.

I am all for your Rights of Man and a Better World, as I shall blooming well show you in due course; what sensible man wouldn't be? But I want it said loud and often that unless we fight like hell *now* against Hitler—much better than we have done so far—all such plans are boloney. Some say that that goes without saying, but it certainly does not. Boobs are

338

already manufacturing a new beautiful let-out for themselves: 'Gimme the New World now or what's the use of fighting at all . . . might as well be run by Göbbels, etc. . . . etc. . . .'

I must say I whistle when you imply, after all you have written and said about Nazism, that you would as soon have Göbbels as the pre-war democracy, imperfect as it was. That doesn't make sense to me. I hate to think of you behind barbed wire.

I refuse to be lost, H.G. Whatever happens, I persist in being your devoted if unwelcome admirer.

Yours ever,
DAVID.

A dank silence, followed a couple of weeks later by a copy of his latest book, with the baffling inscription 'To David, who is always right, from H.G. who suffers from the same tragic lucidity.' Then:

13 Hanover Terrace,
Regent's Park, N.W.1.
July 29, '41.

Dear David,

I quarrelled seemingly with you some fortnight or three weeks ago. I excommunicated you, but now I've forgotten what it was all about. (But you must have been very wrong and annoying.) The excommunication is now cancelled but be very careful not to do it again, and believe me to be as ever,

Your most faithful admirer,
H.G.

Love to Madeline and everybody.
Halo in asbestos box by next delivery.

The whole thing was all very characteristic.

Tempers wore thin in those days. I had been sick of the phoney attitudes being vigorously promoted under the shelter of the so-called 'People's Convention' by the Communists and some cock-eyed strategists who no doubt thought they were doing their best for the proletariat. Upon this I had spoken my mind freely, and in return received my share of abuse. When Hitler attacked Russia, this particular set of asses had had their tune changed for them overnight.

But now the asses of the Right were in full bray. When Russia

339

had been dragged into the war there had been a sigh of relief in Britain at the prospect of no longer having to stand alone. But a sizeable section of the British community resented the company of the Soviet Union as a partner. Here and there, pleasure in the thought that Germany might now lose was balanced by mortification at the possibility that Russia might win. It was evident from the correspondence I was receiving that even moderates felt the new circumstance released Britain forthwith to become a spectator and watch Hitler and Stalin destroy one another. Although Churchill's realism made short work of these ideas, what would in later years have been called a 'cold war' continued under the surface here and there, ready to seethe whenever Göbbels chose to stir the brew.

Incidentally, Beaverbrook's new key importance in the Government, his influence in this connection and his energy in the production of war machines to supply Russia's deficiency, had one curious consequence for me. Suddenly I was in demand with persons who evidently concluded that since a Beaverbrook newspaper printed my cartoons I must have some special access to his Lordship's thoughts. When anyone asked me 'What is Lord Beaverbrook doing?' I always replied, 'The last time I saw him he was signing death-warrants.'

Soon Japan had made her mistake at Pearl Harbour and had brought the United States full into the shooting war; but it would be months before the mighty resources of the new ally would be deployed. Meanwhile the Russians were the only troops actually engaged in fighting Hitler. It was aggravating to have our Polish refugees and their friends, who were hostile to Russia as well as to Germany, apparently wanting to make it a condition precedent to our allowing the Russians to hold the war for us that the pre-war Polish frontiers be rectified forthwith. I drew some reproving cartoons on the subject, particularly one entitled YOU CAN'T DO THAT THERE 'ERE! and was immediately snowed up with protesting postcards in impressive numbers—impressive, that is, until I saw unmistakable signs, by similarity of expression and construction, of the correspondence having been organized.

The Russians, as might have been expected, responded in kind. They had had their difficulties in suddenly having to reverse their propaganda from unfriendly to friendly to fit the new set-up. Heavy military losses had made Moscow more complaining day by day about the delays of first the British and later the United States in starting a second front. It was easy to fall back again into alleging plots and double-crossing intentions among the British.

But when the Russian cartoonists used my Blimp in their cartoons as representative of the British, just to keep the record clear and show the boot was on the other foot this time, I invented a Russian Blimp on the spot, Blimpski, and drew him poisoning the wells of truth. 'There, dammit,' I said to myself as that went off, 'let's see you reprint that.'

Things had become somewhat twisted again and I was not particularly popular anywhere, when one morning I read in the newspapers, out of the blue, an open letter from Efimov, the doyen of Soviet cartoonists, to me. A document evidently approved officially, just cabled from Moscow:

September 17, 1942.

Dear Mr. Low,

Before me are fresh copies of newspapers with your remarkable drawings, which evoked in me the desire to address a few words to you.

I wish to tell you, Mr. Low, with what interest I and other Soviet artists have been and are now following your magnificent work, which has won for you the well-deserved fame of the best cartoonist in the world.

We appreciate your extraordinary skill for its typical features of creative English genius—its steadiness, logic and clever humour, and its subtle sarcasm.

Your visit to Moscow in 1932 afforded me the pleasant opportunity of making your acquaintance. From that day the album *The Best of Low*, with your autograph, which you kindly presented to me, occupies an honourable place among the books of my library.

Since then events of greater and smaller significance have come to pass, some evoking laughter, others the feeling of sorrow and grief. Many achievements have been won and not a few mistakes made.

But never before have we been confronted with problems like those facing us today—problems that will decide our destiny as well as that of future generations. Never before has the menace been so great. The future of history hangs in the balance. On one hand light, progress, democracy, life; on the other darkness, corruption, barbarism, death, that is, Hitlerism. I am happy, dear Mr. Low, that in this decisive hour I am with you—a great artist whose creative work I regard with admiration and from whose works I learn—in one camp, the camp of free people pitted against the corrupt hordes of the Attila of today.

341

My country has mobilized all its resources. Everyone is at his post striking the enemy with the weapon he can best handle. Soviet cartoonists have taken their stand in the general line.

It is difficult for our peoples alone to wage a deadly struggle against the hordes of the enemy—ruthless and armed to the teeth. But our will to fight and win has not been shaken. We have faith in the might and readiness to act of the anti-Hitlerite coalition.

We gladly accept your vows of friendship, sympathy, and the assistance of your people, but our happiness will increase tenfold when we hear that the good Anglo-Saxon battle-axe has struck at our common deadly enemy, who only then will feel what a coalition of peoples defending their life, liberty, and honour means.

I feel sure that the splendid art of David Low will play its part in the achievement of that happy hour.

Yours sincerely,

B. EFIMOV.

P.S. I take the liberty of sending you with this letter one of my drawings.

Assuming the Mantle of Responsibility, I replied in suitably turgid periods. The piquant idea of two cartoonists usurping the functions of diplomacy gave both letters a wide publication on both sides of the world.

September 19, 1942.

Dear Boris Efimov,

I find it difficult to say how highly I appreciate your letter and how grateful I am for the favourable opinions of you and your friends. I have pleasant recollections of the cordial hospitality shown to me when I visited your country ten years ago and of the interesting talk we had together about cartooning and the responsibilities of cartoonists. Believe me, my friend and fellow-craftsman, I have often thought of you in these stormy days.

A philosopher has said that even calamities have a compensation in that they give men the opportunity to realize their highest selves; and I note in your war cartoons, which I see frequently, your own worthy response to the inspiration of the present struggle. Your unfailing wit and lucidity of treatment have a heightened usefulness as an authentic expression of the unconquerable spirit of your people. The drawing you sent me will be a treasured possession. I am proud to find myself associated with you and your fellow-Soviet artists using their talents for such a cause against such enemies—as proud, indeed, as the British people are of the achievements of their allies, your brave soldiers.

There have been, as you say, differences and mistakes in the past, though the Soviet Union has never lacked steadfast friends here who wished only to see her succeed in realizing peace, prosperity and happiness for her people. There may be still misunderstandings to be straightened out in our joint affairs. But all these mean nothing before the present elemental conflict between civilization and barbarism. We are attacked by the bloody bandits of Berlin, who have no discernible principles but to loot and to destroy. The question to be decided is whether human beings may aspire to dignity and freedom or whether they must sink to the condition of animals, looking forward hopelessly to death or that degradation which is worse than death.

Before such an alternative the only reality is our complete unity with you in the struggle, our admiration of the magnificent spirit of your troops, our glory in the epic defence of Leningrad, Moscow, and now Stalingrad, and our eagerness to relieve you of part of what is certainly at present your undue share of the burden. These sentiments, I do assure you, my dear Efimov, are not confined to a section, but permeate the whole of our British people.

It has taken a Herculean effort to develop our power. The British Commonwealth is strong, but in 1939 its war strength was only potential. We entered the war unprepared, spiritually and materially, and we have to organize from the foundations, under fire. We have had to fight delaying actions, to make withdrawals, and suffer humiliations while preparing for the day when in your company and that of the United States we could come forth in complete confidence to defeat Hitlerism and end the war. The enemy has known this well enough and has adjusted his calculations accordingly. Hence his concentrated efforts against you. But jointly with our mighty ally the United States our calculations are capable of readjustment also.

There are many of your friends here who wish with all their hearts that the time for major action had already begun. The spectacle of the enemy ravaging your cities has mixed agony with our enforced patience. Decisions of time and place have had to be influenced mainly by the calculations of professional

343

experts, and their plans are not to be published for Hitler to read.

But be assured that the day is very near when your British and American comrades in arms will seek to match the deeds of their Soviet allies in conditions most carefully chosen to secure the downfall of the enemy. That day I hope to celebrate in a cartoon; and, with your approval, I will give myself the pleasure of sending you the original in return for your gift to me.

Yours sincerely,
DAVID LOW.

On the twenty or so occasions I had broadcast up till then I had always enjoyed it. And I had sometimes wondered what it might be like to have a regular job on the air—to be a Radio Commentator. So now, adding another straw to my somewhat over-loaded hump, I took an opportunity and for nearly two years was a Voice on the B.B.C., winging words of wisdom with periodical regularity to the Pacific and North America. Save for having to get up early in the morning and drive through the icy dawn to catch the right vibrations to send 'live,' it was an exhilarating experience. As pleasant compensation for all the discomfort, I occasionally breakfasted à deux with Ogilvy, the Director, at his flat across the street from Broadcasting House after the thing was over. A gentle, sensible man, with whom I felt in complete accord.

I took much trouble over my scripts, breaking up my sentences to avoid sing-song, and underlining in coloured pencils degrees of emphasis, key words and pauses. I had seen and admired some scripts of my friend Raymond Gram Swing, Britain's pet trans-atlantic radio comforter at that time. There was no reason why a script should not be a work of art. And I remembered words Walter Winchell, the New York Voice of Broadway, had dropped about delivery.

'I talk for 14 minutes, starting at 204 words to the minute, slowing down to 195 and then finishing with a bang.'

'Why?' I asked.

'Why!' he repeated incredulously, 'To get 'em excited of course.'

One morning I arrived at the microphone to find that my producer and his helpers were all laid out with influenza. I had been overlooked in the emergency and I had to produce myself. I found, too, that I had over-written my thirteen-minute script by about five minutes. The circumstances were propitious for an experiment. I beat Winchell by 14 words flat. No war ever had a more rapid appraisal.

Sitting in my little underground niche in the bowels of the B.B.C. talking into the void, there was always a doubt whether anybody heard; or if they did, took any notice. Yet occasionally there was reassuring if astonishing evidence to prove otherwise. It was evident that I was heard by the enemy when there was splenetic reply from Nazi radio 'to the drivelling, meandering, paltry buffoonery of Lord Beaverbrook's little scribbler.' I became involved in a wide and detailed argument over something I said about somebody's post-war plan, with a man in Alberta, Canada. There was an old lady that used to write to me regularly from Singapore. And there was at least one occasion upon which I evoked an adequate response from Australia.

For some time, even before the shooting war with Japan began and especially after the miscalculations and errors of judgment of the Malayan campaign had arrived at the fall of Singapore, I had run a string of newspaper cartoons advocating closer consultation with the Pacific dominions about their defence. Now Britain's position was too obviously tight to do much about it, anyway. One day Britain learned that Australian Prime Minister Curtin found Australia to be in such peril from the Japanese that he said he was going to send for help to the United States 'without any pangs as to traditional links with the United Kingdom.' Amazing as it might seem a decade later, this news was greeted in some important quarters in Britain as though Australia had sold itself to the Yankees and by not going down with a stiff upper lip and a straight bat had betrayed the Empire. This complete misapprehension of realities and relationships in the Pacific seemed to me to require discounting. It was my morning for broadcasting, so, since the responsible authorities had so far kept mum, I directed a few impassioned words to Australia myself for them:

> . . . There are some romantics here left behind the passage of events who are unable to conceive of war except as a John Bull–Britannia affair fought for a closed-shop Empire. The significance of the present war as a common cause of free peoples united escapes them. The noble words of Churchill and Roosevelt fly over their bony heads. Mr. Curtin neither surprised nor shocked realistic observers who looked at the map. Look to America? Yes, of course. Traditional links will look after themselves . . .

345

The blitz disrupted social relationships. Places of meeting blew up, grounds disintegrated, people disappeared, 'sources' dried up, 'background' became fragmentated, constantly sorting out into new patterns like a kaleidoscope.

I was fortunate in having a long-standing friendship with Alexander (or Alistair, as he preferred it) Mackenzie Livingstone. Alistair had a peculiar talent for hospitality, and his usefulness in this respect was appreciated officially in times when it was urgently necessary to 'bring people together' and to promote friendliness with Allies, actual and potential. There were very few important refugees, generals, admirals and air marshals, diplomats and politicians in London who did not pass through his friendly hands, and few whom I did not meet under his auspices in one way or another.

Previously my outlook had been mainly political. It was new and fascinating to find myself sitting at Alistair's round dinner-table with the Top Brass, surrounded with British and American generals and admirals, I tactfully helping Alistair to help them to make good with one another. Generally the conversation was disappointingly innocent. Strangely enough I got on best with Dudley Pound, considering that my ideas about sea-warfare were elementary and he knew nothing whatever about caricature.

Besides this avenue I found plenty of opportunities for sampling the new people, individually and collectively, formally and informally, and getting what 'inside stories' were going. To me, one of the most engrossing narratives of the war was that given by Menzies, the Australian Prime Minister, of the first advance of Wavell's Commonwealth Army along the North African coast in 1941, told to a private dinner at Claridge's; and the most amusing—coming welcome at a dismal time—Harry Hopkins's 'inside story' of how Winston Churchill personally showed him over the Fleet—the 'inside' referred to in this case being his own, which was gravely impaired by the roughness of the waves and the unrelenting energy of his host. A time to remember too, was the day I fell in with the Frenchmen, still in process of freshening themselves up after the fall of France. I found General Lattre de Tassigny congenial, amiable and lucidly informative. Not so de Gaulle, who was excusably doing the Man of Destiny act, and did no social mixing. He looked dramatic and I stood off and made a drawing of him. Small head, patent-leather hair, big nose, small chin disappearing into neck, bulky body, long legs.

Amid the redeployment to meet the altered situations, I touched finger-tips once again with the Ministry of Information. A bright chap from there had had the brilliant idea of adding cartoon posters to the packing material used in the cases of war material being sent to our new Russian Allies via Archangel. Very cunning.

'Wouldn't it be simpler to have them published in the Soviet Press?' I asked innocently.

'Impossible, old boy!'

I gathered it was extremely difficult to get through to the Russians, especially to the Soviet Press. I forebore to mention that I had an exhibition of war cartoons in Russia just then, that one of my originals was hanging over the table in Moscow at which Stalin and Churchill were negotiating at that moment, and that a week or so previously I had had cordial letters signed by what appeared to be the entire staff of the Russian national satirical weekly *Krokodil*, full of editorial goodwill, asking me to contribute cartoons from the Allied point of view. The M.O.I. chaps and I all sat down and I gave them a little educational talk about the 'Tass windows' and the elaborate organization of cartoon propaganda throughout Russia. The poor nincompoops didn't know a thing.

My efforts to be useful to the authorities continued to result in triviality. There was the fine day when Lord Woolton, then Minister of Food, invited about twenty popular cartoonists, representing easy access to about twenty million people, to his offices to ask us to help him to popularize potatoes. In the official view, there was something 'funny' about potatoes which made them a suitable subject for cartoons.

'My dear David,' wrote Herbert Morrison, Minister of Home Security,

> 'We are now faced with the problem of training a rather varied collection of some millions of civilians doing part-time duty as Fire Guards into an organized and disciplined body with a vigorous esprit de corps. I wonder whether it is asking too much ... would you ....'

I did some cartoons 'emphasizing the high importance of the work of the Fire Guards and the cheerful gaiety of their corporate effort.' I did some odd posters for 'appeals,' and in spite of myself I accepted my little social activities, opening little exhibitions, chairing little meetings, making little speeches and in general counteracting despondency and alarm.

On the other hand my private war had widened considerably in scope. Beside my constant flow in newspapers and periodicals I had produced two more Penguin books and, so far as the blessing of the paper control could be obtained, I had more volumes in the press on both sides of the Atlantic. An eager Czech publisher was pushing parcels of my little booklets of appropriately selected and variously translated war cartoons wherever he could find loopholes in Europe and North Africa. What with the pick-up in syndication added to a surprisingly active network of private circulation into sensitive places, enough of my 'paper' was flying about in North Africa at a crucial moment to irritate sorely the Nazi-controlled Paris propaganda. But when Admiral Darlan was assassinated in 1943, it was a bit thick to have *Le Matin* spread it across four columns that I had had something to do with the crime, because I had printed a cartoon a fortnight before reflecting the general desirability of the Admiral's disappearance from the scene at the earliest moment. *Une Preuve Flagrante de la Préméditation de L'Attentat* they called it, on the part of Secretaries Cordell Hull and Eden and, presumably, myself.

Altogether I had become fairly busy for a private citizen. In between times, as a relief from the miasma of war, I wrote a book on *British Cartoonists, Caricaturists and Comic Artists*. My B.B.C. doings had led me to a congenial producer, Stephen Potter, with whom I tried a couple of full-length programmes on the Home Service, followed later (without Stephen) by an experimental series of 'war cartoons' in sound effects, which I regret to say was a monumental flop.

The tide had turned in the war though there was plenty of time for the Allies to lose it, when Göbbels cashed in on the bad blood between Poland and Soviet Russia with allegations that the Russians had murdered thousands of Polish officers at Katyn Forest near Smolensk in 1941. The Polish exile Government in London abandoned diplomatic usage and asked for an investigation, without addressing any enquiry to the Soviet Government. Recriminations. The Soviet Government broke off relations with the London Poles.

This was too much. The war was far from over, yet the disrupters were at full blast to break the Allied Coalition and perhaps—who knows the luck?—switch the war. The splitting campaign was having too much success. I opened up with a few cartoons about rats undermining the foundations of victory. The word 'rat' is an irritant word, like all short, sharp words ending with a 't'. It started off bad temper in various quarters where it had been worked out that to shear away our most powerful fighting ally was a highly patriotic act.

For a while rats were metaphorically thrown back and forth mainly with reference to the same difference of opinion, the exchange culminating in a deplorable uproar about a cartoon entitled NEUTRALITY AT ROME, which dealt with the ambiguous policy of the Vatican. The Church authorities at Rome had just sent a telegram of congratulations to Hitler on his birthday. My sedate drawing showed two figures in priestly frocks standing on cathedral steps, one releasing a dove to Hitler, the other distributing anti-Russian newspapers.

The cartoon reported pictorially the sound facts of the moment. A volume of emotional fury burst over my head the next day. None of my critics, however, was bold enough to contend that the attitudes and policies of a supra-national ecclesiastical power were beyond comment.

Still more or less on the same theme, but more often as a vexation to those who had not observed the passage of time and the significance of events, my cartoons kept cropping up in Parliament:

'SIR A. KNOX (Wycombe, U.) called attention to the cartoon in today's issue of the *Evening Standard*, which, he submitted, was really detrimental to the war effort. The cartoon represented the heads of three allied nations in a most undignified position acting as gangsters ready to sabotage the war effort. . . . Steps should be taken in the interests of the war effort against its recurrence.' (3.5.1944)

'MR. RAIKES (Essex, S.E., U.) said that many in this country felt that this type of cartoon . . . caused nothing but pain and grief to many persons who held these particular individuals in respect in their own countries. . . . The House adjourned.'

(3.5.1944)

'MR. CHURCHILL: . . . Some people think that our foreign policy towards Spain is best expressed by drawing comical or even rude caricatures of General Franco, but I think there is more in it than that. . . .' (24.5.1944)

'MR. C. E. G. EMMOTT (E. Surrey, U.): We are all familiar with that type of caricature which is neither clever nor funny:

odious and characteristic caricatures by Low and all that kind of thing, the whole tone and temper of which is inconsistent with the principle of the maintenance of law. I consider it ought to be strongly condemned.' (26.5.1944)

In the days of Britain's 'finest hour,' under the full burden of bombardment, the British people had risen to unparalleled heights of patience, endurance and unity. The British spirit of cheerfulness under pressure had made history. Now the war was not yet decided, but the desperate peril had receded. The mood changed. Once it became evident that Hitler definitely had over-played his hand, the compelling force of unity weakened. People found less to admire in one another. The emotional exultation had worn off leaving only the personal tragedies and the chores, the shortages and the discomforts. The British have always fancied themselves in the character of growlers. The Spartan spirit was not for them once the pressure was removed. It did not make for popularity to harp on our ridiculously high standard of living, which used up shipping and lives as the Nazi submarine blockade tightened.

The wind changed for me. While the war picture was active, sensational and picturesque, I had been flattered and complimented to the point of embarrassment. 'Thank God for Low' had said a London vicar from his pulpit. 'Low is one of the three forces that hold us together,' said somebody else, meaning as the two others Churchill and J. B. Priestley, whose Sunday evening broadcasts had the ear of the whole nation. I was not used to being written and talked about as though I were a national hero, and this and what I observed happening to other people filled me with dark suspicion about the fortuitous nature of greatness. When I felt called upon to say that people were eating too much and using too much petrol, not working hard enough and shooting off their mouths too much, it was a different story.

The bad-tempered years began. Cheerfulness turned a little sour. Latent disagreements began to reappear. Political party quarrels began to reappear, not only about future developments and directions of foreign policy, but particularly about the blueprints of post-war reconstruction and the use of the opportunity to rebuild 'a Britain worthy of our splendid people.'

Doubtless because of the comparatively quicker impact of pictorial over literary expression, I came in for more than my fair share of attention, acrimonious and otherwise. For a time I became a sort of lightning conductor.

Comments upon the future of controls, and rationing, for instance, were freely discussed in economic and political circles, but the experts were writing and talking for themselves and one another. I had a door to the masses which they had not, but it soon became evident that many people, if they did not positively deplore my giving a wider currency to such matters as socially unsettling, thought that the medium of caricature was unseemly as a means.

Planning, for or against, was going to be domestic question number one for the post-war Britain. Already the opposing legions were lining up and generating steam. Already people who feared that a planned social economy might be detrimental to their own interests were becoming bold enough to make highly coloured attacks on the whole conception.

It all smacked too much of 1919 to me. Same kind of people, same kind of attitude. Nothing learned. I weighed in with a cartoon intended as a reminder, entitled THE GOOD OLD DAYS: Three plump business types reposing comfortably on the upholstery of a large car, over their heads a cloudy effect in which appears a long weary queue of the unemployed of the 1920–1930s, the subject of their discussion. One of the plump types argues: 'Planning would sap enterprise and initiative. It weakens self-reliance and self-respect. We must conserve the best qualities of the British people. Back to the good old days!'

It was symptomatic of the period that the London *Sunday Times* touched off an explosion by according all the dignity of its first editorial to a vehement attack on that cartoon as a 'wicked incitement to class hatred.' That strabismic opinion was contested by other newspapers and debates arose about whether or not the plump types represented the rich class and the queue the poor class? or the capitalist class and the working class? or whom? The *Manchester Guardian* talked sense:

> Is not what annoys the *Sunday Times* the uncomfortable feeling that Low's legend is only the cartoonist's legitimate heightening of current talk in some Conservative quarters? Low's offence seems to be that he got a little too near the bone.

Argument widened across the Atlantic, where the cartoon, rumpus and all, had gone the rounds. Nobody asked my opinion except the *Chicago Sun*, so I gave them the Official Reply:

> I am sick of all this obsolete rot about 'class war.' The only class war I am interested in is that between the sane and the

insane. The figures in my car in my cartoon don't represent plutocracy in particular, but plain stupidity of the type very vocal at present. If the editor of the *Sunday Times* isn't aware of it he should read the newspapers.

Differences of opinion were real often enough; but occasionally my tiffs arose from misunderstanding even among friends, due to my own carelessness in not adequately labelling the figures in my cartoons. For instance:

> 46 Gordon Square,
> Bloomsbury, 13/5/44.

My dear Low,

I was deeply shocked by your cartoon last night. The I.L.O. business is pure hot air which itself achieves nothing. The Monetary Plan is the first major concrete effort at expanding and steadying the export trade, without which full employment is impossible.

It is (I tell you for your private information though you probably know it) the voices of Beaverbrook and the Bank of England you are listening to. For you to obey these voices and picture me as a monetary Blimp is indeed a stab in the back.

> Yours ever,
> MAYNARD KEYNES.

> 3 Rodborough Road, N.W.11.
> 16th May, 1944.

My dear Keynes,

This is very distressing . . . I agree fully that the monetary plan is the really important thing, without which the I.L.O. Charter and policies of full employment could get nowhere; I agree that even as it stands, the monetary plan is a great advance; but I am right, am I not, in believing that the present compromise is a very much more modest step than it could and should be? . . .

Why you conclude that the Blimp talking to me in the background (of the cartoon) is yourself puzzles me. Rather he represents your opponents, as far as I am concerned.

> Yours ever,
> DAVID LOW.

Thus amity was quickly restored. In some other cases it was more difficult. I could not complain of a lack of variety in reception. Sometimes there were inspiring compensations:—

77 Great Russell Street,
W.C.1.
1st October, 1945.

Dear Mr. Low,

I felt I must send you a word to say how deeply touched I was by your 'Palestine' cartoon last week. In these sad times, when our friends are so few, such evidences of sympathy and understanding are beyond all thanks. Yet all I can say is 'Thank you'—both personally and on behalf of my people.

With kindest regards, I am,

Very sincerely yours,

CH. WEIZMANN.

26

FRUGALITY AND DISCIPLINE was no rousing call for a general election. The immediate post-war policies of Britain were dictated by dire necessity. But there was room for difference of opinion about the future. Churchill's advisers gave the Conservative chances away by relying on the negative emotional appeal, the *reductio ad absurdum* of the case for planning. The electorate was not prepared to repeat the 'victory election' of 1919 and the miserable procession of events that followed World War I. The voters preferred the Labour Party, and it took power for five years.

Beaverbrook and his newspapers loyally had upheld Churchill and the Conservatives and I had consistently supported the Labour Party and ridiculed Churchill's attempt to make the prominent socialist Professor Laski the bogey of a scare campaign. Not for the first time the *Evening Standard* and I had been in flat opposition. Yet, as should be in a civilized community, that made no difference to personal relations. It was a stimulating experience to spend one night at Cherkley listening to Beaverbrook and Brendan Bracken (both notoriously concerned with the planning of the Conservative campaign) and another with Harold Laski admiring his collection of seventeenth-century pamphlets.

Many years before I had gone to dinner at H. G. Wells's flat. The other guests were two talkative young fellows I had never met before—Harold Laski and George Catlin. Both of them talked a lot. Sometimes unstoppable, so that H.G. could hardly get a word in and I had to retire behind my knife and fork, moaning 'Heavens, will these fellows *never* shut up?' . . . Curiously, although they differed on many things, I lived to enjoy cordial friendship with both of them.

I would be sitting at lunch in some restaurant when the small

rosy face of Harold Laski would appear over
my shoulder, earnest and a little perspiring,
eyes shining through big spectacles—
'David! Oh, David, you would be interested to hear what Ernie Bevin said
today about your Wednesday's cartoon ...'
and from there Harold would gossip on with
a monologue of chapter length about something which had nothing to do with me or
my cartoon from any conceivable angle.

Harold Laski

Harold Laski's platform manner and
utterance—feet wide apart, unexpectedly
strong nasal voice—'Mistah Chahman . . .' were easy to parody
and there were very few of the bright boys who did not include
him in their imitations. 'So Frank said to me, Harold . . .' 'As I
said to Winston . . .' I had a warm spot for Harold. Who, among
those who knew him, hadn't? He had no ambitions in active
policies. He was a teacher and took pride in it. Like most of his
friends I treasure a heap of correspondence in his microscopically
small handwriting about all sorts of things, from the education of
my daughters to the private life of Mr. Justice Holmes. We did
not always agree:

> Houghton Street,
> Aldwych, London, W.C.2.
> 12th November, 1948.

Dear David,

I am so deep a devotee of all you do that I do beg you not
to join the chorus of those who attack the efforts of Israel to
establish itself as a going concern recognized by the United
States. In all my life I have never known a Foreign Office in
the British tradition act with an ugliness as complete, and a
trickery and malice so devastating, as the Foreign Office has
done in this realm since 1945. I have followed it, I can assure
you, at first hand. I have had many talks with all those concerned on all sides, Arab and English, as well as Israeli and even
American, and I think I could prove to you that this is one of
the tragedies of English policy since the General Election. I
do beg you, therefore, not to lend your great gifts to what has
become the side of revenge and reaction seeking to destroy the
remnant of a pitiable tragedy.

> Our warm affection to you all,
> Ever yours,
> HAROLD.

M*

3 Rodborough Road, N.W.11
16th November, 1948

Dear Harold,

I should be very grieved to think that any expressions of mine were giving you uneasiness. As you know, I think of you as one of the few sane men. I think you take my cartoons farther than they go. Heaven knows I am not about to join any 'chorus of attackers' concerning Palestine. I have always wanted to see the Jews established in Palestine and as soon as possible; but I am disappointed, not to say dismayed, to see how, when they have achieved some power, they use it so ruthlessly; and I want to go on record as believing that we British are not without *any* moral obligations to the Arabs, whatever sort of people they are and whatever kind of tricky Foreign Office we might have. If UNO acts before the world as a rubber stamp on the present military *fait accompli*, I fear that although it may give the Jews happiness, we will have debauched a hard-won instrument once again. It is a sad situation.

We all send you both our affectionate regards,

DAVID.

Looking around the political scene I felt old. After the world war there could be only anti-climax in the return to home affairs, however interesting might be the plans for social improvement. To me Westminster lacked the stimulus of novelty. There were few of the aging actors on the parliamentary stage I did not know inside out. I had seen most of them enter the House of Commons raw, had witnessed their making or their marring. As for the younger fry, I had been hanging around Westminster before some of them were even born. It seemed as though the curtain was going up on my Second Time on Earth.

I had exhausted the possibilities of Churchill and there was no longer pleasure in drawing him. Eden had shaken down to an unsensational formula; Bevin had grown too like his own caricature to incite effort, although, irritatingly enough, he resented my version, and that I thought ungrateful. Attlee I had never been able to get to know more than slightly, which accounted for my failure to abstract his essence. From the day at Margate when the Party made him leader, my impression was of a tight-buttoned little man, shy of ridicule. Someone had told him I was an Australian, so whenever we met he confined the conversation to cricket, about which I knew nothing.

It was thirty years since I had first drawn Herbert Morrison for the *Star* as the Mayor of Hackney. How carefully since then we had both cultivated his hair into the celebrated Morrison quiff. How pleasantly at a joint speaking engagement which we both kept for many years at the Christmas dinners of the Howard Hotel, I marked the development of the bumbling diction which became one of his most endearing social assets. He loved to see himself drawn, although I fear his judgment was affected too much by the degree of sympathy displayed in the representation; and he was Jimmy Thomas's successor as my Fan Number 1. The admiration was reciprocated, for to me he was undoubtedly the most skilful politician in his party. His efficiency at one time gave rise to a belief that he kept a dossier on everybody. 'I'm all right,' a chap was alleged to have said. 'I've just been feeling Herbert Morrison's pulse.' 'You chump,' said his hearer, 'don't you know that's his dodge for getting your fingerprints?'

For the next year or so I was restless and took every opportunity to see at first hand what was happening in the world. I had been vividly conscious of the process of change, not merely in the distribution of power but in the organization of human society. The past was gone. Hitler had not been far out when he foretold that the war would end the old empires. There was a new deal. The atom bomb had blown up far more than Hiroshima.

An acute observer present at the time of the invention of the wheel should have been able from that point to deduce the course of Man—the development of industry, trade rivalries, the rise and fall of nations, power groups, world wars and readjustments, the conquest of space, of time, of life itself, and so on. So far as the people of my century were concerned, the next chapter evidently was to include two items: (*a*) the rebirth of Asia; and (*b*) the development of forces which could make a fool not only of war but also of peace. Was the centre of the world destined to move eastwards? Would the community of nations control the bomb? And if that miracle were accomplished, and the new energies were diverted to peaceful ends, how long could we expect the wages system of a 'free' society to survive? Would the Communist system be insulated from embarrassment, with its total control? On the other hand, were not Lease-Lend and Marshall Aid hints that even hardshell capitalists could make revolutionary readjustments to keep their wheels turning? I was curious to see how Man would approach this future.

Life became a travel sketchbook with occasional sidelights on the

357

prospects for democracy. Here is a drawing made in a shattered German town right after the war. Streets heaped with rubble. I walked in a straight line for half an hour. Every house blasted. Nothing in London like it. Hunched young men with dead eyes, sulky eyes, resentful eyes. Obviously too early to draw conclusions about the future. The respect with which somebody stopped the traffic for me at a crossing was no doubt a tribute to the strangeness of my war correspondent's badge. Might have been somebody important. Shops with nothing in the window but advertisement cards. I was struck by the number of people trying to live on their talents—artists particularly. It was like trailing through a cemetery followed by someone mumbling 'Sketch your portrait, Mister?'

This sketch was drawn on my way to the Nuremberg trials, via Frankfurt, in a busted windowless railway carriage behind a lame engine, sitting bent on a broken seat in the dark surrounded by a sinister company of black shapes, fitfully lit by an occasional station lamp in passing. The train broke down four times, cold as hell, snowing, no nice cup of tea. Arrive at last, am posted to what was once a millionaire's castle, where I find all the special correspondents of all the newspapers I had ever heard of. Aaaaah. Milk and sugar, thank you.

There is a story of a cartoonist who, on seeing for the first time in real life a statesman whom he had been drawing for years, asked: 'Who's that?'

I recognized the men in the dock at Nuremberg instantly, but there were some things about them that were unexpected. After what had happened I did not look, of course, for a set of puffed-up specimens of the Master Race in fearsome uniforms with padded shoulders, swastikas and high heels; but, on the other hand, this lot seemed rather inadequate.

Very ordinary-looking in fact. If you saw them sitting opposite you in the train you would think all was normal. Also they were much too small. As we know, Nazi leaders used to attach great importance to their personal 'presentation,' and under their rule the camera had evidently become the most efficient liar yet evolved.

Where is the great Göring, the jingle of whose medals used to keep the world awake at nights? Tall, broad-shouldered Hess, the very pattern of Nazi body-culture? Burly Streicher, who trod millions under his sadist heel?

Well, Göring turns out to be about 5 ft. 8 in., still fat despite weight lost in prison; jolly, you would say, until you noticed the

Göring at Nuremberg (1945)

cruel mouth, vital, with periods of rumination when the countenance is sicklied o'er with desperate worry.

Göring stands out by a mile as the boss in this company. He is a restless prisoner, leaning this way and that, flapping his pudgy little hands about, patting his hair, stroking his mouth, massaging his cheeks, resting his chin sideways on the ledge of the dock. Göring is not permitted to make speeches, but he manages to get a good deal of expression across with facial action. Nods, shakes, and eye-play suggestive of innocent l'il Hermann wrongfully accused.

359

Sketchbook in hand, I am examining Göring meticulously when he turns his gaze and hooks my eye. After about twenty seconds of mutual glaring it dawns upon me that he is trying to stare me down. The childish vanity of it! How silly! (I win, by the way.)

The appearance of Hess takes me aback. Down to skin and bone, going bald, wild eyes set in deep-sunken cavities, he has a nervous twitch and jerky movements. If, as he now insists, he is not mad, all I can say is that he looks it.

Streicher, the obscene Jew-baiter. Is that him? No loathsome ape, but another little man with another nervous twitch. He has a trick of throwing his head right back and contemplating the ceiling with an air of preoccupation with Higher Things. In prison Streicher has grown a fluff of hair over his horrible baldness, and this, catching the light, gives him a kind of halo. In a white nightgown he could look a somewhat repulsive saint.

In London once we used to know as German Ambassador one Ribbentrop. Later we heard of him as the bawling bully that gave Poland its death notice. Here he is now, changed surprisingly into a meek person like a family solicitor, with disordered hair, pursed lips and large spectacles, fussing shakily with a sheaf of papers.

In a corner Dönitz sits impassive like a little acid-drop, a contrast to his next-door neighbour, Raeder, who shows his anxiety by writhing uneasily. Jodl wears a poker face and moves rarely. Keitel, who now is not, by the way, red-faced but grey, and whose former chest is slipping down to his stomach, turns from side to side, and can't keep for long in one position. During the ten minutes' 'break' the Services get together in earnest conference.

The most pitiful figure in the company is Funk. Funk is the picture of funk. With the earphones clamped like horns to the fat, sick face sagging into the small, dumpy body, he is the perfect model for a gargoyle. In colour he is light green.

The colouring of the prisoners, by the way, is to me not the least revealing indication of their various emotional states. Rosenberg, for instance, is yellowish; Frick, patchy brown. If one were painting the historic scene, one would have to use a palette of drab pigments. It is remarkable how little colour there is in this spectacle of the so-called 'blond beast' on trial. The only reds I could find in the composition were Seyss-Inquart's rusty hair and cheeks, Jodl's nose, and the rims of Göring's eyes.

The next most frightened, I should say, is Sauckel. He is the cartoonist's fat-necked, square-headed German, but on a small scale. His uneasiness is painful to see. To make up for him, at his elbow is Baldur von Schirach, the ex-pin-up boy of the Hitler Youth. Still good-looking, with his scornful, pitiless eye, and mean mouth like an inverted V.

Runners-up for the 'most-perturbed-person' prize are Frick, of the corrugated countenance, and Schacht, who is worried to pieces, too, but in a more refined way. Papen looks more than ever like a fox, shifting his tiny close-set eyes about the room.

Opinions might differ about the award of 'nastiest-person-present,' but I should choose unhesitatingly Frank, the butcher of Warsaw. He wears a fixed sneer and mutters.

The proceedings in court are prosaic and undramatic while I am there, which is how they should be to my way of thinking.

Paris again. I make a little water-colour of the Champs. The beautiful avenue still there; no rubble, thanks be. But it is a drab Paris, lacking in confidence, morose, too many cigarette-stub hunters with stick-and-pin and tin. Juvenile gendarmes, man-power shortage, prices too high, synthetic coffee terrible. I am too soon again to make prophecies. Empty streets at night except for long queues outside the cinemas. Explanation: it is warm inside the cinemas and it is cold at home. All the pimps apparently have gone into the black market. As I tramp to my hotel (no taxis) I am continually accosted by spivs wanting to buy the contents of my suitcase, whatever it may be. Offers on the spot, blind. I beat them off with irritation.

No need to go far for the next scene in the world drama, for the United Nations Organization had thoughtfully arranged to hold its first Assembly at Church House, London, just around the corner.

Tap, tap. Shoosh! The Assembly is in session. Enter the President, cherubic M. Spaak. He's dark-haired and open-eyed, but otherwise he could pass for Winston Churchill's younger brother. He sits at his beige-covered table on his raised platform, a small figure against a vast acreage of blue and white cloth hangings, in the middle of which is a gold medallion with a tasteful device symbolizing something or other.

He sits at an angle of 75 degrees, plump face on plump hand, beaming at the delegates of fifty-one nations airing their eloquence for peace. Here, or outside in his long overcoat, a flat broad hat pancaked on his head, he is made for the cartoonists.

The layout of delegates follows no discernible plan. The Poles, the Turks and the Arabs have the best seats, middle of first row. The Americans sit to the extreme left alongside the U.S.S.R. and behind the U.K. 'Ah, good morning, Mr. Byrnes.' 'Good morning, Tom. Where the heck did you get to last night? Good morning, everybody.' The Americans make noises when they meet. Not like the Russians, who greet silently, or the British, who just nod and growl 'Hullo.'

Byrnes isn't at all the English idea of an American. An unsensational figure, spare, small, dignified. His taste in neckties would stop a clock. Just a suggestion of perkiness. With his coat tail curled, he could be drawn as a bird. He sits between Mrs. Roosevelt, the embodiment of international Mothers' Day, and Vandenberg, with his inseparable cigar stub ('no smoking in the assembly hall,' darn it), who is more what the British think an American looks like. Stettinius is the most personable of the United States delegates. He is irritated to be told he reminds me of Charlie Chaplin in larger size. It's the white hair, not the feet.

In front the United Kingdom. Our Bevin, of course, is the 'big' British personality, physically and otherwise. He looks as though he were about to enter the ring for an all-in wrestling bout. Man-mountain against all comers. When 'Uncle Ernie' has something to say, he champs; and when he is indignant he snorts. Close to Bevin, his second, Noel-Baker, the tall thin eager idealist, and the picturesque pocket-size redhead Ellen Wilkinson. The nearest thing to the eyeglassed spatted Englishman of American comedy is Sir Alexander Cadogan of the F.O., who watches the proceedings impassively with a globous light blue eye.

Next to the Americans are the Russians for contrast. Unsmiling, solemn. Gromyko looks surprisingly youthful. Whatever he may be like at home, in public he seems a gloomy character. They call him 'Mr. Mournful.' Vishinsky, the Soviet top man, is greyed blond with a tight mouth, like Bevin in build, except that he walks with a proud chest, whereas Bevin rolls like a battleship from his knees. Behind Vishinsky's thick-rimmed glasses are pale little eyes that don't miss much. Manuilsky of the Ukraine, old Bolshevik friend of Lenin, a nugget resembling Lloyd George, with all the Gallic movements. Jan Masaryk of Czechoslovakia, large, languid, with a wistful look in his eye.

'Well?' I say to Jan, my good friend.

'I don't think they will,' he says, leaving who and what to be guessed.

The French sit some distance away, in the centre of the floor, where Massigli, the tallest man present, may be seen giving himself a crick in the neck whispering into the ear of little Bidault, who, by his expression, finds being Foreign Minister a job more formidable even than running a Resistance movement.

The Chinese are close by. Wellington Koo is Europeanized, and his immaculate clothes and deportment are strictly Western, though the intermittent sniff which punctuates his public speaking is his own.

Despite preliminary bouts over Iran, Greece and Indonesia in the Council, this first Assembly has concerned itself more with organization than with politics. The cold war has not yet been fully unmasked and summer suitings are still being worn. The place is full of know-alls putting 2 and 2 together and making 22.

After conference hours, I go to cocktails with Molotov. Surrounded by well-brushed satellites all wearing glasses he holds on to my hand and proceeds to run into what seems to be a short sermon suitable to the occasion.

'What did His Excellency say?' I ask.

'He was very complimentary and advised you to go on as you have been going,' answers an interpreter. Since I have been kicking Soviet policy soundly in the pants, I can only conclude that even a superman can't attend to everything, and he hasn't seen the papers.

Stepping aside for the ghost of Geneva as it clanked up the corridor and brushing past the shade of Woodrow Wilson on the stairs, I emerge to rejoin the thousand million people in the outside world. If words could kill, war would be as dead as a doornail. The construction of peace is a different proposition. 'Machinery isn't of the slightest use unless there's a will to work it.'

If it's not one thing, it's another; it's never nothing. Life is a continuous process. The removal of one set of problems reveals another set, *ad infinitum*.

It will always be interesting to speculate on what might have been had Soviet Russia and the United States met in genuine co-operation after the war. Optimists like myself might reasonably have expected the impact of the old doctrine on the new to stimulate the best and depress the worst in both. Many problems of humanity might have been solved without tears upon sensible lines at last. On the most material plane the junction would certainly have been mutually profitable, besides incidentally raising the standard of living for the whole world. The end of nightmare bombs and the beginning of atomic prosperity. But

363

no. These may be the conceptions of sentimentalists concerned with the promptings of the heart. The 'practical' men must have their 'hard facts' for their hard heads.

Yet even on the lowest plane viewing the world as a chess-board for cunning play to win group advantage, a genuine Russo-American association in 1945, with America in friendly, generous, admiring mood, had better possibilities for Russia than for America. But the automatic chess-player had been set long before for a different gambit. The Stalin policy had been to ensure Soviet security by forming a chain of buffer states across Europe. The world might change, the policy might be out-moded, but it remained.

Any intelligent political tipster ought to have been able to foresee the consequences that inevitably, as night follows day, had to flow from the Russian immutability: the replacement of goodwill by suspicion, the bedevilment of the peace, the cold war, rearmament, NATO and the rest. For a space the iron curtain became formidably solid, with the propaganda screen so trans-parent as to be almost ludicrous. The decade of Utter Humbug was upon us, when step by step it became more and more necessary for each side to pretend that the other had no virtue but only villainy. While the air was increasingly filled with denunciations of war-mongering hyenas on the one hand and bestial tyrants on the other; while the rights and wrongs of 'incidents' were disputed in make-believe as though the aims were to serve justice and not some extraneous strategy; and while the scene teemed with the comings and goings of 'peace-loving' delegations whose love of peace partook too much of one-sided sacrifice, I never found any Communist I met that made a dead secret of the 'line' in private. I hooked Bill Rust, for instance, editor of the *Daily Worker*, at a party. 'What's the idea, Bill?' I asked. 'Your people aim even-tually to spread right across Europe to the Channel?'

'Of course,' said Bill, giving me a pitying look.

In the East it was not the Russians that were to drop the bomb whose smoke would swell into the biggest question-mark of all time. Neither was it the Russians entirely that had hardened the United States decision to stay in the Pacific bases to 'protect U.S. interests and world peace,' thereby pledging the Americans to a long grim battle of nerves if ever the régime of Chiang Kai-shek went down before Mao Tse-tung. As it did.

But in the West everybody knew Stalin had had the initiative about world disarmament since the end of the war. He could have settled the whole question of peace or war, bomb or no bomb, whenever he wanted to. But, from his point of view, why should he? Leaving it unsettled paid his Russia handsomely. While he could keep the power of any group to resist his policies below the line of danger to his Russia, no need to change his policies. So long as there was a chance of weakening the American will with moral uncertainties, so long as there was a hope of cajoling the Americans into outlawing, without strict conditions, the nightmare nuclear weapons without which the non-communist world would be outclassed against the huge

Jan Masaryk

Soviet war-machine, hot or cold war could continue.

I had that in mind when the Moscow *Literary Gazette* wired me an invitation to contribute a cartoon giving a Western view on the subject of world peace for their New Year Peace issue, 1948–49. I could not pass up an opportunity like that; so I wired them back a peaceful picture expressing the view that if we peace-loving peoples in the West seemed restless, it was because of the shadow thrown over us (inadvertently, no doubt) by our peace-loving friend Soviet Russia. This was not what was wanted, evidently, for the cartoon was not published, the editor preferring to use a Polish artist's picture of Ernie Bevin as a blood-stained war-mongering hyena. I considered myself free to circulate my drawing throughout my world syndication, with the story and a caption THE CARTOON MOSCOW WOULD NOT PRINT. So that was the end of a beautiful friendship.

Turn the page. I am in beautiful Prague with my daughter Prue for company, being made a fuss of, a guest of the Government. This is not quite behind the iron curtain yet, but halfway. Everybody seems to be talking politics, indoors, outdoors, all hours of the night. The Minister of Information delivers a speech of welcome at me and makes me an official presentation of a pile of books, gramophone records and glassware. (Applause.) So that there shall be no mistake I make a speech, too, explaining that all my own poor efforts had been directed to a victory for freedom of thought and expression. My host's face of smiling approval does not change a muscle. I learn later that he does not understand English.

I took Prue out to dinner with Jan Masaryk, who was then Foreign Minister in that uncomfortable Czechoslovakian set-up. A grand piano took up more space than the table in one of these two rather untidy rooms (bed and reception) which Jan used for living in behind the imposing staircase, halls and bare cold offices of his Ministry at the Czerny Palace.

'Are you happy?' he said.

'Well, I'd be happier if I had a good cigar,' I said.

'Wait,' he said, going down and groping under the bed and coming up with a cigar-box. (Funny place to keep cigars, I thought, and how much more interesting history would be if it were illustrated with unconventional portraits of the butt-ends of foreign ministers reaching under beds.) 'I got these from the Turkish Ambassador.'

Jan Masaryk was an easy and engaging personality, more an artist than a statesman. All he ever wanted to do, he said, was to play the piano, and I believed him. A statesman by the accident of being his father's son. My Government hosts probably counted this as a routine visit for me, but I had known Jan of old. He was glad to see me and we had a grand talk about art. In the privacy he spilled some political beans, too. 'Czechoslovakia a bridge between East and West? No fear! People walk on bridges!'

The year was 1947. He didn't think much of the ability of his communist colleagues in the Coalition Government, but he would remain in it as long as he could to help keep things going . . . he himself was for the Marshall Plan, but Czechoslovakia was next door to Soviet Russia, and, he said, he had to think of that . . . he hoped the communists would not be beaten too badly at the coming elections, as seemed likely, because if they were the Russians might find some excuse to interfere. . . .

We sat at the open window, I puffing the Turkish Ambassador's cigar, looking out across the balcony at the quiet moonlit square. Prue made an idle remark about the ancient Czech custom of disposing of enemies by 'defenestration.' Poor Jan. No shadow marked the spot where in a few short months he himself was to lie there broken and dead on the stones below.

27

THE war had changed a lot of things. The face of Humanity. The *Evening Standard*. Me.

With Trades Unionism strong and well organized, a Labour Government in power with its own majority and socialism shelved for the reformism of the now universally approved Welfare State, a new phase was opening. The old box of cartoonists' dummies, fat top-hatted white-spatted 'Boss,' downtrodden 'Worker,' ragged 'Unemployed,' was obsolete. Into the waste-basket. The question was no longer *whether* to make a better world, but *how*. In that light the political alignment Labour against Conservative was as out-of-date as Whig against Tory or Roundhead against Cavalier. The only contrast that would have made sense and might have produced useful interplay was a Freedom Party against an Order Party, but that was too much to expect. I grew sick of the make-believe of the old party politics, and bored with the many chaps who were so terribly anxious to go 'left' that they bent in a semi-circle and were coming back on the 'right' without knowing it. 'Those damned words Rightism and Leftism!' as old H.G. would say, 'In the most vital human concerns there is no right or left at all, but just straight forward.'

The exigencies of war and the banking-up of masses of potential new readers had sharpened competition among the 'popular' newspapers for mass circulation. Accordingly each paper sought to outdo its rivals in lightness and brightness.

It is a condition of the 'popular' newspaper's survival that the balance it draws between instruction and entertainment must ultimately show a profit. But I felt no compelling need to be ruled by this condition myself. On the contrary. My inclination

367

was rather to step up the 'awareness' of my cartoons, to put in more meat and less mush.

This purely personal feeling was not entirely unrelated to some impersonal conclusions reached after a look around the post-war scene with its conflict of ideologies. If, as was claimed, the basic difference between our 'free' democracy and the totalitarian kind was that the former rested on persuasion and the latter on force; and that we 'free' citizens could think and choose, while the other chaps had to do what they were told; then a certain responsibility was implied for us 'free' ones to keep informed about the conditions of our 'freedom' and its survival. Ignorance was the enemy. Already there was a substantial doubt as to whether this 'freedom' could long survive under the stresses and strains of accommodation to the age of speed and power. How long—in the hands of a non-political generation that could not recognise defeat until it had had it?

The doors might clang, but I did not intend to have it on my conscience that I let democracy die of entertainment. I had before me another decade of active work before lumbering off like an aged elephant to find a resting-place for my bones in the Valley of Silence. I had done my best work so far as the *Evening Standard* was concerned. The whole generation of public men (excepting Churchill) with whom I had been wont to cavort had left the scene, together with their admirers and detractors and the 'disgusted' correspondents who had deplored me and my cartoons for so many years. Beaverbrook had gone to live across the Atlantic. The *Standard's* editorial personnel had completely changed too, and I was the oldest inhabitant. So what?

The time came when I found myself helping to write the last page in the story of H. G. Wells. When he died at 75 and his friends met at the British Association for a Memorial meeting, it was appropriate that speakers should estimate his character in sedate and measured terms. But even as I conformed to propriety my thoughts returned to the little asides and irrelevances that give the public statue warmth and humanity. H.G. slapping a ball; at a party dressed up fantastically for a charade; relating with glee a story against himself (H.G. and Charlie Chaplin waiting at Bishop's Stortford platform for a train, when up comes a local with autograph book. H.G. takes it, but owner wrenches it back. 'Not you—'*Im*!')

I thought of the fun he was, his rudeness ('I have never had a

368

bad oyster, but if I had had, it would have been like Hoover,' he said cheerfully to a Republican Senator, of all people, at an Anglo-American dinner, of all places); I thought of his dissertations, expostulations, sometimes followed by his full-arm swipes of correspondence, which could never damage in the least our friendship.

I thought of the dreadful occasion when a wandering drunk took a fancy to argue with H.G. when we were out supping at a fashionable caravanserai, and we had to skip, leaving half his welsh rarebit. I thought of his high-pitched voice explaining the meaning of the war during the blitz, discovering undemocratic interferences in public affairs by the Royal Family, ex-

A soulful glimpse of Wells

posing General de Gaulle. It rings in my ear still, vibrant with his endless eagerness to put right single-handed the foolishness and stupidities of mankind that obstinately would not be put right.

During the war H.G. had been so impressed at the business-like way the Nazis destroyed books wholesale wherever they went that he feared the possibility of a Dark Age, so that he began to assemble friends and make plans for compiling an Encyclopaedia of Human Knowledge.

This, I gathered, was to be a race against time if individual liberty were to survive and the free spirit to be pursued by future generations. The thought that fools or knaves might seek a short cut to order by shaping and trimming men's minds, stunting their intellects and perverting to utter blindness the power of philosophical reflection on the larger issues of life, was intolerable to H.G. And to me also, as I listened to him. Partly to please him, but partly because I was genuinely moved, I thought up the idea of clarifying the Rights of Man a bit by blocking out a set of posters of the 13 Freedoms. He made it 12, but I made it 13. But H.G. was delighted:

369

13 Hanover Terrace,
Regent's Park, N.W.1.
July 20th, 1943.

Dear Low,

Yours is an intoxicating letter and suggestion. I'd love to do it ... a little booklet ... translations interleaved ... propaganda enlarged into posters ... decorate mess rooms, etc. ...

We had only tentative ideas about what we were going to do with the posters when they were done. Get some millionaire idealist to stick 'em around on hoardings, perhaps, to show people what they stood to lose. But when H.G. died I had no heart for the job, anyway.

The next twenty pages of my sketchbook are full of the American Presidential election of 1948. I went to Butte, Montana, where I was to join the Truman train en route campaigning across the continent. I had flown in the night before and I spent the spare time getting local reactions. This was to be really a first-class box-seat from which to sample the condition of democracy.

Butte was what they called an 'open town'—gambling joints and amusement houses open for business on the main street with everybody free to sin if he felt like it. A few years before it would have been like an old-time Western movie town. But the levelling-out process had set in. The cowboys wore their decorated high boots and patterned shirts but they wore no guns and their ten-gallon hats had come down to uniform fawn quart-size. My own hat was black and, by comparison, wide-brimmed— a social error, for only crooked professional gamblers wore hats like that, I learned later. That hat generated suspicion. The townsmen did not loosen up so readily. I had an instructive time wandering around listening to the local worthies grappling with world problems and preparing for the arrival of the President. Plonked down in the copper belt far from friends, followed by questioning eyes at that blasted hat, and with what seemed only the most casual contacts with the Presidential entourage, I felt like anything but Two-gun Low, the terror of the craps tables.

At last I set off, carrying my suit-case, to take my place at the railway station. What a hope! Crowds blocked the entrance. I had no ticket in my lapel like other important persons. I had forgotten the F.B.I. Strong-arm guards seemed to be everywhere, all suspicious of my hat, obviously fearing the bomb in my suit-case, unwilling to listen to explanations. At last, steeled by necessity, I bailed up the most obvious Secret Service man in sight and shoved my passport under his nose. 'Say, you aren't Low the British cartoonist in the *New York Times*?' It turned out he was a fan of mine. . . . So there I was now among the local V.I.P.s waiting in state to receive Mr. President. What luck! Thank God for syndication.

The President is of the people but, by virtue of his office, a being apart. An American among Americans but not to be held lightly. Although the President's public character was that of the 'ordinary man,' the journey was as royal a progress as could be compatible with popular democracy.

The President seemed a very likeable man, free of what we British call 'side'; willing to play ball with the Press and to co-operate with the photographers to make a good picture. That was very important. My impression was that the people wanted to look at, rather than to listen to the President. This is the visual age.

Cruising alongside the train like a Rival Power were a couple of trucks containing photographic machinery and the picture men. They were the important people, a tough-looking bunch with set mouths, restless eyes and wearing caps and leather coats with an air of desperate resolution, as though there were a war on. Fortunately the Trumans, Harry, Bess and Margaret, made a photogenic family group. 'In America we bank heavily on the Family,' said a picture man to me, as he shot four bulbs at Margaret's bangles, ignoring her father's arguments.

The spectacle of Mr. President at half-past six in the morning (Truman was an early riser) alighting to pick a dewy rose from a railroad track garden for the benefit of the photographers was an affecting sight. But the privilege was not to be trifled with, and there were limits. Mr. President was nobody's mug. For instance: it was Mr. President's custom to pass along through the correspondent's club car now and then to greet old friends and encourage new arrivals. Two solid bodyguards were always right behind him but Truman was so matey one didn't notice them.

One morning a knot of the boys were relaxing with a game of poker, when in popped Mr. President, particularly frolicsome. He paused to talk to Bob over the shoulder of one of the players at a hand of cards.

'Uh-huh!' says he, 'What's here?' Digging into a trouser pocket he produced and playfully waved a handful of dollar bills. 'What will you take for that hand, Oscar?'

Click! The shutter of a camera.

Whoosh! . . . The camera whipped out of the photographer's hands by the bodyguards, the film removed and exposed to daylight. Quickest thing I ever saw.

What a picture that would have made! A circle of hard-boiled gamblers, coats off, disarrayed in neckwear and suspenders, concentrated, grim, chips piled high, with the President of the United States leaning over flashing a handful of dollars, like the boss of some joint. What political repercussions! A picture to alter world history.

The mechanics of the tour were almost routine. The flag-wagging reception on the rear car platform, a tot with presentation flowers, Governor, prominent citizens male and female, handshakes, backslappings, 'a few words,' 'your friend and my friend,' jokes, presentation fishing-rod. . . . all (me too) into a fleet of cars for progress to town centre for official speech, back again to train and off.

So far as speech went Harry was demonstrably better 'off the cuff' than reading from a script, which was a great worry to a curly-headed gentleman who sat secluded away all day carefully writing out the Right Things for him to say according to wherever we were. The Boss was apt to forget and come out with something chipper extemporized on the spur of the moment to loud applause.

The issues, to a stranger like me, were somewhat obscure. The big interest locally was what he thought about, say, building a dam thereabouts, and whether in promise he could out-dam Dewey. Foreign policy was bi-partisan and, short of war, nobody was interested anyway. Nobody mentioned items like America's political relationships with the rest of the world, the lowering of tariffs to enable foreign customers to come to life again, or the adaptation of the machinery of democracy to enable free enterprise to survive the probable development of atomic power in industry. I took it details like that were fixed elsewhere.

And now on to democracy at work, a Republican Convention at Philadelphia.

'Who will be nominated?' I asked.

'Dewey, of course.'

But the preliminaries had to be observed.

A British stranger to American politics might have been excused for mistaking in the milling parades, the singing, buttons, cardboard elephants, waving portraits and slogans, the comic hats and the unstoppable band just a confusion suggestive of Boat Race night and Derby Day held together in the Albert Hall. But sitting aloft in the feverish heat, I was in the right place to discern a certain order in the proceedings. At intervals a hush fell and distinguished statesmen made keynote speeches or named favourite sons, viewing with alarm and pointing with pride, adjusting sectional interests and giving clarion calls. These were listened to with due respect. But obviously the interludes were the thing.

All around me sat perspiring experts making abstruse calculations. The duration of ovations, timed with stop-watch, the movements of key persons, their expressions, their visitings, their tic-tac signals, each had its significance to be carefully watched, added, subtracted and multiplied. The method of repetitive and eliminative voting lent itself to involved negotiation and the grand strategy. The negotiations were continued even more sensationally after the conference adjourned for the day to the smoke-filled back-rooms. And here, as a visiting cartoonist drawing the Convention for the American magazine *Life*, I found my Australian experience in fading myself in and out of places where I should not have been, was of great value. Who was it personally investigated a rumour that Governor Duff had Ed Martin under lock and key? Me. Whose was the third figure on the left when Kim Sigler swung the Michigan delegation? Whose shadow was it behind the screen when the Missouri headquarters were struck by lightning? Mine . . .

And at last there was Mr. Dewey on the rostrum, everybody's unanimous choice, promising to love, honour and obey. Small head and large carnation. My impression was that the whole thing could have been settled over the telephone. All the same I enjoyed it. There is no reason why politics should not be a holiday.

For contrast I went to Hollywood. I had only ten days and I chose to spend them visiting the big executives of the film industry, the producers, directors—the chaps who told the other chaps what to do. I wanted to talk about their educational responsibilities, but they wanted to talk about the ruin of Britain. British 'richugees' from the alleged 'revolution' at home had been busy spoiling Britain's credit abroad. I kept meeting people who seemed to think the British Labour Party had seized power by a *coup d'état* instead of being voted in by a majority of respectable citizens in the usual way.

'Why did you take the government away from Churchill after the way he won the war?' asked a fair charmer, as though I personally had been responsible.

'Lady,' I replied heavily, 'in Britain we have democracy,

meaning that citizens consider the problems and vote for the candidate and/or party that seems to have the best remedies for them. We do not turn over life-and-death power to this or that leader as a sort of present because he has a nice face, because he is good to his mother or even because he won a war. That isn't Democracy. You're thinking of Fascism, Mrs. Hitler.'

In Hollywood there was much perturbation about Communism —which term comprehended Socialism, often Liberalism, and occasionally even Democracy itself. But I had been forewarned, and had provided myself. Joe Schenck started off quite pleasantly by telling me how the Labour Government had ruined the British coal industry, but was a bit nonplussed when I reached in my pocket-book and forked out a budget of facts and figures proving quite otherwise.

I had heard and read for years of this fabulous land of make-believe where stars of the silver screen dwelt in luxurious homes surrounded with polo ponies, halls of mirrors and swimming-baths. But in summer 1948 Hollywood was making heavy weather. The weather was sweltering, the outlook was blue. Big operators had just unloaded film interests and bought into television. The restaurants and night clubs were doing only moderately well.

The indigence was, probably, accentuated to me because of the contrast with my own temporary magnificence. The hospitable and generous American magazine *Life* had arranged for me to live as its guest at beautiful and soothing Santa Monica, in the Yacht Club, a luxurious hotel converted from a splendid house built originally by W. R. Hearst and once occupied by Miss Marion Davies. I had the suite which, I was reliably informed, had been the night apartment of Miss Davies herself. The sitting-room was large enough to house a public meeting and when I retired for sleep into an inner chamber, I felt as lonely as Orphan Annie.

When in the morning, after doing myself at breakfast as well as could be expected from a stomach shrunken in capacity by years of austerity in Britain, I entered my large black glittering limousine which would have put Himmler's famous runabout to shame, to be tenderly conveyed on my lawful occasions, the magnificence of the stars' residences flashing past the window naturally diminished a trifle in impressiveness. While the homes of the gods—Chaplin, Shearer, Pickford *et al.*—gave off an air of calm sure dignity, some of the others seemed almost ordinary. Here and there a swimming-bath was dried up and cracked, a lawn was overgrown, verges were not thinned. Hollywood, in places at least, looked as though the seat was out of its pants.

My driver was an old identity of Hollywood who in his thirty years of driving had carried all the big names of the film world. A companionable man, he was very willing to share his experiences. I listened fascinated to tales about the intimate private habits of the stars, those who behaved themselves and those who didn't, those who could hold their liquor and those who finished a party flopped on his car floor, sick on his cushions. It was a pleasure for me to hear that my own taste in pin-up girls was a wholesome body worthy of any man's respectful passion. Norma Shearer—that was her nice house we just passed—was well fixed. Bing Crosby, Gene Autry, Joel McCrea and Pat O'Brien, I gathered, were the richest stars. They knew their way about. The others, with exceptions, wasted their dough or were taken for it by cleverer people. I was shocked to hear that So-and-so (a genial kindly soul in films) was as mean as cat's-meat—would run his car down a mile of parking line and ease it into a space himself to save tipping the park-keeper a quarter.

In passing I inspected the Hollywood institutions of the time: Louis B. Mayer's enormous desk, which I had heard had a telephone at each end so that contact might not be cut (a gross exaggeration); the M.G.M. Staircase of Sighs with the two endless files of minor hierarchy, those blessed going up, those damned going down; Darryl Zanuck's luxuriously furnished Torture Chamber, and the very riding-whip with which, I was assured, he thrashed yes-men that turned. Sam Goldwyn's big car which, they said, ran by his side in case he swooned as he walked home for his health. The legendary Sam in real life proved to be a genial personality. It was quite true that he consistently misquoted names. 'Glad to see you, Mr. Lee. Take that chair, Mr. Lord. A cigar, Mr. Lincoln? Well, how do you like the coast, Mr. Langworthy?' Fascinated, I felt he might call me 'Mr. High' at any moment.

The salient features were explained to me as we went along. This, said my guides, is where the top men of 20th Century Fox meet for their luxurious luncheon, the very place where Warner Bros., Jack and Harry, reduce their top men to pulp with their comic cross-talk . . . I sat at a modest repast with about a dozen austere and preoccupied shadows. I saw no Bacchanalian debaucheries. Rather was I impressed by signs of apprehension concerning the Johnson Office. I detected in the conversation an exaggerated striving after conventional respectability. There must be no whisper . . .

When I visited Cecil B. de Mille I found him surrounded in a veritable picture-gallery of designs for one of his Old Testament epics, worrying out bosom covering 'improvements' to the costume of Minoan females, to square with the Johnson Office's prejudice against 'cleavage'; and at another studio with an investment of nine million dollars in an epic Joan of Arc I found consternation brought about by some influential columnist having said their Joan had sex appeal, as was proved by the fact that she had to wear armour when doing business with priests and courtiers.

The circumstances did not seem propitious for questionings as to the moral responsibilities of the film industry. Had I expected to illuminate the point Should the Public Have What it Wants or What is Good for it?, I was disappointed. The evidence accumulation from somewhat confused conversation with eight chief executives, six producers and three directors left me feeling that the problem of raising cultural standards is one that must be solved by persuasion rather than by force. As Joe Schenck said, coming to the heart of the matter, 'You must please sixteen millions or it's no good.'

I could not leave Hollywood without doing the rounds of the studios to see for myself the people who divert my daily leisure hour at the cinema. I met a great number of lovely women and clever men. I noted that the stars looked less appetising eating their lunch than on the screen; and that the glamour lies in the lens of the camera; and that it's the director that does the real job. To an inveterate movie fan like myself it should have been a delightful experience to hobnob with companies of my dreams come alive. But I don't think I liked it. How could I ever again take these beautiful people seriously as thugs, gangsters, adventuresses—as anything, in fact, but people? I agreed with Hazlitt—actors should never be seen out of their frames.

As a parting clasp to the United States we went to be dined by the National Cartoonists Society. The company, which numbered about two hundred, was the nearest thing to a trade union artists have ever had. Although I did not quite subscribe to the collective principle applied to the arts, it was a jolly evening, meeting the well-known names. Mostly comic strip men. The hall was hung with flags, seemingly of all nations, Britain, even Ethiopia, too.

'What's this?' I said. 'You have some link with the United Nations?'

'No,' said my host. 'The flags represent the places in which we market our products.'

376

But that's only the West, says a knowing friend. Look now at the awakening East, tomorrow's centre of the world. So off I go eastward with another sketchbook, talking to a lot of people on the way, good and bad, significant and insignificant. I look at Chinese squatters at Malaya. I gaze at plump business men at Singapore. I stare at refugees at Hong Kong. I peep at Americanized Japanese democracy at Tokio. I squint at teeming crowds of thin brown people at Calcutta and thick brown people from the hills of Tibet . . . It is annoying that my impressions are so often only indirectly political or even not political at all. I am so often beguiled by the picturesque variety of the passing scene that I can make no generalizations upon which to base profound conclusions.

Two meetings stand out in my mind as providing matter for reflection : lunch with one of the richest men in the Far East, owner of restaurants, cinemas, newspapers. Smooth, gracious, witty, slim, Chinese, Oxford graduate. The company was mainly business tycoons.

We did ourselves magnificently, tit-bits and dainties, sharks' fins (imported tinned from Europe), bamboo, chicken.

'You seem very cheerful,' I said to our host, 'considering that you live on the slope of a volcano.'

'Slope of volcano very fertile soil,' he said waving expressive hands, meaning no doubt for growing profitable cinemas, restaurants and newspapers. It did not seem a very forward view. I turned to my friend on the right, business tycoon from Saigon.

'Things going better in Indo-China?' I said hopefully.

'No,' he explained happily. 'Everything as usual, war, but nobody win. Of course, if Chinese communists decide to throw in 300,000 troops that would be different, but then they won't. Too busy in Korea.'

'What if Eisenhower patches up Korea?'

My companion dissolved into laughter and passed me some more sharks' fins. I judged there would be a vested interest or two against patching up Korea.

I had come across only one planter with the wide view, relating Malaya to the rest of the world. Most of them, minus the real score, escaped awkward facts by verbal sublimation : there was no cold war, but 'the emergency'; there was 'collective punishment,' not burning of villages; no communists, but 'bandits.' Pretty soon Queen Victoria, Rudyard Kipling and Lord Kitchener would arrive with the Fire Brigade and put 'em out. Everybody had been telling me that the Chinese and Malays had no real interest in politics, only in profiting themselves individually. Then I met a grand old Chinese elder, with a beautiful wispy beard, who patiently explained his people to me, standing on a lawn at Bukit Serene with five lakes spread before us to the horizon. 'You cannot expect them to know what they want yet. What is the use of talking all the time about freedom and responsibility if you never give any real responsibility? People must learn from experience to govern themselves and thus gain pride in themselves and their countries.' That, I thought, made sense.

As a fitting postscript to that particular tour of research I wound up in Korea. Through battered Seoul with its woebegone groups of old women and homeless children, over flattened paddyfields and villages beaten into the earth, past fox-holes to the front line, trying through a hole in the rock to look at the invisible Chinese across the bleakest of battlefields. It was a quiet day barring an occasional shell, which was just as well, because I had a cold. The night before I had slept next to one of the excellent American stoves, but I tried to regulate it and put it out of order. I swathed myself in everything warm-making I had, including towel and newspapers and so filled my sleeping-bag that the top came open in the night, my beret fell off and ice formed on the top of my head.

People, people, people, most of them by no means unhappy, but too many living in what to a western European would be degradation. In all of these manifestations the call of the stomach was obviously more powerful than that of liberty. Fat hopes of expecting a hungry man to prefer freedom to a bowl of soup; but, reasonable needs being satisfied, how to explain to him the conception of individual freedom? How to begin to explain? *Should* one begin to explain? Yes, yes, a thousand times yes.

At this point my own private affairs came to the boil. Paper shortage had kept, and seemed likely to keep, the British newspapers scant of space indefinitely. The *Evening Standard* could no longer afford the room for full-sized political cartoons, and my past had spoilt me for settling down tamely to a life of making small drawings that gave me no pleasure. Anyway I had been in one place too long. Was I not the young man who once vowed he would never take root? Were there not new facets of life? I grew tired of security. I yearned for another taste of the struggle for existence, the spur of uncertainty and the sweet taste of surprise. The technical point decided the issue. No more would I work for one paper alone. I would arrange a home base, expand my foreign connections and take on 'special' jobs abroad. A foreign newspaper had just described me as having become a British institution like the Nelson Column or Guy Fawkes, which seemed to me not quite the right idea. I wanted to be universal. I would cut out the local trivia and adopt the supra-national viewpoint of a citizen of the world. In this elevated mood I went home and sacked myself from the *Evening Standard*.

The consequences were interesting. My business friends concluded I had been offered more money. My political friends concluded I must be after more power. Stoopids who had always thought of me as one of rich Beaverbrook's leg-men assumed that I must have lost favour and been banished, and they fell away overnight. Beaverbrook, from Jamaica:

Dec. 9, 1949.
Black Friday.

My dear Low,

Your letter is an unwelcome message.

I always look over my letters here before opening them myself, for I have no Secy or Typist. Then I select the pleasant-looking lot and read them. The rest I put off until after lunch.

Your letter was in the first batch because I expected to hear that you wished me well for Christmas or that you and Mrs. Low would visit Jamaica or that you had changed your mind about Churchill. Instead I got the worst letter first. That's the way life has treated me far too often.

Your decision is a disaster. It is unnecessary and inadvisable. That's what I think of it . . .

Don't forget your old friend
Yours ever,
BEAVERBROOK.

Green fields and pastures new. To start with, a new association with my old friend Percy Cudlipp seemed to hold agreeably difficult possibilities. Percy, who was now editor of the *Daily Herald*, the mouthpiece of industrial and political Labour, thought the same, and this newspaper became my new headquarters.

As to overseas fields, it was fun to illustrate the serial form of Churchill's memoirs in America, to 'do' Japan for the Tokio *Shimbun*, and to make cartoons for foreign newspapers on distant

'BABY PLAY WITH NICE BALL?' (1945)

great occasions. But there were several miscalculations about my original plan. My agents signed up 250 newspapers to print my work in all parts of the world, but the reproduction methods of some of them were primitive and made me squirm. I had intended continuity of publication for the cartoons, but too many editors made their own selection, and that on entertainment value. Then again, too many newspapers negated my intended universality by giving my cartoons the heading *A British Point of View*. It seemed the hardest thing to convince anyone that in a 'free' Press in a 'free' world there could be a free observer.

My experience with the *Daily Herald* reminded me of some things I had forgotten about newspapers and public receptivity. At home in Britain it was generally, but erroneously, assumed that by virtue of my new 'frame' I would be a Labour Party cartoonist, and when I made no difference whatever in the independence of my viewpoint, there was a touch of asperity among some critics. Not, unhappily, among the readers of the *Daily Herald*. If I had

Beaverbrook and I (1950)

supposed that the average of political interest might not have declined on the Left as much as on the Right, I was soon disillusioned. In the *Daily Herald*, too, the entertainment-versus-instruction battle was in full swing, only more so.

For this reason, perhaps, however congenial I found my colleagues and however much I began to enjoy drawing again in the roomier space, my association with the *Daily Herald* readers was destined to be short.

The T.U.C. Horse

For another, I could evoke no enthusiasm for even mild fun at the expense of trade union leaders and their policies. When, for instance, I repeatedly drew the Trade Union Congress as an honest but simple-minded draught horse ('The T.U.C. Horse') a dispute arose as to whether I was deriding draught horses or the T.U.C. So we parted.

Sitting in my club with some friends discussing the change in Fleet Street, one of them brought in a copy of the *Manchester Guardian* with a completely new make-up of its front page. 'They'll be running cartoons next,' he said. I chuckled inwardly, saying to myself. 'Boy, you don't know it, but how right you are.'

The pattern of my private life had changed, too. My children married and departed for the ends of the earth. I sitting, but still with the same adored wife, in a flat on the top of a tall building in the heart of London, with an excellent view if ever anyone decides to drop a hydrogen bomb. Up here I have time to think . . .

In my mind's eye I see myself returning to my youth, myself at sixty-five rendering an account to myself at twelve in the dry thinking-ditch at Riversleigh.

I started out to be a comic artist. Curiosity to find out how the wheels went around led me to the world of ideas and I became a graphic satirist. Circumstances made me a political caricaturist.

There was a touch of the inevitable about what followed. A life of disputes, quarrels and crises, in a world of infinitely varied opportunity for expressive draughtsmanship concerning the hopes and fears of plain men and women—fear of living, fear of dying, fear of what was around the corner, fear of what might happen, fear of having an atom bomb, fear of not having an atom bomb . . .

The contrast of what-could-be with what-is that is implied in all good satire arises naturally in such touchy matters. It was fitting that they should provide my material and proper that I should oppose shifts and evasions, cruelties and stupidities where I found them. It was equally to be expected that I would receive praise and dispraise according to the passions and prejudices of onlookers.

Coming from overseas uninhibited by reverence for the institutions and traditions of the Old World, I had to be a nuisance, 'irresponsible' to those who understood 'responsibility' to mean loyalty to their established code; and a whiteheaded boy to those who saw gaping imperfections in the *status quo* and chafed at delay in their repairing.

Fortunately for my happiness, in the process-of-becoming I had grown enough self-confidence to be perfectly sure that those who disagreed with me were always wrong. So I survived.

And so at length I found myself on a ringside seat at a crisis of humanity, with a close view of the champions engaged and even a small towel to wave in one of the corners.

If happiness lies in doing what one wants to do as well as one can do it, mine has been a happy life. Not being troubled by a strong possessive instinct or a lust for power, the preservation of my secret integrity was never any problem to me. I could always make enough money to live on and there was no sensible reason why I should betray myself. I can take no pride in affirming that my errors have been due entirely to ignorance.

Although I alone (and I only imperfectly) could know by how much I succeeded or failed to become either the kind of artist or the kind of satirist, or even the kind of man, I wanted to be, it was obviously a help to be living and working during one of the most inspiring and agonizing epochs of history.

If I were asked whether I would rather have had my life in any other period of time, I should say 'No, it has been good to live at a turning-point.' But if I were asked whether I would live it over again, I should say 'No. I've done that bit. Give me the few human relationships without which I cannot imagine myself having any existence, and put me somewhere else. But let it be where things are on the move—and let me be able to draw.'

382

INDEX

385